THE ART AND ARCHITECTURE OF MEDIEVAL RUSSIA

THE ART AND ARCHITECTURE OF MEDIEVAL RUSSIA

By Arthur Voyce

UNIVERSITY OF OKLAHOMA PRESS
NORMAN

By Arthur Voyce

Russian Architecture: Trends in Nationalism and Modernism (New York, 1948)

The Moscow Kremlin: Its History, Architecture, and Art Treasures (Berkeley, 1954)

Moscow and the Roots of Russian Culture (Norman, 1964)

The Art and Architecture of Medieval Russia (Norman, 1967)

Library of Congress Catalog Card Number: 66–13433

Copyright 1967 by the University of Oklahoma Press, Publishing Division of the University. Composed and Printed at Norman, Oklahoma, U.S.A., by the University of Oklahoma Press. First edition.

To David and Ruth

Preface

THE FOUNDING of St. Petersburg in 1703 is commonly accepted as the date marking the passing of Old Russia *(Rus')* and the birth of Modern Russia *(Rossiya.)* For most of the people, however, the pre-Petrine period did not come to an abrupt end in 1703. The cultural and artistic traditions of ancient and medieval Russia left their indelible mark upon successive generations and continued to influence the creative strivings of the Russian artist. In the second half of the nineteenth century the ideas and traditions of Old Russia became the center of the Slavophile nationalist movement leading to the repudiation of Western classicism which had dominated Russia since the end of the eighteenth century. It was this turning away from the West and the rediscovery of the national artistic heritage that led directly to the practical revival of Russian medieval art and architecture, and exerted an influence which is difficult to overestimate in the development of modern art in Russia.

The history of ancient and medieval Russian art embraces more than two thousand years in time and a huge area in space; it is a history of an art with an immense diversity of modes of expression, techniques, and styles. There is hardly any other area in the whole world which has experienced so many cultural and religious impulses of such diverse kinds and forces and of such enduring effect. This most varied cultural development is reflected in the art of Old Russia, although the basic aesthetic conceptions of the indigenous culture which crystallized there in the pre-Christian era have, of course, remained more or less formative.

For a long time the art of medieval Russia was the least studied, and was therefore misunderstood, not only by Western students but the Russians themselves. It was not until the nineteenth century that Russian archaeologists were awakened to the fact that the early centuries of Russia's past present a most rewarding field for study. The Kievan, Novgorodian, Suzdalian, and early Muscovite developments became the subject of scholarly research; the excavations undertaken there and in Siberia since the 1920's have yielded the most surprising and impressive finds in Eurasian art and archaeology.

More treasures of the distant Russian past are steadily being unearthed. The sites of old churches and palaces that disappeared long ago are being excavated and the buildings skillfully restored to their original appearance. The work of cleaning and restoring old icons, begun about a century ago, has been greatly intensified in recent years, thus providing a solid basis for investigating the history of icon painting in the Novgorod and Moscow schools.

I have attempted to include and discuss the most important architectural, painting, and decorative art monuments as they have been created in the territories of Russia by the Russian people and their predecessors. Nearly every work that can be definitely dated, with the exception of manuscripts, has been noted, as well as examples of each of the groups into which the various arts can be satisfactorily divided for purposes of classification. The order of illustrations is approximately chronological, though in the main sections—Architecture, Painting, and the Decorative Arts—items are grouped topically.

Within the limits of a single volume, it is impossible to do more than trace the checkered path taken by Russian culture over the centuries, survey the developments, and show the more important monuments. Despite these limitations, I hope this book will serve the reader as an introduction to the artistic achievements of the Russian people and their predecessors in the pre-Petrine period and afford him a view to a surprising field of art—and a field generally neglected or treated with imperceptive brevity in Western histories.

Much of the research for this volume was done at the Library of the Hoover Institution, Stanford University; and a large part of the material was collected during my visits to the Soviet Union in 1958 and 1961, made possible by the Inter-University Committee on Travel Grants.

My sincere thanks for specific help are extended to the following:

The Joint Slavic and East European Grants Committee of the Social Science Research Council and the American Council of Learned Societies for the 1959 award of a grant for research.

Mr. Joseph A. Belloli, chief librarian of the humanities and social science division of the Stanford University Library, for the help and facilities with which he and his staff provided me in the course of my studies, and for placing so much valuable material at my disposal.

Mr. Adolph E. Anderson for reading the manuscript, for his constructive criticism, and for valuable suggestions.

The State Hermitage Museum in Leningrad; The State Tretyakov Gallery in Moscow; The State Historical Museum in Moscow; and The State Art History Museum in Novgorod for providing me with most of the photographs used in the Iconographic and Decorative Art sections of the book.

The Union of Soviet Architects; and the Archives Department of the State Scientific-Research Museum of Architecture named after A. V. Shchousev for providing me with most of the photographs used in the architectural sections of the book.

The American Council of Learned Societies for assistance in covering a large part of the cost of reproducing the plates.

ARTHUR VOYCE

San Francisco, California
December 1, 1966

Contents

Introduction

General Characteristics of Russian Art

For thousands of years before the rise of the Moscow Grand Principality (middle of the fifteenth century), the land that constitutes modern Russia had been the crossroads of many migrations, the scene of invasions and colonizations, by peoples of diverse origins, faiths, and cultures. They came from all points of the compass either as peaceful settlers or as conquerors, lived there for short or long periods until they, in turn, were subjugated or driven out by invaders of a more vigorous or better-organized race. As Kondakov points out, "The more varied the racial elements of the invaders, the longer their stay, the longer the process of assimilation and amalgamation of the conquerors and conquered into one nation, the richer and more varied became the cultural and artistic treasury of ancient Russia."[1] Large deposits were made by conquerors and conquered, by those who had established themselves permanently, as well as by the nomadic tribes. Into the common pool of cultural wealth, contributions came from the artists and craftsmen of the Greek colonies on the northern shores of the Black Sea, from the Hellenized Scythians and Iranized Sarmatians, the Crimean colonies of the Genoese merchants, and the Syrians, Scandinavians, and Germans who took up residence in various cities of Kievan, Novgorodian, and Suzdalian Russia. The cultural and artistic treasury was further enriched by Arabian caravans bring-

[1] I. I. Tolstoi and N. P. Kondakov, *Russkiya drevnosti v pamyatnikakh iskusstva*, I, preface, 1.

3

ing goods and art objects from the East to the Volga Bulgars, ultimately reaching the Russian settlements of the upper Volga; and no little was added by the workshops maintained by the courts of the Russian grand princes.

There was hardly another land in ancient times where one could encounter so many cultural cross-currents as in Russia. Byzantium, the lands of the Near East, the Caucasus, Western Europe, and Scandinavia were close neighbors, with all of whom contacts were maintained. Persian fabrics, Arabian silver, Chinese ceramics, Byzantine brocades, Frankish swords, and many other strangely foreign things could be found in the marketplaces of her cities. The imported articles represented the accumulated art experience of many periods and schools as well as the techniques of many skilled craftsmen. Needless to say, these importations served not only as objects to be used by the wealthy upper classes of Russian society, but also as models of style for her artists.

Eastern and Western Influences

Because of her geographical position, her extensive trade with the Near and Far East, and the settlement and colonization of her southern provinces by peoples of the highest civilization, the art engendered and cultivated in Russia has preserved the elements of various Eastern sources. There is evidence of the influence of Persia, India, and China, of Greece and Asia Minor, of Byzantium, and lastly of the Mongols and other hordes which in centuries past ravaged these lands. Nor are Western influences to be ignored, although their relative importance, as compared with the purely Eastern elements in the arts of Russia, is disputed among art historians. Thus Viollet-le-Duc arrives at the conclusion that Russian art may be considered as a composite (*un composé*) of elements borrowed from the East to the almost complete exclusion of all others. Russian art appears to him to be the product of three principal elements which constitute its

4

base; the local Scythian element, the Byzantine, and the Mongol. The East, he holds, furnished nine-tenths of these elements.[2]

On the other hand, a number of Russian art historians maintain that the West, and, particularly Scandinavia, exercised a more marked influence on the art of Russia than is commonly supposed. They do not confine this influence to periods later than the sixteenth century, when it became indisputably apparent.

This West European influence is a factor which some art historians underestimate. Russia from the early days of her history was influenced by Romanesque art (at Vladimir), the Italian Renaissance (the early Moscow Kremlin), and the Italian-Polish-German phases of the baroque (the churches of the so-called Naryshkin style at the end of the seventeenth century and the churches and palaces of the eighteenth). Russian art was thus affected by all phases of Western art, with the exception, perhaps, of Gothic architecture, the birth and development of which practically coincides with the period of the Tatar conquest and domination of Russia.

From the middle of the seventeenth century these Western influences, which for a long time were sporadic and superficial, assumed a more and more dominant role at the expense of the Byzantine traditions. Icon painting gave way to the painting of portraits; the shops of the *Oruzheinaya Palata*[3] became crowded with foreign artists and craftsmen. The art of the "Friazin"—that is, the Frankish or West European art—triumphed over that of Byzantium.

It is clear that in the formation of her national art Russia was subjugated to many influences. We shall find evidence, however, that these influences were not merely imported, but usually reworked and recreated. In the apparent predominance

[2] *L'Art russe, ses origines ses elements constitutifs, son apogee, son avenir*, 88.
[3] The Hall of Arms, located in the Moscow Kremlin, is the oldest museum in Russia, housing the finest collections of Russian decorative art. (See Chapter XIX).

of the Byzantine element we must not lose sight of the fact that Russia went for inspiration to the very same cultures by which Byzantium herself had been inspired—the Far East, Persia, and Asia Minor.

We must also note that Russia never relinquished her indigenous elements or distinctive creations. No historical shock, however violent or harsh, completely broke the chain of continuity. There were interruptions, yet they always permitted, even stimulated, a resumption. Ideas, styles, and techniques were accepted, first from one side, then from another, but they were only elements to be adjusted to the established Russian practice, sooner or later becoming absorbed into it.

Recognition of the extraordinary number of facets and the complexity of the Russian cultural phenomena leads to the conclusion that Russian art is the result of many centuries of work and that it was created by the genius of the Great Russian race influenced by a number of foreign races and cultures, yet always remaining unmistakably Russian. We are thus justified in defining Russian art as those works which were produced in Russia, at first under the patronage of the native princes, tsars, and wealthy merchants, and later in response to religious and national sentiment. A Russian woodcarving or piece of jewelry may be Scythian, Sarmatian, or Byzantine or it may be Persian or Hindu in character; it may be conceived in a Western or Eastern style, but the signature of the Russian creativity is there for all to see. The combined influences of the soil, the landscape, the climate, religion, and history have transmuted the diverse foreign elements and out of them have created an art which is quite distinct from any other.

The Russian Selective Faculty

The close contacts with neighboring cultures proved to be of inestimable value, for they brought familiarity with the genius of many races and with the arts of diverse civilization. Geographical situation, circumstances, and national character and

6

temperament have made the Russian artist particularly fit to receive, study, develop, and transform the mingled contributions of the East, the South, and the West. There is much evidence of remarkable discernment in the selection of foreign art concepts and great ability in remolding borrowed forms, imbuing them with a spirit entirely their own.

In spiritual, intellectual, and artistic matters the Russian has always been independent. This was demonstrated as early as the tenth century, when Russia took over the Christian faith from Byzantium, together with its dogma, rites, and art. In religion, art, administration, and jurisprudence it was Byzantium that prevailed at first. But, instead of being overwhelmed by Byzantium from the moment that Orthodoxy was established in Kiev, Russia began to dominate more and more. What Russia took from Byzantium, she took by her own free choice, always conscious and appreciative of the spiritual and aesthetic values of the Mother Church. But she did not remain under Byzantine influence for long. By the second half of the fifteenth century, when Russia assumed the role of defender of true Orthodoxy, she began to draw more and more from her own resources, and her art was rapidly developed into something intrinsically Russian.

It is admittedly difficult to determine just which of the old art objects are purely Russian, because throughout her long formative years ancient Russia was a conglomeration of independent and semi-independent principalities, continually breaking loose from one another, to be reunited under new rulers. The seat of political power shifted throughout the early centuries of Russian history: from Novgorod in the north to Kiev in the southwest to Vladimir-Suzdal in the northeast, and thence to Moscow. Successful princes or chieftains, who rebelled against the central authority and founded principalities of their own, sought to eclipse the splendor of their former suzerains and copied the monuments of the older capitals. They commandeered artists and craftsmen from afar or attracted them by the prospect of lucrative employment. As the central government transferred its residence from one province to another, the art of widely different lands was imported and stimulated by court and church patronage, setting the fashion for the satellite principalities. Russian art ebbed and flowed with the tide of fortune, rising to great heights and suffering periods of decline, but was never entirely submerged, since its strength was sustained and constantly replenished from the rich reservoir of religious mysticism, racial experience, and ideas, and its artists were endowed with the gift for expressing that which moved them deeply.

Some art historians liken Russia to a battleground on which the antagonistic influences of ancient Greece, Byzantium, the East, and the West clashed and fought. Their theses vary, depending on their personal persuasion: some hold that Russian art is primarily Byzantine with an admixture of Far Eastern elements, others, such as Viollet-le-Duc, maintain that it is nine-tenths Oriental. There are those who claim that it took the combined and very powerful influence of Persian and Western art to free Russia from Byzantine traditions. The truth is that none of those premises is fully justified; it was to Russia herself that this liberation was due. She was never content just to sit back and absorb the various art currents which, owing to her geographical situation near the three great cultural centers, were constantly pouring into the stream of Russian art. Russia herself was forever drawing upon her own national substance.

Assimilation and Transformation of Foreign Cultures

As we have pointed out, the Russians were subjected to many influences, but always showed discrimination in selection, proving themselves to be clever adapters and thorough assimilators. Their predilections, their main leanings seem to have been unmistakably Eastern, but the outstanding fact is that, from the heterogeneous elements which they assimilated, a distinct, original, and national art was formed. The evidence of that distinct

8

style, characteristically different from the various origins which may have produced it, can be easily seen in the many examples of Russian art that have come down to us.

Viollet-le-Duc has aptly remarked that Russia has been one of the laboratories in which arts coming from all points of Asia and Europe have been united to form a combination intermediate between the Eastern and the Western worlds.[4] The Byzantine element is mixed with the Persian, the Scandinavian with the Mongol, the Romanesque with the Turanian, but the result is neither Byzantine, Hindu, nor Persian: it is Russian. "Amongst the diverse origins of Russian art," says Viollet-le-Duc, "Byzantine art certainly holds the principal place; but from a time already far distant, other elements belonging to Asia may be perceived—principally in ornament. These Asiatic elements take a more important place when Constantinople is no longer the seat of the Eastern empire, and when the Mongols dominate over Russia without, however, altogether displacing the essential principles of Byzantine structure in architecture and the hieratism of religious painting.

"Without mentioning the secondary elements which appear in Russian art, the two origins that have just been named—the one purely Byzantine and the other Asiatic—dominate, in different proportions it is true, but constitute the base of this Russian art. These proportions may be modified, and have often been, without destroying the unity, for the reason that has been already pointed out: that Byzantine art is itself a composite in which the Asiatic elements largely enter."[5]

As a matter of fact, from very early times the Byzantine influence was opposed and effectively fought by Eastern influences. The Dnieper with its orientation towards Byzantium had a powerful rival in the Volga and the Caspian Sea—the great trade route towards the Orient. We know that, as early as in the twelfth century, the Vladimir-Suzdal principality maintained

[4] *L'Art russe*, 58.
[5] *Ibid.*, 150.

close relations with the civilizations of Transcaucasia, Georgia, and Armenia. A few centuries later, when Russia won its freedom from the Tatar domination, Moscow reopened the Volga route to carry on commerce with Persia. Thus Russia maintained for ages its contact with Eastern cultures and borrowed many a decorative motif from them.

Asiatic influence upon Russian art was so great that, after the Tatar yoke was thrown off, Asia's influence still dominated every other, resulting in works whose originality marks a new period, the longest and most splendid of all those that can be determined precisely in the artistic history of Russia. Thus, while the Eastern empire was disintegrating, while Byzantium was falling into the hands of the Turks, Russia, vigorous and prosperous, was creating an art superbly original and fruitful with masterpieces in architecture, iconography, metalwork, enamels, ceramics, and embroideries.

The special charm and peculiarity of old Russian art lies in the integration of West European art with the Far Eastern and Persian, and this is especially true of its decorative art. This unique interpretation and amalgamation, this union in which, as a rule, the Eastern element proved the more tenacious, not only produced the fine specimens of ecclesiastical woodcarving and enamels in the seventeenth century, but continued far into those periods in which Russian art had begun to attract the attention of European connoisseurs.

Foreign artists and craftsmen have worked in Russia at all times and in all branches of art. They were of diverse nationalities, adherents of various faiths, but most of them succumbed to the spell of the country and let themselves be conquered by her spirit and traditions. They adapted their style not only to the peculiar environmental conditions, but to the whole atmosphere which they found in Russia. Indeed, many of them forgot the land of their origin and became thoroughly Russified.

The Russians in turn appropriated and gave substance to the ideas and teachings of their foreign artists, incorporating them

into the national art. They were never content merely to copy
the foreign models, but always adapted them to their own needs,
tastes, and traditions. In this way the form of Byzantine architecture were refashioned and accomodated to the requirements
of a northern climate, and the decorative elements of the Italian
Renaissance were transformed and mixed with the native Russian motifs.

Russia owes much of her cultural development to the foreign
elements in her population; she is also indebted to those neighboring lands which had outlet markets in Russia. Such foreign
marts were maintained in Olbia, Khersonesus, and Theodosia
(Kaffa), as well as Kiev, Smolensk, Itil, and other cities. But at
the same time, Russian-made art objects were being shipped
abroad as early as the end of the twelfth century. It is also a
curious fact that a great many pieces of Russian silver jewelry,
especially earrings, buttons, and buckles of the twelfth to the
thirteenth centuries, were found in the Kuban province. Evidently the Tmutorokanian principality[6] contained many Russian settlements which greatly influenced the local tastes in
finery.

The Uneven Development of the Various Arts

It remains for us to examine the effect of the general tendencies of Russian art on the development of the graphic and plastic
arts. This development seems to have been quite unequal. At a
time when the arts of the great West European countries were
developing as complete units—that is, when architecture, painting, and sculpture were flourishing simultaneously—certain
phases of Russian art seem to have suffered from lack of nourish-
ment. The richness of its architecture and decorative arts con-
trasts very sharply with the poverty of its sculpture.

Sculpture in the round was comparatively rare and was practiced only stealthily up to the time of Peter the Great; its real
development began in the second half of the eighteenth century

[6] In the Taman Peninsula, established *ca.* A.D. 825.

in the reign of Catherine II. This delayed emergence of the art of sculpture is explained by the attitude of the Russian Orthodox church towards the representation of the saintly figures in the round.

The fear of a possible return of idol worship had sunk too deeply into the consciousness of the upper ranks of the clergy for them to permit sculptured images in the church. Orthodox rulers suppressed the heresies of their laxer predecessors, while high religious authority did not hesitate to use its great powers in upholding the ban and excluding from the precincts of the church any sculptured representations of the saints. We must remember also that the art of the Orient and Byzantium, from which Russia derived so much, traditionally preferred the use of low-relief ornament and polychrome decoration to sculpture in the round. Moreover, good stone and marble materials suitable for sculpture were comparatively rare, and the predominance of wood and brick architecture were not favorable to the development of monumental statuary.

Whatever the reasons may be, the fact remains that, unlike her European neighbors, Russia, up to the middle of the eighteenth century, had done very little in the field of sculpture. With the exception of the low-relief stone carvings that decorate the churches of the Vladimir-Suzdal region,[7] sculpture is almost entirely absent from the façades of Russian ecclesiastical buildings. Nor did ancient Russia indulge in funerary sculpture, an art which, at the end of the Middle Ages and during the Renaissance, played such an important role in the West. This is one of the most conspicuous gaps in ancient Russian art.

Painting, on the other hand, benefited from the relative paucity of sculpture. The iconographic role played by sculpture in the Western churches—the didactic function of the sculptured tympanums and portals of the great Romanesque and Gothic cathedrals—was assigned by the Russian churches to the art of

[7] The sculptured stone wall decorations of the St. Dmitri Cathedral, Vladimir (1194–97) and the St. George Cathedral, Yuriev-Polski (1230–34).

the fresco. The monumental painting, which replaces the stained-glass windows of the Gothic churches, profited from certain characteristics of Russian church architecture. The churches of Russia created especially favorable conditions for the development of fresco painting, in that their walls, in contrast to those of European churches, provided much larger surfaces for painting. Thus the walls of the Uspensky Cathedral in the Kremlin and the vast wall spaces of the Yaroslavl churches are entirely covered with frescoes.

The most striking characteristics of pre-revolutionary Russian painting is the division of this art into two fields: *Iconopis'* and *zhivopis'*, which are diametrically opposite to each other. *Iconopis'*—the painting of icons[8] which was Byzantine in its origin—dealt with religious subjects only, did not know any other techniques than the fresco and distemper painting, and limited itself to the reproduction of the traditional representations of the saints without ever using the living model. *Zhivopis'*—naturalistic painting, introduced into Russia at the end of the seventeenth century by West European painters—is on the other hand characterized by the predominance of secular subjects, the technique of oil, and the study of nature.

Originality of Native Architecture

It is in the field of architecture and the decorative arts that Russia revealed her greatest originality, expressing herself with distinction and imagination. In earlier times wooden struc-

---

[8] Icon—from the Greek word *eikon* meaning image or picture. The Russian religious picture is called *ikona* or *obraz* (pl. *ikony* or *obrazy*), signifying primarily a likeness (*podobiye*) but not a realistic portrait. Originally, the Byzantines applied the term "icon" to every depiction of Christ, the Virgin, a saint, or an incident in the Holy Writ, whether carved or painted, movable or monumental, and whatever the technique in which it was executed. The modern Orthodox church, however, tends to restrict the use of the term to small movable pictures, and this is the meaning it bears in art history.

The Russian icon may be defined as a representation of a sacred subject on a portable plaque of wood or on a metal plate, no matter what the technique employed—painting on wood surfaced with plaster, enamelwork, or mosaic; it is usually painted on a block of nonresinous wood with tempera colors.

tures were favored, and in her "wooden age," she originated and developed certain basic forms, later to be echoed in masonry. In the larger centers wooden and masonry architecture developed side by side, one stimulating and gratifying the love for verticality and slenderness, the other satisfying a yearning for massiveness, monumentality, and lavish decoration in the expression of power and splendor. The Western world knows relatively little of Russia's architecture, especially the ancient wooden structures. The few remaining examples of these testify to the skill and taste of her builders in the composition and grouping of the architectural masses, the keen sense of proportion, expressiveness, and silhouette and the gift for merging and harmonizing the building ensemble with the landscape. It is especially in this field that the Russian architect demonstrated his great talents for selection and adoption. Far from copying the forms of Byzantium, Italy, or Greece, he adjusted them ingeniously to the exigencies of a harsher climate. He reduced the size of the openings and sharpened the pitch of the roof in order to provide better drainage and prevent the accumulation of snow. He replaced the flat, semispherical Byzantine dome, designed for the arid lands of the South, with a bulbous onion-shaped cupola or a pyramid-like spire in the shape of a tent, borrowed from the wooden architecture of the North—forms far better suited to a land of heavy rains and snow.

In the masonry architecture of Russia, which is mostly brick, the architect utilized the lay and bond of the brick, stucco, or polychrome revetments for decorative effect. Polychrome architecture, lavish in its use of varicolored materials, displays the Russian architect's natural predilection for vivid colors. The development of glazes and enamels in designs appropriate to this medium was fostered in architectural ornament. The enamel protected the brick from disintegration and at the same time created an opportunity for beauty of surface, color, and pattern. The elaborate polychrome tile revetments of Patriarch Nikon's time were never relinquished by Russian architects, and the enameled brick ornament also found application in the churches of Moscow and Yaroslavl, notably in the churches of St. Peter and Paul and St. John the Baptist in Yaroslavl. The walls of the apses of St. John are entirely covered with enameled brick patterns, presenting a rich array of designs done with a skill and finish that demonstrate a remarkable feeling for harmony and color.

The Decorative Arts

Decorative art is probably the only other field in which the Russian artistic genius expressed itself as brilliantly as it did in architecture. The explanation is to be found in the fact that these fields are so closely interrelated that it is often difficult to determine just where the creative function of architecture ends and the art of decoration begins. Russia's role in the development of the arts of decoration is particularly interesting because from the very early periods and in all branches of decorative art Russia has shown the combination of the two aptitudes we have aready noted: on the one hand, there is an undeniable native creative genius; on the other, great facility in assimilating foreign cultural contributions. Although these capacities could be mutually contradictory, combined they are productive of great achievements. A widespread and expert appreciation of beauty sustained craftsmanship through the ages. The necessary materials were available within the country, and for many centuries there had been a taste for ornament, a well-developed art of personal adornment, and a great love of color.

Decoration has often been singled out as Russia's most notable artistic achievement. Her craftsmen attained great skill in many media, and her designers through the ages developed a number of patterns based on a few fundamentally national themes which were remarkably viable and prolific. They demonstrated great adeptness in originating and controlling complex and involved groups of motifs and patterns. At the same time they displayed a gift for the dramatic exploitation of expressive silhouette.

Imaginative schemes control the distribution and organization of ornament. The various elements are definitely separated yet clearly related. The decorative motifs, the elements employed in organizing the design, are often geometrical. But geometrical ornament, in whatever form it occurs, rarely stands alone. It is nearly always combined or overlaid with floral and animal forms which constitute the bulk of the actual decorative material. Real and fantastic animals wind through the scrolling, leafy mazes. For the sake of ornamental effect, the artist does not hesitate to place his animals in attitudes which, though sometimes taken from nature, are immoderately exaggerated and often quite fantastic. Shapes are denaturalized and treated as elements of ornament. The main principle is the purely decorative treatment of the animal figure. The vine pattern in its many elaborations is also a constant resource. Every phase of it appears, from the simple undulating stem to complex projections of winding branches bearing fantastic leaves and blossoms.

Animal life has been the dominant theme of Russian artists since time immemorial, and it has always been dramatically exploited. Where natural fauna failed to give sufficient opportunity for heightened effect, some of the old mythical beasts were introduced, including the griffin and the legendary birds of Russian folklore, the *sirin* and the *alconost*.[9] In early days it was common practice to shape the extremities of animals as birds' or griffins' heads. Later the animals developed floriate extensions, and leaves and blossoms were even substituted for natural attributes. But a more effective and characteristic method was to employ the two motifs simultaneously. The feeling of struggle and entanglement so prominent in the Scythian animal style gave way to a more subtle relation. The friezes of coursing animals that ornament the vases, jars, and plates are detached from the foliated background, although enriched and

[9] *Sirin, Sirina,* is the fabulous creature of Russian folklore, half-man, half-bird, inhabiting paradise and entertaining the righteous with sweet singing. *Alconost* is the frightful bird-like creature inhabiting hell, and torturing the damned with her terrible screeching.

bound together by it. The two elements maintain a separate existence that permits the fullest exploitation of the decorative values of each.

That Russia should have sustained an intense and unflagging enthusiasm for barbaric magnificence and colorful art is entirely in character, for Russians love solid splendor and bright hues. The enameled tiled surfaces of their buildings, the gorgeous mosaics, the cloths of gold and silver, the richly colored jewels which in the great days made every court gathering gleam and sparkle, all cater to this taste for imposing beauty. The enduring artistic value of these objects, some of which are shown in this book, indicate that they were created by superb craftsmen. They were, as Maxim Gorky said, ". . . the potters, blacksmiths, goldsmiths, enamelers, men and women weavers, stonemasons, carpenters, carvers in wood and ivory, gunsmiths, painters, embroiderers, seamstresses, and tailors—the people who made the beautiful things that fill the museums and gladden the eye."

The love of ornament and of splashes of vivid color is also found in the simple Russian peasant. It expressed itself in the decoration of his modest log cabin (*izba*), his household utensils, implements, and tools. We have benches and tables, beakers and goblets, flasks, jugs and pots, bowls and ladles, platters, basins of all sizes, shaft-bows and yokes, torch holders and candlesticks, all embodying centuries of popular aesthetic experience. Nor do these exhaust the list, for the peasant craftsman's art became the partner of building, supplying carved posts, balusters, moldings, elements of cornices and gables, window and door frames and grills.

Some of the commonest utensils are rendered with subtle variations and innovations, while certain others are peculiar to a region. Vessels were also made for entertainment, fun, and delight, often too fragile for everyday use. Utility may have been an "excuse," but humor and delight were their real purpose.

Decorative design is deeply rooted in popular feeling; the

creative spirit of the people was kept alive even in the remotest villages. There craftsmanship was very active, and the implements and utensils of daily use were made, carved, and colored by the villagers themselves. One can still admire the touch of the craftsman in the carving of homemade looms and distaffs, the design of linen printing blocks, and the carving of window frames. In the northern provinces laces and embroidery were produced in designs that speak eloquently of the people's natural bent for ornamental art. In these designs the motifs of humans, beasts, and birds are treated with an austere decorativeness, while the Ukrainian needlework has a certain softness and delicacy in its free-flowing, playful, and luxurious design.

Needlework found many applications in the church. The ancient monastery sacristies have preserved for us wondrously worked and embroidered ecclesiastical vestments, altar cloths, and shrouds. Quite often these embroidered pieces, in beauty of composition, finesse of workmanship, and the intrinsic value of their materials, rival those of some of the best icons. In the region of Northern Dvina, in some small church isolated from the world by swamps, one might find elaborately carved icon frames, with six-winged seraphs and patterns that flow in enchanting rhythms. Humble village churches of the Far North preserved carved iconostases, royal doors, lecterns, candle chests, and other bits of decorative carving that never fail to impress the visitor with their "primitive" beauty and charm, and with the taste and dexterity of those village carpenters and woodcarvers, who, with the simplest of tools, could transform those modest interiors into places of sheer delight. The work of these craftsmen had its roots in the distant past and represents the best traditions of folk art; it has given rise to the real masterpieces in the higher forms of Russian art.

II

Geographical Setting

T HE HISTORY and character of Russia's culture and art are so intimately connected with the physical features of the land that we cannot conceive of them apart from their geographical background. We need not enter here into a detailed description, but it will be useful to grasp some of the main features which went to make the culture of Russia what it was.

We can benefit greatly by following the examples of Kliuchevsky and Rambaud[1] in tracing the influence of the plains, forests, and rivers upon the culture of Russia. These are the three basic elements of the physical nature of the land; jointly and separately they played an active part in shaping the country's life and culture.

The Plains and the Forests

The plains of Russia extend into the heart of the Eurasian continent until they reach the mountain masses of central Asia. There is no real natural barrier between the two continents, for the Ural mountain chain is nothing more than a median line that is arbitrarily accepted as a boundary between European and Asiatic Russia. The boundless spaces of the north are largely covered with thick forests, and to the south stretch out the interminable steppes. It is for this reason that Russia is rightly described by Kliuchevsky as "a land of transition, an interme-

[1] V. Kliuchevsky, *Kurs Russkoi istorii*, I, Lecture III; A. Rambaud, *History of Russia*, I, 17–31.

diary between two separate worlds. Culture has linked her indissolubly to Europe, but nature has imposed upon her certain features and influences which have drawn her to Asia, and Asia to her."[2] It is this, perhaps, which accounts for the complexity and diversity of the Russian art elements.

The forests with which northern Russia abounds, and which for many centuries were the setting of Russian life, played a great role in the development and conditioning of Russian culture. The forest rendered many valuable services to the early settler; it provided pine and oak timber for his house and church; it furnished firewood for his hearth; it lighted his home with birchbark torches or pine kindling; it gave him bast for his shoes; and it furnished him with primitive agricultural and household utensils.[3] For countless generations, the entire utilitarian and artistic environment of the Russian peasant was fashioned of wood, and this constant close contact with the surrounding, all-enveloping forests contributed richly to the sylvan lore, the arts of woodcraft, and the great skill of the Russian carpenter. Building in wood acquired a very special place in Russian architecture, its distinctive and most typical forms being closely bound up, in their origin, with the products of the forest, with the essential virtues and limitations of wood.

The relative scarcity of stone on Russia's vast plains had much influence on the development of architecture and sculpture. The pre-Petrine architecture of the country was, for the most part, wooden. Public buildings were, as a rule, of oak and pine—of brick only in the larger centers. The old churches, the mansions of the boyars and the palaces of the tsars, the stockades, and the watchtowers and ramparts of the towns were of wood, and therefore the Russian villages and most of the towns were subject to frequent fires that periodically destroyed the old architectural monuments. The wooden buildings of ancient Russia, because of the limitations inherent in the material, never assumed the imposing dimensions of the castles of France or England or of the

[2] Kliuchevsky, *Kurs Russkoi istorii*, I, 46. [3] *Ibid.*, 70–72.

Rhenish cathedrals. In comparison, the old churches of Russia are small. It has been only since the conquest of the Baltic and the Black Sea that stone architecture has become prevalent.

It has already been noted that the rarity of good stone and marble affected the development of sculpture. Wood or even brick architecture is not exactly favorable to the development of monumental statuary. The Russian sculptor, of necessity, had to concentrate on the use of wood which, because of its natural properties, dictated its own peculiar techniques, restricting the development of sculpture in the round in favor of low relief carving.

The Waterways

In a country as vast as Russia the waterways have always been of paramount importance; for many centuries they were the only means of communication. Russia's rivers, the great arteries with which she is so well endowed, are long, deep, wide, and sinuous, flowing in many directions. In their capacity as trade routes they fostered the growth of commerce and contributed to the development of cultural centers. Russian colonization, trade, and culture everywhere followed the course of the waters.

The tableland of the Valdai is the dominant point in the river system. Here are located the headwaters of all the great rivers, the chief tributaries of Russia's four seas. Near this tableland are the sources of the Volga, which ultimately reaches the Caspian; the Dnieper, flowing to the Black Sea; the Western Dvina, which runs into the Baltic; the Velikaia; the Volkhov; the rivers forming Lake Ilmen; and those which feed Lakes Ladoga and Onega. A glance at the map will show that the Dnieper and the Volga flow south and east—a course which has had its influence on the development of Russian political, economical, and cultural history. This history, indeed, begins in the northwest, near the Valdai hills; the old commercial cities of Novgorod and Pskov are situated on the Volkhov and Lake Peipus respectively. Their connection with the Baltic Sea is a network of rivers and lakes which terminates in the Neva, a short but very wide river on which St. Petersburg (Leningrad), a modern counterpart of ancient Novgorod, was founded in 1703 by Peter the Great.

It is mainly to the Dnieper that ancient Russia owed its contact with northwestern and southeastern Europe. From the northwest, as S. M. Solov'ev points out, came the ruling princes of Russia; from the southeast, Christianity was received.[4] The Dnieper was the main link in the waterway system known as "the great way from the Varangian land to the Greeks," which led from the Gulf of Finland through the Neva, Lake Ladoga, the Volkhov, and Lake Ilmen to the Lovat River; thence by small, shallow streams and across some portages to the Western Dvina, the Dnieper, and finally to the Black Sea and the "Greeks," that is, Byzantium.

The great mass of the Slavonic population occupied the western half of the Russian plain, and it was by the great river Dnieper, which bisects this plain from north to south, that the crafts, industry, and commerce of the population were governed. Because in those days rivers afforded the only means of communication from point to point, the Dnieper became the principal industrial artery of the western half of the plain. It had close communication, through its sources, with the Western Dvina and the basin of Lake Ilmen (the two most important routes to the Baltic), while its lower portion united the central plateau and the shores of the Black Sea; its tributaries, stretching far to right and left and serving as paths of approach to the main road, made the Dnieper region accessible, on one side, from the basins of the Dniester and Vistula, and, on the other, from those of the Volga and Don, that is, from the Caspian and the Sea of Azov. All this served from earliest times to make the Dnieper a busy trade route, and it became still more so under the influence of the Greek colonies, with which the northern shores of the Black Sea and the eastern shore of the Sea of Azov were dotted several centuries before our era. Southern Russia exported grain,

[4] *Istoriya Rossii s drevneishikh vremen*, I, 19.

fish, and honey, receiving in exchange from the Greeks manufactured articles and art objects. Thus the Greek colonies in the Crimea became the advance posts of Hellenic civilization, and the Greek cultural influence preceded that of Byzantium by more than one thousand years.

Kievan Russia, comprising the provinces of the Dnieper Basin, was oriented along the river's course, and its commercial and cultural life was turned toward the Byzantine Empire. It was by the Dnieper that the fleets of war and commerce descended towards Constantinople and that the Byzantine civilization and Christianity reached Kiev.

Centuries later—when the political center of medieval Russia shifted, first to the Vladimir-Suzdal region and then to Moscow —the Volga became prominent in shaping the destinies of the future empire. The central artery of the country, "Mother Volga" exercised a powerful influence on Russian medieval, political and cultural history. The basin of the Volga and its tributaries (the Oka and the Kama), the Russian Mesopotamia, was the nodal point of Moscow colonization, industry, and cultural life. It included nearly the whole of sixteenth-century Russia and played a most important role in the development and fortunes of the land. To quote Rambaud, "From the day that the Grand Princes established their capital on the Moskva, a tributary of the Oka and sub-tributary of the Volga, Russia turned to the East, and began her struggle with the Turks and Tatars. The Dnieper drew Russia towards Constantinople and made her Byzantine, the Volga exerted its pull towards the Orient and made her Asiatic; and it was for the Neva (in later years) to make her European. The whole cultural and aesthetic history of this country was influenced by her three great rivers, and it could be justifiably divided into three periods: that of the Dnieper with Kiev, that of the Volga with Moscow, that of the Neva with Novgorod in the eighth century and St. Petersburg in the eighteenth."[5]

[5] Rambaud, *History of Russia,* 27–28.

The Principal Artistic Centers

The network of waterways, the great river systems, were important factors in fostering interstate and foreign trade and facilitating communications between the various sections of the vast land, but at the same time the long, cold winters, which freeze the rivers and interrupt navigation for months at a time, greatly retard all activities. Above all, the in-between periods of season changes, the spring thaws and the heavy autumn rains which flood the plains, used to transform the land into one vast sea of mud and make roads impassable. Besides, the enormous waste spaces unfit for civilization, the frozen tundras bordering on the Arctic Ocean, the salt-impregnated marshes of the Black and Caspian Sea regions, were factors contributing to the unequal distribution of the population. All this, in ancient times, resulted in the concentration of the population in relatively few centers.

The urban population, in contrast to the rural, was relatively small, and the few large cities were like isolated intellectual oases in the immense expanses of the backward rural countryside. Those familiar with Russian literature of the nineteenth and early twentieth centuries will remember the frequent plaintive reference to this hinterland (*glush*) as the land of mental stupor, intellectual inertia, vegetating life, ennui, and stagnation.

This isolation of the cultural centers and the unequal distribution of population had an enormous effect on the unity and homogeneity of the artistic life of Russia. The cultural life of the upper and lower classes followed divergent trends aggravated by social cleavage. The arts and the crafts developed along two different and distinct lines. On the one hand was the art of the city, the sophisticated art of the Russian upper classes; on the other were the rustic arts and crafts of the common people, the peasantry, engendered and fostered in the quietness of the *glush* and nourished by racial experiences and centuries of tradition. Shut off from the large intellectual centers by the physical

24

barriers of dense forests and marshlands, the vast slow-moving hinterland developed a singularly homogeneous culture which endowed its primitive art with fresh simplicity and a definite indigenous character.

The urban artistic centers were very few in number, and artistic activity was usually concentrated in one region or one city at a time. After the decline and fall of Kiev, art emigrated to the Vladimir-Suzdal region, then to Moscow, and later to St. Petersburg. When the torch of learning and art was extinguished in one center, it was lit in another.

As may perhaps be expected, the finest and most inspiring periods of Russian art and crafts were also the periods of renewed enthusiasm and quickened spirit. The establishment of a new political center, the advent of a strong ruler or a new dynasty almost invariably caused an upward sweep of the artistic curve. On the other hand, decline followed fast upon the waning powers of the state, tsar, or emperor.

If we follow the evolution of Russian art across the centuries, from antiquity to our own days, we find four successive centers, or foci of art:

1. The Crimea and the northern shores of the Black Sea.
2. The region adjoining "the great way from the Varangian land to the Greeks," that is, from Scandinavia to Byzantium via Novgorod and Kiev.
3. The region of Moscow, comprising the basin of the Upper Volga and the Oka with the cities of Vladimir, Moscow, Yaroslavl and Rostov.
4. The region of St. Petersburg (Leningrad) and Moscow again.

Part One

The Pre-Christian Era

III

The Scythians and Greeks in South Russia

THE ESTABLISHMENT of a settled order in Russia is usually assigned to the middle of the ninth century, and Russia's cultural beginnings are commonly dated from the tenth century, when Christianity became the state religion. There is, however, ample evidence that Russia, as an organized state, existed long before the ninth century and formed part of the civilized world, even in the classical period and the period of migrations.[1] Archaeological studies of the ancient cities of southern Russia reveal that they were flourishing centers with an elaborate pagan culture. They indicate an unbroken process of development of the people who had occupied the region around the Dnieper, to the east and west of it, from the Carpathians to the Don—a continuity of culture in this territory from the Scythian to the Kievan state. The objects which were found in the large cemeteries speak eloquently of the wealth and taste of the inhabitants and the great commercial activities of that period.

The region of South Russia was a merging point of many influences—Oriental and Southern influences arriving by way of western Asia, the Caucasus, and the Black Sea; Greek influences spreading along the Dnieper and the Don routes; and Western influences passing down the great Danubian route—resulting in the formation of mixed civilizations which in their turn influenced Central Russia on the one hand and, on the other,

---

[1] For the pre-Christian history of Russia and of the proto-Slavic and Slavic people, see G. Vernadsky, *Ancient Russia.*

Central Europe, especially the region of the Danube.[2] Here cultures succeeded each other from prehistoric times onward: the Cimmerian[3] yielding to Scythian, later to Sarmatian, Gothic, and Hunno-Antic. It may be reasonably assumed that these cultures did not vanish without leaving a trace, nor succeed one another without intermingling. It is more likely that one culture overlaid the other and that the survivors of the earlier population remained in their former domains, even when the region was overrun and subjugated by fresh intruders. The transmission and diffusion of cultural stimuli between the Oriental and Greek elements continued for centuries. The diffusion process was vast and two-directional, so that Greek motifs and concepts which were borrowed and reworked by Eastern peoples eventually were adapted by the Eastern Slavs.

The beginnings of the Greek civilization of the Crimea and the northern shores of the Black Sea date from about the same time as the first appearance of the Scythians in South Russia. The Greek outpost city of Olbia at the mouths of the rivers Bug and Dniester (opposite the present city of Nikolaev) was founded in 644 B.C. Shortly afterward a number of other cities destined to play important roles, in the cultural history of ancient Russia were founded. Among them the more important ones were Khersonesus (Korsun'), close to the present city of Sevastopol; Palakion (Balaclava); Theodosia (Feodosiya); Panticapaeum, on the site of the city of Kerch; Tanais (Azov), at the mouth of the Don; Scythian Naples (Neapol Skifsky), near Simferopol; and many others.[4]

The Greek cities played an important role in the development of international commerce, serving as a link between the Medi-

---

[2] M. Rostovtzeff, *Iranians and Greeks in South Russia*, 7.

[3] The Cimmerians (1000–700 B.C.), until their conquest by the Scythians (*ca.* 700 B.C.), were in control, for a considerable time, of the whole northern littoral of the Black Sea from the Dniester River to the Kerch Strait. To them belong the scanty remnants of bronze culture found in South Russia, dating from the beginning of the first millennium before Christ.

[4] For an illustrated study of the history, art, and architecture of these cities, see V. F. Gaidukevich, *Antichniye goroda severnogo prichernomor'ya*.

terranean and Eurasia. Some of them were large communities in which not only commerce but also art and crafts flourished, while in the neighboring regions agriculture achieved a high level of productivity. Thus the Greek cities of the period became important cultural centers in more than one aspect. They were, moreover, closely bound to the cities of Greece proper as well as to those of Asia Minor, remaining part of the Hellenic world at large. They served therefore as a bridge between the Hellenic world and the Scythians, paving the way for the Hellenization of a considerable portion of the region and contributing no little to the arts of the early Slavic people.

The origin, rise, and progress of the Scythians and how far they are to be identified with the Slavs are questions best answered by anthropologists, ethnologists, and archaeologists. Although excavations of the Scythian burial sites have done much to clarify their culture and constantly bring to light new facts, the origin of the Scythians is still a matter of debate.[5] There are several theories, each of which may have some validity, since it seems that the name "Scythians" has been used to designate tribes of various ethnic stock.

According to the Greek chroniclers, the Scythians originally dwelled in northern Turkestan, and once were dominant in that region; they belonged to the white race and spoke an Aryan or Indo-European language. From Turkestan they spread outward in many directions with momentous effect upon all surrounding countries, forming the first wave of Oriental nomads to sweep across the Black Earth region in historical times. The Scythian

[5] M. Rostovtzeff has advanced the theory of the Iranian origin of the Scythians; the Russian scholars V. V. Grigoriev, I. E. Zabelin, and D. I. Ilovaisky suggest that the Scythians must have been of Slavic origin. (See Ellis H. Minns, *Scythians and Greeks,* 35 ff.). Zabelin believes that the Scythians were the ancestors of the Slavs; he points to the striking resemblance of the figures—their features, haircuts, and clothes—on the Kul-Oba and Nikopol vases to the modern Russians. (I. E. Zabelin, *History of Russian Life* in Russian, I). The Soviet academician B. D. Grekov also claims that genetically the Slavs are related to the Scythians, especially to the Scythian plowman. (B. D. Grekov, *The Culture of Kiev Rus,* 18).

hordes overran all of southern Russia and penetrated even to the center of Europe. The ruling horde, the so-called Royal Scythians, was probably of Iranian origin; some of the auxiliary hordes may have consisted of Ugrians and Mongols; and it is quite possible that other groups known under the name of Scythians— as, for example, the Scythian plowmen *(Aroteres)* and the Neuri —were of proto-Slavic stock.[6]

By the sixth century B.C. the Scythians had firmly established themselves in southern Russia and in the valley of the Kuban and entered into trade with the Greek colonies on the shores of the Black Sea. Their empire included within its domains a large number of different tribes of Scythian origin in addition to many different groups of subjugated people. As conquerors and as a dominant minority, the Royal Scythians developed a highly efficient military organization under the command of their king, who possessed great power. Being nomads—warriors, hunters, and cattle breeders—and preferring to preserve their nomadic way of life, they chose to remain in the steppes stretching between the lower reaches of the Don and the Dnieper, a region suitable for grazing and horse breeding but not for agriculture. The agricultural sections of their empire had to pay tribute in kind. For purposes of administration and tax collection the Scythian state was divided into four provinces, each province being subdivided into nomes or districts governed by tribal chieftains.

In their prime (fifth and fourth centuries B.C.), the Scythians were the masters of all the peoples of South Russia from the Volga to the Bug and of a large part of the Danubian region. These nomad warriors controlled the vital centers of the most important river and overland routes for foreign and international trade. Through the Greek cities of the northern shore of the Black Sea, they were in constant contact with the Hellenic world

6 The Neuri were a tribe which inhabited an area between the upper Dniester and the middle Dnieper rivers, the above area extending to the basins of the western Bug and Vistula. This tribe is generally regarded as Slavic (Niederle, *Slavianskiye drevnosti*, 36.)

and carried on an important trade with the Greeks of Asia Minor and the Balkan peninsula, exporting large quantities of grain, hides, furs, and slaves. In return for this merchandise the Scythians received Greek jewelry, metalwork, and pottery.

In their turn, the Greek colonies found it advantageous to maintain friendly relations both with the Scythians and with their successors, the Sarmatians. The prosperity of Olbia, Panticapaeum, and Khersonesus depended on the existence of a stable kingdom in South Russia, guaranteeing these cities unmolested commercial intercourse with the people inhabiting the basins of the great rivers.

The Scythian domination of the steppes lasted some five centuries. Their protracted stay in South Russia and the establishment of relative peace and order resulted in the development of material cultures combining elements of the indigenous Greek culture and the Iranian elements brought by the conquering nomads, who, as we shall see, were endowed with an acute artistic sense.

The Scythian People and their Culture

History has left us but little record of the early culture of the Scythians. Our knowledge of them largely depends on secondary sources, since the Scythians did not have a system of writing or a coinage. Our firsthand information is, of necessity, based on deductions derived from analyzing the great variety of objects found in their graves. These objects shed much light on the Scythians' way of life, on their peculiar beliefs in the hereafter, and on their habits and occupations, but, above all, they reveal the Scythians' great artistic talents and help us to assess their contributions to the art of southern Russia and Western Europe.

Herodotus gave many details of their habits, occupations, clothing, and arms, their behavior in warfare, their religious belief, and funeral rites, but so incredible seemed his tales that, until late in the nineteenth century, many scholars tended to dismiss them as utterly fantastic. However, recent archaeological discoveries have produced corroborative evidence to support many of his assertions. His description of the embalming process and the funerary ceremonial has been largely confirmed by the embalmed bodies and the various furnishings recently found in the frozen tombs of the Pazyryk region in eastern Altai.

According to Herodotus, the Scythians were polytheists, worshiping a number of different gods and goddesses. Their main devotions were paid to the great goddess, Tabiti-Vesta, the goddess of fire and perhaps also of beasts. She alone figures in their art, presiding at the taking of oaths, administering communion, or anointing chieftains. Rostovtzeff found that she had been worshiped in southern Russia long before the Scythians appeared there.[7] In Scythian art she sometimes appears as half-woman, half-serpent, sometimes standing, sometimes seated between her sacred beasts, the raven and the dog, or sometimes with an attendant or in conversation with a chieftain.

The great goddess is often shown seated on a throne while a nomad chieftain stands before her prayerfully either to invoke her help or else to be invested by her with regal powers. The most impressive rendering of this scene of initiation or anointment appears on a felt hanging found in the Pazyryk Mound No. 5 in the eastern Altai region. There the goddess is shown seated in majesty on a throne with a sacred tree set at her side, while a mounted warrior faces her.

The ceremony of the sacred oaths taken by the Scythians, as described by Herodotus, had some peculiar religious significance. When the Scythians made a treaty and a solemn oath had to be taken, "a large earthern bowl is filled with wine and the parties to the oath, wounding themselves slightly with a knife or an awl, drop some of their blood into the wine; then plunge into the mixture a scimitar, some arrows, a battle-axe, and a javelin, all the while repeating prayers; lastly the con-

[7] *Iranians and Greeks*, 107.

tracting parties drink each a draught from the bowl, as do also the chief men among their followers."[8]

Herodotus also noted that the Scythians had no images, altars, temples. Instead, they lavished much of their attention and veneration on the tombs of their dead. Their burial rites, especially for their kings and chieftains, were elaborate, savage, and cruel. The deceased was accompanied in his grave by one of the royal concubines who was ceremoniously strangled on this occasion, as were his servants, such as his cup bearer, his cook, and head groom, and the horses which he had personally used during his lifetime. His prized possessions and all that was thought to be needed for future life were stored in his grave: meat in large quantities in big caldrons, wine and olive oil in large jars, insignia of his power (scepters, axes, and other regalia), his best arms, his best robes and ornaments, in fact, objects of all descriptions.[9] The profusion of gold and of rich jewelry found in the graves is impressive.

A characteristic aspect of the Scythian culture is the placement of the departed's horses about the funeral structure. The graves of the archaic epoch from the Kuban district are especially characteristic: in them the horses encircled the tent-shaped wooden tomb on all four sides.

The Scythian and Sarmatian domination in South Russia has left us an illustrated record of the culture, arts, and customs of that age. The more prosperous period of that age is well documented by the magnificent treasures which have come from the rich tumuli (*kurgany* in Russian) scattered all over the steppes and along the rivers of South Russia. A vast number of them are located about the mouths of the Danube and the Dniester, stretching upward along the Bug to Mogilev-Podolsky; along the Dnieper and its tributaries up to Smela (west of the Dnieper, near Cherkassy) and Romny (northeast of Kiev); all over Cri-

---

[8] Herodotus, *History*, 225.

[9] For a description of the ritual, see Herodotus, *History*, 225; Minns, *Scythians and Greeks*, 87–88; Rostovtzeff, *Iranians and Greeks*, 45.

SOUTH RUSSIA

KURSK

VORONEZH

0 20 40 60 80 100 miles

• Kharkov

KHARKOV

Starobelsk

Migulinskaya

Golubinskaya

Donets River

EKATERINOSLAV

LAND OF THE
DON COSSACKS

Don River

Tanais
Taganrog Fedulovo
Novocherkask
Elizavetovskaya

Sea of Azov

KUBAN

STAVROPOL

Cimmerian Bosporus

Novokorsunskaya
Ladozh Kazanskaya
Maryin Ust-Labin
Seven Brothers Voronezh Ulski Kuban
Ekaterinodar Vozdvizhen Stavropol
Anapa Siver:
Panticapoeum Karagodeuashkh Kelermes Kostromskaya
Novorossisk Maikop Yaroslavskaya
Kurdzhips Tsarskaya
River

Sea

mea; along the Don and the shores of the Sea of Azov; and along the Kuban and its tributaries as far as the Caspian Sea. Many of these tumuli are concentrated around the various ancient settlements, along the old trade routes and transfer points, and some stretch out in belts near the sites of ancient Greek cities and colonies. Nearly all of them show the same burial arrangements, and in those which were not plundered soon after the burial a wealth of bejeweled arms, costly utensils, diadems, collars, ornamental plaques, rings, and necklaces have been found. There was much gold and silver in all of them, bronze being used only for common utensils and iron for heavy arms and the chassis of chariots. As a rule, the parade arms and vessels, the horse-trappings and personal costume accessories were made either of solid gold or covered with gold plaques.

Items that have come down to us, including the most utilitarian objects, arrest attention, first because of the skill with which they were fashioned, and second because of the strongly individual style of the animal representations with which most are decorated. These figures reveal a preoccupation with the animal world and an ability to express this world's essential features with a directness, ingenuity, and power that are seldom found in nomadic art. Indeed, the animal forms which the Scythians created are so alive and attractive that the modern eye is instantly caught by them.

To the period of the latter part of the fourth century B.C. belong the most imposing tumuli of South Russia. The richest among them are: Kul-Oba near Panticapaeum; Karagodeuashkh in the neighborhood of Novorossisk; the graves to the east and west of the lower Dnieper, Chertomlyk, and Solokha; the group at Serogozy; the group on the middle Dnieper near Smela, province of Kiev, and near Romny, province of Poltava, scattered graves farther to the west near Ryzhanovka, province of Kiev; and an interesting group on the middle Don.

To these must be added the treasures found in the graves scattered all over Siberia and central Asia. Together they constitute a very important part of the decorative art collections of Russia, and at the same time the most national, springing, as it were, from the cradle of the race.

The Gold Treasure Gallery of the Hermitage Museum in Leningrad, where the bulk of the finds has been concentrated, and museums in Moscow, Kiev, Dniepropetrovsk and other cities possess rich collections of antiquities from the Scythian and Sarmatian periods. The remains of these ancient cultures, in their wealth of precious metals and their peculiar character, demonstrate the diverse influences to which they had been exposed. We can distinguish the Greek and Iranian elements, the impulses emanating from the Caucasus and Asia Minor, and also those from Western Europe. We find that, despite the particular intensity of the Greek influence, an independent native element, strong and indeed dominating, had been at work.

IV

Scythian Art

SCYTHIAN ART is large in scope but relatively little known. The museums of Russia are filled with large quantities of gold and silver plaques, reliefs, and full-round sculptures in wood or bronze, sarcophagi, and domestic utensils; but the study of this assortment of material from a bygone artistic world is only in its preliminary stage. The greater part of the objects, in Russian and other European collections, came from chance finds or through excavations carried out during the nineteenth century. A number of graves were opened and robbed by Russian treasure hunters in the seventeenth and the eighteenth centuries. Some, however, remained either hidden or only partially plundered, while others have been but recently discovered by Soviet archaeologists. Details of the discoveries are usually meager. A truly scientific method of excavation has been undertaken only in relatively recent times.

As excavations in Russia multiplied, producing ever more examples of Scythian art, it became evident that the whole of the Eurasian steppe had a life which stretched far back into the past and that, in the Scythian period, all parts of it had been linked by close and regular contacts.

The origin of Scythian art is much disputed. Rostovtzeff, who analyzed the subject in great detail, is inclined to consider central Asia the source of the style, A. M. Tallgren points to Russian Turkestan, G. Borovka to northern Siberia, H. Schmidt to the ancient Orient, and M. Ebert to Ionia and the coast of the Black Sea.

The Soviet scholars M. I. Artamonov and S. A. Zhebelev have yet another opinion. Concerning the Scythian or animal style, they point out the presence in it, from early times, of elements pertaining to all the above regions—especially the elements that had penetrated from the East and then from the antique classical world—built around a distinct indigenous core. Regarding the features common to the art of the extensive territories where the so-called Scytho-Siberian art prevailed, they point out that both the Scythian and Siberian arts are characterized not only by the diffusion of the same foreign influences but by the interchange of forms and motifs of indigenous origin. Stressing the thesis that "in the first stages of its existence the animal style was prevalent among the upper layers of barbarian society," Artamonov and Zhebelev express the opinion that this art was stimulated and developed by the need of decorating and embellishing various objects of ceremony and parade.[1]

Other scholars believe that Scythian art is completely original and autonomous, and tend to minimize the influences of the outside world. As so often happens, the truth eludes exact determination.

Scythian art came under the influence of both the Far East and Greece, and the problem of its origin can be better understood when we consider the extensive importation into Scythia of Greek and Iranian objects of all kinds of various periods. As we have already pointed out, Greek colonies existed in the Crimea and along the northern shore of the Black Sea at a very early time. Greek artists had workshops in those cities, where local artists and craftsmen worked side by side with craftsmen from metropolitan Greece or from the Greek cities in Asia Minor.

Nevertheless, while Greek influence was considerable, it did not overwhelm the indigenous artistic idiom of a people whose

[1] S. I. and N. M. Rudenko, *Iskusstvo Skifov Alta'ya*, 11.

temperament differed greatly from that of the Greeks. Certainly the Scythians' reactions to these influences, in the course of time, depended upon the circumstances and places in which they were located. Drawing widely on available material, they were stimulated by a variety of sources. But despite certain obvious similarities, the style of representing a borrowed theme or motif seems to change on closer inspection of the object, and two very different worlds or concepts become apparent. The character of Scythian art retains an individual flavor that is immediately sensed and is sometimes very impressive.)

In investigating the gradual evolution of Scythian life and art, Rostovtzeff differentiates four periods in the history of Scythian civilization, each of them marked by some peculiar feature.[2] These periods are:

    1. The Archaic Period (the end of the seventh, the sixth, and the beginning of the fifth centuries B.C.).

    2. The Transitional or the Perso-Ionian Period (the fifth and the early fourth centuries B.C.).

    3. The Classical Epoch or the Panticapaeum Period, the highest stage of Scythian prosperity (the fourth century B.C.).

    4. The period of decay displaying some new features and influences (the end of the fourth and the beginning of the third centuries B.C.).

A significant prelude to Scythian art is found in the material produced in the early Iron Age. In the eighth century B.C., a civilization commonly referred to as the Minusinsk culture (named for a region in the upper Enisei where large Scythian necropoli had been discovered) extended and developed also throughout a considerable part of Siberia. The earliest objects of art in bronze, iron, and gold—found there in large quantities —are decorated with simple geometric motifs: straight or broken lines, triangles, and swastikas.

The prosperous life of the Scythians in the fourth century B.C. is evidenced by the magnificent treasures which have come from

[2] M. Rostovtzeff, *The Animal Style in South Russia and China*, 23–24.

the Kuban mounds. The tombs are the final resting places of kings and chieftains to whom the finest objects in bronze, silver, and gold were offered for their life beyond the grave.

Greek influences, predominantly Ionian, attained supremacy in 500–400 B.C., for in this period the objects placed in tombs (vases, diadems, collars, and perfume vessels) were products of Greek workshops. These Greek imports were the basis for the diffusion of Greek motifs in Scythian products; the repertory of local artists gave way to a preference for the most varied, fantastic animals—sphinxes and winged lions—whose complex form and sinuous lines appealed to the imagination and taste of the Scythians. But the marks which Hellenism left have remained ineffaceable.

The Scythian Animal Style

The life of the Scythians—as herdsmen, hunters, and warriors —was of necessity so closely bound up with nature in its wilder forms that the tribesmen developed a profound understanding of the animal world. It was this constant close contact with wild life that became instrumental in evolving an art mainly concerned with animal forms. It was an art essentially decorative in character, and the productions of this style display a sensitive feeling for space, a skillful adaptation of the ornament to the shape of the object to be decorated, and a fine understanding of the properties of the material employed. The stylization of its forms, its vivacity, dynamism, and color, corresponds in some measure to the artistic trends of our own day.

Scythian artists had little interest in an art of volume, but compensated for this by endowing their figures and compositions with lively movement. Their predilection for stylized form frequently led to a preference for relief rather than full-round sculpture. Their animal reliefs are endowed with an exuberant and vital elasticity and strength, a powerful suggestion of struggle and action. For the sake of ornamental effect, the artists do not hesitate to place their animals in attitudes which, though sometimes taken from nature, are immoderately exaggerated and occasionally quite fantastic. Bodies are deliberately distorted, legs elongated. The accent is on rhythm and swift motion. The supple, sinuous lines of these reliefs are truly exciting.

The Scythian animal style is at once primitive and highly sophisticated. Its salient characteristic is the purely stylized treatment of the animal figures; its principal features strongly suggest that the style had been developed by a race of hunters. Favorite motifs are:

1. Single figures of beasts of prey or herbiverous animals depicted in various poses: standing, crouching or reclining, or curled up in a circle.

2. Beasts or birds of prey depicted as attacking other animals or as clasping and devouring their victims.

3. Animals linked in combat.

4. Animals in pairs or in groups.

5. Parts of animals; that is, individual members of the animal's body, especially heads or legs.

6. Figures of the animal covered with other complete or partial animal shapes.

Some of these motifs were borrowed from Oriental art; others were transformed by Greek artists and reached South Russia in a modified form. Three main currents are observable in the animal style of South Russia: Assyro-Persian, Hellenic, and Scythian. These currents influenced each other and gave rise to hybrid forms.

The Scythian current, although affected by the two others, has a distinctive individuality; its outstanding feature is its purely decorative quality. The animal figure is subordinated to its ornamental purpose. The paws, the tail, the ends of the horns, and the ears, seldom retain their natural form; they are usually transformed into heads of other creatures. The heads most frequently used are those of birds of prey, lions, panthers, elk, wild goats, and rams. These heads are reduced to their essential elements and stylized. In some motifs all that remains of the bird's head is a beak; of the lion's head, the ears, eyes, and a vestige of the muzzle.

Beasts of prey, especially those of the cat family, play a prominent role in Scythian art. The representation of these animals must be attributed to foreign influence since neither the panther nor the lion is a native to southern Russia. However, in northeastern Russia and Siberia, the bear, an animal as much at home in those wooded regions as the elk, occasionally appears in motifs which in Scythia portray the feline beast.

The chief herbivorous animals in Scythian art are those belonging to the reindeer family. Stags and elks are common, usually shown in crouching positions with their legs bent under their bodies; they appear upon quiver cases, breastplates, shields, on top of standard poles, and on bridle cheekpieces and other trappings.

The wild goat is quite common, especially on Siberian articles. Figures of these animals in the round were often used as decorations, perched on rims of vessels and crowns. (See, for example, the Novocherkask diadem, Plate 8.)

The motif of animals linked in combat is widespread, but nowhere was it expressed with such fervor as in the Altai region. An early Scythian version, as opposed to an Altaian one, comes from the Seven Brothers Barrow in the Kuban, where a wooden rhyton of the early fifth century B.C. was decorated with four gold plaques. Each plaque shows a bird of prey or another carnivorous animal attacking a herbivorous one. A winged lion is seen attacking a mountain goat; its claws have gripped the victim's flank as it takes a bite out of its back. The agony in the goat's eye is particularly expressive.

The bird is also a favorite subject, sometimes with wings spread to form a gold plaque for sewing on clothes, more often a mere head or beak, upon standards and horses' cheekpieces.

Significantly, the ox—the animal associated with the plowman—hardly ever appears as a motif.

The rich variety of the animals themselves is no less impressive than the diverse aspects in which they appear. Real and imaginary beasts jostle each other, intertwine and intermix in such an unfettered, fanciful manner that a new, unexpected world unfolds before us.

The conventionalized transformation of the antlers of the deer or the horns of the ram and the wild goat into decorative shapes was another favorite device. It originated a series of variations and diverse combinations in which animal motifs are interwoven with floral motifs, especially palmettes. The horns of an elk may form a palmette, or the horns of a stag may be transformed into a floral ornament above its head.

The Art of the Sarmatians

In the last centuries B.C., a new group of warrior tribes—the Sarmatians—appeared on the steppes of the Black Sea. Like the Scythians, they were a nomadic people, horse and cattle breeders in the region of Kazakhstan. Their social structure and mode of life had much in common with those of the Scythians. The Sarmatian tribes began to move westward, toward the Pontic steppes, in the third century B.C., gradually breaking down Scythian resistance. By the middle of the second century B.C. the Sarmatians replaced the Scythians as rulers of South Russia.

Being nomads, the Sarmatians depended on local and neighboring populations for their supplies of agricultural products and luxury items. Like the Scythians, they were traders and therefore found it profitable to maintain peace and protect the commercial highways. As in the Scythian period, the Greeks of the Black Sea area played an important part as middlemen between the inhabitants of the South Russian steppes and the Mediterranean world. The Greek towns on the Black Sea kept their position as centers of production and exportation. Their artists and craftsmen continued to work for customers in the South Russian steppes.

Like their predecessors, the Sarmatians revealed their artistic talents mainly in the field of the decorative arts and crafts (utensils, costume jewelry, armor, weapons, and other items). They developed the art of combining precious metals with colored gems and brought it to a high degree of perfection. Their principal motifs were still those derived from the animal style, but in the hands of their artists the style acquired a more conventional and richly decorative character, leading to the appearance at Panticapaeum and in the Siberian steppes of the polychrome style of jewelry.

The gold diadem from Novocherkask (Plate 8) is a characteristic specimen of this jewelry. The shape and the cameo which adorns the front of the diadem are Greek, as are the pendants attached to the lower part of the diadem. But the upper row of figures representing the sacred trees flanked by goats and deer is in pure animal style and reminds one of the motifs found in Siberian jewelry.

The most favored color combinations were gold with red stones: garnets or red chalcedony (carnelian). Horse trappings were usually decorated with gilded bronze plaques set with red chalcedony stones.

The characteristic feature of the polychrome style at Panticapaeum and in the Sarmatian world is not merely the use of precious stones to adorn jewelry but something more important and distinctive. Instead of merely providing settings for precious stones, it incrusts gold objects and ornaments surfaces with gems and cut stones, occasionally enamels. The surface gradually becomes no more than a field for incrustation and for the production of polychrome effects. The goldsmith uses inset gems of various shapes and sizes and glass and enamels of various hues. The result is a surface ornamented with precious stones, in which the color scheme is of primary importance.

Compared with the original, more primitive stages of the Scythian animal style, this later phase is distinguished for both strength and refinement. It includes some new motifs: a series of fantastic monsters whose bodies are composed of the members of various beasts and birds. Prominent is the Iranian winged griffin with a horned lion's head or with an eared eagle's head, both heads crested. This motif begins to play a very conspicuous role and becomes the progenitor of diverse variants. The style reveals a new trend and a new force; it is no longer Scythian, but represents the decorative skill and artistic concepts of the Sarmatians. It spread all over central Asia, Siberia and South Russia. From South Russia and Siberia it entered central, eastern, and northern Russia and developed there a vigorous offshoot in a highly conventionalized animal style. From this phase of the style we may trace threads which lead us right into the foundation of South Russian civilization.

V

Major Scythian and Sarmatian Tumuli in South Russia

THE SCYTHIAN and Sarmatian antiquities discovered in the tumuli of South Russia can be divided into four principal groups: the Dnieper River, the Strait of Kerch, the Kuban River, and the Don River. The distribution of the tumuli reaches from the Podolia and Kiev provinces southwards toward the Black Sea and eastward to the valley of the Kuban on the northern slopes of the Caucasus. The finest are at the bend of the Dnieper, near Alexandropol; a few occur about the towns of the Bosporus on each side of the Strait of Kerch. Objects of a type resembling the barbarian element in Scythian tumuli can be traced right across Siberia to Krasnoyarsk beyond the Altai mountains.

The Dnieper Group

Among the tumuli of the lower Dnieper region, the most remarkable are those of Alexanderopol, Chertomlyk, and Solokha.

The tumulus of Alexandropol (mid-fourth century B.C.), known as the *Lugovaya Mogila* (the Grave of the Meadow) and discovered in 1851, is in the region of Ekaterinoslav (Dniepropetrovsk at present). It was pillaged by thieves, and only a few objects—remains of two chariots and bronze standards—were left for archaeological study.

Chertomlyk (fourth century B.C.), about twelve miles northwest of Nikopol, was excavated by Zabelin in 1859–63. It is perhaps the richest of the group, both in the variety and in the artistic quality of the objects found in it, and also in the fabulous intrinsic value of the goldsmith work. The tumulus contained a central burial chamber with four minor chambers radiating from it. Not only the king's grave but the queen's grave was found there. A bronze torque encircles the king's neck and gold rings were on all his fingers. An ivory-handled dagger, a gorytus[1] containing bronze arrowheads, a golden hilt of a sword, a scabbard, and a whip lay within easy reach of the body.

The jewels worn by the queen are extremely rich, very heavy and valuable. Her costume is loaded with gold, especially the great conical tiara, of the Irano-Greek type. Near her was a bronze mirror set in blue paste. It was here that the famous Nikopol vase of Chertomlyk (Plate 7) was discovered, in addition to two bronze caldrons, numerous stamped gold plaques and roundels (bractae[2]), and several saddles and bridles.

The Nikopol vase—about 28 inches high and about 15½ inches at its greatest diameter—is a silver, partly gilt, amphora with two handles. The arrangement of the outlets, plugs, and strainers suggest that the vase was meant for some liquid which forms a scum or sediment, probable *kumys*.[3] The whole of the surface with the exception of the neck and handles is covered with a *repoussé* decoration consisting of foliage, amongst which are placed on each side two large birds and two smaller ones. Both the fauna and the flora are those of the steppes; the larger birds seem to be the cranes which abound there, and the smaller a kind of pigeon-hawk or rook.

The ornaments on the two sides of the base are similar in design, but the figures in front are in fairly high relief, while as we follow the designs toward the back, the *repoussé* work shades

[1] A case for bow and arrows, made of wood or leather. The bow cases of Scythian chieftains were covered with gold or silver plates decorated with elaborate designs usually depicting military scenes.

[2] Also spelled bractea, small dress ornaments of gold or electrum, they are mostly round thin plates pierced with holes for sewing. The ornament is *repoussé* or die-stamped.

[3] A drink made from fermented mare's or camel's milk.

off and becomes quite flat. The whole of the foot, the neck, and the *repoussé* work are heavily gilt. It is evident that this vase was made for some great Scythian chief, probably during the fourth century B.C.

The artist must have had firsthand knowledge of the Scythians, their dress, customs, occupation, and the flora and fauna of their land, as shown by the figures in relief. The most interesting part of the decoration is the frieze (Plate 7) which runs around the shoulder, below the handles, and beneath a group of a stag and griffins. This is composed of a number of figures forming two distinct scenes, one on the front and the other on the back of the vase. They portray a most important part of the daily occupation of the nomad Scythians: the breaking-in and training of the wild horses of the steppes.

All the figures, five bearded men and three youths, are evidently Scythians, dressed in their belted blouses and full trousers tucked into boots. The hair is cut Russian fashion; their features and characteristics are similar to those found among the present-day dwellers in that region.

The bractae consists, for the most part, of small thin plates of gold or electrum,[4] pierced with holes for sewing. They are of various sizes and shapes, *repoussé* or stamped with simple designs of flowers or with figure subjects; with animals, such as winged dragons, hippocampi, panthers, stags, wild boars, dogs, or winged horses; with sphinxes or sirens; with groups of dancing women or domestic subjects; or with martial or hunting details of Scythian life. Some were meant to be worn as single ornaments; others, sewn on in lines, formed regular borders or designs on robes.

The scabbard and gorytus found in the Chertomlyk grave (Plate 3) are made of a thin plaque of gold or electrum; *repoussé* in very slight relief with figures and scenes. The form of the bow-case is like that of the cases carried by the figures

---

[4] Alloy of gold with one-fifth part of silver; its color is paler and more luminous than gold.

on the Nikopol vase or the small Kul-Oba vase. It is a work of great delicacy executed by Greek craftsmen to a Scythian pattern.

The bas-reliefs on the Chertomlyk gorytus may be described as an ensemble of illustrated metallic plaques. In the narrow upper compartment we see a stag brought down by a lion and a panther devouring a gazelle. Below, there unfolds a frieze in two tiers, the bas-reliefs depicting mythological scenes.[5]

Of the two caldrons, the larger is about three feet in height. Six beautifully modeled ibexes range round its rim, serving as handles.

The Kerch Group

The most celebrated tumuli in the region of the Strait of Kerch are the Royal Tumulus (*Tsarsky kurgan*), the Golden Tumulus (*Zolotoi kurgan* or Altyn-Oba), and, most important, Kul-Oba (the Mound of Cinders of the Ash-Heap). These tumuli, dating from the late fifth and early fourth centuries B.C., were explored in 1831 by the Frenchman, Dubrux. The grave of Kul-Oba contained the bodies of a king and his queen. The diadem, bracelets, armlet, medallions, and collar found on their bodies, the gorytus, vases, and other art objects that were around them, are of great beauty and originality.

The small vase (Plate 4), found at the feet of the queen in the Kul-Oba tomb is an extremely interesting piece ethnographically as well as artistically. It is of electrum, somewhat globular in shape, with a small foot. On the lower part is a gadrooned and guilloched ornament, and on a band encircling the center are the Scythian genre scenes which give so much interest to the piece. These are exquisitely executed in *repoussé* and chased, all rendered with great attention to detail; they depict characteristic episodes from Scythian military life and portray with great

---

[5] According to Mr. Stephani, former keeper of antiquities at the Hermitage Museum, it is the legend of Alope, daughter of Cercyon, king of Scythia (cited by A. Maskell, *Russian Art and Art Objects in Russia*, 58).

fidelity the native costumes, arms, and accouterments of those days.

The scene to the right (Plate 4) depicts in great detail the field operation—the bandaging of the Scythian chief's wounded leg. The chief is in Scythian costume—blouse belted at the waist, full trousers tucked into his boots—a costume which has descended almost unchanged to the Russian of recent years. The attending warrior wears an almost identical costume, with his head covered by a *bashlyk* (a kind of a hood coming over the shoulders) which is also popular in Russia. This is, as on the Nikopol vase, an almost photographic portrayal of the Scythians of those days: the long hair, the scraggly beard, the blouse, the *bashlyk*, and the boots.

The next scene depicts another field operation—a tooth extraction being performed on the chief by his attendant, acting as camp dentist. Most notable are the expressions of attention, pain, and comradely solicitude. The clothing of the Scythian warriors appears to be ornamented with small geometrical figures arranged in rows. The bow-cases are of the usual Scythian form, similar examples of which are found in the regalia (Plate 167) of seventeenth-century Russian tsars.

Another scene depicts a Scythian warrior occupied in bending a bow, apparently the chief's bow because the warrior has another at his side.

The bracelet is one of a pair. The band of each is formed of a cable terminating at the open ends in two figures of sphinxes. The lower parts of the bodies of the latter enter into the collared ends of the band, which are ornamented with filigree and were at one time partly enameled. The sphinxes hold in their paws a serpent in thin wire which joins together the open ends.

Among the other objects found at Kul-Oba the most interesting are a gold belt clasp, a gold earring, and an electrum plaque with a figure of a dying stag on it.

The figures on the belt clasp represent two Scythians embracing, each holding with one hand the same drinking horn. The two men wear the characteristic clothing of their nation. The horn appears to be an ordinary ox-horn. Rostovtzeff is of the opinion that the scene represents the Scythian ceremony of the sacred oath performed at the conclusion of a treaty of alliance or of making a contract.

The gold earring dates from the fourth century B.C. The medallion contains a relief figure of a woman modeled after a statue by Phydias (Plate 5).

The electrum plaque with *repoussé* ornament depicts a dying stag in his last agonies (Plate 2). There are figures of various wild animals placed on different parts of the stag's body as if ready to devour it. The plaque is thought to have been executed, some time during the fourth century B.C., by a Greek artist who tried to emulate the Scythian example found at the Kostromskaya Stanitsa in the Kuban district.

The Kuban and the Don Groups

The Kuban Group includes the tumuli of the Seven Brothers *(Semibratskaya Mogila* at Cape Ak-Burun), those of Karagodeuashkh (near the Krymskaya railway station, twenty miles northeast of Novorossisk, discovered in 1888), Kelermes, Maikop, Kostromskaya (seventh to sixth centuries B.C.), and others. Farther north on the Don are the tumuli of Novocherkask (first century B.C.–first century A.D.) and Elizavetinskaya (fifth to fourth centuries B.C.)

The richest archaic finds were discovered at the tumulus of Kelermes. The objects found there are of great intrinsic value. Prominent among them are a battle-axe of iron plated with gold, its handle decorated with a series of animals, standing or at rest;[6] another is a massive chased gold plaque in the form of a half-crouched lion which probably adorned the breast-piece of a corselet. Each of the lion's paws has the form of a curled lion, and the tail is covered with six figures of the same kind. The

[6] Rostovtzeff, *Iranians and Greeks,* plate VIII.

ears, eyes, and nostrils of the beast are inlaid with amber, the ears in the technique of cloisonné work.

From the tomb of Kostromskaya Tumulus comes one of the most famous examples of the Scythian animal style: the Sitting Stag (Plate 1).

The portrayal of this animal has the characteristic peculiarities of the Scythian style. The legs are tapered and doubled up under the body, while the neck and head are stretched far forward and upward. The antlers, with their hooked branches, are arranged in waves extended along the back. The artist, instead of portraying the animal literally, attempted to present his vivid impression of the stag under particular circumstances. His representation, though stylized, fully conveys the high tension and elasticity of the body, the grace and yet the strength of the legs, the extended and agitated neck and head, the quivering ears— all the result of the keenest observation conveyed in expressive and simple forms. The motif was often repeated with all its peculiarities by other Scythian artists (Plate 2), but none surpassed the creator of this example.

From the graves of the Seven Brothers a rich and large collection of precious objects was brought to light in 1875. Rostovtzeff ascribes them to the fifth and early fourth centuries b.c.

An outstanding example is a helmet or headdress of pure gold weighing nearly two pounds avoirdupois (Plate 6). It is demi-ovoid in shape, and the ornament is of *repoussé* and pierced work. The band at the base consists of acanthus stems and tendrils. The design above, three times repeated, represents Ionic volutes curling outward, with a lily-like flower between them. The volutes, the acanthus, and the scallop work are undoubtedly of Greek inspiration. But the whole was transformed by the Scythian craftsman into an object truly representative of Scythian art.

The treasure found near Novocherkask (1864) on the lower Don included the famous diadem and collar, a gold box and perfume bottle, and many other art objects.

The diadem (Plate 8), ascribed to the first century B.C.–third century A.D., is of pure gold, set with large pearls, amethysts, and garnets ornamented with a large carved amethyst stone representing the bust of a woman. Under the band are a number of pendants; over it is a row of figures representing three sacred trees, flanked by goats and deer. Although the shape of the diadem is Grecian, as are the amethyst bust and the pendants, the ornaments on the upper edge of the diadem are in a pure animal style. The whole is a strange mixture of different elements and workmanship—an adaptation of the art of Greece to indigenous barbaric taste.

The collar is formed of three plain rings of solid cast and hammered gold encrusted with colored inlays of coral and turquoise. A part of it is hinged to open. On the upper and lower tiers of the collar, for about half its circumference, is an open-worked ornamentation consisting of animals alternating with bird-headed monsters. The paws are four-clawed and the tails are long and twisted. The thighs, shoulders, and ears are encrusted with turquoises and pink stones, and the eyes are of topaz. The basis of these motifs is the animal style, but a new Iranian-Sarmatian element is strongly noticeable, bringing with it the opulence of varicolored incrustation so dear to the hearts of the Orientals.

The perfume box is almost hemispherical in form; a smaller box fits within the outer casing and is hinged to it. On the lower part of the box an eagle and an animal of the cat family are represented, both occupied in devouring an elk. On the cover three animals of the wild ass family are symetrically disposed, their feet resting on the filigree mounting of a gem which is now missing. The incrustations of gems on this box are of the usual character.

The gold perfume bottle has a nearly globular body and a rather long plain neck. A cover or lid fits on the latter like a cap and is fastened to it by a short chain passing through four rings or staples, two each on the lid and body respectively. Seed

pearls are on the ends of the chain. The whole of the outer surface is chased in a manner similar to the perfume box, and the
subject is an elk being torn to pieces by an eagle and some kind
of a wildcat.

VI

The Art of the Siberian Nomads

SIBERIAN ART is important because it provides a clue to the origin of the Scythian style. The character of the excavated objects seems to suggest that we must look to central Asia, to a place from which both South Russia and Siberia could be easily reached. Some scholars are of the opinion that western Siberia, and particularly Altai, although it may not have been the cradle of the Scythian animal style, was at any rate the center of its development. The fauna of the animal style, with its profusion of cervoids, points to a land of mountains and forests rather than to a plain suitable to agriculture. That the originators of the style were nomads—hunters and warriors rather than tillers of the soil—is indicated in their portrayals of the wild, predatory beasts and birds, not the domesticated animals of an agricultural life. Yet they were at the same time in touch with the civilized life of the Near East, especially that of the Persian Empire. Some motifs of their animal style and the technique of incrustation with colored gems were borrowed from Persia or from peoples subject to Persia.

The culture of the nomadic tribes who inhabited Siberia resembled that of the Scythian tribes in South Russia. Their origins are still highly conjectural. Our earliest knowledge of these groups came with the first recorded visits of European explorers to Siberia in the early eighteenth century; the important investigations of archaeologists and anthropologists did not begin until the second half of the nineteenth century.

At that time much research work was carried out by Russian archaeologists in southern Siberia, especially in the district of Tomsk and in the Yenisei basin, as far as Lake Baikal and the Altai mountains. The best-studied and richest area is Minusinsk. Its museum contains many articles found both in the nearby graves and in fields. Chronologically, the Bronze and early Iron Age at Minusinsk coincides with the Scythian period in South Russia, especially the early period of Scythian domination—the sixth and fifth centuries B.C. The Scythian and Minusinsk civilizations are very similar, most notably in military equipment.

In decoration, there is also a close resemblance between the art of Minusinsk and that of South Russia. The animal style plays an important part in the Minusinsk art and is of the same type prevalent during the archaic and ripe Scythian period. Rows of animals are used to fill space; beaks and eyes of eagles and eagle-griffins appear as ornamental motifs; and there are the same stylizations of animals, the same crouched or curled positions of the bodies, and the same stylization of the extremities of an animal body. Animals of the Scythian type are used as tops for various objects: the boar so similar to the boar of Alexandropol, and the eagle so typical of the Seven Brothers tumuli.

The objects found in the tumuli of the regions of Amu-Darya, Tobol, Irtysh, and Ob also show a striking similarity to those found in South Russia. We find the same jewelry and funeral ornaments, the same *repoussé* or open-work plaques and trappings with which the Scythians loved to adorn themselves and their horses. There are the same attitudes in the animals, the same decorative devices, and the same treatment of antlers, legs, claws, and tails. However, some of the Siberian plaques (Plates 9–12) exhibit a tendency toward naturalism and ethnographic realism: animals grouped with human beings and placed in a landscape setting—a development foreign to the Scythian style, which is essentially ornamental. It is quite understandable that the influence of the art of Asia was much stronger in this region than in the neighborhood of the Black Sea Greek colonies.

Perhaps the most striking aspect of the Siberian finds is their wealth in gold. Although finds of gold objects in the Siberian tumuli have been extremely rare of late, there is documentary evidence that fabulous wealth was buried and later stolen from those graves. Native Siberian mound diggers (*bugrovshchiki*) and Russian immigrants, especially in the eighteenth century, systematically plundered these graves and melted down the gold and silver they found. Peter the Great's attention was called to the continued grave plundering, the high artistic quality of the objects, and the clandestine traffic in the melted-down gold objects. He issued an *ukaz* ordering that the thieves be severely punished and all retrieved and discovered art objects be surrendered to the *Kunstkamera* (Art Chamber) at St. Petersburg. In obedience to his order several collections were sent to the *Kunstkamera* by the provincial governors. Shortly after his death the collections were transferred to the Academy of Sciences in St. Petersburg. In 1764 Catherine the Second added considerably to the collection which, upon being transferred to the Hermitage Museum, became known as the Siberian Collection of Peter the Great.[1]

The Hermitage Museum in Leningrad contains thousands of items, nearly all of gold, some set with stones, which are classified under the general description of "objects from Siberia," mainly the basins of the Ishim, the Irtysh, and the upper Ob. The Siberian collection includes collars, frontlets, plaques, and belt buckles displaying men, birds, animals, curious animal forms, and combat scenes. Although the scene on each object is different, the scenes are generally uniform in outline: each is rounded along the sides and in the shape of a B (in a horizontal position) on top, with one loop of the letter always smaller than the other.

Prominent among the B-shaped gold plaques is one depicting a struggle between a tiger and a fantastic creature with the paws of a beast of prey, the head of a stylized bear, and antlers, the

[1] See M. Gryaznov *Drevnee iskusstvo Altaya.*

branches of which, like the ends of the creature's tail, are eagle-griffin heads (Plate 12).

Interesting for its subject matter is the plaque depicting life in the forest (Plate 10). The scene represents two horsemen hunting a boar. One is shooting an arrow from his bow at the boar in full flight. The other hunter, ambushed in a tree, holds his terrorized horse by the bridle. He tries to make the horse climb the tree which has saved his own life. The plaque is inlaid with blue paste, and pink coral; the eyes of the men and beasts are in black enamel. The work is probably of the third century A.D.

In the depiction of combat of a lion-griffin and a horse (Plate 9) we have a good example of a favorite device by which the creature's hindquarters are decorated with a pattern of a circle between two triangles, and of another by which an animal is represented as having its hindquarters twisted right around in the agony of struggle for life.

Among the numerous other gold items is a plaque portraying an episode from the life of the early Siberian nomads (Plate 11). The plaque is of massive gold, openworked, showing three persons beneath a tree on which one of them has suspended his bow-case and bow. One figure, seated on the ground, holds the reins of two saddled horses. A second is lying, his head resting on the lap of the third person, a woman. Only one of the three is seen at full length, the warrior who lies on the ground; of the others we see merely the busts or half-lengths. The reclining warrior appears to be dressed in a short close-fitting tunic with leggings and sandals. His hair is short and he wears a long straight moustache. The facial features of the man behind him are similar. The woman wears an open, long-sleeved robe, and her headdress is high and of curious form. The horses and the tree seem to be of a kind peculiar to those regions. In spite of the realistic portrayal of the scene, the story it sought to convey is not clear. Some think that the scene depicts the death of a tribal chief. Others believe that it is simply a detail from the daily life of the early Siberian nomads.

An important step in Scythian archaeology was in the Siberian explorations during the 1860's of V. V. Radlov, who supplemented surface observations of the mounds with excavations. In 1865 his researches brought him to Katanda, in the southern Altai, a site so rich in barrows, and with barrows of such unusual construction, that he decided to open some of the largest. Instead of being topped with just earth, as were the barrows in southern Russia, they were covered with an additional layer of great boulders. Radlov had been at work on the largest of these mounds for but a short time when his men struck a layer of ice. This was especially surprising since they were in a region which is not subjected to perpetual freezing. Radlov had stumbled upon the first of the frozen barrows which are now known to be peculiar to this particular area of the Altai.

The formation of ice in these barrows was caused by the layer of stones which caps them. The autumn rains penetrate this layer and filter down some distance through the earth beneath. During the intense cold of the winter months the moist layer of earth is thoroughly frozen and never melts, even in the summer, because of the insulating layer of the stones above. As a result, most of the bodies and many wood, leather, and fur objects buried beneath the layer of ice have survived for nearly twenty-five hundred years. Radlov found the dead with some of their clothes well preserved and their household objects lying virtually intact.

The most surprising and exciting finds were those in the recently (1924–49) excavated tumuli in the Pazyryk Valley of eastern Altai. The finds revealed a great variety of objects and utensils, dramatic in nature and often, at first sight, quite abstract in design, but all unmistakably the artifacts of a unified society.

The Pazyryk Valley lies on the southern slopes of the Chulishman range in the Altai mountains, about a mile from the Ulagan River. The group of mounds was discovered in 1924 by an expedition of the Russian Museum of Leningrad, but actual excavations were begun under the leadership of S. I. Rudenko in 1929. Rudenko found an important burial ground of some forty mounds. They varied in size and shape, some being round, others oval, but all were topped with boulders. Five mounds were exceptionally large, and nine of the smaller ones closely resemble them both in shape and construction. Although the contents of the graves proved to be sensational, the work was abandoned at the end of the first season. It was resumed in 1947 and continued for two additional years.

The excavations brought to light the story of a people who were not only endowed with an acute decorative sense and with a great skill for expressing it in a wide variety of materials, but who had also attained a relatively high degree of culture involving life in elaborate tents and log houses, fine horsemanship, the use of wheeled carts, and the ability to produce skillfully woven textiles.

The Altai tribes were nomadic, but their pastoral way of life depended to some extent on the existence of agricultural communities. It is more than likely that, by the fifth century B.C., a section of each tribe lived in permanent encampments which served the nomadic members of the tribe as a base. Recent archaeological discoveries indicate that some of the Altaians of the Scythian period (middle of the first millennium B.C.) lived in permanent log houses. The construction of their burial chambers shows a highly developed carpentry technique and the use of many typical details of house construction. The nomads in both the European and Asiatic sectors of the plain appear to have had a very similar way of life and to have followed closely analogous occupations. This seems to be borne out by the similarity in the clothing and equipment of the two groups. The art of the two groups is similar but distinguishable by certain local features resulting in part from the geographical position of each section. Thus, in the Far East, the influence of China was an important factor in the nomadic culture of the area; in the center, Persian elements were more influential; and in the west, those of

Greece. Yet, in spite of these foreign influences, the nomadic culture predominated throughout, tending to express itself with greater power in the Altai region and with greater refinement among the Royal Scyths of southern Russia. The influences were not entirely in one direction, for the indigenous culture of the steppe in turn made itself felt in both the eastern and the western worlds.

The Altai nomads maintained extensive cultural and economic ties with the other tribes of the steppe region. They borrowed much from their near and far neighbors and in turn transmitted to them many elements of their own culture. Consequently their own art contains much that is common both thematically and stylistically to the art of their culturally close kinsmen, the Scytho-Sarmatians and other nomad tribes. The tribesmen of the Altai region developed a culture with a rich artistic expression, sometimes powerful and dramatic, sometimes fine and delicate, but always alive (Plates 13–16). The art is one that had something to say, and what the artists made was not only useful but expressive—telling part of the story of a whole culture. Even for products made to serve practical purposes, the shapes and decorations were devised to have meaning. The objects in gold, silver, iron, bronze, wood, horn, leather, and felt all have a vitality that is striking. It was the intimate knowledge of the animal world, both carnivorous or herbivorous, that contributed so much to the nomad's skill in rendering animals in their characteristic poses—whether resting, crouching, galloping, preparing to attack, or engaging in mortal combat with other animals—always displaying the hunter's keenness of observation and an unerring eye for interesting details.

The art of the early Altai nomads, like that of their western cousins, was essentially decorative and ornamental. Although their animal figures served as embellishment for various objects, it would be wrong to assume that the Altai artists had only decoration as their objective. Their repertory included the telling use of spirits and mythological images.

The world was seen by the nomads as the habitation of a multiplicity of spirits, where the human spirit slips almost imperceptibly into those of various animals, and vice versa. The human aspects of animals can often be recognized in the conventions of representation; the relation between man and certain animals was an intimate one. Often the whole animal was not represented, but was indicated by a part or a number of parts which stood for the whole. Thus a bird of prey might be completely depicted or might be suggested by a head or a beak, or by the eye alone.

Although animal forms were at times presented naturalistically, it was generally the idea or the concept of the animal which the artist expressed. Frequently the expression of that concept might include details of other beasts and birds of prey.

The motif of the eye was given great importance. Animal heads appear in nearly all designs, and the full front view of the open eyes is emphasized. These eyes stare with various degrees of intensity from the objects they adorn, investing them with an impressive sense of inner life.

It is difficult to identify the animals or combinations of animals used on some objects. The identities may have been known only to the patron for whom it was made and to the artist who made it. This is especially true also of the symbolic significance of the totemic figures. They had a multiplicity of meanings which varied with the person using them and with the uses to which they were put.

Many of the representations are fabulous creatures presented in the image of this or that real beast. Therefore the selection of the beast image was limited to those animals whom the nomads believed to possess certain distinctive attributes which especially attracted the attention of ancient men. Those were the tiger and the wolf from the predators, the elk, the stag, the mountain goat and the wild ram of the ungulates, the eagle and the cock of the bird family, and the burbot of the fish. In very ancient times these animals were looked upon as totems—as ancestors and patrons of the clan. With the passing of time the animals lost their particular significance, and in the age of the early nomads they were evidently looked upon as mythical creatures endowed with special secret powers. The horse, goat, antelope, saiga, rabbit, swan, and goose were used as subjects less often.

Fabulous beasts, such as winged lions and sphinxes, entered into the Altaian artistic repertory from the East. The Altaian nomadic imagination seems constantly haunted by these fabulous creatures, and, in this respect, we recognize a preoccupation which is common to the Orient. Generally speaking, Scythian art never ceased to favor a zoomorphic art.

It is significant that the Altaians borrowed from Iran certain mythical motifs. Among them was the griffin, which became one of the perferred subjects in local art. However, the Altaic griffin differs from his Iranian prototype both in style and in content. In Altaian art the griffin is represented in the form of a winged tiger, with a mane or cockscomb on his neck, with long ears, with the horns of an antelope ending in little balls or volutes, and sometimes with the head of an eagle and with feathers on his neck.

Through the intermediary of Iran, Altaian art was also enriched by certain ornamental motifs from the vegetable kingdom which were widely used in the Near East and the Mediterranean. These ornaments were also modified to suit the tastes and techniques of the Altaian artists—the silhouette cut-outs of their felt and leather applications.[2]

---

[2] For an extensive, richly illustrated discussion of the art of the Altai nomads, see S. Rudenko, *Kul'tura naseleniya Tsentral'nogo Altaya v skifskoye vremya,* and, by the same author, *Kul'tura naseleniya Gornogo Altaya v skifskoye vremya.*

VII

The Scytho-Iranian Legacy

ALTHOUGH THE SCYTHIAN PERIOD is not directly connected with the history of the Eastern Slavs, a number of features from the Scythian period were conveyed to and took firm root in the life of the Eastern Slavs. The cultural legacy of the period manifested itself in various aspects of the life of the early Slavs as expressed in social organization, religious beliefs, superstitions, funeral rites, dwellings, dress, and decoration. The early phases of Russian art are bound by many ties to the Scythian and Sarmatian world; in Russian folk art and handicrafts Scytho-Iranian traditions have been kept almost to our own day.

Aside from their immediate contact with both Slavs and the Finns, the Scythians and Sarmatians occupying the steppes of South Russia served also as a link between the Greek and the Persian civilizations on the one hand and the peoples of central and northern Russia on the other. It was due to the facilities of commercial intercourse established through the Bosporan Kingdom that objects of both Parthian and Sassanian origin found their way north up the Volga River. This explains why so many silver vessels of Greco-Bactrian and Sassanian craftsmanship have been found in the southern Ural region.

Archaeological research has given us a picture of the tastes of the early Slavs, examples of their handicrafts and of the kind and quantity of their material possessions. Excavations at Tsarskoe Gorodishche, the site of the ninth-century city of Rostov-Veliki, have revealed not only spinning wheels, axes, potters' implements, and other tools, but also moulds for fashioning articles in silver, bronze, and copper. The objects which were produced by the early Slavs retained many very ancient features in their decoration; especially characteristic are variants of the great goddess and the tree of life, geometric forms of symbolic content, and of the female figure combined with bird attributes, whether derived from a pigeon, duck, or swan. Other popular motifs show the influence of Scythian and Goth designs; the Slavs also probably derived from them such Oriental motifs as the griffin and the siren—the female, sweet-singing bird with a human face.

The influence of Scythian art spread over much of Europe; but it especially affected the lands of ancient Russia, where the diffusion of the Scythian and Sarmatian motifs laid the basis for what we know as the art of old Russia. Some motifs and patterns of the most ancient pagan origin have persisted into the twentieth century—notably in embroideries, in wood and stone carvings, and in the pottery and horse-harness decoration which the peasants adapted for their own use—often showing little change from pagan times.

With the passing of centuries, certain patterns became distorted, representational forms having been transformed into geometric ones; in other instances, change seems to have been intentional, ideograms having been substituted for pagan symbolism at a time when the latter was being ruthlessly eradicated by the Christian clergy. However, some of the patterns have retained their original names, and these give a clue to their meaning by disclosing that certain designs, which are now abstract, are known as the goat, the cock, the calf's eye, and, more significant still, the antler pattern.

The horse and the cock, both of them solar symbols, became prominent in ancient Slavic art. Horses, believed to be endowed with magical powers, found a place in the Slavic sagas, and were soon joined by the fire-bird (*zhar-ptitsa*) and by the cock. The latter took the firmest hold on the people's imagination, and its form survived longer in Slav art than any other ancient motif, retaining its prominence throughout the Slav world to modern times. The versions which appear in Russian and Balkan embroideries trace their descent to the cocks of the Scythian Altai. The Scythian blend of abstraction and realism is also characteristic of Russian decorative art, and designs which come very close to the Altaian examples were produced in the nineteenth and early twentieth centuries, long before the discovery of the Pazyryk tumuli. The antler-like element in the Pazyryk cock's combs likewise survives in Slav art, and the kinship remains clearly marked in other respects.

The chief subjects represented are woman, the horse, as well as the bull, deer, goat, bear, and bird. Man is portrayed very rarely and only as an appendage to the horse. The repertory of subject matter is not accidental. It may be explained as a legacy from pre-Christian times, more precisely from the period of Iranian control over the Slavs. The horse, the bull, the goat, and the bear all played an important role in the rites and mythology of the ancient Slavs. The bird had a special significance in Iranian mythology.

Woman's portrayal in old Russian toys and figurines is to be explained by the ancient Irano-Alarodian cult of the mother goddess. The worship of feminine deities by the Scythians is mentioned by Herodotus. It is characteristic that clay figurines similar to the later Russian toys have been found in some of the old Kievan burial sites. Woman, the horse, and the bird play an important role as subjects of these figurines. The sites of these finds date from the sixth to the thirteenth centuries A.D. Similar figurines and weapons were found in the Gnezdovo burial sites at Smolensk, of the seventh to tenth centuries. Some figurines, such as the bird found at Toporok in the upper Volga region, were undoubtedly used in pagan rites and ceremonies possibly as symbolic offerings. Others may have been used as amulets (Plates 18, 19).

The ornament of Russian folk embroidery has its origin in

dim antiquity. We owe much to the skill and innate taste of the Russian women, needleworkers who have preserved for us in various embroidered articles a pictorial record of figures and scenes depicting the many layers of folk culture and ways of life of the Russian people from pagan times onward. Each period of culture, and especially the Iranian, is reflected in the various ornamental motifs. These embroidery records derive from the nomads of the steppes, the forest dwellers of eastern Asia and Scandinavia, the classical antiquity of the Roman Empire, the barbaric period of pagan Germany, and the art traditions of Byzantium.

The image of the great mother of Iranian times is a prominent motif in old Russian embroidery. The woman in these embroideries is always standing in the center of the picture, always facing the spectator in the characteristic Parthian manner. In the upper part of the typical picture are usually two swastika symbols representing the sun and the moon. The horses, generally placed on either side of the woman, apparently have a symbolic meaning also, since there are usually swastika signs at the bottom of their hoofs. In some scenes deer are represented instead of horses; occasionally, the lion and the panther are shown. Such embroideries contain interesting parallels to certain objects of Scythian and Sarmatian art, such as the famous gold plaque of the tiara from the Karagodeuashkh tumulus, as well as the fragments of a drinking horn from Merdjany in the Kuban region.[1]

Each ornamental motif, every line, every form had its own symbolism which with the passage of time lost its original meaning and peculiar significance, but whose forms were preserved and handed down from generation to generation. The embroiderer followed tradition and worked mostly from memory. It is difficult to trace dates or determine localities, as the figures and ornaments are similar to those found in textiles of many other peoples all over the world, and dating from various periods.

[1] Rostovtzeff, *Iranians and Greeks,* plate XXIII.

However, a comparison, of some figures, such as the fantastic birds and quadrupeds, with similar figures in illuminated manuscripts suggests that the designs of this kind of needlework go back to the earliest times of Russian history. In designs which are composed of geometrical patterns in which the figures are conventionalized, the signs and emblems of religion, of good wishes, and of good augury common to the East can be traced. In addition to geometrical motifs we often find the representation of the sacred tree (the tree of life) embellished with flowers, human figures with raised arms, and scenes depicting votive offerings and the decoration of idols with branches and flowers. In many scenes the sacred tree is flanked by representations of symbolic animals—peacocks, lions, unicorns, birds of paradise— and symbolic signs of augury—swastikas, circles, and rosettes— figures indicating a long ancestry. In later times the subjects for ornamentation were various architectural motifs.

The design of the patterns, embroidered in several techniques, consists of various motifs, the most popular being derived from the animal kingdom. Next in popularity are floral and geometrical motifs. Bilibin points out that in the pattern composed of animal and human figures the most favored motifs are birds and horses and their riders, more rarely various beasts, and almost never fishes.[2] The birds are usually of the fantastic kind and highly ornamented. The peacock, considered to be the most sumptuous motif in design, is usually presented in a highly elongated form with a huge tree-like tail. We also find short-tailed birds, pullets, and chicks. The cock's comb, although of relatively recent date, appears often beside the other motif, the bird of paradise.

There are many varieties of the equestrian motif in design, with the horse usually playing a more important role than the rider. The rider is reduced to secondary importance and becomes insignificant in stature. Sometimes the little fellow is

[2] Bilibin, "Ornamental Motifs in Russian Folk Embroidery," *Mir Iskusstva*, No. 11, 1904.

represented as an odd appurtenance or as a plant. It is for this reason that the equestrian motif group is called "horses" (*Koni*).

The beast motif is quite varied. There are lions, bears, and deer, all represented fantastically: their tails are strung with little birds and their backs are sowed with flowers. Certain animal figures point to a derivation from the distant past. There is an oft-found creature represented with a long body, the head of a horse at each end, and with four or sometimes more legs. Figures of this kind were discovered quite often in the tumuli scattered all over Russia.

The representation of floral ornament was as far from realism as that of the animal. In general, one feels that in folk ornament there is not the slightest attempt at realism.

The design of the Russian peasants' ceremonial towels, which had been for centuries of a devotional character, closely followed early prototypes, with the goddess invariably forming its main motif. She often appears in the same pose as that in which she is shown on Scythian metalwork, being generally flanked either by two princely horsemen, who sometimes have birch twigs twined in their hair and hold offerings, or by mounted priests, the reins of whose horses are firmly grasped by the goddess. The background is filled in with various solar symbols such as cocks, horses, ducks, hares, and fire-birds.

Woodcarving in Russian national architecture has deep pagan roots dating probably to the fourth century B.C. The representation of the benevolent spirits in the form of a horse, bird, snake, or dog are put at all entrances to the house—over the door, window, at the door lock, and near the stove—for the purpose of driving away the malevolent spirits and preventing them from entering the house. The roof is always decorated with a magic symbol—the figure of a horse, sometimes the figure of a bird perched on a vertical support. Horse and bird figures are particularly common in the decorations of the Belorussian peasant huts and on pictures of buildings appearing on the spinning wheels of the Russian North.

Horse forms were introduced into folk art by the sun-worshiping pagan Slavs who used pictorial renderings of the horse to symbolize the golden-maned steeds who drew Apollo's chariot on his daily course across the hemisphere. Spinning wheels, drinking vessels, combs, gingerbread moulds, and children's toys are usually decorated with the figure of a horse. Often these figures are accompanied by those symbolizing the sun: disks, rhombes, and rays. The moulded silver gilt figure of a horse (Plate 19), of sixth-century date found in Martynovka, near Kiev, still retains many features proper to Scythian art, although it is more stylized.

The head of the horse had a religious significance. Planted on long poles, arranged around the house, the skulls of horses were regarded as potent charms for warding off evil spirits. This custom, although greatly modified by the passing centuries, remained in force almost to our own day. In many villages of northern Russia, the carved wooden head of a horse, set on a long pole, used to be placed near the house for exactly the same reasons as the real horse's skull of ancient times. Such carved heads could be found on house roof ridges (Plate 90), near the stoves, and even in the "red" corners of the peasant *izba*, as well as on many household articles.

Examples of the animal-style motifs can be found in the silver temple pendants *(kolty)* of the twelfth century, in various objects of daily home use, in arms and armor; it can also be seen in chapter heads and chapter tails of Russian medieval manuscripts. The influence of the animal style can also be detected in the sculptured decorations on the early Russian churches. It can be observed in the bas-relief series that adorn the walls of the twelfth- and thirteenth-century churches of the Vladimir-Suzdal region, notably the Church of the Intercession of the Virgin on the Nerl and the Cathedral of St. Dmitri at Vladimir (Plates 27, 29). On both of these buildings curious beasts of a heraldic type stand amidst a profusion of Christian and other symbols. The manner of their disposition on the walls is Western rather than Eastern in conception, but the Christian elements and the general style are derived either from Byzantium or from Armenia and Georgia. The animals themselves, however, bear a very close resemblance to the creatures evolved by Scythian designs. They represent a revival of local forms which were reanimated and transformed into something wholly new by the Christian artists of the region.[3]

It is worthy of notice that the decorative arts were flourishing in ancient Russia, especially that branch of the artistic crafts which was traditional with the peoples dwelling along the northern areas of the Black Sea—the art of the metalsmith and the jeweler. The peculiar variants of the animal-style ornament, in which the representation of animals acquired the character of pattern endowed with bright coloring, became widespread.

Until the westernizing reforms of Peter the Great altered the course of the country's civilization, Russian decorative art retained a great many Scythian motifs. Although zoomorphic elements and stag forms were abandoned, many bird patterns persisted, appearing as decorations on various examples of metalwork, ceramics, and needlework. Some domestic utensils, especially spoons and winetasters, retained Scythian shapes and continued to display the arrowhead motifs which are so characteristic of Scythian ornamentation.

[3] Lazarev, in Grabar', *Istoriya russkogo iskusstva* (1953), I, pp. 419–26.

VIII

The Emergence of the Slavs

I T IS DIFFICULT to state just how and when the Slavs appeared on the historical scene. Information on their early history is somewhat nebulous and scarce. Some Russian historians, including Grekov, assert that their origin dates back to pre-Scythian and Scythian times, when various Scythian and Sarmatian tribes and peoples, through long-continued and varied intercourse, gave rise to new ethnic groups, one of which was the Slavonic.[1]

While early Russian annals contain information on the Russian tribes of the ninth and tenth centuries A.D., little is known about their ancestors. It is assumed that their respective ancestral groups consolidated themselves in the Sarmato-Gothic period (200 B.C.–A.D. 370), while the process of their consolidation must have started even much earlier in the Scythian period. According to Jordanis, a Goth who wrote in the sixth century A.D., the Slavs were well known to the Romans, and were divided into three groups: the Wends, the Sclaveni, and the Antes. During the domination of the Goths in South Russia, the Slavs formed a part of the Gothic Empire, under a kind of vassalage. Jordanis, who was well acquainted with the condition of northeastern Europe, knew of their numerous settlements in the Dnieper region and of their occupation of the steppes as far as the Black Sea.[2]

[1] B. D. Grekov, *The Culture of Kiev Rus*, 13.
[2] Cited by Rostovtzeff, *Iranians and Greeks*, 219.

There is some evidence that there existed in ancient times three groups of proto-Slavic tribes: West Slavic, Middle Slavic, and East Slavic. They differed from one another in dialect and customs. Each group controlled its own territory and had its own neighbors, and so was subject to admixture of different foreign ethnic features.

The fall of the Western Roman Empire, followed by the mass migration of Slavs across the Danube into the Eastern Roman Empire, left its impress on the fate of the Slavs as a whole and, in particular, on their East European branch. A new epoch began in the history of the Eastern Slavs, who, from this time on, figure in source material as the Antes.

The Eastern Slavs, the progenitors of the modern Great Russians, Ukrainians, and Byelorussians, are thought to have left their homeland in the Carpathian mountains and to have been living, by the third century A.D., in the territory between the Baltic and Black Sea, and the Don and Danube rivers. Archaeological evidence points to a certain continuity of culture in this territory for the period from 500 B.C. to 500 A.D. The clans of the Eastern Slavs spread along the northern fringe of the steppes, over the area which in pre-Soviet Russia was known as the Left Bank Ukraine and the provinces of Kharkov, Kursk, Poltava, and Voronezh. The Eastern Slavs founded a state of the same type as that of their predecessors. They naturally inherited the towns, the trade relations, and the Greco-Iranian civilization of the Scythians and the Sarmatians, slightly modified. But before the Slavs could evolve and develop their own culture they had to wage a hard struggle with the nomad tribes sweeping over Europe. New invaders of the same stock as the Huns, the Avars, (Western Turks) tried to overpower them, but the young Slavonic state was strong enough to repulse this attack. They drove out the Goths, the Avars, and successfully resisted the onslaught of the Pechenegs (Turko-Tatars). The important point is that the Slavs settled firmly in Eastern Europe.

In the fifth and sixth centuries A.D. Russia was swept clean of her German, Iranian, and Mongolian rulers and inhabitants. Small fractions of the Alans remained on the Kuban, where they still dwell under the name of Ossetians; some Gothic tribes were left behind in the Crimea and on the Taman peninsula; scattered bands of Huns, after their downfall, came back to Russian steppes; but not one of these groups played any part in the future destinies of Russia. The place of the Germans was soon occupied by the Slavs.[3] From the scanty information available about these people, it may be assumed that they were of hardy stock, capable of great feats of endurance, notably hospitable, and, in times of war, great fighting horsemen.

They took firm root on the Dnieper and spread widely to the north and east, occupying all the old highways of commerce. In the north they developed Novgorod, in the east they founded Rostov, in the south opposite Panticapaeum, Tmutorokan. They organized military protection for their Dnieper commercial fleet carrying goods to Constantinople. In the southeast, the rule of the Khazars, the new masters on the Volga—the peaceful rule of a trading people—guaranteed them the oriental market.[4] They developed a lively trade with the German north, the Finnish northeast, the Arabic southeast, and especially the Byzantine south. This was, as with their predecessors, the main source of their civilization and their wealth, and it conditioned and determined the forms of their culture and their arts. Their centers remained the same great cities on the Dnieper, the most important of these being Kiev, favored by her advantageous geographical situation in the middle of the Dnieper basin, midway between the Baltic and the Black Sea.

The cultural development of the Slavs was similar to that

[3] *Ibid.*, 218.
[4] Khazars (Kozary, 650–737) were probably of Turkish origin (the ethnic composition was mixed). At first their home was in the Caucasus. Later they controlled the lands between the Caucasus Mountains and the Volga and the Don rivers and even beyond the Dnieper and the Crimea, collecting customs duties from the caravans and ships plying north and south, west and east. They were conquered by the Russians in the tenth and eleventh centuries. On the Khazars, see M. I. Artamonov, *Ocherki drevneishei istorii Khazar.*

of many other nations. They began with the deification of the forces of nature: the sun, the moon, the stars, and the winds, but for the Slavs the deities did not acquire the characteristics of human beings.

The religion of the early Russian Slavs was not a unified system of dogmas but rather a complex body of heterogeneous religious beliefs. It had its heaven and hell where souls were said to go after death, but preserved its primitive natural character right up to the conversion of the Slavs to Christianity. It was rooted in the simple worship of nature: water, trees, and "Moist Mother Earth."

The worship of clan ancestors was an important element of Slavic religious beliefs. This was connected with a more general idea of propagation as the basic force behind each clan *(rod)* and family; hence the worship of *Rod* and *Rozhanitsy*—deities representing the forces of reproduction inherent in each clan. Specifically, each clan venerated its progenitor *(prashchur)* and each household invoked the protection of its guardian, the *domovoi* (house sprite).

The belief in wood sprites *(leshei)* and river nymphs is as old as that in home sprites. The worship of trees was widespread. The custom of decorating holy copses of trees with embroidered towels, at the time of folk festivals held in the woods, was kept in some remote parts of Russia even as late as the nineteenth century. The belief in wood and water sprites was part of the general veneration of forces of nature.[5]

Generally speaking, the veneration of the forces of nature was adapted to the cycle of labors in both agriculture and cattle breeding, and from it came what may be called the agricultural religion of the ancient Russian Slavs, with its primitive symbolism and periodic festivals.

The pre-Christian Slavs believed that each wood, stream,

[5] The river and tree nymphs were known in old Russia as *rusalki*. Festivals in their honor were called *rusalii*.

well, even each individual tree possessed its own soul, its own spirit. They believed that each house in the village was under the protection of a spirit that watched over the cattle, and over the fire in the oven. It was the daily chore of the housewife to put some delicacies near the oven so the house sprite could enjoy them on his nightly prowls. In each barn, in the mysterious light of the underground fires, dwelt the souls of dead forefathers and kinsmen. Each living creature in the household was endowed with special traits. The cock, who announced the dawn with his singing, was considered to be a soothsaying bird. Cocks were offered as a sacrifice at every sacrificial rite. The golden cockerel played a prominent role in folk tales or songs about animals. Ducks and geese symbolized water; in ornamentation we often find long rows of these birds swimming one after the other in single file—representing a river. A bull depicted as turning up the soil personified fertility. The horse, that noble, impetuous animal, was merged in the mind of the ancient Slav with the image of the sun god or a fighting horseman. In general, the horse was a favorite motif in ancient art.

The beasts of the forests were thought of as werewolves, mainly as enemies of mankind. Sorcerers were always turning into wolves. A hare crossing the road betokened trouble. But the bear—the principal predatory beast of the Russian forest—was held in high esteem. Clay figures of bear paws were interred with the dead; bear's teeth were worn as necklaces. The picture of a bear was adopted by many Slavic chieftains as their coat of arms. The name of this lord of the forest was never mentioned by the superstitious Slav. The Russian word for bear *medved'* (one who knows honey) is an allegorical description of the beast. Apart from the beasts, the woods, in the mind of the Slavs, were filled with innumerable hostile spirits. Each swamp, river, and forest harbored its own special evil spirits. The Slav plowman used dozens of charms—hardly half of them understood by us—to guard his family and his cattle from the hostile forest elements. In his art we find many figures of various amulets and special talismans designed to protect man from the spirits of the forest.

To protect themselves from the evil spirits lurking everywhere, the ancient Slavs used all kinds of bronze amulets and charms: miniature figures of beasts, horses, birds, fishes, keys, small hatchets, knives, and silver claws and teeth of the lord of the forest, the bear. Amulets were put into the cradles of newborn babies. Every important stage in a boy's life was marked by an elaborate ritual: a sword was put in his bed in the belief that it would help him to become a great warrior. His training in horsemanship would begin at the age of three, and the event was celebrated by a sumptuous banquet. Marriage, as the beginning of a new life, a new family, was celebrated with elaborate ceremonies and incantations, exorcising the evil spirits and invoking the gods to bring good fortune to the newlyweds. Death was attended by weird rites resembling those of the Scythians. Tools and implements of the deceased—his arms, food and drink, all that was believed necessary to him in the future otherworldly life—were put into his grave. The graves of the well-to-do were fitted out with wooden replicas of their houses. The wife of the deceased, wearing her wedding gown, would be killed and interred with him. Over the tomb a high barrow would be made and some of the dead man's arms laid upon it. The funeral rites included combat games and a memorial feast celebrated at the place of burial, when large quantities of sacrificial birds and animals were consumed. Every year, at appointed times, the near of kin would assemble at the grave with sacrificial offerings to the memory of the deceased, who was believed to have passed on into the realm of mysterious spirits.

The cycle of the seasons was marked by special festivities and dances. In winter, there was the festival in honor of Koliada, the fierce god of winter and the hunt. Spring was celebrated by a series of festivals in honor of the sun deity. The dances and the ceremonies were important means of passing on the cultural traditions as expressed in myth and legend.

During the height of the pagan period the festal rites were grave and solemn. Old women and grayheaded warriors—the guardians of traditions—took part in the sacred dances and in the chanting. The participants wore animal masks, and the dances were performed slowly and gravely, as in a divine service. Later, when paganism began to lose its grip on the people and the fear of evil spirits was on the wane, the observance of these rites assumed a character of fun and entertainment. During the celebration of the New Year, girls and boys, dressed in inside-out sheepskin coats, would go from house to house singing and dancing and collecting gifts of food and sweets. In the spring, at Easter time, the young men and women would be reveling: jumping over specially lighted purifying bonfires, and merrily dancing around a lone birch tree standing in a clearing. The tree would be decked in a woman's dress and decorated with towels embroidered with the figure of the Scythian great goddess, her attendants, and attributes. The early Slav artist provided the masks, costumes, and accessories for these rites.

The pagan Slav pantheon had a very complex origin. At least two different cults were practiced in ancient Russia: that of Svarog (god of the fiery sky) and Khors (the sun god), and that of Perun (the terrible god of storm and war) and Volos (the benevolent god of cattle and patron of herdsmen).[6]

As a result of sun worship, the horse and cock, both of them solar symbols, became prominent in Slavic art. The horse grew in symbolic importance, and stables were built close to the solar temples to house the holy animals. Horses endowed with magical powers found a place in folklore poetry, and were soon joined by the fire-bird and by the golden cockerel. The latter captured the people's imagination, his representation in many versions surviving longer in Slav art than any of the other ancient motifs. The versions which appear in Russian embroideries can be

[6] Niederle, *Slavianskiye drevnosti,* 268–97.

traced to the leather cutout silhouettes on the coffins found in mound I of the Pasyryk burials.

In addition to the cult of Svarog, Khors, and the other deities there was also practiced the worship of the great goddess, Mother Earth, and Mokosh, the mysterious goddess of weaving and water elements. The cult of the great goddess was widespread in South Russia in the Scythian and Sarmatian periods. The representation of the goddessses became a popular motif in old Russian folk art.

The first period known to us is the worship of vampires and river gods, then of *Rod* and *Rozhanitsy*, that is, the forefathers. This is followed by the spread of the Perun cult. With the advent and strengthening of the warrior clans, Perun was adopted by the military and became the god of the ruling prince and his retainers. The god of cattle, Volos, evolved into a god of wealth and trade, as cattle turned into a means of exchange and as a kind of monetary unit in trade. And finally, when the Kiev state was at its height, an official pantheon was adopted for the entire country as a step towards internal unity, and the prince's god became the state god, though the cult of the other gods continued to exist. Statues of the gods were erected on city squares and sacrifices of birds and animals, and occasionally humans, were made to them. Temples were built, and worship was conducted by priests and sorcerers.

Not only did religious elements of the Iranian and Finnish peoples fuse with those of the Eastern Slavs at a very early date, but also those of more highly developed religions, such as the Jewish, Mohammedan, Roman Catholic, and Byzantine Greek Orthodox. Ancient Russia was acquainted with all these religions through her established intercourse with the Khazars, the Arabs, and the peoples of central Asia, western Europe, and Byzantium.

When the Slavs established commercial and cultural relations with Byzantium at the dawn of their history, they were drawn into the circle of world trade associated with the culture of the dying Hellenic world. Though this acquisition of culture came later in eastern Europe than in the West, the Slavs moved rapidly along their path of development, even outdistancing other nations.

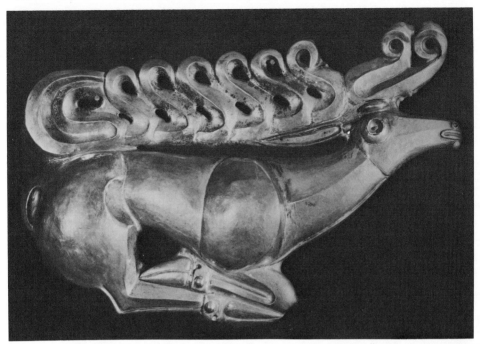

PLATE 1: *Sitting Stag*, a hammered solid-gold shield ornament, from Kostromskaya Tumulus, seventh-sixth century B.C.

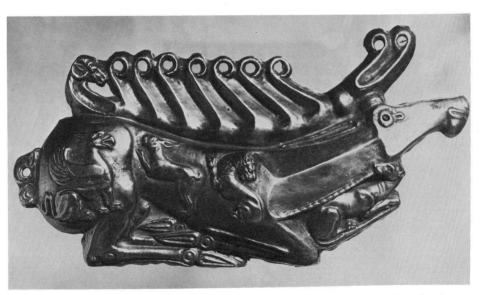

PLATE 2: *Dying Stag*, a gold ornament from a shield, from Kul-Oba Tumulus, fourth century B.C.

PLATE 3: *Gold Gorytus Casing*, from Chertomlyk Tumulus, fourth century B.C.

PLATE 4: *Electrum Vase*, from Kul-Oba Tumulus, fourth century B.C. and (below) detail of frieze.

PLATE 6: *Gold Helmet*, with *repoussé* and pierced work, from Tomb of the Seven Brothers, fourth century B.C.

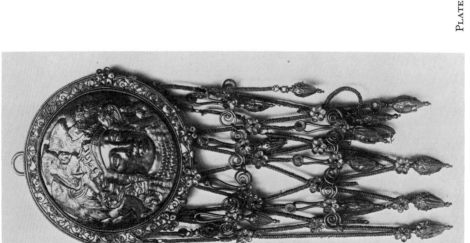

PLATE 5: *Gold Earring*, from Kul-Oba Tumulus, fourth century B.C.

PLATE 7: *Nikopol Vase,* from Chertomlyk Tumulus, fourth-third century B.C.: front view (above) and detail of frieze (below).

PLATE 8: *Diadem*, from the Treasure of Novocherkask, first century B.C.-third century A.D.

PLATE 9: *Lion-Griffin Attacking a Horse,* one of a pair of cast-gold belt buckles with stone insets, from western Siberia.

PLATE 10: *Hunting Scene,* in a **B**-shaped belt buckle of pierced-gold plaque inlaid with blue paste, pink coral, and black enamel, from western Siberia.

PLATE 11: *Scene from the Life of Early Siberian Nomads*, of open-work gold plaque, from western Siberia.

PLATE 12: *Dragon Engaged in a Fight with a Tiger*, of gold plaque with turquoise inlay, from western Siberia.

PLATE 13: *Figure of a Lion*, from a felt saddlecloth, from Pazyryk, eastern Altai.

PLATE 14: *Eagle-Griffin and Lion-Griffin in Combat*, from a leather cutout appliqué ornament on a saddlecloth, from Pazyryk, eastern Altai.

PLATE 15: *Pole Top*, with head of a stag in the beak of a griffin, of wood and leather, from Pazyryk, eastern Altai.

PLATE 16: *Swans*, decorative figures on a felt tent cover, from Pazyryk, eastern Altai.

PLATE 17: *Early slavic Stone Idol,* from the tumulus near the Village of Akulinnino, Moscow region.

PLATE 18: *Figure of a Man,* cast silver, from Martynovka Tumulus, near Kiev, sixth century.

PLATE 19: *Figure of a Horse,* cast silver, from Martynovka Tumulus, near Kiev, sixth century.

PLATE 20: *Cathedral of St. Sophia,* east façade, Kiev, 1037.

PLATE 21: *Central Nave,* looking east, Cathedral of St. Sophia, Kiev.

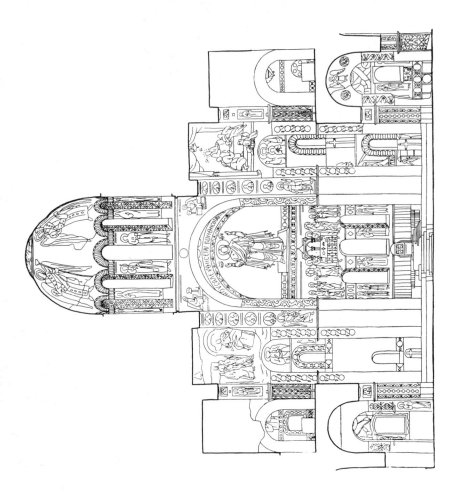

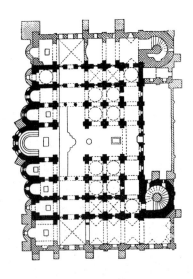

PLATE 22: *Cathedral of St. Sophia, Kiev*: plan (above) and cross section (right).

PLATE 23: *Cathedral of St. Sophia*, Novgorod, 1045–52, and plan (right).

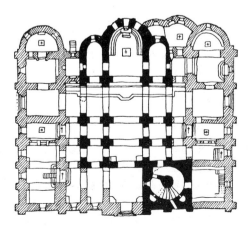

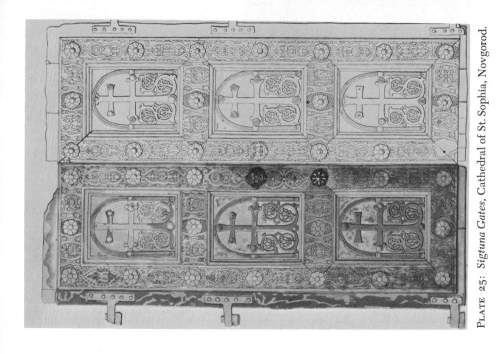

PLATE 25: *Sigtuna Gates*, Cathedral of St. Sophia, Novgorod.

PLATE 24: *Korsun' Gates*, Cathedral of St. Sophia, Novgorod.

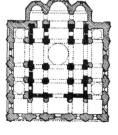

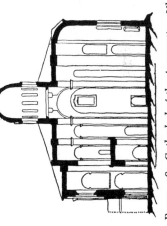

PLATE 26: *Cathedral of the Assumption,* Vladimir, 1185: panoramic view from the northeast (top), closer view (right), plan and cross section (above).

PLATE 28: *Tower of Palace at Bogoliubovo, near Vladimir*, 1160.

PLATE 27: *Church of the Intercession of the Virgin on the Nerl, near Vladimir*, 1165.

PLATE 30: *Church of the Transfiguration*, Novgorod, 1374.

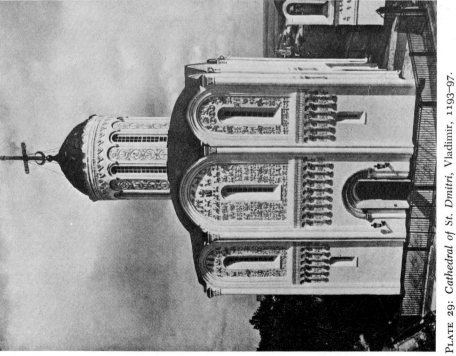

PLATE 29: *Cathedral of St. Dmitri*, Vladimir, 1193–97.

PLATE 31: *Cathedral of St. George*, Yuriev-Polsky, 1230: south-porch portal (left), detail of relief carving of a saint's head (middle), detail of relief carving on the west-porch wall (right).

PLATE 32: *The Virgin of Vladimir*, Greek, early twelfth century.

PLATE 33: *St. Dmitri of Salonica* (mosaic), from Monastery of St. Dmitri, Kiev, 1051.

PLATE 34: *The Virgin Orans*, Yaroslavl School, twelfth-thirteenth century, and detail (right).

PLATE 35: *St. George the Victorious*, Novgorod School, twelfth century.

PLATE 36: *Mandilion Portrait of Christ*, "The Image Not Made with Hands," Norgorod School, twelfth century.

PLATE 37: *The Annunciation of Ustiug*, Novgorod School, twelfth century.

PLATE 38: *Archangel Gabriel,* "Angel with the Golden Hair," Novgorod School, twelfth century.

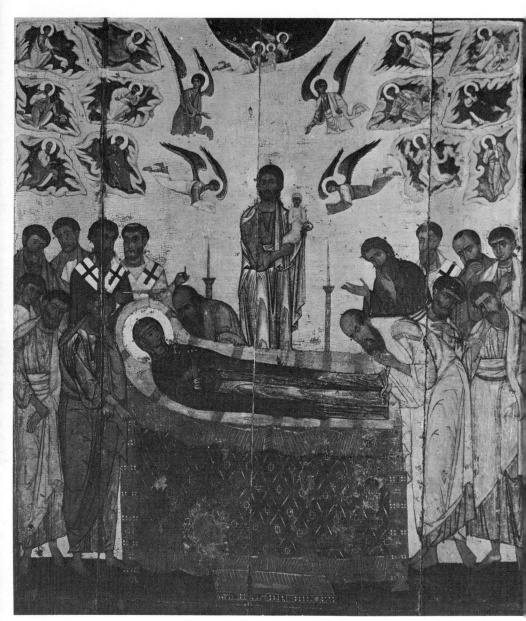

PLATE 39: *Dormition of the Virgin*, Novgorod School, thirteenth century.

PLATE 40: *Dormition of the Virgin*, detail from Plate 39.

PLATE 41: *St. Demetrius of Thessalonica*, Novgorod School, fourteenth century (?).

PLATE 42: *The Dormition of the Virgin,* Novgorod School, ca. 1380.

PLATE 43: *The Prophet Elijah*, Novgorod School, late fourteenth century.

PLATE 44: *The Virgin of the Don,* attributed to Theophanes the Greek, late fourteenth century.

PLATE 45: *The Transfiguration of Christ*, by Theophanes the Greek, fourteenth century.

PLATE 46: *The Transfiguration of Christ,* detail of figure of Christ from Plate 45.

PLATE 47: *The Transfiguration of Christ*, detail of figure of Apostle Peter from Plate 45.

PLATE 48: *Christ with the Angry Eye*, Novgorod School, fifteenth century.

PLATE 49: *The Miracle of Saints Florus and Laurus,* Novgorod School, fifteenth century.

PLATE 50: *The Nativity of Christ*, Novgorod School, fourteenth-fifteenth century.

PLATE 51: *The Miracle of St. George the Victorious*, Novgorod School, first half of the fifteenth century.

PLATE 52: *The Battle between the Suzdalians and Novgorodians*, Novgorod School, late fifteenth century.

PLATE 53: *The Battle between the Suzdalians and Novgorodians,* detail from Plate 52.

PLATE 54: *Entry into Jerusalem*, Novgorod School, early sixteenth century.

PLATE 55: *The Forty Martyrs of Sebastiya*, Novgorod School, early sixteenth century.

PLATE 56: *The Saviour with the Wet Beard*, Novgorod School, sixteenth century.

PLATE 57: *Four Saints*, Pskov School, late fourteenth century.

PLATE 58: *St. John Chrysostom, detail from Plate 57.*

PLATE 59: *St. Nicholas*, Pskov School, early fourteenth century.

PLATE 60: *Dormition of the Virgin,* Tver School, first half of the fifteenth century.

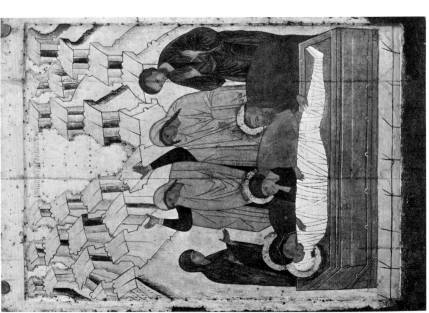

PLATE 61: *Entombment*, Northern School, last quarter of the fifteenth century, and detail (above).

PLATE 62: *Descent from the Cross*, Northern School, fifteenth century.

PLATE 63: *Trinity-Sergius Monastery, Zagorsk:* Assumption Cathedral, 1554–85, view from the east (left); Church of the Trinity, 1476, view from the southeast (right).

PLATE 64: *Cathedral of the Assumption, Kremlin, Moscow, 1475-79.*

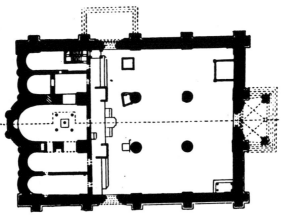

PLATE 65: *Cathedral of the Assumption,* Kremlin, Moscow: floor plan (above), detail of west portal (right), longitudinal section (below, left), and detail of south portal (below, right).

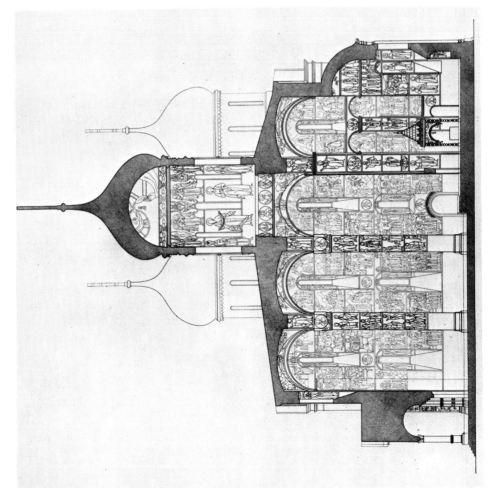

PLATE 67: *Cathedral of the Annunciation*, Kremlin, Moscow, 1482–90, and floor plan (right).

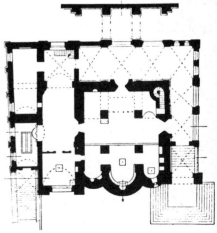

PLATE 66 (opposite): *Interior*, Cathedral of the Assumption, Kremlin, Moscow.

PLATE 69: *Cathedral of Archangel Michael,* Kremlin, Moscow, 1505–1509, and floor plan (right).

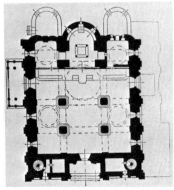

PLATE 68 (opposite): *Interior Gallery,* Cathedral of the Annunciation, Kremlin, Moscow.

PLATE 70: *Church of the Consecration of the Chasuble*, Kremlin, Moscow, 1484–85.

PLATE 71: *Drum and Cupola Detail,* from (left) Church of the Virgin's Nativity, Kremlin, Moscow, late fourteenth century, and from (right) Small Cathedral, Donskoy, Monastery, Moscow, 1593.

PLATE 73: *Church of the Ascension,* Kolomenskoye, near Moscow, 1532, and cross section (right).

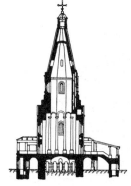

PLATE 72 (opposite): *Belfry of Ivan Veliky,* Kremlin, Moscow, 1532–1624.

PLATE 75: *Church of St. John the Precursor, Dyakovo, near Moscow, 1553–54, view from southeast.*

PLATE 74: *Church of the Transfiguration, Ostrovo, near Moscow, 1550.*

PLATE 76: *Church of St. Basil*, Moscow, 1555–60, east elevation.

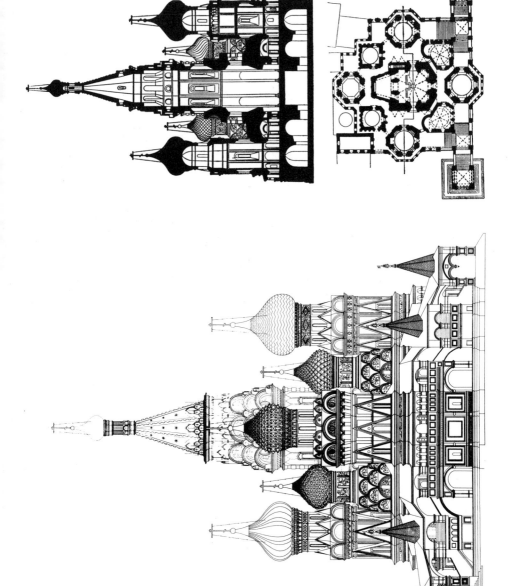

PLATE 77: *Church of St. Basil*, Moscow: west elevation (far left), section (upper left), and floor plan (lower left).

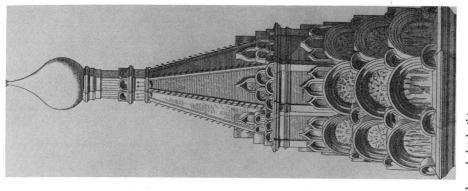

PLATE 78: *Church of St. Basil*, Moscow: detail of drum and cupola supported on kokoshniki (left); cupolas viewed from the southwest (middle); detail of octagonal tower-tent roof and cupola supported on kokoshniki (right).

PLATE 80: *Church of St. Paraskeva, Shuya, Archangel province, 1666.*

PLATE 79: *Nikolskaya Church, Panilovo, Archangel province, 1600.*

PLATE 81 (left): *Uspensky Church*, Varzug, Archangel province, 1674.

PLATE 82: *Church of the Resurrection*, Ust-Padenga, Archangel province, 1675.

PLATE 83: *Window Frame,* Church of the Assumption, Village of Cherevkovo, Vologda province, 1683–91.

СОБОРЪ
УСПЕНІЯ ПРЕСВЯТОЙ БОГОРОДИЦЫ
въ г. Кеми, Архангельскои губ.
постр въ 1714 г.

CATHEDRALE
DE L'ASSOMPTION DE LA VIERGE
à Kème, ville du gv. d'Archangel,
constr en 1714.

РЕСТАВРАЦІЯ. RESTAURATION.

1.2.двери
Флора и Лавра и
Архангельскои

церквей
Благовѣщенія (XVIIc)
губ. Шенкурскаго у.

1.2.portes des
Sts Florus et Laure et de
gv d'Archangel, distr

églises des
l'Annonciation (XVIIᵉs)
de Chenkoursk

ЗАПАДНЫЙ ФАСАДЪ. FAÇADE OCCIDENTALE.

PLATE 84: *Cathedral of the Assumption of the Holy Virgin,* west façade, Kem, Archangel province, 1714. Shown upper left and upper right are doors from two other contemporary churches,
the Church of Florus and Laurus and the Church of the Annunciation, Archangel province.

PLATE 85: *Church of Saints Florus and Laurus*, Rostovsk Village, Archangel province, 1755: view from the northeast (left) and from the northwest (right).

PLATE 86: *Church of the Transfiguration*, the twenty-two-cupola church, Kizhi Island, early eighteenth century.

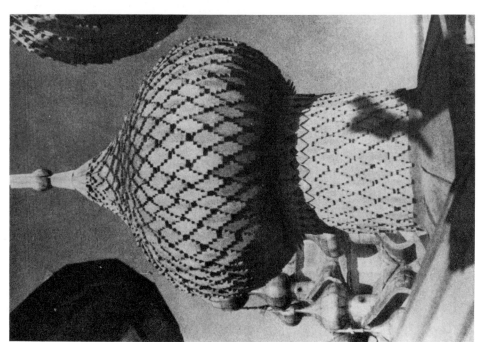

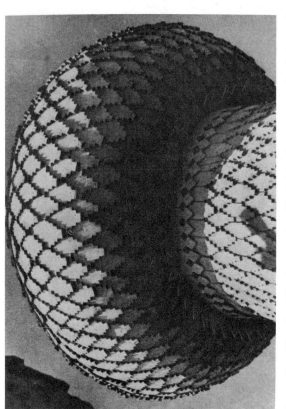

PLATE 87: *Church of the Intercession*, Kizhi Island: corner cupola (left) and central cupola (above).

PLATE 88: *Palace at Kolomenskoye*, Moscow suburb, seventeenth century.

PLATE 89: *Roof Construction Details, izba* in the Vologda province. In the upper-left and upper-right corners are shown two decorated chimneys. Legend: 1. ridge beam, 2. tie beam, 3. bargeboard, 5. strips of wood over the rafters to which the sheathing is nailed, 8. bracket formed by corbeled logs serving to support the roof edges, 9. gutter, 10. gutter-supporting rafter, 11. rafter, 14. the layer of logs forming the gable triangle.

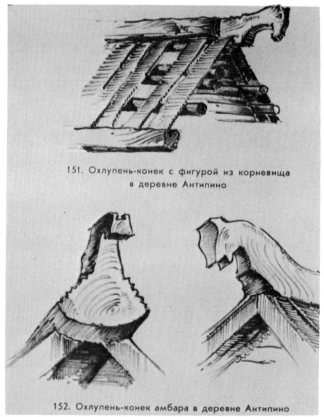

PLATE 90: *The Horse-head Motif,* in the decoration of the ridge pole of peasant cottages in western Siberia.

151. Охлупень-конек с фигурой из корневища в деревне Антипино

152. Охлупень-конек амбара в деревне Антипино

PLATE 91: *Teremok*, inn and pub, on the highway between Kostroma and Yaroslavl, eighteenth century, from a lithograph by André Durand.

PLATE 92: *Church of the Georgian Virgin,* MOSCOW, 1653.

PLATE 93: *Cathedral and Belfry*, the New Jerusalem Monastery on the Istra, 1656–85.

PLATE 94: *Church of the Holy Trinity, Ostankino, near Moscow, 1668.*

Part Two

The Byzantine Period

The Architecture of Kievan Russia

B Y THE MIDDLE of the ninth century the Russian annals begin to give us a systematic record of the Russian people and its princes. Kievan Russia emerges as an organized state possessing its own peculiar political, social, and economic structure. "The Russia of Kiev," writes Rostovtzeff about the eighth- to twelfth-century period, "was the last link of an ancient historical chain and the first of a new one. Kievan Russia was the immediate successor of the series of commercial states which had replaced one another in the steppes of south Russia from time immemorial, and at the same time the mother of the subsequent Slavonic Russian States in Western Russia [the Galicia of today], on the upper course of the Dnieper [the modern White Russia], and, most important of all, between the upper Volga and the Oka, Great Russia, the Russia of modern times."[1]

The state consisted of several important commercial cities situated partly on the Dnieper and its tributaries, partly in the far north on Lake Ilmen, and partly in the east on the upper Volga. It was based economically on the control of the Dnieper waterway and functioned as an intermediary between the inhabitants of the northern forests, the southern steppes, and Byzantium. The trading of the Kievan state with Byzantium was organized. Every spring expeditions of traders set out down the Dnieper from Kiev in large boats. They carried furs, wax,

[1] *Iranians and Greeks*, 220.

honey and slaves, receiving in exchange articles of luxury and objects of art.

Byzantium, which had first attracted the Russian princes and traders by its riches and the brilliance of its capital and the imperial court, affected them in many other ways as well. It was not long before the Russian upper classes and merchants fell under the spell of Byzantium's spiritual and artistic culture. In 957, Princess Olga, grandmother of Prince Vladimir of Kiev,[2] was baptized in Constantinople, and by the second half of the tenth century a considerable number of the Russian aristocracy had been converted to Christianity. The pagan religion was gradually breaking down and a need arose for a solution to the religious crisis which all Russia was experiencing. The ancient Russian chronicles contain an interesting account of Russia's conversion to Christianity (989 A.D.).[3] According to the chronicler, Vladimir was visited in 968 by religious missions of different faiths: Mohammedans from the Bulgars of the Volga, Roman Catholics from Germany, Khazars professing Judaism, and a Greek philosopher of the Orthodox faith.

The prince, after listening to the representatives of the various faiths, was impressed with the profundity of the Orthodox dogma (including the most fearful picture of Judgment Day and the tortures that awaited the damned), as expounded by the Greek philosopher. Before making a decision, however, he dispatched a mission to the seat of each religion in order to observe "by whom and how God has worshiped." The emissaries whom Vladimir sent to Constantinople returned entranced with the solemn beauty of the Orthodox services, which have ever since made so powerful an appeal to Russian hearts. The splendors of St. Sophia, the brilliancy of the priestly vestments, the magni-

[2] Vladimir Svyatoslavovich, known as Saint Vladimir (of the Orthodox church), but celebrated as the hero and center of a wonderful cycle of epic tales *(byliny)* in which he figures not as Vladimir the Saint and Baptist of Russia, but as a solar hero: *Krasnoye Solnyshko,* the Beautiful Sun of Kiev.

[3] The *Ancient Chronicle,* written at the end of the eleventh century by the monk Nestor.

ficence of the ceremonies, heightened by the presence of the Emperor Basil II and his court, the patriarch and the numerous clergy, the incense, the chanting—all that deeply impressed the Slav emissaries who, in describing the beauty of the service, said: "We did not know whether we were on earth or in heaven."

Their report was so enthusiastic that Vladimir promptly decided to accept Orthodox Christianity as the official faith of Russia. He was baptized at Khersonesus (Korsun') in the Crimea in 988, and forthwith proceeded to baptize his people in droves. He married Princess Anna, the sister of Emperor Basil, who brought to Kiev many artists, architects, and craftsmen, many icons, rare manuscripts, and church furnishings. Russian works of art produced in the eleventh and twelfth centuries, especially in the domain of goldsmith work and enamel, are witness to the powerful effect produced by the Byzantine craftsmen, who not merely made precious and beautiful objects, but created schools of local artists who founded in Russia a tradition modified by native ideals.

History and legend are inextricably mingled in the records of the Russian chronicles, but the story has many credible elements. Vladimir was well able to hear and weigh the merits of various religions discussed in Kiev, which was a meeting place for travelers of many nations.

It would, of course, be naive to believe that conversion to the new religion, imposed on the Russian people by an edict of a Kievan grand prince, abolished paganism overnight. The conversion of Russia to Orthodox Christianity was ordered arbitrarily by a ruler for reasons of state as well as for personal reasons.[4] The acceptance of the new religion by his subjects was primarily an act of obedience. But in general, Christianity, in the urban centers at least, was received willingly. It was in the hinterland

---

[4] Among the inducements and attractive concessions offered by Byzantium to Prince Vladimir were the autonomy of the Russian church and the promise of the hand in marriage of the Byzantine Princess Anna, Emperor Basil's sister. This was a most significant and tempting honor, since the princess was a Porphyrogenite (born to the purple) and in those days was considered sacred.

that paganism lingered longest. According to many Russian historians, even as late as the twelfth century, Christian rites were practiced only by the upper stratum of the society. The peasants kept their old pagan ceremonies, and for them nature was still the home of a whole world of deities. Orthodox Christianity was able, at first, to affect only the exterior phases of the people's religious practices. Yet the fact that Russia received Christianity from Byzantium and not from Rome was of immense importance in the future development of her arts, and brought in its trail consequences of great significance.

Russia's conversion to Christianity was a protracted process and resulted not only in a religious dualism (dvoeveriye) until the new faith was absorbed by the whole nation but also in a cultural dualism. By the eleventh century, however, the new religion had taken root in the country, and Byzantine thought became the main intellectual influence in the land. Two elements of the Orthodox dogma must be singled out: the overpowering mystical fear of the All Highest Judge and the emphasis of the church on the physical splendor of its edifices. They were cardinal factors in determining the characteristics of Christian culture in ancient Russia.

It should be remembered that the baptism of Russia took place at the time when the iconoclast movement (see Chapter XII) had come to an end, and when the medieval Byzantine renaissance was flourishing. Russian art of the period was permeated with the genius and personality of the Byzantine painters and craftsmen. It was vigorous and exuberant, as though the native artists had caught something of the buoyant spirit of the new religious teachers and were impatient of delay. Art, inspired by Byzantium, entered upon a period of great achievements. This current became powerful and soon made itself felt throughout Kievan, Novgordian, and Suzdalian Russia.

Russian acceptance of Orthodox Christianity was not entirely devoid of complications. In Byzantium the church and the state were closely united—the emperor heading both the empire and the church. It is therefore understandable that the metropolitan sent to Kiev by Byzantium became not only the head of the Russian Orthodox church, but also the representative of the authority of the Constantinople patriarch and, hence, of the Byzantine emperor. The dependence of the Russian church upon Byzantine policies became in time so galling that it developed into a source of friction between Kiev and Constantinople. The grand prince and the Christianized upper classes of that time were eager to transform the Greek faith into a national religion as quickly as possible. The canonization of Vladimir who was declared to be a saint, "the equal of apostles" and the true teacher of the newly converted nation, despite the opposition of Constantinople, shows that the Russians did not wish to be led by the Greeks but claimed the right to choose what suited them from the Byzantine church.

To emphasize the independence of the Russian church, Prince Yaroslav (1016–1054) appointed, without asking permission from the Greek patriarch, a Russian priest, Hilarion, as the metropolitan of Kiev. Yaroslav even declared war on Byzantium, but failing to win, he set out to compete with Constantinople, to enhance the importance of his own capital and eclipse the envied splendor of his rivals. He embarked upon an extensive building program and laid the foundations for a new Kremlin, building the Golden Gates[5] and erecting the Cathedral of St. Sophia and a number of other churches and monasteries which he enriched with rare icons, gold vessels, and other art objects.

Thus the prosperity and splendor of Kiev were due as much to its political ambitions as to its being the center of Russian trade. It became a mecca for foreign artists and craftsmen, a cosmopolitan center where representatives of Southern, West-

[5] The main entrance gates in the wall that surrounded Kiev. The structure was a combination defense tower, arch of triumph, and church. The name "Golden Gates" (*Zolotyie vorota*) is derived from their gilded copper mountings and their function, serving as the principal entrance to the city on triumphal, festival, or formal occasions. Nothing but ruins remains, but many legends, serving as a basis for poems, pictures, and musical compositions, are connected with this structure.

ern and Eastern cultures met, mingled, worked, and exchanged ideas.

Under Yaroslav, Kiev reached its highest state of splendor. In addition to building St. Sophia and the Golden Gates, the Grand Prince founded the monastery of St. George, repaired the Church of the Tithes, built the Cathedral of the Annunciation, the Church of St. Irene, and surrounded the city with ramparts. The capital city became a Russified copy of Constantinople, a Ravenna of the North. S. M. Solov'ev cites Thietmar of Meresburg, a writer of the early eleventh century, who described Kiev as an extremely great and powerful city, possessed of "four hundred churches and eight markets," and another western writer of that period, Adam of Bremen, who declared Kiev to be the rival of Constantinople, "the brilliant ornament of Greece," that is, of the Orthodox East.[6]

The Architectural Monuments of Kiev

The principal monuments of Kiev were erected during the reigns of the three grand princes: St. Vladimir (reigning 978–1015), his son and successor Yaroslav the Wise (1016–1054), and Izyaslav (1054-1073). It was St. Vladimir who placed the cornerstone of the Church of the Assumption of the Virgin, or Church of the Tithes, usually known as the Desyatinnaya Tserkov,[7] in 989. Yaroslav founded the Cathedral of St. Sophia in 1037 in commemoration of his victory over the Pechenegs. Prince Izyaslav founded the Monastery of the Caves (Kievo-Pecherskaya Lavra). All these churches were, in the main, Byzantine buildings, although certain influences which came from Georgia and Armenia are to be discerned.

The Desyatinnaya Church, the first and oldest stone building in Russia, was designed and constructed by imported Greek artisans, and its ground plan reflects the features of Byzantine

[6] *Istoriya Rossii s drevneishikh vremen,* I, 245.

[7] It was given this name because the prince endowed it with a tenth part (*desyataya*) of his revenues. It was consecrated in 996 and destroyed by the Mongols in 1240.

church architecture most prevalent in the tenth century. The basic plan of these churches was a Greek cross inscribed in a rectangle, surmounted by a cupola over the intersection and sometimes with subsidiary smaller cupolas between arms of the cross. An essential element of Byzantine church architecture of this period was the handling of the cupolas. The central cupola was raised upon a circular or polygonal drum, usually pierced with windows lighting the nave. The minor cupolas were lower and smaller than the central one, thus providing a pyramidal silhouette. This huge church was girdled on the outside by galleries and, according to available sources, was crowned with twenty-five picturesque cupolas. Excavations have revealed the tragic way the building was destroyed by the Tatars in 1240, when the last of the city's defenders locked themselves up in the church and tried to dig an underground passage to safety. They were buried alive when the vaults crashed down on them.

Of the few architectural monuments of that time that have survived in Kiev, the Cathedral of St. Sophia, perhaps the most interesting of all, still exists (Plates 20–22). The cathedral was the main center of cultural, social, and religious life in Kiev, and it stood in the same relation to the palace and the person of the Kievan grand prince as the great St. Sophia of Constantinople did to the Byzantine emperor and his palaces. In the course of its nine centuries of existence, the cathedral has been sacked and pillaged over and over again and all but destroyed. The Kievan princes were continually at war, not only with the nomads of the steppes but among themselves, and the capital city was of course the principal target for each invading army. During the fratricidal struggle, Kiev was laid waste and the cathedral was robbed of many of its treasures. In the thirteenth century the cathedral was sacked during the Tatar invasion; in the fourteenth, during the Polish-Lithuanian conquest, when it was practically wrecked. In these early years of the fourteenth century St. Sophia fell upon hard times. The rising power of Moscow, both political and ecclesiastical, eclipsed that of the parent city, and it naturally affected the importance of St. Sophia as a metropolitan seat. The virtual desolation of the church occurred in the sixteenth century. Its upkeep was almost totally neglected, and it was continually plundered by the inhabitants, becoming in the early part of the seventeenth century scarcely more than a heap of rubble.

The original central part of the cathedral was in the form of a Greek cross, the arms of which are about 96 feet long by 26 feet wide.[8] The four piers of the central square support the four-arched vault, which carries the principal cupola. On each side of the nave is a series of cruciform pillars which carry the arches sustaining the choirs. The cathedral was practically square in shape: it contained five aisles terminated in semicircular apses. In the seventeenth century two more aisles were added on each side, thus giving the cathedral an extraordinary width.

The present exterior of St. Sophia—the silhouettes of the cupolas and the wealth of ornament—is not medieval Russian (nor Byzantine) but Ukrainian baroque, a result of restorations undertaken by Metropolitan Peter Mogila in 1632. The remnants of antiquity in St. Sophia are largely confined to its interior, and only an imperfect idea can now be formed of its original eleventh-century exterior. The exotic exterior and silhouette completely disguise the original outline. According to G. Pavlutsky, the cathedral, when first constructed, had thirteen cupolas (symbolizing Christ and His apostles).[9] The central cupola was surrounded by four smaller ones: two over the chief lateral altars and two over the tribunes. Outside these four smaller ones there were eight others: two over the extreme north and south corner altars and three respectively at the north and south corners of the tribunes outside the larger ones which adjoin the central cupola. The present-day building has nineteen cupolas of various sizes and designs.

---

[8] The cross inscribed in a square at ground level has long been known as the "Greek-cross plan" derived from the domed basilica.

[9] In Grabar', *Istoriya russkago iskusstva* (1909), I, 148.

In its primitive state the cathedral was one of the rare examples of ecclesiastical edifices in which architecture, decorative sculpture, mosaics, and monumental painting contributed to artistic unity. The interior of the building—originally designed to be flooded with sunlight and thus bring out the beauty of its deep-toned mosaics—is darkened by the many additions which surround it on all sides and at all levels.

Mosaics and Frescoes

Although only a small part of the original cathedral and its mosaics have survived, there is still much to be admired in the imposing dimensions of its interior, its fine proportions, and the luxuriant mosaics and frescoes. Many of the latter, still in a good state of preservation after nine hundred years, are wonderful specimens of a great age in ecclesiastical art. But the work of restoration (1853–54), while approached by Professor F. G. Solntsev with piety and respect for the original, was executed rather crudely.[10] Many of the frescoes were disfigured; and in the 1880's some of the mosaics were also subjected to restoration, and in the process the original elements were covered over with paint.

The frescoes which have been preserved or restored are numerous and cover the columns, the walls, and the vaulted ceilings everywhere. The subjects conform to the liturgical scheme of the eleventh century. The eleventh-century mosaics, which are of particular brilliance and impressiveness, were probably done by Greek artists; the inscriptions and titles of the scenes are in Greek.

The mosaics decorate the apse and the areas under the main cupola, the best lighted surfaces of the cathedral. These mosaics are the first to attract the attention of the beholder and thus

[10] Professor F. G. Solntsev (1801–92), painter, archaeologist, student of Russian antiquities, member of the Imperial Academy of Fine Arts; discoverer and restorer of the ancient mosaics and frescoes in St. Sophia, Kiev; member of the committee for the publication of the *Drevnosti rossiiskago gosudarstva*, 1849–53, to which he contributed many excellent drawings.

determine the character of the decorative scheme. In the main cupola the mosaic shows Christ as Pantocrator surrounded by four archangels. His right hand is raised in blessing, while His left hand holds a book. The pendentives at the corners are occupied by the evangelists. In the conch of the altar apse, traditionally known as the indestructible wall *(nerushimaya stena)*, is the majestic mosaic of the Virgin Orans. The outline of the figure of the Virgin against the shimmering gold background of the apse is one of the first mosaics to come into view. The image is of heroic proportions (some sixteen feet in height) with arms upraised in prayer. She stands alone, clad in a purple *maphorion*[11] which is thrown over her head and around her shoulders. Beneath it, her robe falls in graceful folds to the tips of red slippers contrasting with the simplicity of the robe itself. Personifying the Terrestrial Church she, together with the figure of the Panthocrator in the cupola, before whom she intercedes for the sins of humanity, dominates the entire decorative scheme. Below the figure of the Virgin is a mosaic of the Last Supper, with a double apparition of Christ presenting to six of His disciples the bread and to six others the wine. On either side of the arch of the altar apse is a mosaic of the Annunciation.

The renovated frescoes are in bright luminous colors. But the original frescoes, especially those in the semidark side chapels, lighted by the faint glow of the icon lamps and flickering candles, impress one with the severe beauty of the ancient images, as though specially conceived to put fear into the heart of man and confound him with the realization of his own utter pettiness in the sight of the Deity.

The mosaic images are suffused with the same mood as that of the frescoes; they have the same severe solemn expression heightened even more by the dark gold of the background. The faces seem to stand out especially clear and sharp, stern and somewhat

[11] A large shawl covering the head and shoulders. Originally the costume of Palestinian and Syrian women, it was then worn by the early Christian deaconesses. Decorated with the Virgin's star, it forms an essential part of the Virgin's garment in icon painting.

rigid with wide-open eyes looking into the distance. It seems as though they were frozen in this attitude of contemplating the face of God. They are unworldly, far removed from the cares and worries or the petty happiness of mere mortals.

Besides the various complex elements of religious portaiture and symbolism shown in the mural decorations of St. Sophia, there are on the walls of the staircases leading to the galleries some striking frescoes which represent carnival scenes and circus spectacles. These frescoes are of peculiar interest; they depict in considerable detail elaborate spectacles similar to those presented at Christmastide in the hippodrome at Constantinople before the Byzantine emperor and his suite. The stairways probably connected with the prince's palace, which has long since disappeared. The passage from the palace to the church was decorated, as in Constantinople, with scenes of hunting, music making, dancing, and other amusements. These frescoes are perhaps the most interesting to be found in Russia, showing as they do purely secular scenes of medieval court life. There are jugglers and comedians disguised as fantastic animals, hunting scenes, wild beasts, curious trees, a circus scene in which charioteers are preparing for a race, folk dancing to music, and many others —truly surprising unholy pictures for the walls of a sacred edifice.

This cycle of frescoes contains more than 130 figures of merrymakers. The spectators are also depicted occupying several loges —the princes with their entourages enjoying the performance. The figures are presented frontally against a vertical perspective. The subjects must have been taken from the favorite amusements of that period. Kliuchevsky cites many references in Russian folklore to the games played at the court of Kiev on Sundays.

The Kiev Monastery of the Caves (Kievo-Pecherskaya Lavra), oldest and most famous monastic establishment in Russia, was enlarged by Abbot Theodosius in 1073. It served as a retreat for many members of the upper clergy and the nobility who wanted to spend the rest of their lives in seclusion and religious meditation. They lived in cells or caves hollowed out of the limestone cliffs overhanging the right bank of the Dnieper (hence the monastery's name). Many of the anchorites sealed themselves up in their cells, leaving only small apertures through which they received their sustenance. This ascetic community steadily grew in numbers, wealth, and power, and by the end of the eleventh century became the center of ecclesiastical authority in Kievan Russia. As Kliuchevsky points out, "Everything that was powerful, influential in Russian society of that era, everything that contributed to the making of Russian history was centered in that monastery."[12] It was instrumental in introducing certain specifically Russian features into the divine service; it also developed its own standard types for churches and monastic buildings.

Of special significance for Russian architecture was the monastery's Church of the Assumption, one of the first above-ground buildings. Finished in 1075 and consecrated in 1089, it was seriously damaged by fire in 1484 and 1718, rebuilt in the Ukrainian baroque style between 1723 and 1730, and almost totally destroyed in the Second World War. This three-naved church originally had but one cupola placed over the central square, with six internal masonry piers, thus adumbrating the single-cupola type of church of fairly simple design which became the standard type for church architecture in the Vladimir-Suzdal principality.

Somewhat younger than the Church of the Assumption of the Monastery of the Caves was the Church of St. Michael with the Golden Roof (Mikhail-Zlatoverkhei), founded by Prince Svyatopolk Izyaslavich (baptized Michael) in 1108. It was originally conceived as a single-domed church with three apses and six internal piers. But like St. Sophia and the Assumption, its many additions and alterations have changed its original aspect.

[12] The Monastery of the Caves became the first home of the Russian Chronicles, which were systematized at the beginning of the twelfth century. The monk Nestor, celebrated as the compiler of the *Ancient Chronicle,* became an inmate of that institution in the year 1074. (Kliuchevsky, *A History of Russia,* I, 92–94.)

The church was dismantled during the construction of the new plaza in Kiev, but its few surviving medieval mosaics were saved. Some of them were transferred to the St. Sophia in Kiev, others to the Tretyakov Gallery in Moscow. The extant mural decorations are the mosaic of the Eucharist, a figure of St. Thomas, fragments of three other apostles, and single figures of St. Dmitri of Salonica (Plate 33) and St. Stephen. Of special interest is the mosaic of the Eucharist, attributed to a group of Greek-trained Russian mosaicists led by the legendary Russian icon painter Alimpi,[13] a many-gifted inmate of the Pechersk Monastery. The representation of the Eucharist shows a deviation from the treatment in the mosaics on the same subject in St. Sophia; the conception of this sacred scene is highly original. The portrayal of the apostles lacks the stiff ceremonial formality which characterizes the mosaic of the St. Sophia Eucharist. In contrast to the stereotyped figures of the apostles, the figures here are more varied, the individual heads more diversified, and their facial expressions and gestures more animated. P. P. Muratov points out that the manner of execution of these mosaics demonstrates the naturalistic tendency that had begun to creep into the Byzantine art of mosaics of the twelfth century.[14]

The districts of Ovruch, Pereyaslavl, Vladimir-Volynsk, and Novgorod-Seversk contained some of the most interesting churches of this period; a few of them are still standing, others are in complete ruins. Descriptions in the chronicles and traces of ruins uncovered in recent archaeological excavations indicate the influence these structures had on the subsequent architectural history of the Kiev region.

The twelfth-century Church of St. Basil (Vasili) in Ovruch, restored in 1908 by A. V. Shchusev, was a single-domed structure with three apses and four internal piers. The restored build-

[13] Alimpi (Alipii, Olympius), mentioned in the *Pechersk Paterik*. This monk is credited with being a great icon painter and physician. Yu Shamurin, *Kul'turniya sokrovishcha Rossii*, I, 33.
[14] In Grabar', *Istoriya russkago iskusstva* (1909), VI, 125.

ing gives us a true picture of the development of ancient Russian architecture and the original appearance of its remarkable monuments.[15]

Of the old monument of Pereyaslavl (now Pereyaslavl-Khmelnitsky) there is nothing left but earthen walls, the remains of fortifications. Only the chronicles speak of considerable building that was started there at the close of the eleventh century. Excavations showed that in the eleventh and twelfth centuries the city had many monumental stone structures. These included the big and unique St. Michael's Cathedral, the remains of stone fortifications with a tower, small churches in the residences of boyars, and so on. In one of them were found splendid specimens of applied art—a bronze candelabra and a large candlestick ornamented with cast lion's heads. Thus, in virtually a desert place were resurrected monuments of the hitherto completely unknown but vigorous school of Pereyaslavl architects.

The Architecture of Chernigov

The architecture of Chernigov is of particular interest. Several of its churches from the pre-Mongol period survived into the twentieth century. The most interesting were the eleventh-century Cathedral of the Transfiguration and the twelfth-century Church of St. Paraskeva.

The Cathedral of the Transfiguration (Preobrazhensky Sobor) in Chernigov was founded about 1017 by Mstislav of Tmutorokan, Prince of Chernigov and younger brother of Yaroslav. It was originally a three-naved basilica with three semicircular apses and five cupolas, one large one over the center and four smaller ones at the corners. The basic ground plan, exclusive of the narthex which extended the full width of the three naves, was of the cross-in-square. A striking feature of the interior design was the use of marble on a considerably larger scale than

15 Grabar' considers the work of this restoration, that is, the techniques, the meticulous care, scientific and perceptive approach of the restorer, as something of extraordinary interest and value. (For plan and elevations, see Grabar', *Istoriya russkogo iskusstva* (1953), I, 154–55.

that seen in St. Sophia at Kiev. The columns that supported the altar arch and those that supported the central cupola were of marble, and the arches that supported the smaller cupolas rested on impost blocks of the same material. Chernigov was burned by the Tatars in 1237, and the cathedral was nearly ruined and remained in a dilapidated state until 1675, when it was drastically rebuilt. It was again damaged by fire in 1750 and restored in 1798; finally, it was all but destroyed in the Second World War. Little of the original decoration of this cathedral has survived but among the remnants of the antique frescoes is a female figure robed in a stole. It is considered one of the outstanding examples of early Russian frescoes.

The twelfth-century Church of St. Paraskeva (Church of Good Friday) in Chernigov, designed by the Smolensk architect Peter Miloneg is a most interesting Russian version of the canonical type of Byzantine church. Miloneg's building, as reconstructed by P. D. Baranovsky, introduces a few bold structural innovations and some fresh concepts in Russian architectural aesthetics.[16] The Paraskeva plan is that of the usual four-columned, three-apsed, single cupola church, but the structural system used in raising the cupola over the square base is radically different. Above the four arches resting on the sides of the square, further tiers were raised, each corbelled out inwards from the tier below, gradually roofing in the space and forming support for the elements of the superstructure. Externally the transition from the walls to the base of the drum is achieved by the use of a second tier of vaulting parapets (*zakomaras*)[17] and rising rows of purely decorative *kokoshniki*,[18] one at each

[16] Reproduced in Grabar', *Istoriya russkogo iskusstva* (1953), I, 153.

[17] The parapet over the extrados of the vaulting, conforming in outline to the type and number of vaults, and thus dividing the wall parapet into several arched sections.

[18] *Kokoshnik, Kokoshniki* (pl.), was originally a structural feature, a series of corbelled-out, round or pointed arches arranged in receding tiers for the purpose of supporting the elements of the superstructure. Later it developed into a purely decorative feature used as ornament for all kinds of articles.

side of the square base of the cupola drum, thus reflecting the stepped tiers of arches in the interior.

The restorer of the St. Paraskeva has ventured the opinion that the design and decoration of this monument were inspired by the native wooden architecture of the period.

The trend toward the multi-tiered, tower-shaped superstructure, reflected in Miloneg's Chernigov structure, became the generating force for Russian architecture of later centuries. It blazed the path for the pyramidal Church of the Ascension in the village of Kolomenskoye and the St. Basil Church in Moscow.

A remarkable characteristic of the architectural style prevalent in Chernigov is the use of Romanesque ornament in architectural details. The Chernigov churches represent the first attempt to combine the Byzantine and Romanesque styles. True, the Romanesque features appear on a very modest scale. Nevertheless, it is quite apparent that the union of Byzantine and Romanesque forms began in Chernigov, much earlier than in the Vladimir-Suzdal region, where, as we shall see, the builders in adapting one style to another were able to create such an outstanding work as the Cathedral of St. Dmitri (Vladimir).

The Decorative Arts and Crafts

The Kievan period witnessed the rise and development of a brilliant school of the decorative arts and crafts, revealed especially in the arts of niello, filigree, and enamel. Byzantine decorative techniques and patterns were assimilated and new ones evolved in response to the change in national sentiment.

The decorative articles and ornaments excavated at Kiev and other great Russian cities are specimens of an indigenous, highly flourishing art. They are proof of the existence of a high state of culture in certain provinces of Pre-Mongolian Russia. Modern research has shown that even such delicate and highly refined articles as *cloisonné* enamels were produced in Kievan Russia. Although some of these articles are similar to those of Byzantium they were not always of Greek importation. Most were products of local industries, made for very definite purposes, specially designed and decorated in a manner that had personal significance for the individual owner.

The extraordinary works of monumental art, the mosaics, and the frescoes of the Kiev cathedrals were executed by groups of Byzantine artists and their Russian pupils; but most of the decorative articles in common use were of local manufacture, or were the products of Greek-Eastern industry imported into Russia via the Crimea, the Caucasus, and the River Volga. Asia Minor and Syria were the principal suppliers of southern and eastern Russia during the grand princes' period. This is attested by the great number of metal articles, textiles, and glazed earthenware found in those regions. But, at the same time, Russian-made art objects were being shipped abroad as early as the end of the twelfth century. An inventory compiled in 1143 by the Monastery of St. Panteleimon on Mount Athos lists many precious objects donated by Russian princes: books of the gospels, icons in expensive encasements (*Oklady* or *rizy*), chasubles, stoles, reliquaries of gold incrusted with precious stones, and a number of Russian books. Many of these listed objects are described as of Russian workmanship.[19]

By the twelfth century the national decorative art of Russia reached a high state of development. The skill of its craftsmen became known beyond its borders. The travelers Carpini (Giovanni de Piano) and Rubruquis (William of Rubrouck) speak of the splendors of Russian cities. From them we learn that the Tatars of the Golden Horde employed Russian artists to make rich ornaments and decorative objects for the courts of their rulers. A Russian craftsman made for the Khan an ivory throne ornamented with precious stones, metalwork, and carving.

The Tatar invasion administered a heavy blow to Kievan institutions and culture, but the development of culture and art was not altogether stopped. The traditions of the Kievan period were maintained and developed in Novgorod and Pskov, in the

[19] Tolstoi and Kondakov, *Russkiya drevnosti*, VI, 7–8.

Ukraine and Byelorussia, and even in the principality of Muscovy.

The Tatars occupied all the highways of commerce towards the East, seized the mouths of the great Russian rivers, and drove the Russians from the Dnieper and made them their vassals. The Russians were forced to retreat and seek new homes in the swamps of the upper Dnieper and the Pripet in the northwest, and in the forests of the upper Volga and the Oka in the east. But in retreating, they carried with them the traditions and cultural achievements of Kievan Russia developed from their constant relations with the Greek and Oriental world during the centuries in which the Kievan State had existed. The wonderful effloresence of art in the Vladimir-Suzdal region, during the eleventh, twelfth, and thirteenth centuries, and in the Galician Russia of the same period, shows how deeply the classical civilization had taken root in Russia.

X

The Architecture of Novgorod and Pskov

NOVGOROD occupies an important place in the history of Russian culture. The city is celebrated not only because of its stormy political history, but because it was the birthplace of a unique and quite original Russian art that lived on long after the political death of the city. In comparison with Kievan Russia, Novgorod had its own uniquely individual and expressive art style. It was only at the end of the sixteenth century that it relinquished its importance as an art center to Moscow. For many years this shift was, in a sense, only geographical because Moscow continued to nourish itself on the art treasures she inherited from Novgorod.

From the eleventh to the fifteenth century, Novgorod had been the political center of the Russia of the northwest. Situated on both sides of the Volkhov River, at the head of the ancient Dnieper water route leading "from the Varangian land to the Greeks," the city had a "business quarter" on the right bank and a "Sophia quarter" on the left. On the right bank were the Yaroslav Square market, the business establishments and commercial arcades. This was the aristocratic side of the city. The left side, where the Cathedral of St. Sophia and the citadel (the *Kreml* or *Detinets*) stood, was the democratic.

The social and political organization of Novgorod in its prime was unique among Russian cities and principalities. The city, "Lord Novgorod the Great," was essentially a democratic city-state. During the tenth and eleventh centuries Novgorod was governed by the grand prince of Kiev through his representative, usually his son. But after the death of Vladimir Monomakh (1125), when his heirs weakened themselves by internecine wars, the Novgorod popular assembly (*Veche*) demanded and obtained the right to select its own prince. The prince played a minor role, being held in the background by the local mayor (*Posadnik*), who was elected by the popular assembly. Because no dynasty of princes could establish itself for long at Novgorod, the city was able to keep its liberties and customs intact under the short reigns of its rulers.

In their pursuit of commerce, the Novgorodians penetrated the northern and northeastern parts of Russia, even beyond the Urals. They were not only in regular and constant touch with Byzantium, but, what is most important, they also maintained close relations with the Germanic world. The trade with the West was at first in the hands of merchants from Gothland, but during the thirteenth and fourteenth centuries it was taken over by the Hanseatic League of northern Germany, and Novgorod became a very important member of the Hansa—the only member which commanded a large and rich hinterland.

Nowhere is the aesthetic character of Old Russian civilization so obvious as in Novgorod. Its art-living merchant aristocracy succeeded in making it something like a Russian Venice. As an independent cultural entity it lasted only from the middle of the thirteenth to the end of the fifteenth century, but during this period it was by far the most brilliant and flourishing spot in Eastern Europe. It produced an artistic movement of great fertility and originality—a very original architecture and a school of painting, which is, together with the Tuscan and Greek schools of the same period, one of the three great schools of the fourteenth century.

Christianity entered Novgorod shortly after the conversion of the Kievan State. St. Vladimir was then the Prince of Kiev, and his son, Yaroslav ruled as his representative in Novgorod. The chronicles tell us that "churches were erected and priests were ordained in the towns." A wooden church with thirteen *Verkhi,*[1] forerunner of the Cathedral of St. Sophia, was built. From the description contained in contemporary chronicles, we have reason to believe that it was similar in type to the churches found in the remote northern villages of the sixteenth and seventeenth centuries.

Ecclesiastical Architecture

In its early stages, the prevailing ecclesiastical architecture of Novgorod is simpler than that of Kiev. Its churches are heavy-set, "cubic" in form, small, and modest in decoration, reflecting the conservative tastes of its democratic burghers. The severe climate and heavy snowfalls of the north caused certain modifications of Byzantine architectural forms. In the course of time, windows were narrowed and deeply splayed; roofs became steeper; and flat-domed profiles assumed the bulbous form which, in different varieties, became eventually the most notable feature of Russian church architecture. Scandinavian and German influences were also important factors in the formation of Novgorod architecture; their structural and decorative devices are frequently encountered in the gabled roofs and the saw-toothed friezes that encircle the drums just below the cupola.

As in Kiev, the ecclesiastical architectural history of Novgorod begins with the Cathedral of St. Sophia (Plate 23). The cathedral functioned not only as the seat of religious activities, but also as the center of political, social, and cultural life. It was built between 1045 and 1052 by Vladimir (son of Yaroslav, then grand prince of Kiev), replacing a wooden church of the same name (erected by Archbishop Yoachim of Khersonesus in 989). The new cathedral followed its Kiev namesake in plan, but it diverges from Byzantine practice in that it has only three apses and two double aisles, each outer aisle ending in a straight wall. (The two semicircular projections at the northeast and south-

---

[1] Fancy roofs; literally tops, or fancifully shaped roofs. Some historians are inclined to interpret the meaning of the word as domes or cupolas.

east corners are one-story chapels.) As originally built, it was of the cross-in-square, Byzantine form, with six piers of cruciform section and five cupolas, exclusive of that surmounting the staircase tower of the west facade. Except for some minor additions (an extra chapel added to the east end in the sixteenth century), St. Sophia preserved substantially its original aspects, since Novgorod and its "younger brother," Pskov, were the only towns of importance that escaped the fury of the invading Tatar hordes. Novgorod's historical monuments remained the most remarkable examples of ancient Russian architecture until the Second World War, when many of them were totally or partially destroyed by the Germans.[2]

The white, austere, almost windowless walls, the bare buttresses, the semicircular parapets, and the marvelous silhouettes of the five cupolas rising above the simple mass of the cathedral make a strikingly effective composition. Especially beautiful is the silhouette of the central cupola, quite matchless in the delicacy of its outline. The walls are very thick and laid up Byzantine-fashion of gray-yellowish stone interspersed with courses of thin red brick. (The external stucco coat was applied in 1152.) Recent examination of the ruins of this cathedral, almost destroyed by the Germans in 1942 and restored in 1948,[3] disclosed that the wall fill contained many pieces of shaped and carved stone and ornamental fragments from ancient Novgorod buildings that were torn down before 1045, and whose material was used in constructing the cathedral. This fact would lead us to believe that the Novgorodians had much experience in masonry building long before the introduction of Christianity.

The centuries were kind to this structure and even the addi-

[2] A. Udalenkov, "O mirovom znachenii russkogo natsionalnogo zodchestva," Arkhitektura i Stroitel'stvo, Moscow, October, 1948.

[3] The restoration of the destroyed monuments and the rebuilding of the city were begun soon after the war under the supervision of a specially appointed commission composed of archaeologists and architects. The work on the exterior of St. Sophia and its belfry was finished in 1948. Work on the interior continues. S. Davidov, "Izucheniye i vosstanovleniye pamyatnikov arkhitektury Novgoroda," Arkhitektura i stroitelstvo, December, 1948.

tions and alterations did not disfigure it. On the contrary, as A. Shchusev puts it, they added character, liveliness, and picturesqueness.[4] It lost its primitive Byzantine appearance but gained something genuinely Russian in the silhouette of its masses and various elements.

The interior is impressive: four massive cruciform columns support the great drum of the central cupola. The choirs, arranged along the north, south, and west walls, are reached from the stairway in the tower, and are supported on a series of arches. The walls of the central, elongated, semicircular apse are faced, to about a man's height from the floor, with mosaics of a rich geometrical pattern. Centuries ago the walls were completely covered with frescoes, but of these, little remains except the image of the Christ Pantocrator in the main cupola and the recently discovered figures in the drum. Much interest is centered on the image of Christ Pantocrator; his right hand is shown raised but closed, and thereby hangs a poetic tale. Thrice, says the legend, the painter tried to represent the Pantocrator's hand open in benediction, but thrice it miraculously closed. Then a mysterious voice was heard saying: "Do not paint me with my hand open in benediction, but leave it closed, as in this hand I hold the destinies of Great Novgorod, and when the hand would open, it would be the end of Novgorod."[5] It seems that this prophecy came to pass: a German shell destroyed the cupola and most of Novgorod was destroyed as well.

The cathedral contains many outstanding works of old-Russian decorative art. The epoch of Ivan Grozny (1533–84) left beautiful specimens of woodcarving and metalwork. Art of that period, enriched by its contacts with the art of the Orient, acquired a high degree of craftsmanship, an extraordinary variety of ornamental forms, and a wealth of decorative devices. We notice in the principal Russian churches the appearance of elaborate iconostases, royal doors, altar canopies, tsars' and patriarch-

[4] In Grabar', *Istoriya russkago iskusstva* (1909), I, 169.
[5] Tolstoi and Kondakov, *Russkiya drevnosti*, VI, 106.

al thrones, all embellished with fine carving, most of them indubitably of Oriental derivation. The thrones of the tsar (1572)
and the metropolitan (1560) in St. Sophia stand facing the royal
doors of the iconostasis. Both are carved, painted, and gilded
wood, and date from the period of Ivan Grozny. A still older example of woodcarving is the Chaldean furnace (*Khaldeiskaya
peshch*, Plate 185), which was removed to the Russian Museum
in Leningrad (formerly the Museum of Alexander III).

The sacristy of St. Sophia, in spite of much looting, contains
many magnificent objects of great historical and artistic value.
They are especially valuable because of their antiquity, as almost
all of them date from the thirteenth, fourteenth, and fifteenth
centuries, while the articles in the churches and monasteries
of the Moscow region belong mostly to the sixteenth and seventeenth centuries.

Two other works of ancient decorative art must be mentioned.
These are two sets of bronze doors which, in the style of their
design, illustrate vividly the duality of influence—Byzantine and
Germanic—to which the Novgorodians were subjected. The so-
called Sigtuna (*Sigstunsk*) bronze gates (Plate 25), at the entrance to the chapel of the Nativity of the Virgin, have a legendary history. They are said to have been brought to Novgorod
as a trophy from the Swedish city of Sigtuna, pillaged in 1187.
The design of the doors is of an Italo-Byzantine character and
the damascene workmanship (deeply incised design in the metal
with laminations of gold or silver, similar to that of many Byzantine doors at Amalfi, Salerno, and Rome) is of the eleventh century. There are six identical six-sided crosses placed in rectangular niches which probably constitute the portion of the original doors. The bordering floral forms and rosettes are later
additions.

The so-called Korsunian gates (Plate 24) on the west front
of the cathedral are traditionally supposed to have been brought
from Korsun' by St. Vladimir in 988.[6] Actually, they are the work

[6] According to Kondakov this legend of the origin of the doors has persisted

of a Magdeburg artist, Master Requinus, who lived in the second half of the twelfth century. The doors, eleven feet eight inches high consist of twenty-six cast bronze high-relief panels placed over a massive oak backing. The bronze reliefs present scenes from the Old and New Testaments and other subjects surrounded by scroll work, and form a kind of sculptured iconostasis. The inscriptions are in Latin and in Slavonic—the latter added in the fifteenth century. A few of the panels are signed by a Russian craftsman. Modern research has disclosed that the doors were originally ordered by the Bishop of Polotsk for his local church and later purchased by the Hanseatic merchants of Novgorod for presentation to St. Sophia.

The earlier Novgorodian churches had a cubic shape, with three semicircular apses projecting at the east end. The exterior walls were devoid of decoration. Gradually, however, certain modifications in the design of these box-like structures begin to appear. In the second half of the twelfth century, the changes affected primarily the east front and, later, the remaining walls. The two lateral apses are shorter than the altar apse; the walls are broken into three vertical divisions (*Trekhdol'noye deleniye*) by bands of stone or brickwork forming blind semicircular arcading. The number of internal columns supporting a single cupola is reduced from six to four.

The small Church of the Saviour at Nereditsa, near Novgorod, was a good example of this architectural modification. Built in 1198, it was totally destroyed during the Second World War. The church was of great importance architecturally and, especially, because of the fine mural paintings that adorned its interior. The space given over to the frescoes was so large that the painters had to evolve many scenes and cycles to fill it. Though not arranged in the traditional order, the scenes followed the Byzantine convention; many figures were depicted in rigid atti-

for a long time, because in ancient Russia anything outstanding in ecclesiastical art, whether it was an icon, cross, sacred vessel, relief, or ornamented door, was believed to have come from Korsun' (Khersonesus). Tolstoi and Kondakov, *Russkiya drevnosti* VI, 112.

tudes, but there were some that foreshadowed the more supple movements of later periods of Byzantine style.

Toward the middle of the fourteenth century, the Novgorodian builders still further modified their original cubic design in order to adapt their structures to northern climatic conditions. Most important among the modifications is the appearance of the high-ridged, eight-sloped roof with four gables, examples of which are the Church of St. Theodore Stratilates, 1360, and the Church of the Transfiguration, 1374 (Plate 30). Next was the gradual replacement of the large windows of Byzantine and south Russian architecture with small openings with mica panes. The same century brought other developments. The heads of the niches in the walls became trefoil and half-trefoil in shape. (In the earlier churches they were semicircular.) The number of apses was reduced to one, as in the Church of the Saviour in Kovalevo, 1345, and the Church of the Transfiguration in Volotovo, 1352.

In any discussion of the outstanding characteristics of the architecture of Novgorod, the question of the origin of the bulbous cupola looms large. The date of its innovation is uncertain, but we can reasonably suppose that all cupolas built before the middle of the thirteenth century were originally of the flat-domed Byzantine type. Since this hemispherically shaped cupola was not practical in a region of heavy snows, it has been inferred that a rational substitute was found in the favorite feature of Russian native wooden architecture—the roof with the ogee-shaped section (*bochka*). According to M. V. Krasovsky, the Russian carpenters designed these roofs by drawing a circle and removing a segment at the bottom equal to approximately a quarter of its diameter, then adding this amount to the height of the roof above the upper arc of the circle.[7] Slightly concave lines were then drawn in to connect the peak with the tangents to the circumference of the circle. The size of the removed segment determined the outline of the base of the bulb. Some his-

[7] *Kurs istorii russkoi arkhitektury,* 86.

torians are of the opinion that this section was first used for the silhouette of polygonal cupolas, and later applied to circular cupolas.

Pskov

Pskov, "the younger brother of Novgorod," on Lake Peipus, between Novgorod and Riga, was the center of a vast territory from its very inception. Its lands were fertile, particularly in comparison with those of neighboring Novgorod. Pskov's geographical situation was a major factor in its rise as an important commercial and industrial center. It was linked with the Baltic through Lake Chudskoye and its tributaries. The city must have originated in the eighth century, although the legend of the invitation of the Varangian princes does not mention Pskov but Izborsk, which was ruled by the legendary Truvor. At first, living in the shadow of the Novgorod republic, it showed strong tendencies toward political independence; *Veche* practices must have developed there at an early period. In the fourteenth and fifteenth centuries, Pskov became a boyar republic which held sway over the entire Pskov territory.

Pskov's earliest section, the citadel, stood on a high and narrow headland where the Pskov River empties into the Velikaia. Subsequently, the town grew toward the south in the area between the two rivers, although the other side of the Pskova (Zapskovye) was also settled at an early period. The old chronicles record that, as early as the twelfth century, rich monasteries were located in the Zavelichye district, on the western bank of the Velikaia. Larger-scale stone construction, almost equal to that of Novgorod, was going on throughout the twelfth century. Among its stone buildings are the Cathedral of the Transfiguration in the Mirozhsky Monastery in Zavelichye, which was built and decorated with frescoes in 1156; and the thirteenth-century Cathedral of St. John the Baptist, also in Zavelichye.[8] In the fourteenth and fifteenth centuries, the Pskov

[8] Grabar', *Istoriya russkogo iskusstva* (1953), II, 314–15.

area had more masonry citadels than the whole of the principality of Muscovy.

Although politically (until 1348) and commercially dependent upon Novgorod, Pskov shows some significant architectural innovations. Smaller than Novgorod and not so prosperous, she could not afford large and luxurious buildings. Her architects therefore concentrated upon developing a small type of church, and in so doing demonstrated both practical expediency and artistic sensibility. The churches are relatively tiny and squat and usually have three low apses. The cupolas, roofs, and decorative elements are similar to those of Novgorod.

Pskov's greatest contribution to medieval Russian architecture was evolved in the fifteenth century. Its diminutive churches were too small to contain interior columns for the support of the cupola. Some way had to be found to permit the transfer of the cupola load to the side walls. The Pskov builders developed the structural device of corbeled-out superimposed tiers of arches for the support of cupola drums. These tiers of semiround or pointed arches, which became known as *kokoshniki*, were at first visible only inside of the structure, but eventually their highly decorative possibilities were realized, and their form permitted to appear externally. The feature was destined to become a favorite decorative device in Russian architecture. Its appearance became so popular that often multiple rows of semicircular or pointed *kokoshniki* were added for effect, when they were not required for support.

The church porches, the exterior galleries (*paperti*), and the arcaded belfries (*zvonnitsy*) were Pskov's other outstanding contributions to Russian architecture. The porch, serving as entrance to the galleries, first appeared in the twelfth century. Novgorod was quick to adopt this feature and from that time on the builders in both cities erected porches with squat columns which supported steep two-sloped roofs.

The Russian exterior galleries (*paperti*) are a development of the Byzantine narthex. In the mild climate of Byzantium those galleries were usually open, but in the cold regions of northern Russia they were walled in, so they could serve as shelter to worshippers coming from distant villages, who were often forced by bad weather to remain for many hours indoors. The gallery also functioned as a refectory and became known as *trapeznaya*.

The arcaded belfries were at first simple appurtenances in the form of open-arched wall extensions built over the church facades or over the galleries. In the fifteenth century they were replaced by separate storied and arcaded structures. The latter type of belfry elaborated by the Pskovians, was adopted by the Novgorodians. The bell tower of St. Sophia of Novgorod, added to the cathedral in 1439 and remodeled in the eighteenth century, is of pure Pskovian type.

In their escape from the Mongol invasion, Novgorod and Pskov remained the only cities in Russia where building could go on without interruption until the fifteenth century. Pskovian builders were employed in many cities. Their skill and fame were so great that in 1480 Grand Prince Ivan III summoned them to Moscow to undertake the reconstruction of the Cathedral of Annunciation in the Moscow Kremlin.

XI

The Architecture of Vladimir-Suzdal

W<small>E HAVE NOTED</small> the cultural trends prevalent at the two nodal points of the Dnieper trade route, first Kiev, then Novgorod. Another center of medieval Russian cultural and artistic life, the principality of Vladimir-Suzdal, is of special interest because it included most of the area later to form the Grand Principality of Moscow—the nucleus of the modern Russian state.

At the beginning of the twelfth century the political and cultural center of pre-Mongolian Russia began to shift toward the northeast. Under pressure by the nomads of the steppes, the Russians began to migrate from the lands of the Dnieper basin to the forest regions of the upper Volga, most of them settling in the triangle formed by the upper Volga and the Oka (the territory comprising the pre-revolutionary provinces of Moscow, Vladimir, Kostroma, Yaroslavl, and Tver and the district of the White Lake). Although the colonization of the Volga began in the first decades of the eleventh century, the greatest activity dates from the middle of the twelfth century when the various settlements coalesced into the principality of Vladimir-Suzdal, opening the Moscow era.

The newcomers completely changed the complexion of this area, which in the past had been occupied largely by Finnish tribes. This territory became the Slavic-Finnish melting pot, and it was the mixture of the Slavic settlers with the Finns that eventually brought into existence the Great Russian (Velikorussian)

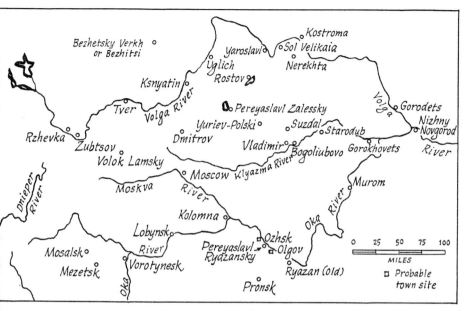

VLADIMIR-SUZDAL AREA

branch of the eastern Slavs who assumed state leadership in the Muscovite period. Many national characteristics of the Great Russians are to be explained by the Finnish strain in their blood.

Moreover, this migration to the northeast was destined to become one of the most important events in the history of Russian civilization. Kiev and Novgorod had been, up to the very end of the twelfth century, under the influence of Byzantium. This influence markedly declined in Russia of the Volga region.

"Mother Volga" (*Matushka Volga*), as she is affectionately called by the singers and narrators of Russian folklore stories (*byliny*)[1]—this central artery of the country—became prominent in shaping the destinies of the future empire. It exercised perhaps the greatest influence on Russian medieval political and cultural history. The basin of the Volga and its tributaries (the Oka and the Kama) became the nodal point of Moscow colonization, industry, and cultural life. It included nearly the whole of sixteenth-century Russia and played a most important role in the development and fortunes of the land.

The ethnic, social, and political structures of the Suzdal province were quite different from those of Kiev, and this divergence became even more marked through the economic and cultural influences which were exercised upon Suzdal. Her relations with Constantinople were limited, and contacts with the German Hansa or with Scandinavia were difficult.

In contrast, there were established, via the Volga and its tributaries, very active exchanges with central Asia and the Caucasus. The Volga, on which the Suzdalian princes maintained a fleet, became the great commercial and civilizing route of the New Russia; and as Kiev was naturally drawn by the Dnieper toward Byzantium, Suzdal was oriented by the Volga's course towards Asia.

---

[1] The word *bylina* is derived from the Russian verb *byt'*, to be, and connotes "that which has occurred." It is a popular narrative or epic poem or tale relating to historical events in Russia from the tenth to the nineteenth century. The *byliny* (pl.) are all anonymous and have been handed down by oral tradition. The narrators recite merely what they have heard from one another.

The first important city that the Suzdalian merchants encountered on the Volga was Bulgari, the capital of the Volga Bulgars (not far from Kazan). The pagan Bulgars had been converted to Mohammedanism and were under the influence of Mussulman civilizations. They were in a strong position to serve as intermediaries between the Russians, the Persians, and the Armenians. It should also be pointed out that there were direct relations between Vladimir and the Caucasus. A son of Prince Andrei Bogoliubsky, Prince Yuri (1212–28), married Queen Tamara of Georgia. This Georgian marriage had a significance for Suzdalian art comparable to the influence on the art of Moscow resulting from the Byzantine-Italian marriage of Ivan III, prince of Moscow, to Princess Zoë Paleologue which took place more than two centuries later.

The Vladimir-Suzdal region emerged as an important political center when Suzdal was organized as a principality and assigned to Vladimir Monomakh, later prince of Kiev (1113–25). He, in turn, allotted it as a domain to his youngest son, Yuri Dolgoruky (George Longarm). During the first half of the twelfth century, many towns were founded and largely populated by emigrants from southern districts of the Kievan principality. Among them were Moscow itself (1147), as yet an unimportant fortified border village, Yuriev-Polski (Georgetown in the fields, 1152), named for Prince Yuri Dolgoruky, and Tver and Kostroma on the Volga. Construction on a large scale, begun by Yuri, was continued by his son, Andrei Bogoliubsky, (1157–75) who made Vladimir his capital city, and by Andrei's younger brother, Vsevolod III. It is with the works of these three twelfth-century Vladimir autocrats, great warriors, but even greater builders, that we are chiefly concerned.

The Architectural Monuments of Vladimir-Suzdal

The twelfth- and early thirteenth-century structures under consideration were all erected before the characteristic northern innovations were carried through at Novgorod. Hence the dominating influences were still Kiev and Byzantium. But we shall observe that in this remote district western and Caucasian influences also made themselves felt. Another important factor in the development of local architecture was the supply of white stones from the quarries of the Kama River, which relieved the local architects of the restrictions imposed by the use of brick in Kiev and stimulated the use of carved stone decoration.

Monumental buildings were erected in the capital city of Vladimir and a new princely seat, the town of Bogoliubovo, arose during the reign of Prince Andrei. The outstanding architectural monument of the Vladimir-Suzdal region is the Uspensky Sobor (Cathedral of the Assumption)[2] at Vladimir, built by Prince Andrei Bogoliubsky in 1158–61 (Plate 26). The cathedral was projected by the ambitious prince not only as a metropolitan see of the Vladimir-Suzdal principality, but as the principal cathedral for all of Russia, whose head the prince strove to become. The chronicles tell us that "with God's help he was able to gather masters from all lands."[3] Among them were West European architects, lapidaries, and carvers and Byzantine painters and craftsmen.

Much of the prince's treasury was lavished on this structure, and the chronicles relate that for sheer splendor it was the most magnificent and ornate ever seen in Russia. It was reduced to ruins by the great fire of 1183 which destroyed most of the city of Vladimir. Andrei's brother and successor, Vsevolod, reconstructed and enlarged it (1185–89) by building an outer shell around the original church. The old walls were breached through, creating arched openings, and the original three naves

[2] A better translation of the Russian word *uspenie* would be dormition; hence, Uspensky Sobor should be called "The Cathedral of the Dormition of the Virgin." However, in deference to long usage, the word "Assumption" is used throughout this work. *Sobor* is commonly translated as cathedral; literally it connotes a "bringing together"; hence (a) a synod or great council of church or state; (b) a service conducted by several priests; (c) a collegiate church, and so the principal churches of towns and monasteries, but not necessarily a bishop's seat.

[3] Grabar', *Istoriya russkago iskusstva* (1909), I, 314.

were extended to five. New galleries were built on all three sides and at the corners four helmet-shaped cupolas were added to the original single one. The windows and portals of the extant cathedral are of the Romanesque type, deeply recessed and richly decorated. The three semicircular apses projecting from the eastern end are decorated with blind ornamental arcades running around the tops of the apses, with some of the engaged colonnettes extending the whole height of the apse. On the lateral façades, vertically divided into four panels, this decoration is repeated.

Similar decorative devices appear on the Church of Pokrov Bogoroditsy (Intercession of the Virgin) built in 1165 on a bluff overlooking the river Nerl, a short distance outside Vladimir (Plate 27). It is a small four-piered, three-apsed church with a single dome, and looks like a miniature edition of the original Uspensky Cathedral. The blind ornamental arcades and the decoration on the cupola drum are similar to those of the Uspensky Cathedral. But this new version of the traditional form is done with extraordinary finesse. It is one of the loveliest architectural creations of Vladimir-Suzdal and is a summation, as it were, of the artistic searchings and experiences of the period.

The church is slightly elongated along its east-west axis and thus loses the heaviness of the traditional cubic mass. The proportions of the altar apses are lightened, setting off the shape of the principal elements of the decorative carving scheme repeated on all three facades. The central motif is the figure of the psalmist, King David, playing a stringed instrument. On his sides are the doves and lions so often mentioned in the psalms. The female masks seem to be traditional with most of the twelfth-century churches dedicated to the Virgin. The griffins (in the lateral tympanums), each devouring a lamb—motifs reminiscent of the Scythian animal style—are probably also inspired by the symbolism of the psalms. The portals, the capitals of the pilasters, and the colonnettes of the central frieze are decorated with carving.

Recent archaeological excavations have brought to light the white-stone foundation of the gallery, supported by graceful arches surrounding the church, and a massive wall in which was the staircase leading to the galleries and the balcony. Archaeologists have also reconstructed the very interesting history of the building. It was erected on a riverbank which was always inundated during spring floods. In order to raise the building above the level of the flood, the architects built a high foundation for its walls and pillars, enclosing them in an artificial embankment. The slopes of this embankment were faced with white stones. Thus, the famous church on the Nerl originally was an extraordinarily striking edifice. Its tiers, which are reminiscent of the design of St. Sophia's Cathedral in Kiev, were brought into greater relief by the white stone hill on which it stands. The church at the confluence of the Nerl and Klyazma rivers, which were plied by the vessels of ambassadors and merchants, was an architectural introduction, as it were, to the ensemble of the Bogoliubovo castle (Plate 28) and the capital of Prince Andrei, the town of Vladimir.

The purely decorative aspect of the Nerl church is modest compared with the ornamental lushness presented by the Cathedral of St. Dmitri in Vladimir (Plate 29). It was built by Prince Andrei's brother, Vsevolod III, between 1193 and 1197. In plan it is almost square and, like the Nerl church, is a four-column structure with three apses, but it lacks the slender elegance of the latter since the sweep of its vertical lines is interrupted horizontally by a wide decorative band consisting of small arcatures supporting a delicate frieze. The arcature niches contain reliefs of plants and birds, and the spaces between the capitals of the engaged colonnettes are occupied by figures of aureoled saints. St. Dmitri repeats the decorative features of the two churches discussed above, but greatly elaborates upon them. The cupola is of the flat type and rests on a richly molded cornice, below which is a fringe of denticulated chevrons. The cupola drum contains a number of narrow, arched windows alternating with recessed panels filled with relief ornament.

St. Dmitri was built as a church adjunct to Prince Vsevolod's new palace, units of which flanked the cathedral to the north and south and were connected with it by stone galleries. The cathedral thus formed the central element of a complex and sumptuous architectural ensemble of the prince's palace. It followed the favorite twelfth-century type of single-cupola, four-column church. But this old scheme was given a new and brilliant interpretation by the Vladimir architects. Majesty and quiet strength permeates the interior of the cathedral, its spacious cupola drum, the paced rhythm of its arches, and the finely ordered exterior masses. Though the principal elements are of massive proportions, the cathedral as a whole conveys the impression of lightness and gracious elegance.

It is in the tympanums of the upper division panels that the most striking decorations are found. The symbolism is that of Psalm 148.[4] In the central tympanums on the north and south façades, King David is represented, as on the Nerl church, surrounded by animals interspersed with plants and trees. Besides the biblical scenes, there are representations of apocryphal stories, such as that of Alexander of Macedonia ascending to heaven on a chariot drawn by griffins. The mythical animals, basilisks, and dragons follow the medieval conception of the animal kingdom exhibited in the Physiologus.[5]

The façades are covered with carved stone reliefs extending from the top of the drum of the cupola down to the central frieze. The ornamentation is like a gorgeous heavy woven fabric pro-

[4] Verses 7–12: Praise the Lord from the earth, ye dragons, and all deeps: Fire, and hail; snow, and vapours; stormy wind fulfilling His word: Mountains, and all hills; fruitful trees, and all cedars: Beasts, and all cattle: creeping things, and flying fowl: Kings of the earth, and all people; princes, and all judges of the earth: Both young men, and maidens; old men, and children.

[5] The title of a collection of allegories compiled in Alexandria in the second century A.D., based on the peculiarities ascribed to various animals, real or imaginary, and explaining certain scriptural passages.

ducing an extraordinary rich effect, but at the same time not detracting from the clarity and harmony of the architectural elements.[6]

Certain motifs and the style of some of the reliefs suggest a similarity to the plastic arts of the Caucasus, Romanesque sculpture, and to some of the decorative art objects of Byzantium and the Balkans. Doubtless the stone carvers who decorated this cathedral had access to the rich collection of art objects in the princes' treasury and the sacristies of the churches, where various liturgical furnishings, precious ornamental utensils, and fabrics were kept. They must have used those ornamental motifs as models for their carved reliefs. But here again we see the hand of the Russian carvers, trained in flat relief-carving on wood, transforming the foreign motifs into something intimately Russian. The figures of the animals, shrubs, and flowers acquire a flat ornamental character.

The main theme of the bas-reliefs is a rounded picture of the world in all its colorful aspects, a kind of poetic glorification of the universe. In both churches of Vladimir the psalm-singer, David, is shown surrounded by earthly creatures. But in the St. Dmitri Cathedral there are also hunting scenes, galloping riders, a fist fight, and Alexander of Macedonia rising to heaven, while next to him is St. Nikita chastising the devil, and all sorts of animals, birds, griffins, and harpies, in a word, life in its varied manifestations, as imagined by man in the twelfth century.

The reliefs in the tympanums of the upper central panels are assigned to the glorification of the Creator receiving homage from all creatures; they are arranged in even horizontal rows, and, as a rule, rows of foliate motifs alternate with those composed of conventionalized beasts and birds, recalling the ornamental devices of Russian folk embroidery. The entire ensemble is a compound of semiprofane, semisacred, pagan, and Christian deco-

[6] For a discussion of the sculptural reliefs at the Vladimir-Suzdal churches, see V. N. Lazarev in Grabar', *Istoriya russkogo iskusstva* (1953), I, pp. 396–441.

rative motifs, quite different in spirit from those of the austere and simple decorative elements of the Uspensky Cathedral. The mixture of the exotic, fantastic animals, beasts, holy warriors, saints, angels, and bloody fighting scenes leads us to believe that the sculptured reliefs of St. Dmitri were conceived primarily as a strictly decorative composition aiming to heighten the splendor and the majesty of the cathedral.

The frescoes of St. Dmitri, of which only remnants have survived, are part of a large cycle depicting the Last Judgment. In the central vault under the choirs, the apostles are presented surrounded by hosts of warrior angels; on the southwest vault, paradise and musician angels. The paintings are ascribed by Russian art historians to Byzantine masters of the Comnenian period (1081–1185) and to their Russian pupils. The cross crowning the cupola is made of open-work gilt copper on a forged iron frame. It is ascribed to Russian metal craftsmen of the twelfth century.

About thirty-five years after the erection of St. Dmitri, the Church of St. George at Yuriev-Polski was built. There the sculptured ornament covers the walls like a blanket of some creeping plant spread over the entire field of the façades, from cornice to base. It consists of a sprawling hieroglyphic design of strapwork, flowering buds, birds, and chimeric monsters (Plate 31).

In essence, the principal elements of Suzdalian decoration consist of fantastic animals and of designs of a very pronounced Oriental character. The animal sculptures of St. Dmitri are composed of heraldic eagles, lions with tails in the form of flowers, griffins, centaurs, and basilisks. The strolling griffin of Yuriev-Polski with his tail plaited in the form of a palmette is particularly remarkable for the stylization of forms. These animals are either interlaced or arranged face to face on each side of the tree of paradise. The portal archivolts are decorated with strapwork braided bands and delicate rope moldings. Of all these motifs, spread in profusion over the Suzdalian churches, some were evidently inspired by the carved ivories and embroideries of Byzantium, others by the silverwork of Sassanid Persia, and still others are strongly reminiscent of the decorative features of Armenian and Georgian architecture.

Analysis of the architectural forms and the decorations of the churches of Vladimir reveals a general Byzantine background and certain additional elements, some that seem to have been borrowed from the Romanesque architecture of the West, others from the Georgian and Armenian art of the Caucasus. From Byzantium the Suzdalians adopted the general features of the square plan with three semicircular apses, and the four columns supporting a flat cupola with its circular drum. Instead of the brick used so widely in Byzantium and Kievan Russia, however, they used cut stone, and instead of polychrome revetments they used carved stone embroideries. These divergencies can be ascribed to the influence of Western architecture. For when Prince Andrei Bogoliubsky tried to eclipse the splendor of rival capitals he brought in architects, painters, and sculptors from many lands, Western European included.

To the influences of Byzantine and Romanesque art must be added the third factor: the arts of Caucasian Georgia and Armenia. We know that Armenia possessed an original architecture that reached a high state of development in the tenth and eleventh centuries. We also know that the Suzdalian princes were in active communication, via the Volga trade route, with the lands of the Caucasus, and that a son of Andrei Bogoliubsky married a Georgian princess.

Those familiar with the monuments of Georgia will have no difficulty in recognizing the similarity of certain features in the cathedrals of Vladimir and those of Armenia and Georgia. There seem to be the same well-conceived, harmonious proportions, the same decorative devices in the employment of wide horizontal bands of blind arcading, and a very similar treatment of the relief ornament covering the walls like a rich embroidery.

It is interesting to speculate on the possible further developments of the art of the Suzdalian region, and the direction it might have taken, had it not been for the Mongol invasion. As the Vladimir-Suzdal principality was in the path of the invading Tatars, it suffered very heavily. Horde followed horde with the relentlessness of a swarm of locusts, settled for a while to gather loot, and passed on, leaving a track of burned cities and waste lands. The invaders swept across the country with such devastating violence that it seemed as though Russian civilization could never recover from the blow.

In 1238 the cities of Suzdal, Rostov, Yaroslavl, and Vladimir were pillaged and burned. The elimination of the capital of Andrei Bogoliubsky as a factor in Russian art can be dated from that year. But the genius of Russia, at first shocked into stillness, reasserted its vitality and a new civilization rose from the ashes of the old. It was then that Moscow took over.

XII

Icon Painting

THE AESTHETIC CULTURE of pre-Petrine Russia is best reflected in the art of that period. It was a religious art, guided by reverence for ecclesiastical tradition, yet strongly influenced by the native arts of the Russian people. This was especially manifested in the sphere of religious painting.

From the tenth century until the end of the seventeenth century painting was virtually confined to icon painting, an art introduced to the newly converted nation in the tenth century in the form of models sent to Kievan Russia from Byzantium. Both in Byzantium and Russia this art was limited to the representation of the Deity, sacred personages, and the scriptural events. It was never an attempt to achieve realism or authentic portraiture. The fundamental principle of this art is a pictorial expression of church doctrine, to represent sacred events and indicate their meaning. Being primarily an object of veneration and an auxiliary to worship, the icon was as formalized as the sequence of the liturgy or the ritual of a sacrament. Nevertheless, despite strict rules governing their painting, icons exhibit a variety of styles, subjects, compositional characteristics, and moods. In spite of the devoutness with which the Russian icon painters regarded their Byzantine models, they contrived to give them a popular appeal, both in line and in color.

The Byzantine Legacy

To understand the particular character of Russian icon painting and to follow its development it is necessary to consider the Byzantine art from which it sprang, and by which it was nourished during the first three centuries of its existence. It should be borne in mind that there were three epochs in Byzantine art: first, the Justinian age of the sixth century; second, the Byzantine Renaissance in the age of the Macedonian and Comnenus dynasties, tenth and eleventh centuries; and third, the second Renaissance of the fourteenth century in the Paleologue era. Throughout the many centuries of its history, Byzantium was a blending of two essential traditions amalgamated with the Christian idea: the Hellenistic, which was prevalent in Constantinople, in parts of Western Asia, and in Greece itself; and the Oriental, which was predominant in Syria and Anatolia. The Hellenistic was characterized by a greater attention to elegance and realism, the Oriental by its accent on abstract arrangements, ornamental motifs, and decorative symbolism.

The development of icon painting was greatly influenced by the search for a style suitable for the presentation of the religious image. The search was particularly intense during the fifth century and, after decades of zealous activity of this period, resulted in a distinctive style for the portrayal of the Christian celestial world. At this time were created images of Christ and the Virgin Mary, portraits of the apostles, prophets, and angels, and scenes representing the chief events of the Bible and the Gospels. These images and scenes belong to that type of realistic art which takes its observations from life and is very Hellenistic.

Since the baptism of Russia took place at the time when the iconoclast movement had come to an end, the Russians did not see and did not copy any Byzantine icons until the end of the tenth century. However, we must consider the far-reaching changes in Byzantine icon painting during the iconoclastic movement, the final elaboration in 843 of a special doctrine of images, and the effect of the latter on Russian icon painting.

Ever since Old Testament times there had been an aversion

to the "graven image" in the East Christian area. Opinion on the value and permissibility of sacred images had been divided, and in 726 a violent dispute on the subject arose in the Eastern Roman Empire which divided the clergy into two camps, image worshipers (iconolaters) and image breakers (iconoclasts). For over one hundred years, the dispute flamed up repeatedly, but the iconolaters became finally victorious in 843. This victory not only firmly established the image in the Eastern church, but had another consequence of far-reaching significance, namely, the elaboration of a special doctrine declaring that religious images were to be venerated as sacred objects and, as such, were to be under the control of the Church. It also indicated the manner in which the artist was to handle religious themes.[1]

The new doctrine established a canon for religious painting and brought forth a comprehensive set of prescriptions covering almost every detail of subject choice and form selection for the proper creation of religious pictures. As a result, icon painting became almost an affair of dogma, in which nothing must be left to chance. One of the main requirements was that the painting should faithfully reproduce the characteristic features of the persons or scenes portrayed—features whose authenticity were established by tradition. This involved not the application of naturalistic principles, but the evolving of characteristic types, which, once established, were scrupulously adhered to and copied over and over again.

The Church did not allow any scope for the caprices and originality of the individual. The formal language of the new Christian art became subject to strict laws. Pictures of the Divinity and the events of the Bible had to be constricted into rigorously determined compositions, governed by precise formulas.

Rules governing the making of an icon were set down in a manual. A standard guide, it dictates to the painter the minutest details of technique, not forgetting the color of the

[1] For a discussion of the Doctrine of Images, see L. Ouspensky and V. Lossky, *The Meaning of Icons*, 27ff.

saint's hair or the shape of his eyelids. The authors of the manual for iconographers realized the dangers inherent in such sensuous art creations as had been produced by the ancient Greeks. Obviously they thought it preferable to distort nature, and to cut out all the libidinous stimuli of fleshly pagan art, fearing that such art, instead of remaining a window to God, might turn into an idol and a goal in itself.

The manual guided the artist and kept him close to the scheme of compositions approved by the Church; it also simplified the problem of the representation of individual saints. The Church required their absolutely abstract images, which could hardly be told one from another without each saint's prescribed "symbol of attribution." The icon painters—monks of many lands, Greeks, Serbians, Russians, and other East Europeans—considered themselves not as interpreters of the dogma, but simply as humble servants of the Church who must follow the prescribed rules.

For expressing the invisible the icon painter used a number of procedures and devices. For example, in portraying the human figure, he usually gave it a severely frontal pose, with the result that the eyes seem fixed intently on those of the spectator. The leading figures were commonly magnified; thus Christ is usually at least a head taller than those beside Him. An altar is as large as the church that houses it; and the hand of a saint making a gesture of benediction is greatly enlarged. Care was taken that no part of the leading figures should be obscured by intervening persons or objects; they are depicted full length and well in view. Even a landscape of mountains or buildings is arranged to show the leading figure to the best advantage.

Most figures are represented with their faces turned towards the congregation. The artist deliberately "dematerialized" his personages; the bodies seem to have no weight or substance. The saints are generally depicted in rigid attitudes, each with his familiar canonical features and strictly defined attributes: gospels in the hands of the saints, swords or lances for the soldiers. The figures live and move in the air of an unknown world, where mountains, trees, and flowers are fantastic, where conventional garments in conventional folds fall over abstract bodies, where every miracle is possible and acceptable. The icons convey to the onlooker neither a natural perspective nor the feeling of atmosphere. The colors are rich, but there are relatively few of them, and there are no shadows. Inverted (reversed) perspective was used in order to make the human figures in the foreground appear smaller than those in the background, when the latter are more important than the former. According to this system figures of greater importance either in heaven or on earth are made larger, and those of lesser importance smaller, irrespective of their situation in the picture plane.

Architecture plays a peculiar role of its own in the icons. While it serves, as does landscape, to denote that the event depicted in the icon is connected historically with a definite place, it never contains this event inside itself, but merely serves as a background to it, for, according to the very meaning of the icon, the action is not enclosed in or limited to a particular place.

Architectural and landscape symbols helped to form the ornamental silhouettes in the background—a roof with cupolas is a church, a single frontlet means a whole building, a piece of cloth draped from one wall to the other indicates the interior of a house or of a church. Movements and emotions, such as joy and despair, are stressed by nature and backgrounds. For instance, in the "Entombment" (Plates 61, 62), the lifted arms of the crying woman are accentuated and echoed by the silhouette of two mountains.

During the Middle Ages, Byzantine Church decorations, whether in painting or mosaic, had two invariable characteristics: they were practically always iconographic, and every detail was regulated by an iconographic program, rigorously laid down and formulated. This program allowed very little latitude; all church decorations of the eleventh and twelfth centuries were much alike, all the more so because the architectural layout of the churches also conformed to a standard type. The structure was invariably crowned with a central dome (sometimes with other domes as well) and was intended to symbolize the Christian cosmos. The church was both an image of the cosmos in an ordered hierarchy and a calendar of the Christian year. Christ Pantocrator reigns in the dome, the Virgin intercedes or shows the way in the apse, below her and in different parts of the church the saints and prophets of the church are revealed in the order of reverence due them, and the twelve feasts of the church adorn the walls of the narthex. Unlike Western schemes of decoration, the program was not intended to be primarily narrative or didactic, but to mirror the liturgy.

Under the early Palaeologi, Byzantine artists enlarged the field of the mural narrative picture in churches, chiefly by drawing on the iconographic repertory of the illuminated book. This change linked up with a certain relaxation (end of the twelfth to the beginning of the fourteenth century) of the uniform control by the church which was set up in the ninth century after the defeat of the iconoclasts. Strict control was not again enforced, it seems, until about the mid-fourteenth century, when the conservative-minded, rigorist monks known as Hesychasts gained the upper hand at Byzantium.

Early Russian Icons

Together with Christianity, Kievan Russia received from Byzantium an established liturgical image, a formulated doctrine concerning it, and a mature technique worked out in the course of centuries. The first architects, artisans, and icon painters at Kiev were Greeks, masters of the classical period of Byzantine art, under whom local artists and craftsmen were trained. Greeks and Russians worked side by side. Thus were formed the Byzantine-Russian workshops which decorated the churches of Kiev with mosaics, frescoes, and icons. These workshops became centers not only of Byzantine inconography but also of the Byzantine manner of icon painting.

Since Russia was Christianized in the time of the Renaissance of the Byzantine Empire in 988, it is understandable that the essential Greek iconographic traditions of that epoch became the basis of early ecclesiastical art in Russia. The eleventh and twelfth centuries were a period of assimilating Byzantine principles and forms, but as early as the thirteenth century the ecclesiastical art produced in Russia began to assume a Russian aspect. By the last quarter of the fourteenth century, the borrowed art forms had become unmistakably national.

The search for a solution of the religious problems connected with icon painting and for greater freedom in interpreting the principles of the Byzantine style was an important factor in leading to the formation of local artistic groups. The new cultural and artistic centers—Novgorod, Vladimir-Suzdal, Yaroslavl, and Pskov—became the starting points of artistic deviation, developing the legacy of Kiev. Each region developed along its own lines, thus laying the foundation of several schools. Each local school of painting was pursuing a well-defined aesthetic trend peculiar to itself, and soon distinctive features began to develop in the iconography, the composition, and especially in the coloring. The crystallization of specific idioms and the movement away from Byzantine Greek form towards a more native Russian expression became especially pronounced in Novgorod.

The new chapter in the history of Novgorod art begins in 1108, when the painting of frescoes in the Cathedral of St. Sophia, in the spirit of Byzantine art of the Macedonian epoch, was commenced. By the second half of the twelfth century, Novgorod's own style, which combined the severity of Byzantium with a popular picturesqueness, reveals itself in the frescoes of the Church of St. George in Staraya Ladoga and in the Church of the Saviour at Nereditsa.

The Novgorod artists treated the Byzantine models with great independence. In the images of their saints Russian characteristics began to be evident: bodies of a well-defined national type, with strong and sometimes even coarse features. The faces became less stern, the bodies less elegant, but the outlines were more concise than in the Byzantine icons. As Igor Grabar' puts it, "The ideal of the man of Novgorod is strength and beauty—the beauty of strength. His art is at times clumsy, but always magnificent, for it is strong, majestic, overwhelming. Such is the iconography of Novgorod——vivid in color, strong and daring, with sure brush-work, with outlines made by a confident hand, decisively and imperiously."

The early Novgorod icons—*St. George the Victorious* (Plate 35); *Dormition of the Virgin,* the so-called *Blue Dormition* (Plate 39); *Archangel Gabriel* (Plate 38)—belong to the Byzantinizing trend which was fairly strong in the twelfth century, was still evident in the thirteenth century, and, under the influence of popular art, disappeared in the course of the fourteenth century. Novgorod art of the fourteenth century experienced the influence of the final brilliant stage of Byzantine art—the Palaeologue Renaissance. This reached its highest point in the last quarter of the fourteenth century, and is reflected in the works of the highly gifted Theophanes the Greek, who migrated to Russia about 1370.[2] He seems to have fallen in love with the country of his adoption and assimilated many of its characteristics. Like his compatriot, Domenico Theotocópuli (1541–1614), surnamed El Greco, whose long stay in Toledo, Spain, made him a typical representative of Spanish art. Theophanes' artistic genius reached its highest development in his adopted home. Little is known of his origin and early training, although recent research indicates that before his arrival in Russia he had worked in Constantinople, Galata, and Kaffa (Theodosia) in the Crimea. He brought to Russia the latest innovations of the Palaeologue Renaissance, and it is known that he attracted the admiration of his contemporaries by his individual style and ability to draw and paint living beings freely, without recourse to manual patterns, models, or accepted Byzantine prototypes.

---

[2] For a detailed discussion of the frescoes and icons of Theophanes the Greek (Feofan Grek), see V. N. Lazarev in Grabar', *Istoriya russkogo iskusstva* (1953), III, p. 148ff.; see also I. Grabar', *Feofan Grek.*

His best known, still extant, works are his frescoes painted in 1378 in the Church of the Transfiguration in Novgorod, and his icons: *The Dormition of the Virgin* (Plate 42), *ca.* 1380; *The Virgin of the Don* (Plate 44), late fourteenth century; and *The Virgin Mary*, 1405, in the Cathedral of the Annunciation, Moscow.

In their painting the Novgorod masters introduced a number of elements of realism in depicting human figures and details of life. They avoided the complicated symbolic subjects which were so widespread in later Russian icon painting. The composition of fourteenth-century icons is still mainly very simple and laconic, limited to a small number of characters and conveying but a sketchy idea of events. However, there gradually grew a desire for more detailed narration in painting, as a means of providing more material for the imagination and the emotions. In *The Dormition of the Virgin* (Plate 42), for example, we find a large group of people at the deathbed of the Virgin. A fourteenth-century icon, *Descent into Limbo*, depicts Christ freeing the righteous from hell as related in one of the apocryphal gospels.[3] The painter not only uses a considerable number of characters but conveys their share in the events by their poses, gestures, and facial expressions.

The Novgorod school reached the height of its development at the turn of the fourteenth century and during the fifteenth, when its finest works were produced. Icon painting acquired certain clearly marked national characteristics, to which were added specifically local, Novgorod qualities. The Novgorodians developed a lively anecdotal style related to the dramatic narrative manner of the Palaeologue Renaissance, yet colored by the native traditions of northern Russia. Many icons were devoted to the saints associated in the popular mind of that time with agriculture, handicrafts, and trade. In this connection, the fifteenth-century icons of *The Miracle of Saints Florus and Laurus* (Plate 49) is of special interest. The saints, considered to be the

[3] Reproduced in color, K. Onasch, *Icons*, plate 39.

protectors of horses, stand in the upper row at each side of the archangel with two saddled horses beside them. The second row of the icon shows the three saints on horseback spurring on a herd of grazing horses. Other examples are *The Prophet Elijah* (Plate 43), whom the people revered as the "Rainbearer" and the protector of their homes from fire; and icons of *St. George* (Plates 35, 51), who was regarded as a patron of the peasantry, a guardian of cattle, and the very embodiment of saintly knighthood.

The well-known fifteenth-century icon *The Battle between the Suzdalians and the Novgorodians* (Plate 52, 53) has many interesting features.[4] It deals with an historic event, the attack launched on Novgorod by the Suzdalians during the reign of Andrei Bogoliubsky, and with the legend of the miraculous deliverance of the city by an icon of the Virgin, *The Virgin of the Sign* or *The Virgin Orans* (see Plate 34).[5] In order to narrate the story in a consecutive way the icon is divided into three rows. In the top row we see how in the moment of danger the Novgorodians take the icon from the Church of the Saviour in the trading quarters of the city and bear it solemnly to the other side of the city, to the Cathedral of St. Sophia under whose walls the enemy stands. In the middle row the icon is shown as set up on the city walls, and envoys of Novgorod are shown going out for parleys with the Suzdalians, from whose ranks arrows are being shot at the icon of the Virgin. According to the legend, when the icon was hit by an arrow, the figure of the Virgin turned away, striking panic in the ranks of the Suzdalians. The victory of the people is depicted in the bottom row: the Novgorod guards are passing through the city gates to put the Suzdalians to flight.

This work, with its interesting subject matter, provides us with many realistic, historically true details, such as the rendering of costumes, weapons, and local topographical features, the bridge over the Volkhov, the Novgorod Kremlin, and the Cathedral of St. Sophia. All these are represented as they existed during the

[4] Reproduced in color, *ibid.*, plate 41.
[5] Reproduced in color, *ibid*, plate 66.

life of the artist. The icon as a whole represents a typical product of feudal ideology. The principalities fight each other; each has its own heroes and saints who defend their own towns and defeat their enemies. It is quite understandable that this historical painting, which dates from a period of acute conflict between the separationist policy of the ruling boyars of Novgorod and Moscow's policy of unification, possessed a propaganda function. It may have been intended to strengthen local patriotism by recalling the miraculous aid Novgorod had once received.

All these Novgorod icons are characterized by their free and confidant drawing, their simple and clearly constructed composition, and by their brilliant unmixed colors—pure reds, yellows, and greens—intense and vibrant tones with flaming vermilion predominating. It is in the clarity and brilliance of these colors that the artistic taste of the Novgorod school is best expressed.

Pskov painting of the fourteenth and fifteenth centuries, while reflecting the general manner of the development of north Russian art in the Novgorod tradition, had its own local characteristics. Its works display a tendency toward decorative features and the use of a very different color range, in which intense shades of green and orange-red predominate.

A particularly fine and typical example of Pskovian painting is the *Four Saints* (Plates 57, 58). The bodies of the saints are rendered in two dimensions and treated as decorative geometrical patterns. The icon's strong accents of black and white clearly indicate its northern origin, the degree of independence from Byzantium, and the high level of development of a national style.

Part Three

The National
or the Moscow Period

MAJOR RUSSIAN TOWNS, TWELFTH AND THIRTEENTH CENTURIES

XIII

The Rise and Aggrandizement of Moscow

HE NAME OF MOSCOW (Moskva) appears in the Russian chronicles for the first time in 1147. It is recorded that the Grand Prince Yuri Dolgoruky, on a visit to the domain of a boyar named Stephen Kuchko, caused him to be put to death on some pretext or other,[1] and—impressed by the natural beauty of the spot and advantageous location of one of the villages on the Moskva river bluff, the very spot where the Kremlin now stands —he founded the city of Moscow. For more than a century after its founding, Moscow remained an obscure and unimportant village of the Suzdal province. It emerged into the light of history (1272) as a small principality when Daniel, the son of Alexander Nevsky, became prince of Moscow. Daniel increased his appanage[2] by acquisition of Pereyaslavl-Zalieski, which belonged to one of his nephews, and by the addition of Kolomna, which he seized from the Ryazanese princes, and thus became the founder of Muscovite Russia.

Around the Moscow principality under the Mongol domination, a new state was organized. A dynasty of rival princes grew

[1] Several versions of the story are given by I. Zabelin, *Istoriya goroda Moskvy,* I, 22–41.

[2] The Russian custom of inheritance was equal division among all the sons; hence, each son of a prince received an appanage, or *udel,* a portion of his father's territory with full sovereign rights. The practice was particularly characteristic of the period from the twelfth to the fifteenth century, which some Russian historians distinguish as a special "appanage period" (*Udel'naya Rus'*) —the Russia of small domains, as compared to the Russia of the grand principalities (*Veliko-Kniazheskaya Rus'*).

up—hard, cunning, and persevering. They kept up their personal feuds, brother fighting brother, hoarding wealth in their treasuries, and administering their states as private possessions. A few giant figures among them were destined to become the founders and builders of the Moscow state, the future Russian Empire.

Although it is not our purpose to follow the political history of Moscow, a few of the more important events and significant personalities, so far as they influenced the development of the arts, must be singled out.

Moscow's ascendancy began in the Mongol period, and its dominance was recognized in 1327 when Ivan Danilovich Kalita,[3] Prince of Moscow (1327–41), obtained from the Tatars the title of *veliki kniaz* (grand prince). Later he managed an appointment as general tax collector for the Tatars, thus rapidly increasing his wealth as well as his power. Kalita, whom the Russian historian N. M. Karamzin called the "Consolidator of Russia," extended the territory of the Moscow principality by purchases and other acquisitions, a policy continued by his successors. Although the city of Vladimir was still the official capital of Russia, Moscow had become the real capital, and Kalita endeavored to obtain legal recognition of the fact.

A decisive move for both church and state occurred at the beginning of the reign of Kalita. From the time of the destruction of Kiev through the continued shock and confusion of the domination of the Tatar horde, the need had grown to establish a new seat for the metropolitan of the church. The move from Kiev to Vladimir at the beginning of the fourteenth century was significant; the next move, in 1326, from Vladimir to Moscow, was much more so.

The metropolitan of Vladimir, Peter (1305–26), passed most of his life in Moscow: His successors, Feognost (Theognostus)

---

[3] The surname *Kalita*, "Moneybag," was given to Ivan because of the bag he always wore at his belt, his frugality, and his habit of haggling over scraps of land.

and St. Aleksei, made it their permanent residence. Then the Holy See, and with it the religious supremacy which had first belonged to Kiev and later to Vladimir, moved to Moscow, so that it became the ecclesiastical capital of Russia long before it became the political capital.

The church, whose power radiated far and wide over the Russian land from the Holy See, now began to draw the various segments of the country toward Moscow, while the great wealth of the church also gravitated toward the city. Moreover, the transfer of the Metropolitan See gave the economic supremacy of the princes a moral authority that helped to ease the bitterness engendered by their unscrupulous policies.

An important factor contributing to the rise of Moscow was its exceptionally favorable geographical position—at a junction of several highways leading from southern Russia to the north, and from the territories of Novgorod to those of Ryazan. Colonists from the southern provinces passed through Moscow and settled in the neighborhood for a time at least before resuming their journey north. In this way the principality of Moscow was enriched by large numbers of pioneering and enterprising people. The Moskva River connected the upper Volga with the middle Oka, and the Novgorodians used this route to ship to their own territories grain, wax, and honey from the richest sections of Ryazan. Moscow's location also facilitated communication with the trading centers on the lower Volga and the Caspian Sea. Relations with the West were maintained through the Crimean colonies of the Genoese merchants. The city thus became a center of international trade and a source of wealth and power for her princes, whetting their appetites for additional territory.

The cultural development of Moscow had begun long before the fourteenth century. It had its roots in the brilliant culture of the Vladimir-Suzdal principality of the age of Prince Andrei Bogoliubsky which, in turn, derived from the cultural wealth of Kievan Russia with its many-sided international connections. Important progress was made in the first half of the fourteenth century, during the reign of Ivan Kalita, and his successors. There were certain features in Kalita's activities that roused the admiration of some of his contemporaries, especially among the clergy. This may be seen in the prince's eulogy, which says that his accomplishments in Russia were like those of the Emperor Constantine in Byzantium. The authors of the eulogy heap further praise upon Kalita for ordering many books to be written.

The age of Kalita and his successors was a period not only of political consolidation but also of the development of art. The construction of the Kremlin masonry cathedrals and churches was an outstanding achievement in Russian architecture of the first half of the fourteenth century. In 1344 the walls of the Assumption (Uspensky) and the Archangel Michael (Arkhangelsky) cathedrals were covered with frescoes by Greek and Russian painters. The participation of these artists shows Moscow in a unique double roll—as a center of Russian culture and, at the same time, a center of international art.

The cultural gains accomplished in the age of Kalita and his successors were further enhanced in the second half of the fourteenth century during the reign of Dmitri Donskoy (1362–89).

Dmitri was the first Russian prince who had the audacity and the organizing ability to defy and defeat the Tatars. The memorable battle of Kulikovo (1380) on the upper Don, which gained for Dmitri his surname of Donskoy, proved to the Russians that the dreaded enemy was not invincible.[4] But Kulikovo was far from being the end of the Tatar horde.[5] Dmitri had won an epic victory, but the might of the Tatar horde was not yet broken. Only two years later, under the command of Tokhtamysh, one of Tamerlane's generals, the Tatars surged for-

[4] The battle of Kulikovo, also known as the "Mamai Massacre" (*Mamaevo poboishche*), is regarded by Russian historians as having broken the back of the Tatar domination.

[5] Horde (*Orda*)—the camp of a Tatar tribe, figuratively used as the name of the Mongol government. The capital of the Great Horde was Karakorum; its subsidiary, the "Golden Horde" (*Zolotaya Orda*), was established at Sarai on the Volga.

ward again across the steppe. Moscow was sacked and burned, the whole principality was plundered, captives were carried off in great numbers, and Dmitri was obliged to resume the payment of tribute.

It was a frightful experience, but Moscow rose from her ashes and gradually regained strength and importance as the capital city of the Moscow principality. There was no stopping its economic and political advance. Neither the rival Russian principalities nor the decaying Tatar horde had the strength to impede her progress.

The city was quickly rebuilt. New large mansions in wood and stone made their appearance. Contemporary chronicles and other documents mention the stone palace of Prince Vladimir Andreevich (a cousin of Dmitri Donskoy), decorated with a mural panorama of Moscow by Theophanes the Greek. The "Golden-roofed" Palace-on-the-Quai of Prince Donskoy, gutted and sacked by Tokhtamysh, was rebuilt and luxuriously refurnished by Vasili I, the son of Donskoy. When Dmitri died the principality of Moscow was by far the largest of the northeastern states. Vladimir, the former capital, had receded into the background, and the importance of Moscow as the national capital was firmly established.

The authority of the Tatar horde continued for some scores of years. Dmitri's successors were some times in open rebellion, but more often submitted humbly to the Tatar khans. Submission and a transient acquiescence paid in some ways, for the Mongols understook to protect Moscow from conquest by her western neighbors. While Russia was working out her unity, the horde, after the death of Tamerlane in 1405, was torn by internal dissensions and dismembered into three khanates, which were soon to disappear from the political scene.

Its close ties with distant Constantinople explain many phases of Moscow's cultural life in the fourteenth century. Russian visitors to Constantinople had a chance to meet many other merchants and people of various nationalities. Most important were the Genoese merchants settled in Galata, a suburb of Constantinople. We begin to see evidence of an Italian influence in the Russian icons of the period; and Theophanes the Greek, who decorated a number of Galata and Sudak churches with frescoes, was invited to continue his work in Novgorod and Moscow.

The fifteenth century was a very difficult period for Moscow. The pillage and destruction of the city in 1409 by the Tatar horde under Edigei, the long internecine wars, the rivalry between the princes Vasili the Dark and Dmitri Shemyaka, and the frequent, devastating fires and epidemics retarded the growth of the city and hampered its cultural development. But in spite of all that, Moscow was able to extend its power and influence.

Ivan the Great

In the second half of the fifteenth century, the Moscow principality was still surrounded by the hostile Lithuanian empire on the west, the lands ruled by the Tatars on the east, and the Swedes and the Teutonic Knights holding the shores of the Baltic. In spite of the century and a half of efforts by the Moscow princes to extend their domains, to unite and consolidate the various principalities into one state, there was still much dissension and strife. Novgorod and Pskov were independent and troublesome. Moscow, with no direct access to the sea, had only intermittent relations with the centers of European civilization.

This was the age of the early Renaissance period in Western Europe, the crumbling of feudalism, the emergence of two sharply divided and hostile religious camps, and the beginnings of the national power-states. In the East it was a period of transition from Byzantium to Russia, from Constantinople to Moscow, from the Second to what was regarded as the Third Rome. Although widely separated intellectually, Western and Eastern Europe had very much the same atmosphere; a new age had begun, revealing the first signs of an epoch of reciprocal cultural penetration.

Russia, just emerging from Tatar domination and waking

from a long nightmare, found herself still in the Middle Ages. To achieve unity and progress, a strong and far-sighted leader was needed. The man who was to assume this role and who was to bring his country closer to the culture of the West was the resourceful and crafty Prince Ivan III (1462–1505), whom Karamzin called "The Great Gatherer of the Russian Land"—the precursor of Ivan the Terrible and Peter the Great.

Ivan succeeded in annexing almost all the hitherto independent principalities and cities of northern Russia—Novgorod, Tver, and the minor appanages on the upper Oka. He was victorious in Lithuania and Livonia, acquired territories which had not been included within the boundaries of ancient Russia, and pushed the frontiers of the Moscow principality as far as the frozen seas of the north and toward the Ural mountains on the east. Muscovy became an important factor in the international politics of Western and Eastern Europe, and its importance grew steadily during the reign of Ivan. After the fall of Novgorod, the boundaries of the Moscow state reached the Gulf of Finland and thus became a Baltic power.

Perhaps of greatest importance to Russian political and social life, art, and architecture was Ivan's marriage to Byzantine Princess Zoë, daughter of Thomas Palaeologue (a brother of the last Byzantine emperor) who had, after the fall of Constantinople taken refuge in Rome at the court of Pope Sixtus IV. When both Thomas and his wife died around 1462, their children were brought to Rome and left in the care of the Pope, who entrusted Cardinal Bessarion, a prominent Greek scholar converted to Roman Catholicism and an ardent supporter of the Florentine Union, with the task of supervising their education.

On the death of his first wife in 1467, Ivan began to look for a spouse of exalted degree. Marriage to a Byzantine princess, a "branch of the imperial tree which formerly overshadowed all Orthodox Christianity," seemed highly desirable; it would further the aggrandizement of the throne of Moscow and, at the same time, entitle him to the right of administering the Russian church. Although fully aware that Zoë's education had been contaminated by Latinity, he swallowed his religious scruples and asked the Pope for her hand. The Pope, who was hoping that the princess would bring Russia over to Rome, eagerly agreed.

The marriage was consecrated in 1472 and Zoë Palaeologue took the name of Sophia Fominichna. With her a multitude of priests, artists, architects, and all sorts of professional people came to Moscow, not only from Rome but from Constantinople and other cities. They brought with them Greek and Latin books, priceless ancient manuscripts, icons, and ecclesiastical art objects, thus laying the foundation for the great "lost" library of Ivan IV and the Vestry of the Patriarchs.

Sophia's portrait, brought to Moscow in 1470, seems to have disappeared. On a 1498 Moscow embroidery depicting a Palm Sunday procession, Sophia is shown leading the grand princely family. She appears to be pretty, but we do not know whether it is an accurate likeness. The Italian Princess Clarissa Orsini, who called on her in Rome in 1472, found her beautiful, though the Florentine poet Luigi Pulci, who was present at this meeting, described her in a letter to a friend of his as abhorrently fat.[6]

Although the lady may have been less than glamorous, Ivan's marriage to her was a diplomatic triumph. With it the aura of sanctity, which the sovereign princes of Russia had originally acquired from Byzantium, returned in a heightened form. As tsaritsa, Sophia intended to use her marriage to elevate the tsar of Moscow to the position of inheritor of all the power and prestige which hitherto had belonged to the emperors of Byzantium. She enjoyed the right of receiving ambassadors accredited to Moscow and the opportunity of entertaining Italian visitors

---

[6] The pen portrait of Zoë, drawn by Luigi Pulci (1432–84), is decidedly ungallant. The art historian Louis Réau quotes him as follows: "*Une montagne de graisse, deux grosses timbales sur la poitrine, une paire des joues de truie, le cou enfoncé dans les timbales. Je ne sache pas avoir jamais vu chose aussi onctueuse, grasse et glasque. Apres cela je n'ai plus reve la nuit que de montagnes de graisse et de suif et autres choses degoutantes.*" Réau, *L'Art russe*, I, 236.

and Italian residents. The latter called her *"Despina"* (feminine of "Despot"), in the Byzantine fashion, and she appears to have loved that title, as she preferred to think of herself as a Byzantine rather than a Muscovite princess. Thus, following her marriage, the princely court of Ivan III was introduced to Byzantine court etiquette and the pomp and glitter of a formerly powerful imperial dynasty.

Moscow came to regard herself not only as an Orthodox kingdom, but as the exclusive Orthodox state and the depository of the "True Faith" in the world. This attitude resulted from a number of events and movements outside as well as inside Muscovite Russia which, coinciding as they did with the consolidation of the state by the rulers of Moscow, made those rulers, in Muscovite opinion, the successors of the Byzantine emperors. The first of these events was the Council of Florence in 1439, when the Greeks, in the hope of obtaining papal help against the Turks, agreed to a union with Rome and recognized the primacy of the Pope.[7] The metropolitan of Moscow, the Greek Isidore, gave his assent to the union; but he was deposed by the authorities in Moscow, where no need was felt to seek favors from the Latins. Canonical relations between Constantinople and Moscow were temporarily suspended, for the Russians were unwilling to communicate with anyone who might be infected with Latin heresy. Somewhat later (1446), the Russian church was declared autocephalous and independent of the Greek patriarch —a decisive step toward national independence and toward domination of the Orthodox world.

When Constantinople fell to the Turks in 1453, the Russians preferred to regard the catastrophe as God's punishment for the sins committed by Byzantium in compromising with the Roman Catholic church at the Council of Florence. Byzantium fell, it was said, because it had betrayed the true faith and embraced

[7] At the Council of Florence—a council of the Orthodox and Catholic clergy at Florence in 1439—a union of the Eastern and Western churches was proclaimed. The union left the Greeks in possession of their Church ritual, but obliged them to recognize the Catholic doctrines and the primacy of the Pope.

Latinity, leaving the Russian church the only independent Orthodox church. Moscow felt stronger than ever, proud of her unshakable fidelity to a faith she held unquestionable. This conviction was strengthened by the rapid growth of the principality of Moscow, which coincided with the gradual decline of the Byzantine Empire.

Now that all the Eastern states and churches were in the hands of the infidels, Moscow proclaimed herself the successor to Constantinople, the Second Rome. Ivan III, as heir to the Byzantine emperors, became the effective ruler of all Great Russia and threw off the last remnants of Tatar supremacy (1480). This succession of events produced a revolution in the Orthodox world, which was immediately seized upon by the Muscovites and made the basis of their political philosophy. Moscow became the Third Rome, the sole depository of all imperial power and the only receptacle of unsullied Orthodoxy.

The theory of the Third Rome was first formulated by the monk Filofei (Philotheus) of Pskov, who in his epistle to Grand Prince Vasili III (1505–33) wrote: "The first Rome fell because of the Apollinarian heresy, the Second Rome, Constantinople, was captured and pillaged by the infidel Turks, but a new Third Rome has sprung up in thy sovereign kingdom. Thou art the sole king of all the Christians in the world. Two Romes have fallen, but the Third Rome, Moscow, will stand, a fourth is not to be."

The new political outlook also derived no little from the late fifteenth-century violent religious conflicts which gave rise to the so-called "Josephite Doctrine," establishing close unity between church and state and declaring that "the Tsar was similar to humans only by nature, but by the authority of his rank similar to God: he derived his authority directly from God, and his judgment could not be overruled by that of any prelate." The conflict was at first mainly between the party of bishops and abbots, headed by Joseph, abbot of the Volokolamsk Monastery, who fought for the preservation of all the privileges and landed possessions of the church and advocated the sanctification of autocracy, and the party of the Trans-Volga hermits headed by Nil Sorsky, abbot of the Sorsk Hermitage, who denied the right of the monasteries to own lands and preached asceticism and complete renunciation of the political functions which the Josephite faction was proposing to assume. In the end victory went to the Josephites, who contrived to win the support of secular authority.

Relevant legends were revived, and an imperial genealogy was later officially devised, according to which the Rurik dynasty was descended from Prussus, a brother of Augustus Caesar, so that the ruling dynasty of Russia was of Roman imperial origin. Ivan III's marriage to Zoë Palaeologue added no little to the transfer of primacy from the Second Rome to the Third. The ruler of Moscow took up the role of successor of the Byzantine emperors and the Roman Caesars, and became the head and protector of the Orthodox faith. The visible signs of grandeur surrounding the grand prince were multiplied. To the orb and scepter and other insignia of the Russian heir to Byzantium, including the cap or crown of Vladimir Monomakh, was added the Byzantine double-headed eagle. Access to the sovereign within the Kremlin walls was invested with an elaborate ritual; the whole ceremonial of the court, thickly overlaid with Byzantine custom, took on a fantastic pomp. For dealing with foreign courts the title of tsar was assumed; in internal acts this title was accompanied by the word *Samoderzhets* (the counterpart of the *Autokratos*). In 1589 the idea of Moscow as center of the one true faith received its final affirmation when her metropolitan was raised to the rank of patriarch with the sanction of the four Eastern patriarchs, who now looked to Moscow and her mighty tsar to protect Eastern Christendom.

The new, greatly enhanced status of the crown had to be made manifest by the embellishment of the capital city. Thus Moscow launched a program of building new and magnificent cathedrals, great palaces, and residences commensurate with her international importance.

Tsaritsa Sophia enthusiastically supported the vast building program. While she was too young when Constantinople fell to have known the real splendor of the Byzantine court, she was familiar with the magnificent Roman palaces and quite naturally desired to have something similar built in Moscow, both as a means of impressing foreign ambassadors and visitors and as a suitable setting for the elaborate ceremonial at the court.

In 1474, spurred on by his wife, Ivan III sent a mission to Italy headed by one of his boyars, Simeon Tolbuzin, to recruit the best architectural engineering talent available. Tolbuzin was able to bring back with him Ridolfo Fioravanti of Bologna, who, like Leonardo da Vinci, was at once an architect, an engineer, and an expert in hydraulics, military fortifications, pyrotechnics, and metal casting.[8] His fame had spread beyond the boundaries of his native land, and many municipalities and reigning dukes were clamoring and competing for his services. Fioravanti declined all invitations in favor of going to Moscow, where, he felt instinctively, there were greater opportunities for a full expression of his many and varied talents.

In 1488 Ivan again sent emissaries to Italy, this time the Greek brothers Demetrios and Manuel Rhalev to find architects, jewelers, metalsmiths, and arms manufacturers. These brothers deserve credit for securing the services of another great Italian architect, Pietro Antonio Solario (or Solari) of Milan, who was one of the principal builders of the Kremlin. In 1493 another mission, sent to the court of Ludovico il Moro of Milan, persuaded the Milanese architect Alevisio to work in Moscow.

[8] The Russian chroniclers seem to be of the opinion that Fioravanti *(Fiore-vanti)* was called Asistotle because of his many and various accomplishments in the fields of art and science. (See Russ. Biog. Sl. Vol. 21, p. 141.) The *Enciclopedia Italiana* gives his name as Aristotele Fieravanti della Alberti (1415–86). See above *Enciclopedia* (Edizioni Instituto G. Treccani, 1932–40), XV, 237–38.

The Structures of the Kremlin

The principal architects of the Kremlin structures as they existed up to the seventeenth century were Fioravanti, Marco Ruffo, Pietro Antonio Solario, Antonio Friazin, and Alevisio the Milanese. There were other architects, but very little information about them exists. There is no definite record that Fioravanti participated in the building of the fortifications of the Kremlin; but the facts that he was famed in his day as a specialist in military engineering and that the construction of the new Kremlin was begun during his stay in Russia, justify the supposition that he took part in its construction or, at least, acted as consultant in design. The undertaking of such a large group of masonry structures in the Moscow of that day became possible only after Fioravanti organized a plant for brick manufacturing, taught the Russian builders how to prepare good mortar, and introduced a number of technical building processes.

The Italian architects and engineers were put in charge of the Kremlin reconstruction. The walls and towers of the Kremlin (but not their superstructures) are their work (Plates 102, 103), as is the Granovitaya Palata (the Palace of Facets). The fact that most of these architects were northern Italians hailing mainly from Milan (Marco Ruffo, Solario, Alevisio) may explain the resemblance of the early sixteenth-century Kremlin walls and towers to those of the castles of northern Italy. The reconstruction of the Kremlin cathedrals and churches was a quite different matter. Instead of building in the Renaissance style, which, in Western Europe they masterfully imposed everywhere, these Italians had to follow Russian models and to build as their Russian patrons ordered.

The triangular enclosure of the Kremlin contains within its relatively small area the Russian counterparts of Reims, Saint Denis, and Sainte Chapelle of France. Few places, except the Athenian Acropolis and the Roman Capitolium, contain within a small area all the significant monuments of a nation's past.

The cathedrals are grouped around Cathedral Square (Sobor-
naya Ploshchad'), which has since the end of the fifteenth century been the heart of the Kremlin and its most picturesque
spot (Plates 64–70). East of the main façade of the Grand Palace stands the Cathedral of the Annunciation (Blagoveshchensky Sobor), and opposite this is the Archangel Cathedral (Arkhangelsky Sobor). Behind the Palace of Facets (Granovitaya
Palata) the great dome of the Cathedral of the Assumption (Uspensky Sobor) rises from among the cupolas and crosses of surrounding churches. The Palace of the Patriarchs stands on the
north side of the square; on the east rises the Bell Tower of
Ivan Veliky, rebuilt by Boris Godunov in 1600. Nearby are two
other bell towers, one of which was built in 1532–42 by the Italian architect Bono.

On Cathedral Square, against the background of the huge
bulk of the Grand Palace, surrounded by a tall early nineteenth-
century metal screen, stand the architectural monuments of medieval Moscow—edifices that have served as a starting point, a
stimulus, and an inspiration for the architectural activities and
for the development of the aesthetics of Moscow. These monuments were built and decorated by men of diverse backgrounds,
schools, and tastes; yet, in spite of this diversity in aesthetic approach, there is a remarkable harmony in the ensemble. The
beauty and charm of the scene seem not the result of a haphaz-
ard contribution of this or that architect, but an expression of
medieval Russia. The forms are austere, the masses restrained
and heavy, the interiors dimly lighted, and the vaulting almost
lost in semidarkness. A faint silvery light plays on the gold
frames and nimbuses of the icons and on the moldings and carving of the iconostases. The stern figures of the saints and elders
of the church gaze with wide-open eyes and seem to threaten
even as they bless. The effect is awesome, evocative of the unique
religious feeling of the fourteenth and fifteenth centuries per-
vaded with meekness and the fear that hung so heavily over the
heads of the Moscow populace of those days.

The Cathedral of the Assumption of the Virgin (Uspensky Sobor) is the most celebrated of the Kremlin churches (Plates 64–66). From the fifteenth century the Russian sovereigns were always crowned in this cathedral, which is thus the Russian counterpart of the Cathedral of Reims; the church metropolitans and the Moscow patriarchs are buried here. Its dimensions are rather small—in the West it would be called a chapel rather than a cathedral—but it is so fraught with recollections and so crowded with furnishings, frescoes, and icons, from the floor to the cupola, that its size is forgotten in the fullness of its contents. The fine situation of the cathedral, its splendid domes, and its internal grandeur all excite attention. Its connection with the ecclesiastical, civil, and political history of Russia gives it more than ordinary importance.

The construction of this cathedral was begun in 1326 (in the reign of Grand Prince Ivan Danilovich Kalita) by Peter, the metropolitan of Moscow (the titular saint protector of Moscow), who may therefore be called its founder. When the Italian architect Fioravanti was summoned by Ivan III to reconstruct the old church in 1475, he was advised to go to Vladimir and study the Uspensky Cathedral, built in 1158.

Russian historians Solov'ev and Zabelin point out that neither Fioravanti nor the other foreign architects had a free hand in the design of the commissioned buildings. The fact that the Uspensky Cathedral at Vladimir was suggested to Fioravanti as a model can be explained on the ground that the design of a great cathedral, the very see of the Orthodox faith, could hardly be entrusted to a foreigner, a Roman Catholic at that. Byzantine traditions were still very strong, and the Russian clergy, ever on guard against any possible heresy or the slightest sign of "Latinity," would not tolerate revolutionary innovations in church design. On the other hand, many wooden churches in the Moscow of that period had little in common with Byzantine forms—suggesting that there were no fixed types of church architecture.

Fioravanti visited not only Vladimir but also Rostov and Yaroslavl, where he became acquainted with the local masonry cathedrals and churches. On the shores of the White Sea he saw many of the ancient wooden churches. On his return trip he visited Old Ladoga, with its twelfth-century churches, and undoubtedly passed through Novgorod and saw St. Sophia Cathedral built in 1045–52. Thus the Italian architect had an opportunity to get firsthand information on Russian religious architecture and to grasp the essential features of its traditions.[9]

The Moscow cathedral, completed in 1479, resembles its Vladimir namesake but is far from being a literal copy. The two cathedrals are of the same width, but the one in Moscow is much longer; the Moscow cathedral has five apses, the Vladimir three; furthermore, the latter's choir galleries are suppressed. The vaulting of the Moscow cathedral rests on six pillars, four of which—huge circular columns—support the central cupola, which rests on a flat roof and is surrounded with four smaller cupolas. This very simple disposition produces a grandiose effect, and the massive pillars give an extraordinary stability without heaviness to the body of the cathedral. The influence of the Vladimir architecture is noticeable mainly in the façade, decorated at mid-height with a band of arcatures forming small niches (kiotsy) that the architect used very successfully as window embrasures.[10]

The plan of the Moscow cathedral, the system of its vaulting, and the disposition of its five cupolas became in time traditional and, in the sixteenth century, served as a model for the Smolensky cathedral in the Novodevichei Convent in Moscow (1550) and

[9] The archives of the city of Milan contain a letter, written by Fioravanti on February 22, 1476, to the Duke of Milan, describing the former's travels in northern Russia. (See Ettore lo Gatto, *Gli artisti italiani in Russia*, I, 20.)

[10] The *kiot, or kiotsy* (niche, frame, or cupboard in which icons are housed), usually has a pediment at the top and is glazed in front. It may either be a shrine by itself or form part of a triptych, often with appropriate religious scenes painted upon the doors.

in the Assumption cathedral in the Trinity-Sergius Monastery (1585) at Zagorsk (Plate 63).

The whole interior of the cathedral is covered with paintings in Byzantine style, upon gold backgrounds; the pillars themselves are covered with figures painted in zones as on the columns of Egyptian temples and palaces. On the columns are gigantic figures of the martyrs and figures from the New Testament; on the walls are scenes from the Gospels and the *acathist* to the Virgin; and in the window embrasures of the north wall are portraits of Saints Vladimir and Olga, the first Christian prince and princess of Russia. The entire west wall is occupied by a painting of the Last Judgment, an incredibly complicated composition containing hundreds of figures. One gets the feeling of being surrounded by a mute multitude of thousands of figures, ascending and descending the walls, walking in files in Christian processions in attitudes of hieratic stiffness, following the curve of the pendentives, of the vaulting, and of the cupolas. The mysterious effect is increased by the paucity of light. The great grim saints of the Greek calendar, assume in their tawny, ruddy shadows, a formidable life-like look; they gaze upon you with their fixed eyes, and seem to threaten you with their hands outstretched in blessing. The militant archangels, the holy knights with elegant and bold mien, mingle their brilliant armour with the dark robes of the old monks and anchorites.

According to the "Sophia Annalist," the frescoes were so wonderfully executed that when the grand prince, the bishops, and the boyars entered the temple they exclaimed, "We see heaven!" We must remember that the rapturous remarks of the annalist pertain to the years 1514–15, when the cathedral was for the first time embellished with wall paintings. A few of these can still be seen on the masonry partition separating the sanctuary from the nave. They are hidden by the high iconostasis, first built in 1482, rebuilt in 1690, and renovated in 1813 and again in 1881–83, when it was covered with *repoussé* silver ornament.

In 1642 and 1643 the cathedral was done over with a new set of wall paintings on the gold background, some of the finest Russian painters of the period participating in the work.[11] The paintings have been frequently restored, but not always in the strict spirit of the original. In the 1920s a number of important experiments were conducted in cleaning and restoring certain eighteenth-century paintings in the cathedral. During these experiments an excellent seventeenth-century fresco in fine condition was uncovered. In spite of the many renovations and restorations, the Uspensky Cathedral interior is still the closest in expression to the aesthetics of the fifteenth and sixteenth centuries; it is the most rewarding and inspiring of Moscow churches.

The present smoke-gray wall coating probably did not exist in the sixteenth century. The interior of the cathedral was undoubtedly aglow with warm, bright colors and clear-cut, sharp outlines, recalling the churches of Yaroslavl. The faces of the images must have been less stern, less grim than they appear now. The main efforts of the ancient Russian prince-builders and artist-decorators were concentrated on imparting to the church a sense of opulence and magnificence, an equivalent to an imagined "dwelling in paradise," the "Lord's Temple."

The wall paintings of the Uspensky Cathedral served as a prototype for the works of many Russian painters of later generations. In wall painting as well as in architecture, it was regarded as a model as late as the reign of Empress Elizabeth (1741–61). The St. Petersburg architects of the early eighteenth century perfected their own type of single-cupola church, but during Elizabeth's reign an order was issued making the Uspensky Cathedral a prototype for future churches. Even the great Rastrelli, the favorite architect of the empress, had to incorporate the basic forms of the cathedral in the design of his most elegant baroque churches.

[11] I. M. Snegirev, *Uspensky Sobor v Moskve.*

Several religious furnishings of the Uspensky Cathedral and its sacristy are of great artistic value. Many of the ancient icons were painted by some of the great Russian masters, but they are so nearly covered by gold sheathings incrusted with precious stones that only the faces and hands of the saints are visible. There are several icons by F. N. Roshnov, who was active during the late decades of the seventeenth century. Over the altar there is his large painting of the Crucifixion, on each side of which is a painting of "The Passion" of each one of the Twelve Apostles. The present iconostasis (Plate 143) was erected in the middle of the seventeenth century; curiously, it contains none of the woodcarving that was popular at the time and that was widely used in other contemporary churches. Among the icons of the five tiers of the iconostasis there are many extremely rare works of great art, but here again golden sheathings cover up most of the images, thus depriving the beholder of the full appreciation of some of the best medieval Russian ecclesiastical painting.

The iconographic material illustrates two themes: church and state. The religious theme stresses the idea of the Universal Church—the union of the Old Testament with the New. The state theme dwells on the importance of the unification of all the Russian states by Moscow. Through apertures in the gold and silver encasements appear the heads and hands of the saints. Their aureoles, incrusted with precious stones, stand out in relief. The images have breastplates of gold and silver and collars and pendants of diamonds, sapphires, rubies, emeralds, and pearls. From the center of the ceiling hangs a massive circular, silver chandelier, which was installed after the original had been carried off during Napoleon's invasion.[12]

[12] One of Napoleon's cavalry units was stabled in the cathedral during the French occupation of Moscow. The French removed five tons of silver and five hundred pounds of gold from this cathedral alone. Fortunately, the Cossacks recovered most of this booty, and in gratitude presented to the cathedral a silver chandelier with forty-six branches that weighed nine hundred pounds.

Near the south portal of the Uspensky Cathedral stands the canopied tsar's stall or throne of Vladimir Monomakh.[13] This throne, a curious monument of the epoch that ushered in the change from the period of the appanage to that of the grand prince, was traditionally used as a coronation chair for the Russian rulers. Legend claims that it was originally built for Vladimir Monomakh, grand prince of Kiev, and that it was transferred from Kiev to Vladimir and from there, during the reign of Grand Duke Ivan Danilovich Kalita, to Moscow. According to most Russian historians, however, the original throne was built in 1551 for Ivan the Terrible and, because of the damage it suffered during the Time of Troubles and the Polish occupation,[14] was rebuilt for Tsar Mikhail Feodorovich (Plates 180–182).

The throne is justly considered one of the finest examples of medieval woodcarving. It is made of walnut and lime and is decorated with relief and pierced carving painted dark brown, although traces of gold visible here and there indicate that it was once gilded. On the cornice frieze, just below the base of the canopy and on the door leaves, a series of inscriptions in interlaced and cursive Slavonic characters add a decorative touch.

Four sculptured mythical beasts serve as supports for the throne. The contemporary chronicler speaks of them as awe-inspiring savage beasts rendered so realistically as to give the impression of being alive.

The twelve carved bas-reliefs on the side panels and door leaves are masterpieces of decorative art depicting scenes from the campaigns, battles, and other activities of an unidentified

[13] Vladimir Monomakh, grand prince of Kiev (1113–25), was the last outstanding ruler of Kiev. He was the father of Yuri Dolgoruky, and has been idealized in Russian chronicles as a prince of great wisdom and many virtues.

[14] Time of Troubles (Smutnoye Vremya), sometimes designated as the Epoch of Disorder, is the name given to the tragic events that took place in Russia beginning with the murder in 1591 of Tsarevich Dmitri, son of Ivan IV. The famine of 1601–1603 was followed by the struggle between the supporters of the contender to the throne, the False Dmitri, and the followers of Boris Godunov. The civil war was further complicated by Polish and Swedish intervention, and ended by the establishment of the Romanov dynasty in 1613.

ancient Russian prince. The composition, with a keen sense of rhythm and mass organization, is reminiscent of ancient icon painting, except for a marked quality of dynamic realism lacking in the icons. The sense of movement is especially strong in the battle scenes, where the attacking knights are depicted in full war panoply, including sabers and lances, on their galloping chargers.

The octagonal, tent-shaped canopy, its form somewhat reminiscent of the crown of Monomakh, rises above the square stage of the throne in a series of receding tiers of *kokoshniki* and steep gables (Plate 181). Derived from the forms of the wood architecture of northern Russia, this canopy (*shatyor*) served as a prototype for later ones.

The Cathedral of the Archangel Michael (Arkhangelsky Sobor), originally built of wood in the middle of the thirteenth century, was rebuilt of stone in 1333 as a final resting place for the Moscow princes (Plate 69).

In 1505 Ivan III decided to build a new and larger cathedral worthy to stand beside the newly erected Uspensky (Assumption) and Blagoveshchensky (Annunciation), entrusting the design and construction to the Milanese architect Alevisio Novyi. Like Fioravanti before him, Novyi was compelled to incorporate the basic features of Orthodox church planning and design into the new cathedral, but in the exterior decoration he succeeded in introducing Italian architectural forms of the fifteenth century, which were adapted and reworked by Russian artists of later generations. The Arkhangelsky Sobor rests on a stone base; its walls are of red brick, but the decorative elements are of white stone. The lower story is embellished with pilasters and arcatures containing small windows; the upper is divided into rectangles crowned with elaborate cornices. Novyi treated the *zakomary* (roof parapets) as purely decorative features by converting them into scallop-shell niches. The result was a structure endowed with a beauty radically different from that of the preceding Moscow churches. If the Uspensky Cathedral can be considered the epitome of the past and the embodiment of the traditional Moscow and Vladimir forms, the Arkhangelsky was the first step toward a new art—the incarnation of the contribution that Italian art made to Moscow architecture.

Ivan III removed to this cathedral the remains of the earlier princes who had been buried in a more ancient church built by Ivan Kalita. Russian sovereigns were interred here until the time of Peter the Great. Along the wall the tombs of princes and tsars, from the founder of Moscow to the predecessor of the founder of Petersburg, are arranged in genealogical order, and form "a sepulchral chronicle of the Russian monarchy." (Only Boris Godunov is absent—his tomb is in the Troitsko-Sergievskaya Lavra.) Ivan the Terrible and his two sons occupy the most sacred spot, the narrow, fresco-covered diaconicon next to the altar. Above each brass-covered coffin is a figure painted in a long white robe with a halo round his head—not the halo of saintly canonization, but of imperial investiture. These figures have been repainted and renovated many times and, in the process, have lost much of the quality of the original.

The sacristy and library of the cathedral contained some of the great treasures of Russian ecclesiastical art, including the famous twelfth-century Mstislav Book of the Gospels that belonged to the Novgorodian Prince Mstislav Vladimirovich (Plate 147).

The Cathedral of the Annunciation (Blagoveshchensky Sobor), built by Pskov architects in 1482–90 on the site of the original founded by Grand Prince Vasili Dmitrievich (1389–1425), differs in certain details from the other two cathedrals of the Kremlin (Plates 67, 68). The central cubical element, surmounted by five cupolas, closely resembles the forms of the Vladimir Uspensky Cathedral. In the Blagoveshchensky, however, the Pskov architects introduced an architectural motif destined to play an important role in the development of Moscow architecture of the sixteenth century and to become a theme for endless variations in the field of the decorative arts—the *kokoshnik*. The form, borrowed from the ogee-shaped roof, indicated a tendency to replace the forms of the Byzantine arch by more elongated silhouettes. The Pskov architects supported the elements of the superstructure with corbeled arches arranged in tiers and receding in steps. The cupola drums consequently seem to grow out of these elements, and the semicircular *zakomary* of the Vladimir and Moscow Uspensky cathedrals acquire the characteristic shape of the ogee arch.

In 1547 the Blagoveshchensky was damaged by a fire. While it was being repaired, open porches were added to three of its sides. This was the first such use of porches in a Russian church, a feature that became popular in the Moscow and Yaroslavl churches of the second half of the seventeenth century.

At the time of the construction of the porches an anonymous Italian built the deep-shadowed portals with their engaged columns, pilasters, and archivolts, and decorated them with the richly carved, dark blue and gold ornament that winds and twists around the arches, columns, and door architraves. The Russians restudied and reworked this ornamental vocabulary, transforming it into something more suited to their taste and introducing their own ornamental elements—the *busy* (a type of beading) and the *perekhvaty* (a type of belt or band ornament).

The Blagoveshchensky is much smaller and of a more intimate character than either the Uspensky or the Arkhangelsky; its proportions and decorations are in better taste. The internal arrangement is similar to that of the other Kremlin cathedrals. The floor is paved with mosaics of jasper and agate, and the wells are covered with frescoes by Feodosi (1518), Ivan Filatov (1648), and others. The altar is elegant and richly adorned; the iconostasis is decorated with the works of Theophanes the Greek, Andrei Rublev, Prokhor, and Daniil Chernyi.

In 1487 Ivan III commissioned the Italian architect Marco Ruffo to build the Palace of the Facets (Granovitaya Palata), which was to serve him and many of his successors as a formal location for throne and audience chamber (Plates 104–106). This gray stone building, the oldest civil structure in Moscow, stands on the west side of Cathedral Square, adjoining the huge cream-colored mass of the nineteenth-century Grand Palace. Its construction was begun by Marco Ruffo, but was finished by his compatriot Pietro Solario. The diamond rustications of the original façade recall the wall treatment of the Castello in Ferrara and the Pitti Palace in Florence. The Granovitaya, together with the Holy Vestibule to the west of it, is all that remains of the old palace of Ivan III. The Holy Vestibule (Sviatyia Seni) was renovated during the construction of the Grand Kremlin Palace in 1848.

The Granovitaya contains a large, square, vaulted chamber, about seventy-seven by seventy feet, whose size and effect of spaciousness are greatly accentuated by the single central massive pier, which made possible the use of four cross vaults to span the entire room (Plate 105). The chamber was admirably adapted for the great formal receptions of foreign ambassadors, the installations of the metropolitans and patriarchs, and the openings of the national assemblies. In 1552 Ivan IV celebrated the conquest of Kazan in this room; in 1709 Peter I gave a banquet here to celebrate his victory over the Swedes at Poltava; here in 1761 Catherine II opened the first conference of the commission to draft the new law code (*ulozheniye*).

The throne formerly stood on the south side of the chamber. In the west wall of the chamber, close to the ceiling, is a curtained opening through which the distaff members of the royal family who were not present in the hall itself could observe the ceremonies from an upper-level secret chamber without being seen.

The base of the central pier is surrounded by shelves forming a buffet; on great occasions the magnificent treasures of ancient gold and silver plate and vessels from the royal household were displayed here.

It must be noted that the buildings designed by the Italian

architects stand apart from the general trend of late fifteenth-century Russian architecture; they inspired a reaction against the traditions of Byzantine art and thus served to make Russian art and architecture independent. Early in the sixteenth century, Italian architects, artists, and artisans began to lose favor with the Russians. Perhaps the main reason for this was the fear of "Latinity," fear of the persistent efforts of the popes to effect a union between the Roman and the Orthodox churches. The Italians were naturally suspected of aiding the Pope, and so they were replaced by Germans, English, and Dutch. Not until the eighteenth century, under Peter the Great, was an Italian architect again invited to Russia.

XIV

Wooden Architecture

THE TATAR INVASION almost put an end to the rapid architectural evolution that had taken place in southern and northeastern Russia during the twelfth and thirteenth centuries. But with the gradual disintegration of the Tatar power, the artistic interests of Russia, which lay dormant for over a century, steadily began to reassert their vitality. The Russian builders became conscious of their own architectural inheritance—the centuries-old forms preserved in their wooden structures; and it was this primitive art of the country that formed the basis for the Muscovite architecture of the national period.

From the beginning of the sixteenth century, the history of Muscovite architecture is largely the history of nationalizing the forms created in Kiev, Vladimir-Suzdal, and in Novgorod and Pskov; most important, it is the history of modifying and transforming those essentially Byzantine forms by introducing fresh elements derived from the primitive native wooden architecture. To understand the particular character of the Moscow masonry edifices of the sixteenth and seventeenth centuries, it is necessary to consider the character of the primitive architecture and the construction methods of the wooden buildings from which the Moscow edifices originated.

We have noted earlier that from the eleventh to the sixteenth centuries, the Kievan and Novgorodian Russias were artistically, in many respects, dependencies of Byzantine art. The St.

Sophia cathedrals of Kiev and Novgorod were designed, built, and decorated by Greek architects and artists. The scheme of the Byzantine church—the dome on pendentives—was the accepted standard for Orthodox churches. But we must not exaggerate either the importance or duration of Byzantine influence. On closer analysis, the two St. Sophias in Kiev and Novgorod show marked differences from their namesake in Constantinople,[1] and there is strong evidence that, after the twelfth century, Russian masonry architecture began to develop on independent lines.

In trying to adapt the imported Byzantine forms to the local climatic conditions, the Russian architects transformed the flat half-spherical Byzantine dome, designed for the sunny lands of the Mediterranean, into a bulbous cupola better adapted to the heavy snowfalls and rains of the North. In the sixteenth century the bulb-shaped cupola was replaced by the tent-shaped roof, which was even better adapted to the climatic conditions and the landscape of Russia. By the middle of the seventeenth century the architectures of Byzantium and Russia had hardly anything in common. It suffices to compare the great flat dome of Constantinople's St. Sophia with the multifarious, varicolored cupolas and "tents" of St. Basil (Plate 77), the lovely pyramid of the church at Kolomenskoye (Plate 73), the pagoda-like silhouette of the church at Fili (Plate 95), or the mass of rhythmically upsurging cupolas of the church at Kizhi (Plate 86), to become convinced that early Russian architecture became thoroughly emancipated from its model.

There were other powerful impulses from alien sources, notably, the influence of Romanesque architecture on the twelfth-century churches of Vladimir-Suzdal, and of the Italian Renaissance on the fifteenth-century Moscow Kremlin. The Russian architectural and ornamental vocabularies were enriched, and

---

[1] Santa Sophia (Church of Hagia Sophia), the masterpiece of Byzantine architecture, was built in Constantinople under Emperor Justinian (A.D. 532–38).

new construction methods were introduced by the invited Italians,[2] but the truly vital revolutionary movement that took place in Russian architecture of the sixteenth-century was the resurgence of popular art expressing the ideas, tastes, and building techniques of the common man. It was the wooden architecture of northern Russia that affected the design of masonry architecture by transforming its proportions and decoration and even its structural methods. It was this revolutionary architecture which produced in Moscow the churches of Dyakovo, Kolomenskoye, Ostrovo, and St. Basil, with their wealth of ornamental forms that have found reflection in many of the decorative arts.

The Techniques and Forms of Wooden Architecture

Centuries ago, in her "wooden age," Russia originated and perfected certain basic forms and techniques which enabled her to develop an architecture distinguished by a quality of vertical continuity, picturesqueness of mass, and rich decoration. Those forms—the tent-shaped spires (*shatry*), the "barrel" (*bochka*) and "cube" (*kub*) roofs—have been echoed through the centuries, by the pyramidal roofs, cupolas, and steeples on most Russian churches and public buildings.

There is no whole wooden building of any importance remaining from either the pre-Christian era or the period from the eleventh to the sixteenth century. Our esthetic appraisal must be, to some extent, conjectural and based on somewhat uncertain reconstruction. But judging from the monuments dating from the seventeenth to the nineteenth century, we can see that the builders of northern Russia employed their own structural methods and evolved many characteristic architectural forms so structurally sound, so logical, that their development may reasonably be assumed to be the work of centuries.

[2] The architects, artists, and technicians who were brought to Moscow from Rome, Venice, and Milan during the reign of Ivan III and his son, Vasili III, to direct the reconstruction of the Kremlin fortifications and some of its churches and palaces. They were most active and influential during the half century from about 1475 to 1525.

The development of Russian wood architecture is a fascinating story of the mutations and combinations of the various forms of "blockwork": the rectangle and the polygon; the shed, the wedge, the ogee barrel-vault, and the tent roof; and the storied belfries, the pinnacles, and the cupolas. In the period of the rise of Moscow this development was so influential that the history of Moscow architecture is, to a great degree, that of the translation and adaptation of wooden architectural forms to masonry structures.

Using the axe, without the aid of the saw, and without the use of metal nails, the ancient Russian builder erected very complex structures, often of great height, strength, and stability. According to the historians of Russian architecture F. Gornostaev and I. Grabar':

> All the timbers and boards of the galleries and stairways were surfaced and finished only with the axe. All the jambs, heads, and sills of the doors and windows, all the floor, ceiling, and roof planks and boards were also only axe-finished. When you examine these structures and their various elements—work that must have required an enormous amount of patience and perseverance—you wonder at the skill and dexterity that was necessary to do all the rough and finished work with just an axe.[3]

This very difficulty of preparing board lumber served as a discipline, preventing the craftsman from becoming petty or finicky in decoration, and trained him to think in large forms. Most often the decoration was done directly on the structural elements of the building, as on the jambs of the doors and windows, and on the columns of the gates and stairways.

Since all construction was of timber, the very nature of the material established certain practices and evolved definite building methods and forms. The timber was usually pine, not always seasoned, and generations of practice had taught that with such material the structure was best built by laying the logs hori-

[3] *Derevyannoye zodchestvo russkago severa,* in Grabar', *Istoriya russkago iskusstva* (1909), I, 341.

zontally, one on top of the other, so that in the process of drying and shrinking the weight of the logs transmitted downwards would prevent the formation of chinks and crevices.

The basic form in Russian wooden construction is the "block-work" rectangular frame (*srub*)[4] formed by round logs laid in ranges and interlocking at the corners. Each log is somewhat hollowed on the lower surface, to fit down over the one below, and the interstices between them are filled with moss or oakum, thus making the walls proof against cold and moisture. Each range of logs forms, as the Russians call it, a crown (*venets*), and the entire pile of crowns rising to the desired height, is called *srub*. The frames thus assembled are very solid and do not need any nails. Exterior surfaces of the logs are left in the round; the interior surfaces are axe-hewed to smoothness, hewed so expertly as to seem sawed. The assembled box-like structure comprising floor, roof, doors, and windows is called *klet'*.[5]

These blockwork frames are square or oblong in plan. Their dimensions are limited by the length of the timbers. The rectangular *klet'* was the unit of wood construction forming the principal element of the Russian peasant's house, the *izba*. It was covered by a shed or gabled roof, and in olden times had no ceiling (Plate 89). In the development of Russian wooden architecture this simple *izba* had an importance greater than that of the more pretentious edifices.

The Izba

The *izba* is essentially a heated chamber, in its earliest and simplest forms lacking a chimney, the windows serving as an outlet for smoke. For protection against cold and dampness, door

[4] Derived from the Russian verb, *rubit'*, to cut, to hew with an axe, *srub* connotes a structure formed of axe-hewed logs or timber.

[5] The primary meaning of *klet'* is enclosure, that is, a fully assembled, quadrilateral or multilateral blockwork unit; however, it also implies a part of the house or a unit of the structural and planning system. The peasant's hut consisted of one or two units, and the house of the well-to-do, the mansion or the palace, of a number of these basic units interconnected and arranged side by side or one on top of the other.

and window openings were reduced to a minimum. Living quarters of the well-to-do were on a second floor (*gornitsa*)[6] built over a substructure called the *podklet;*[7] the substructure, or the first floor, being reserved for the servants, livestock, and the storing of provisions. Large houses consisting of several units and two or three floors were called *khoromy* (mansion) or *dvorets* (palace).

The simplest form of roof was the gable, but the Russian craftsman, with his flair for the picturesque, was quick to see possibilities for modifications and variations which evolved from the simple, low-pitched roof of the common hut to the wedge-like roofs, peaked gables, and ogee-shaped, pyramidal, and multi-domed roofs of the great churches.

The pitch was governed by the gable pediments, which could be built up and shaped to any desired angle and thus give the roof any slope or profile section. The carpenter, by shortening each successive layer of the logs in the gable wall, and shaping their ends to the desired angle, built up the gable triangle.

By flaring the walls outward, in a somewhat bell-shaped fashion, at the eaves level, the builder was able to provide a projecting shelf foundation for his steep roofs, thus breaking the main pitch of the roof and furnishing large eaves of gentle slope. Through his shaping of the profiles of the gables, he was able to give the roof almost any desired form. Thus it was not long before he evolved the ogee-section roof, the so-called *bochka*.

The end of the ridge beam overhanging and crowning the front gable was usually carved, in the shape of a fantastic bird's head, the head of a goat or deer, or usually, the head of a horse (Plates 89, 80). The opposite end of the ridge beam was shaped in the form of a tail. This type of figure decoration was applied to dwellings only; it is never found on church roofs or on barn roofs. The ornamented ridge beams and the carved forms of

[6] Derived from *gora*, hill, elevation; hence *gorny yarus*, elevated or upper tier and, by extension, *gornitsa*—upper-story room.

[7] From *pod*, meaning under; hence *podklet* means the structure supporting the *klet'*.

birds perched on long poles erected near the house were especially popular in the north regions—the province of Perm and in
the territory along the Onega River. Quite possibly they are "left-
overs" of pagan symbolism, derived from the animal style of
Scythian-Sarmatian ornamentation.

Much ingenuity and skill was lavished on the decoration of
the bargeboards and rakes, the "towel-and-tassel" board suspended from the ridge and masking the bargeboard joints, the
ends of the top ridge beam and the eave elements. In some parts
of the provinces of Vologda and Archangel the house roofs are
ogee shaped, resembling the *bochka* roofs of the churches.

The window became the focus for rich decoration that often
extended several feet on each side of it, sometimes over the entire height of the building. In brick buildings the window might
be set into fancifully arched frames, the whole incrusted with
colored tiles. The cottage or the *izba* window was also accentuated and often was treated in a delightfully gracious way.
In this the Russian builders have persevered through the centuries, so that in the village and small-town cottages the most
beautiful things are the windows framed by masses of carved
and painted ornament, relieving the severity of unadorned log
walls. Even in the worst periods of borrowed sophisticated "city"
ornament, when florid contortions of line and complexity of
forms were in vogue, the windows of rural cottages, churches,
and mansions still retained much charm (Plates 83, 109, 116, 118).

Carved wooden chimneys are characteristic of many houses.
They rise high as slender rectangular flues, terminating in fancifully shaped tops crowned with gabled roofs, large projecting
eaves and carved ridge beams. The propensity for picturesqueness expressed itself in the design and decoration of these flues,
and, in houses otherwise severe and simple, one finds a touch
of fantastic playfulness in the chimneys.

The stairway, also, was a functional and decorative element
of the Russian *izba*, and especially of the more elaborate houses
of the well-to-do. In Russia, of old, the role of the exterior stair-

way was not limited to the merely practical function of affording a way of getting up to or down from the upper floors of the house. The stairway and its landings served as a setting for the display of hospitality, manners, and customs. On the landings the formal welcoming of guests and visitors took place, and it was there that the ceremony of bidding them goodbye was performed. Thus etiquette gave importance to the arrangement, construction, and decoration of the stairway.

Church stairways are usually monumental and symmetrical. The flights are arranged either parallel or at right angles to the walls of the structure, and some are free standing, at a considerable distance from the walls, recalling the great formal stairways of the boyars' *khoromy* or the tsar's palaces.

The Ancient Russian Nobleman's Mansion

It is difficult to visualize the domestic architecture and the home furnishings of the Russian nobility before the Petrine reforms. The only sources of information are descriptions and allusions in the chronicles of those days and in the heroic poetry of ancient Russia,[8] the few models, measured drawings, and paintings of the now-vanished wooden palace of the Stroganovs at Solvychegodsk and the tsar's palace at Kolomenskoye.

The basic elements of even the very sumptuous mansions were still the blockwork units and their connecting passageways. Most of the units were two storied—the lower story serving as a foundation for the upper. Thus the appellation *khoromy*, in a proper sense, referred only to the upper stories which contained the private apartments of the owner.

As in the yard of the peasant, in the very extensive court of the nobleman, each blockwork unit was built separately, and at

---

[8] The *bylina* of the Kiev cycle, "The Youth of Churilo Plenkovich," contains a description of the splendors of the mansion of the youth's father, the doughty old merchant Plenko. No doubt allowance must be made here for poetic license, but this description of a suburban mansion coincides in many respects with the drawings of Meyerberg (1661), depicting a seventeenth-century boyar manor in the village of Nikolskoye near Moscow.

some distance from the others, the space between the units depending on their functional relationship and the available ground. As a whole, the wooden *khoromy* was nearly always an ensemble of units of a decorative and picturesque character, more or less flamboyant. Instead of the West European single-unit type of mansion or palace, the Russian builder usually erected a group of interconnected structures. Although he evidently had little feeling for formal symmetry, he was endowed with a surpassing sense of balance. At the same time he never suppressed his love of romantic composition, play of light and shade, and vivid colors.

Perhaps one of the best examples of ancient *khoromy* architecture is the celebrated, but now-vanished, tsar's palace—"the Russian Versailles"—at Kolomenskoye near Moscow. We can get some idea of it from the model and the Hilferding engraving made from measured drawings prepared shortly before the aging and crumbling structure was taken down in 1768 by order of Catherine II (Plate 88).

The palace, set in gardens on a high bluff overlooking the Moskva River, was in reality a small city complex of 270 blockwork dwelling units of various shapes and sizes. It contained all the characteristic elements of the great mansions: the vestibules with their elaborately decorated stairways, passageways, arcaded balconies, towers, and observation platforms. Here also were all the roof forms, the varied shapes of doors and windows, and the multifarious decorative entablatures developed throughout the centuries.

According to the extant detailed descriptions, the oak gates and the door and window pediments were beautifully carved and heavily gilded, as were the heraldic eagles over the apartments of the tsar and tsaritsa. The architraves of the doors and windows with their bright colors and gilt enlivened the otherwise smooth surfaces of the walls, blending with the sky-blue coloring of the shingle imbrications of the roofs over the banquet room unit and the towers of the tsar's and tsaritsa's apartments.

The imbrications of the *bochki* over the covered stairways and those of the tent roofs were painted green. Adding still more color were the roof ridges bristling with weather vanes and the golden chain-braced crosses over the cupolas of the palace church.

Much like the seventeenth-century Moscow Kremlin, the palace at Kolomenskoye was a product of national art. Its architectural forms reflect the imagery of the folk poetry and the fairy tales of the magic fire-bird (*zhar-ptitsa*) palace glittering with gold and bright colors.[9] The roots of this architecture can be traced to the mythical age of pagan Russia, and its growth and perfection to the provinces of the North.

The elaborate and ornate stairways, observation towers, communicating arcades, and galleries influenced the design of many structures, in masonry as well as in wood. The model of the palace served as reference source for the architects of the nineteenth century who tried to revive the architecture of Russian antiquity, and it is evident that the architects of the Historical Museum (V. Sherwood) and the Municipal Duma (M. Chichagov), in Moscow were inspired by it.

The Wooden Churches of Northern Russia

Long before Christianity became its official faith, Russia had Christian churches, and there is little doubt about the material of which they were constructed. It was mainly in the North that the forms of wood building were perfected, and, as Gornostaev and Grabar' remark, "These forms became the inexhaustible source from which the arts of Russia, in their anemic periods, drew new blood; their significance has not been as yet fully appreciated."[10]

[9] The *zhar-ptitsa* is a fabulous golden-feathered bird of Russian folklore; the tale is of the handsome young prince transformed by the ogre, Koshchei, into a bird and imprisoned in an inaccessible golden palace.

[10] *Derevyannoye zodchestvo*, in Grabar', *Istoriya russkago iskusstva* (1909), I, 332. For an informative, richly illustrated study of early Russian wooden architecture, see P. Maksimov and N. Voronin "Wooden Architecture in the XII–XVI Centuries," in Grabar', *Istoriya russkogo iskusstva* (1953), III, 245, 281.

The construction methods and terminology were evolved early. The ancient word *khoromy* was later also used to indicate a *khram*, or mansion, but in this usage meaning a dwelling of not just an ordinary mortal but a temple, a "house of God."

For early masonry structures (the cathedrals of St. Sophia in Kiev, 1037, and in Novgorod, 1045–52), Byzantine church architecture, with its well-established forms of plan and elevations, was accepted as basic. But in the North the local builders had no ready examples which they could adopt or imitate. They had to draw either upon their own imagination or upon the traditional forms of domestic architecture, especially those of the large wooden mansions of the wealthy boyars. Even when masonry churches became more numerous, they could not be "copied" in wood, for the very nature of the material precluded the adaptation of masonry forms to wood structures. Although certain general plans, dictated by the special requirements of the Greek Orthodox church, had to be followed, even these were greatly modified and changed to suit the native building precepts, the topography, and landscape. Thus was developed a folkish understanding of what a "house of God" should look like, and how it should be built. These factors irresistibly directing the development of wooden church architecture away from alien traditions gradually brought about its liberation from Byzantium and influenced modification of the borrowed forms.

In this struggle between the native architectural idioms and the precepts of the clergy, the latter was able to hold to the general outline and principal elements of the basic Byzantine church plan: the central space for the congregation, the sanctuary, and the narthex. But even these took on local characteristics. The narthex was replaced by the spacious refectory (*trapeznaya*), and transformed into the vital house element, the vestibule of the *izba*. Together with their homey functional significance, these church elements also acquired the construction forms of the *izba*. Finally, like the large *izba* or the *khoromy* of the boyars, the church was elevated one floor above the ground and erected upon a substructure (*podklet*). The church also inherited the more showy part of the *khoromy*, the stairways with their covered landings. The structural frames of the church, in the form of blockwork rectangles similar to those of the *izba* units, required the *izba* methods of construction; and the various heights and spans of the individual units necessitated separate roofs.

Although the church was built in the fashion of an elaborate nobleman's mansion, it was felt that it required further distinction, which found expression in the addition of cupolas and crosses to the roof. The cupola was borrowed from the masonry church, but the method of roof construction in wooden buildings consigned it to the role of a purely decorative superstructure. The wooden cupola, although given the circular form of the masonry domes, was modeled along different lines. Its walls were flared outward, and its top was drawn upwards and thus molded somewhat in the shape of an onion-bulb (*lukovitsa*). Another feature of the masonry churches, the semicircular form of the parapet built directly over the extrados of the roof vaulting (the *zakomara*), found its equivalent expression in wooden architecture. The possibility of using the parapet form to accentuate the masonry roof vaulting suggested itself to the Russian builder, ever alert for novelty of design. He became cognizant of its functional virtues as well as its decorative possibilities, and proceeded to adapt it to the wooden roof.

The masonry *zakomara* became the progenitor of the ogee-shaped wooden roof, popularly known as the *bochka*, or barrel-vault roof. Before long the barrel-vault roof was molded to the taste of the builder in wood. The original semicircular section became an ogee section; its outline was refashioned—the walls were pushed in at the base, flared out at the center, and drawn together and shaped into a sharp ridge line at the top. This became a favorite motif of the Russian builders, who varied its profile, combined it with other motifs, and used it functionally and decoratively. The *bochka* roof was usually applied to the church sanctuary and the narthex. Occasionally it served as a base for the cupolas, and often it was used over the main landing of the stairway. The profile of the *bochka* roof—its front elevation—became known as the *kokoshnik,* a form which had acquired great popularity in the decorative arts, ecclesiastical and secular. The degree of its popularity can be judged by the widespread use of the form in the profiling of the upper part of the icon frames, wood and metal diptychs and triptychs, baldachins, and women's hair ornaments and headdresses.

The church cupolas and cupola drums were covered with scale-like wooden shingles called *lemekh.* These shingles were made of aspen, cut into very thin, narrow pieces, the ends shaped in the form of a cross. Such a roof, seen against the gray northern forest, is suffused with a peculiar beauty, giving, in the shimmering light, the impression of being covered by some silvery substance (Plate 87). The roofs—whether painted or unpainted and weathered, wedge or ogee shaped, tented or domed—are always the most original, spirited, and fascinating part of the structure.

The load-carrying members—the columns which supported the ceilings of the refectories, church vestibules, or stairways—were decorated with carved braided bands interspersed with heavy melon-shaped forms that helped to underscore, as it were, the subjection of the columns to the strains and stresses of the loads. In contrast, the colonnettes and small timbers, which carried the relatively light loads of the stairway and balcony elements, were slimmer, of more delicate proportions, and decorated with high-relief carving.

The carving which decorated these members in the early periods was austere because it had to be done with the axe, the chisel, and the knife. The appearance and the application of the saw, especially the band saw and fret saw, and the brace and bit, opened up new possibilities in piercing and carving, and brought in a series of new ornamental motifs in the decoration of door and window architraves, gables, bargeboards, and rakes, at the same time enfeebling the character of ornamental design in relation to material.

Inside the church, color decoration was used extensively on the mullions and the moulded horizontal strips marking the tiers of the iconostases, the royal doors, the icon niches (*kiotsy*), the columns in the church vestibule, and occasionally the ceiling beams. The purpose was to bring the decorative elements of the church into harmony with the painted icons, and to accentuate the ornamental values of the carvings, which otherwise would be lost in the dim interior of the church.

On the exterior, color decoration was used in places where it could be protected from rain and snow. It was, as a rule, applied to the underside of the roof eaves, the upper parts of the walls, the deeply incised outlines of the carving on the door and window architraves, and the stairway columns.

The horizontal arrangements of the wall beams is an invariable characteristic. Timbers hewn from whole trees are laid in ranges, one on top of the other, to form the walls. Here is the mark of close kinship between church and *izba*, the indigenous contribution of the "primitive" builder. The well-articulated logs, the visual elements of the wall surface, are the units of scale which emphasize the hugeness of the structure. Because the upper elements are usually formed of smaller timbers than the lower, the tall blockwork frames of the church seem taller than they are. This impression of great height is accentuated by the deft arrangement of the roof shingling covering the pyramid-shaped spires, on which the plank-like shingles of each succeeding row are made shorter than those below them. A similar device is used for the interiors in the design of the iconostases and in the manipulation of the size and arrangement of the tiers.

The rectangular block units with their deep overhanging eaves, the units piled high in tiers one on top of the other; the roof forms, variously combined, ingeniously varied, and crowned with a multitude of cupolas all around and about the dominant central body of the church and its smaller dependencies; the hanging arcaded galleries; the beggar's porches; and the stairways with their ogee or tented roofs—all provided a field for the display of imagination and an opportunity for spirited articulation and expressiveness of silhouette. These churches, the product of an original culture, were the mainspring of a great artistic movement and contributed much to the evolution of Russia's architecture of the sixteenth century.

The extraordinary variety of forms in the many old wooden churches still extant in northern Russia is indeed remarkable. In spite of their seeming dissimilarities, one can perceive characteristics which suggest that these churches can be divided into two basic types, with a further subdivision of two other types. The difference between the basic groups becomes especially clear if we turn from the complex specimens to the simple—from the large spectacular wooden cathedrals to the tiny and humble roadside chapels of the villages.

The Izba and Shatër Types of Churches

The commonest type of chapel is a blockwork rectangular structure similar to the village peasant house, the *izba* with a simple porch in front. Churches of the rectangular type were evolved by the placing, in a straight line, of several units. The basic framework is a square or oblong box, and the most usual form has three units, of which the central one—the largest and tallest—is the nave; the other two, added to the east and west ends, are respectively the sanctuary and a kind of vestibule or porch (*trapeznaya or pritvor*), corresponding to the narthex of Byzantine and Romanesque churches. In this type, the central compartment was usually given a steep wedge-shaped roof, crowned by a small bulbous dome covered with shingles.

No doubt the first Christian churches and chapels in Russia were of the primitive rectangular type. But at some remote period, one cannot state just when or how, a new form for a different type of church structure came into being, the octagon. This form apparently was used exclusively for religious purposes. Such a church, even if it lacked the crowning cross, would attract attention by its unusual form. Its rows of logs are arranged to form a "circle," or rather the nearest equivalent, an octagon, and the entire blockwork unit is covered over by a roofing system that had never been applied to an *izba*—a roof having eight slopes, something akin to a tent (*shatër*).

The origin of this type of structure was probably the nomadic tent. Starting from this form of structure, so simple in appearance, the Russian builder developed a number of spirited variations. The essential feature of the building is an octagonal tower. The roof for such a tower was invariably, and quite logically, an octagonal pyramid, which was destined later to be translated into brick and stone. The great height of these tent-shaped roofs required, just as wedge-shaped gable roofs did, an easing of their sharp slopes at their bases—shelf-like eaves of a more gentle pitch, eaves that would project several feet beyond the walls, shed moisture, and protect the structure.

The tent-type church, while keeping the three traditional parts—sanctuary, nave, and narthex—differed from the *izba* type in that its central element forms an octagon; being much taller, it was also distinguished by a quality of soaring verticality. The practical advantage of octagonal form is, of course, the larger floor space, gained in using timbers of the same length as those used to frame the rectangle. Moreover, it is stiffer structurally, offers greater resistance to wind stresses, and therefore can be carried to a considerable height.[11] The same is true of the tent-shaped roof, which can withstand stronger winds than the large areas of the steep gable roofs. But the most important advantage of the tented churches was inherent in the focusing or centering effect of the octagon, to whose principal axes could be added various projections giving the structure a cross-shaped form. Furthermore, it could be easily surrounded with many secondary

[11] There were churches reaching a height of 245 feet. A height of 140 feet was quite common.

elements—chapels, porches, galleries, and stairways. The subsidiary ridged *bochka*-shaped roofs and decorative *kokoshniki* over the secondary elements gave the ensemble an unusually picturesque and expressive silhouette (Plates 79, 81).

This type of church was the most striking Russian creation in the field of architecture. It is remarkable how rational, how carefully thought out is this deeply national form of a church. The tent-type church, although simple in its primitive form, led to greater things. Most of the novel stone forms of sixteenth-century ecclesiastical architecture seem to have been influenced by the tent-type wooden churches of North Russia. It was the favorite design probably because it satisfied a basic craving for verticality and vigorous silhouette. It was also this particular form that the church authorities objected to so strenuously and tried to suppress. In the eyes of the upper ranks of the clergy, the tent roof did not express the essence of the church; it seemed to them too folkish, too playful, implying too great a self-assertion on the part of the individual builder. This attitude finally culminated in a church edict, issued in the middle of the seventeenth century, prohibiting the construction of tent-type churches.[12]

Each one of the two basic types of wooden churches—the *izba* and the tent—passed through several stages of development but never lost its basic distinguishing characteristics.

The Multi-Cupola and the "Cube" Types of Churches

In addition to the two principal types, there are the multicupola and the "cube" types of churches, which were brought about mainly by the edict prohibiting the building of tent-type churches.

These two subsidiary types were developed largely because of the desire of the Russian builder to introduce some spirited element, something dramatic that would take the place of the for-

[12] Quoted by P. Miliukov, *Outlines of Russian Culture*, III, 13. See also I. Zabelin, *Cherty samobytnosti v drevne-russkom zodchestve*, 138.

bidden tent. The first of these two types was the multi-cupola type church, which appeared in the second half of the seventeenth century, at first with nine cupolas, increasing to seventeen, as in the Church of the Intercession near Vytegra (1708), and culminating in the twenty-two-cupola Church of the Transfiguration at the Kizhi Church Yard (*Pogost'*) overlooking Lake Onega (Plates 86–87).

This church was erected in 1714, and it is perhaps as unique in the field of wood architecture as is the Church of St. Basil in the field of masonry. In plan it follows the traditional form of the tent church: an octagon to which, on every other side, were added square projections, thus converting it into a cross (Plate 85). Instead of crowning it with the tent, the builder chose to break away from tradition, and superimposed octagon upon octagon in a series of receding steps, crowning each step with a *bochka,* drum, and bulbous cupola. The four flights of cupolas lead one's eye upward to the central topmost and twenty-second cupola, whose supporting drum is planted directly on the roof of the octagon. On the western side is a huge double stairway with a common platform giving access to the narthex.

The result of this extraordinary combination of simple and complex elements is a fairy-like structure recreating the deeply rooted folk idea of a house of God, the multi-cupola church,[13] and at the same time preserving the favorite pyramidal silhouette. One may truly say that this is the work of a master builder endowed with an imagination of a high order, however fantastic it may seem.

The second subsidiary type is the highly picturesque, so-called cube-shaped church, whose roof forms are found extensively in the Onega region. The central square element in these

[13] The practice of having two, three, five, seven, nine, and thirteen cupolas dates from the eleventh century. The numbers are symbolic: two signifies the two natures of Jesus Christ; three represents the Trinity; five Our Lord and the Four Evangelists; seven the Holy Sacraments, or the seven gifts of the Holy Spirit; nine the nine celestial hierarchies; and thirteen Our Lord and the Twelve Apostles.

churches is surmounted by a roof which has, in vertical section (or in silhouette), the stylized form of a bulbous dome (Plate 84). Its square plan, flared out sides, and heavy mass must have been responsible for the nickname of *kub* (cube shaped or cube form). This roof form is probably derived from the combined and modified forms of the *bochka* and the cupola. It became a great favorite among the masses, as it was the nearest in silhouette to the beloved but forbidden tent. It was in reality a kind of a substitute for the tent and the *bochka*—and a form at least sufficiently acceptable to the upper ranks of the clergy.

All these church forms were being built, with minor innovations, up to the end of the eighteenth century. The innovations, if any, were but the reflection of those fleeting tastes and vogues that were popular in the bigger cultural centers, in Moscow and St. Petersburg. Short lived fashions, fortunately, could not change nor radically influence the very stable traditions, nor the basic construction methods evolved by the builders of the North. Yet there is no escaping the fact that "progress"—in the form of better-processed building lumber, smaller more refined sizes, and elaborateness of decorative forms—had begun to corrode and destroy one of the most significant, original, and beautiful phases of national creativity. The older the monuments, the more apparent the creative power of their builders. These old enormous structures, built of huge timbers, are suggestive of an age of giants. The work was largely anonymous, mostly the effort of cooperative, builder-guilds (*arteli*), sometimes of whole villages and townships. And the results took on the flavor of the soil.

XV

Muscovite Architecture, 1500–1600

THE SIXTEENTH CENTURY was the turning point in the history of Muscovy. Profound historic events and social upheavals marked that period. It is indispensable to bear in mind the historical facts of the latter if one is to gain insight into the cultural milieu which produced the old Russian works of architecture and formed the aesthetic taste of the Muscovite society.

The first decades of the sixteenth century brought to completion Moscow's absorption of the separate patrimonial appanages into a single state under the central authority of an autocratic grand prince. Moscow became a great metropolis, with the largest population of any city in Russia, and a center of social and religious life, learning, and art.

In the second half of the sixteenth century, during the reign of Ivan IV (commonly known as The Terrible), when many more territories and peoples were annexed to it, Russia acquired the characteristics of a multinational empire. These fifty odd years (1533–84) were a period of expansion and further centralization of the state, the establishment of absolute monarchy, and the introduction of reforms in all phases of economic, cultural, and social life.

Ivan the Terrible (Ivan Grozny), grandson of Ivan III, became grand prince of Moscow at the age of three, and in 1547 was crowned tsar—the first Russian ruler to use this title formally and fully. His grandfather, Ivan III, had used the title of tsar from time to time, but without the full significance that Ivan gave to it. The official assumption of the title was an expression of the great historical transformation which had taken place in the political position of the Moscow rulers. In the month following his coronation, Ivan took as his tsaritsa a gentle, quiet, and attractive maiden called Anastasiya Zakharin-Yuriev, of an ancient noble family—the same family that two generations later, as a direct outcome of this first marriage, was to give Russia a new dynasty, the Romanovs. Alone among the seven wives he was to take, she gave him the calm, companionship, and love that he craved and returned, and to her he was always a devoted and tender husband.

The tsar has been and will remain a source of controversy. He was an extraordinary, complex character, extreme in conduct and in speech. His temper was violent and revealed many of the symptoms of the manic-depressive, but he also demonstrated on many occasions that he was capable of affection, kindness, and tolerance. His true character is shrouded in mystery and the role played by him has been and still is very differently assessed by historians. Most paint him in the blackest colors. Leroy Beaulieu describes him as a "strange compound of craft, mysticism, inhuman in his piety, monstrous in his atrocities, bloodthirsty in his reforms, bred in the midst of plots and suspicions, possessed of a mind singularly free and inquiring for his time and country, combining the Russian's practical sense with the ravings of a maniac."

On the other hand, the Soviet historian R. Wipper points out that "in foreign historical literature the meaning of the term Grozny has been utterly distorted by its translation as 'Iwan der Schreckliche,' 'Iwan der Grausame,' 'Jean le Terrible,' or 'Ivan the Terrible,'" thus emphasizing the accusation that Ivan IV was inhuman. In the sixteenth century, however, the term Grozny (from Groza—storm) had a majestic and patriotic ring. This appellation had been previously applied to Ivan III."[1]

[1] R. Wipper (translated by J. Fineberg), Ivan Grozny, 28.

Karamzin and other Russian historians have divided his reign into two periods: the first or "beneficient" period, embracing his minority, and the period of the "reforms," which began after the death of his wife, Anastasiya.

Ivan believed himself the descendant of Augustus Caesar and, according to Josephite doctrine, God's vicar upon earth. He assumed the dazzling title of tsar and bitterly fought anything that challenged his one obsessing idea—the divine character of the power and the mission entrusted to him. He believed, for example, that all wars waged by him were, in a sense, religious wars, directed against the heretic or the infidel. Again, he believed that any act of disloyalty against the tsar, the protector of the church's truth, was also an act of disloyalty against Russian Orthodoxy. In his desire to establish an absolutism based on military and financial power and not on the sanction of the scheming boyar cliques and the wealthy monasteries, he proceeded to break the power of the formerly independent princes of the other branches of the house of Rurik, pursuing a policy of grisly terror against the aristocracy by executing hundreds upon hundreds of boyars, their families and retainers.

Ivan was one of the first Moscow rulers to appreciate the value of foreign cultures and to discover that the East as well as the West had something valuable to contribute. The conquest of the Khanate of Kazan in 1552 brought into the state a territory with a relatively dense population of Moslem and pagan non-Russians. By this conquest Russia annexed a segment of the Orient and, with the annexation of Astrakhan in 1556, itself became an Oriental state. Muscovy now extended not only to the Urals but to the Caspian. The barrier to the Far East was lifted. The great trade routes that Kazan controlled—the Volga highway to the Caspian and Caucasian markets and the Kama road to the Ural Mountains and the lands beyond—were at last opened.

There was a great influx of Oriental wares from the Caspian zone and Persia. The trade axis of Moscow stretched from the

Caspian to the Baltic by way of Astrakhan, Kazan, and Moscow, through Novgorod, Narva, and Pskov toward the ancient terminal of the road "from the Varangian land to the Greeks." A new land bridge between Europe and Asia was coming into being. The task was to take what could be taken from the East and West alike.

A far-reaching result of those conquests and annexations was the fusion of national and racial stocks. Ivan started the process of bringing together and blending the peoples of the Russian Empire and placing them all, as far as human rights are concerned, on the same level. Immediately after the conquest of Kazan he brought high-born Tatars to his court. For the new administration of the state he enrolled Tatars, Germans and members of various tribes in the Russian south, and may new men of obscure origin in the places of the boyars of ancient line. He gathered experts of all sorts about him and made them a part of his entourage. Ivan was trying to create a new type of Russia for this reconstructed empire.

Shortly after the fall of Kazan, Russia received unexpected visitors from across the seas. The English Trading Expedition, headed by Richard Chancellor, arrived in Moscow to make the first contacts Muscovite Russia had with England.[2] The route opened by the Expedition along the Northern Dvina through Archangel added one more window to the West and provided an opportunity for trade, for greater understanding, and for cultural exchange between England and Russia. The trade arrangement made a great contribution to Russia's economic development, and consequently to its political and cultural development as well. In exchange for a promise to ship military supplies and other goods through the mouth of the Northern Dvina, the Eng-

[2] Richard Chancellor was commander of one of three vessels under Sir Hugh Willoughby sent by Edward VI of England to find a northeastern passage (1553). Willoughby and many of his crew were frozen to death in the Arctic, but Chancellor made his way to Moscow, thus discovering the trade route around Norway. In 1555 Chancellor was sent to Russia again, this time as an envoy of Mary and Philip; he was drowned off the coast of Scotland on the return voyage (1556).

lish obtained exclusive rights to use the northern route, the right to trade duty-free all over the Moscow State, right of free entry and departure, and also right of free transit by the Volga route to Persia and central Asia. They acquired a firm footing, established warehouses in all the large towns, and became the most favored foreign merchants in the Moscow State.

In spite of Dutch attempts at competition, the English controlled the Russian market and managed to influence the political thought of Russia as well and to give the nascent process of Europeanization a character in keeping with their national interests. More than this, Russia's attitudes toward the European powers were colored by English advice. Ivan became a strong Anglophile and even considered the possibility of marrying Queen Elizabeth or, if that were impossible, Lady Hastings. He wanted to provide an asylum in England for himself if his dynasty should fall. It is not surprising that he was called the "English Tsar" by his intimates.

The conquest of the Volga trade routes and the coming of the English mark a new era: Russia ceased to be a land of "natural" economy; capitalism became a dominating economic force. Moscow became a thriving metropolis, the largest city in Russia, a center of trade, religion, learning, and art. The eventful and turbulent age of Ivan the Terrible witnessed not only the great political and commercial expansion of the Russian state, but also the growth of cultural consciousness and the burgeoning of national art and architecture. It was at this time that the printing press was introduced (1563), that literature and the decorative arts were flourishing, and that woodcarving, gold and silver work, enameling, and casting of metals reached a high degree of craftsmanship.

The passion and controversy that flared up in the church and the state clearly reflected the richness of intellectual life and the abundance of talent among the laymen and clerics who surrounded Ivan IV in the early years of his reign. Among the outstanding figures of Russian culture of that period were the first printer and enlightened scholar, Ivan Fedorov; the writers Peresvetov, Yermolai-Erasmus, the Metropolitan Makari, compiler of the *Grand Cheti Minyei*,[3] Archpriest Sylvester, editor of the *Domostroy*,[4] and the tsar himself, who was a voracious reader and a passionate bibliophile;[5] the oligarchic statesman Prince Andrei Kurbsky;[6] the metal-casting specialist Andrei Chokhov; and the architects Barma and Posnik (Postnik) Yakovlev,[7] builders of the St. Basil Cathedral.

Masonry Structures

The sixteenth century, in the artistic life of Moscow, was particularly notable for its searchings and probings in many directions, its daring and innovations. The Italian architects, Ridolfo Fioravanti and Alevisio Novyi, had just built the Uspensky and

[3] *Cheti Minyei*—religious reading matter arranged by days of the month. The *Grand Cheti Minyei* includes biography and instructive and eulogistic discourses, and consists of about twenty-seven thousand large-size pages.

[4] *Domostroy* is literally a house orderer; by extension a guide for living, a book aimed to regiment behavior to the smallest detail, providing a religious, moral, and practical life pattern for the family under the guidance of the master of the house, the father and husband. It determined the usages and customs of the land for generations and was instrumental in excluding women from public life, relegating them to separate quarters in the house, the *terem*.

[5] It is said that Ivan IV, who inherited a fine library from his grandfather, Ivan III, augmented this collection by rare Greek, Hebrew, and Latin volumes which he procured through his agents in the capitals of Western Europe. There is some evidence that he commissioned the German scholar, the Dorpat pastor, Vesterman (Vetterman), to translate some of the works into Russian. This collection and its whereabouts have been the subject of speculation by many bibliographers. In 1891 searches were conducted throughout the subterranean passages of the Kremlin, but nothing was ever found. (See Bartenev, *Moskovsky Kreml'*, II, 201–211.)

[6] Prince Kurbsky (d. 1583) was a descendant of the House of Rurik, associated with Sylvester and Adashev in the Elected Council during the reform period of the reign of Ivan IV; commander-in-chief of Muscovite armies in the Livonian War. In 1564 he suffered an ignominious defeat at the hand of the Poles and, fearing the tsar's anger, defected to Lithuania. From there he wrote a number of letters and a *History of the Great Muscovite Prince*, vilifying and revealing a malevolent hatred for his former sovereign. Kurbsky's calumnies have darkened the image of Ivan through the centuries.

[7] Barma was evidently the senior architect as he is mentioned in seventeenth-century chronicles as working with a group of collaborators or "comrades" (*s tovarishchi*).

Arkhangelsky cathedrals in the Kremlin. Marco Ruffo and Pietro Solario erected the Granovitaya Palata. Moscow was flooded with new art forms, technics, and devices, and together with a richer art vocabulary and better workmanship, a clearer creative consciousness emerged, a sense of liberation from the Byzantine traditions. In looking about for sources of inspiration, the Russian architects turned to the indigenous forms of wooden church architecture, examples of which abounded in and about Moscow. These wooden churches were the most numerous, most attractive, and closest to the heart and aesthetics of the city. Their graceful, slender, tent-shaped roofs, their clusters of chapels, galleries, and porches with their picturesque stairways, their *kokoshniki, bochki,* and cupolas—all these distinctive features must have captivated the imagination of the local builders.

The experimenting with wooden building forms and their adaptation to and incorporation in the masonry architecture of Novgorod and Pskov went on in a leisurely manner for a long time, but in early sixteenth-century Moscow this process speeded up. In the suburbs of Moscow a number of memorial and votive churches appeared in rapid succession, and many of the wooden forms were reflected with increasing boldness. The influence exerted by wooden architecture also brought about the substitution of the wooden tent tower for the traditional Byzantine cupola and a number of other important changes: increased emphasis on height; introduction of entrance porches and the use of external galleries; combination of the pyramidal spire with the cupola; and the introduction of separate freestanding belfries.

The first church in the neighborhood of Moscow which exemplifies an attempt at adapting the forms of wooden architecture to brick construction is the Church of the Ascension in the village of Kolomenskoye erected by Vasili III in 1532 (Plate 73). Here the most characteristic and most expressive of national wooden architectural forms—the "tent"—was incorporated, for the first time, into ecclesiastical masonry architecture. The architect succeeded in translating the wooden forms—and imparting to them the poignant feeling of national architecture. The whole building has the firmness and compactness of a monolithic pyramid, recalling the form of the great wooden "tent" churches. There is the same foundation course of the arcaded porches, the same cruciform plan, the same octagonal central element, and the same tent-shaped roof. The kinship of this masonry structure with the wooden churches of the north becomes especially clear when compared with the Church of the Assumption at Vartsug (Plate 81). It is a significant monument in the history of Russian architecture. Its deep debt to the past was inevitable, since it was the product of an enthusiastic Russian Renaissance. Though its elements were gathered from a variety of sources, they are fused and transfigured into national substance.

A second tent-type church, somewhat similar to the Ascension at Kolomenskoye, is the white stone Church of the Transfiguration at Ostrovo, a suburb of Moscow, built in 1550 (Plate 74). It has some of the elements of the older masonry churches combined with the new features derived from wooden construction. The outstanding feature of this church is the large number (nearly two hundred) of *kokoshniki*. They are combined in lively rhythmical groups forming the transition from the square to the octagon, and above it to the "tent." In semicircular form their corbelled tiers support the cupola drums over the chapels at the eastern corners, and in ogee form, of which there are seven tiers, they provide a transition from the square base to the octagonal superstructure, and from that to a short "tent" spire surmounted by a drum and cupola. The carved decorative bands of apses and drums recall the ornament of the cupolas of the Cathedral of Annunciation in the Kremlin.

Another kind of tower is seen in the Church of St. John the Precursor at Dyakovo (Plate 75), near Kolomenskoye, built in 1553–54. The architect evidently attempted to build a tall tower-like mass with subsidiary shapes at its base, which would give the church a pyramidal appearance. But it seems that he hesitated, not quite daring to depart from the traditional cupola type. The result, though a compromise, marks a decisive step in the history of Russian architecture, pointing the way to bolder innovations. Ingenious, richly decorated, altogether unusual amongst the older Moscow masonry churches, this church gives the impression of being as spirited in design, as uniquely different as that of Basil in Moscow. It remains pentacupolar just as tradition demanded, but by clever manipulation of the height of the corner chapels in relation to the central element, the architect succeeded in giving the structure the general silhouette of a pyramidal tower. The transition from the base to the tower is accomplished by two recessive rows of decorative *kokoshniki*, the upper pointed and the lower semicircular, which greatly add to the beauty of the upper elements. The wall surfaces are embellished with rectangular frescoed panels and colored tiles. Over the west wall the architect placed a sharply profiled belfry, of the type developed by the Pskovian builders, but with the Muscovite decorative treatment.

In the general architectural masses of the church the architect succeeded in retaining the austerity and somewhat heavy characteristics of early Moscow, but to the decorative elements he brought much variety, richness, and a generous amount of textural and color values. It is interesting to note that the Church of St. Basil, though differing greatly from the Dyakovo church, borrowed much from the latter.

The Churches of Kolomenskoye, Ostrovo, and Dyakovo served as prototypes for the most striking monument of this period— the Church of Basil the Blessed (*Vasili Blazhenny*, 1555–60), best known in the West for its marked difference from Western tradition (Plates 76–78). It occupies an exceptional place in Russian architecture and deserves to be considered at length. This boldest departure from classic or Byzantine architecture violates the laws of symmetry and proportion as understood by the Western world, and the structure is uniquely medieval Russian in content, form, technique, decoration, and feeling.

Long the subject of heated discussions, the architecture of St. Basil's has been either greatly ridiculed and termed "the dream of a diseased imagination" or highly praised as a unique expression of the medieval Russian genius. Theophile Gautier, the French writer, compared the agglomeration of its many elements to the crystals of a giant madrepore. Other Western observers, notably the French De Gustine and the German Blazius, described its ensemble of towers and cupolas as "a bush, a plant, or a bouquet of varicolored flowers." However it strikes the beholder, there is no denying that, in spite of its seemingly incongruous jumble of architectural elements and decorative details, the church is uniquely original in conception, design, and execution. Furthermore, some observers believe that the architecture of the church, in its departure from the traditional plan and distribution of masses of the Kremlin cathedrals, reflected the beginning of the new, national epoch in Russian art—an expression of the aesthetics of the rising middle classes and no longer that of the dwellers inside the Kremlin, the formerly powerful boyars. Its very location on Red Square points to the steadily growing importance of the districts beyond the Kremlin.

St. Basil, originally known as the Cathedral of the Intercession of the Virgin (*Pokrovsky Sobor*), is a votive church built by Ivan IV in commemoration of the conquest of Kazan and Astrakhan. At that time Russia was passing through a particularly intense phase of religious fervor. The Stoglav Council had recently met; the young tsar, flushed with victory, wanted to signalize his military success as a triumph of the Cross over Islam.

At the suggestion of the Metropolitan Makari, Ivan decided to erect a masonry church dedicated to the Intercession (*Pokrov*) of the Virgin. Because this was to be a memorial church, easy of access to all of the people of Moscow, Ivan decided on a site on Red Square at the edge of the ditch along the Kremlin. With the church as the central, dominant element, he planned eight smaller but separate churches (not chapels) of wood, each with its own altar and iconostasis, dedicated to a saint whose feast day coincided with one of the days of the eight decisive victories over the Tatars. These temporary wooden churches were later replaced by masonry structures. In 1588 another church was added on the northeast side of the cathedral to house the crypt of Basil the Blessed. One of the most venerated altars in the church—the third in importance—was dedicated to the entry of Jesus into Jerusalem. Foreign visitors to Moscow during the seventeenth century were impressed with the colorful Palm Sunday (*Verbnoye Voskresen'ye*) processions and referred to St. Basil's as the Church of Jerusalem.[8]

St. Basil, for whom this extraordinary church was named, was a popular mendicant prophet and miracle worker of the sixteenth century who claimed as his distinctive glory that he was "idiotic for Christ's sake." This church contains relics of another saint, John the Idiot, as well as the chain and cross worn in penance by St. Basil. Idiocy was a common form of religious fervor in Russia, and these dedicated idiots (*urodivyie*) were treated with reverence.

Begun in 1555, St. Basil's was finished and consecrated in 1560. It was designed by the Russian architects Barma and Posnik Yakovlev, who, in the words of the chronicler, were "very wise and eminently fit for this marvelous work." According to a persistent legend, St. Basil was designed by an Italian architect, who was then blinded by order of the tsar so that he would not be able to produce a more beautiful church elsewhere. Another version of the same legend says that the tsar asked the architect if he could build an even finer, more magnificent church. When the architect replied that he could, the tsar or-

---

[8] On Palm Sunday, before the communion service, a holy procession, from the Cathedral of the Assumption in the Kremlin, depicted the entrance of Jesus into Jerusalem, in which the patriarch rode upon an ass to the Church of St. Basil and thence to the *Lobnoye Mesto* on the Red Square. In this procession—headed by children singing Hosanna, followed by white-robed priests carrying church banners, processional crosses, and icons, by boyars waving palm branches—the patriarch's mount was humbly led by the magnificently attired Tsar.

dered him beheaded so that St. Basil's would remain an unrivaled monument.

The St. Basil group of churches is basically cross-shaped, the arms of the cross extending from a square center—the main church—over which rises the central tower covered with a tent-shaped roof and crowned with a gilt cupola (Plate 77). At each arm of the cross, along the principal axes, is an octagonal church. Four other secondary churches (two square and two of irregular outline) are along the diagonal axes. All these elements are placed over a tall, vaulted substructure—the typical lower story of the Russian wooden churches. The pyramidal belfry at the southeast corner is separated from the church. The plan and the general massing of the elements are unusual, not only in the accepted concept of church design but in the distribution of the main masses. Rather than being merely the result of some fanciful caprice, the arrangement and grouping were probably planned by Metropolitan Makari.

The main church is of stone and brick and covered with stucco. In the seventeenth century the entire structure, originally white, was painted in variegated colors, the stairways were roofed over, the sheet iron covering of the cupolas was replaced with tile, and the old belfry was replaced with the present tent-roofed bell tower.

Like the church at Kolomenskoye, St. Basil embodies the characteristic architectural features of the wooden churches of northeastern Russia translated into masonry. Here, too, the transition from the square substructure to the main octagonal tower is accomplished by recessive, interspaced tiers of ornate *kokoshniki*. The same method is used to form the transition from the massive base to a smaller octagon supporting the tent-shaped spire surmounted by a small bulbous cupola. The eleven steeples are banded together like an immense bundle of fantastically shaped plants. The eight cupolas, dominated by the central pyramid, are all of the same general silhouette but are different in design—as if to single out each of the component churches in the complex.

Some, with their twisted, variegated shapes, are reminiscent of oriental turbans; some are decorated with ribbed or interlacing designs; others are faceted, giving them the appearance of pineapples; still another has imbrications reminiscent of the aspen shingles of the wooden churches. All the cupolas are bulbous and project beyond the diameter of the drum. This diversity of forms and decorative features is further heightened by the lavish use of colored tile.

The interior is by contrast somber and cavernous. It produces the impression that the church was sculptured from one huge block of stone. Each of the nine church chambers is prolonged upward in a kind of drum surmounted by a dome. The chambers, suggestive of ancient frescoed catacombs, are connected by low, vaulted passages within the thick walls, with a narrow, vaulted corridor around them. The low, arched doorways and windows are of various forms, all deeply recessed and flanked with engaged columns. The interior of the central church was frescoed in 1784 during the reign of Catherine II; the other surrounding churches were frescoed between 1839 and 1845.

St. Basil's is understandably strange, puzzling to Western eyes; yet it was well suited to the age and its former surroundings. It still exercises a singular attraction at all times of the year, but is especially fascinating in winter. Seen in the pale sunshine, with its clump of pinnacles and cupolas illuminated against the sky, the building is most impressive.

As one of the first monarchs to make systematic attempts to exploit art for state propaganda, Ivan gave great impulse not only to architecture but to the development of icon painting and the applied arts and crafts. He had a keen appreciation of the arts of the jeweler, the goldsmith, and the enameler, and was fully conscious of their value in enhancing the prestige of his regime. He established a settlement on the outskirts of Moscow for all the German metalworkers who had been captured in his Livonian wars, and in 1567 imported a number of goldsmiths from England. The first mercenaries, enlisted from the prisoners, were the precursors of a long line of military leaders, administrators, physicians, and architects who entered the service of the Russian government (many becoming naturalized citizens) and exercised great influence on the course of Russian civilization.

When he annexed Novgorod in 1570, Ivan resolved to curb its turbulent spirit by transferring its population. Thousands of families were exiled, and many of them were brought to Moscow. These new arrivals included certain Hanseatic merchants who formed the nucleus of the foreign colony in the capital, which a century later became instrumental in opening a new era in Russian cultural life.

A conscientious dilettante and collector, Ivan had the gift of discovering talented Russian artists and craftsmen, putting them to work, and getting the best from them. He accepted or rejected commissioned works of art according to his personal likes and dislikes. During his outbursts of piety and repentance, many churches and monasteries were the recipients of gifts of icons, iconostases, vestments, and church vessels. The icon encasements, relic containers, ciboria, chalices, and censers made during his reign are among the finest examples of the art of embossing, chiseling, engraving, filigree, enameling, and niello work. Until the closing years of the sixteenth century, when the Stroganovs came to the fore as patrons of the arts, the tsar, with his immediate advisers among the clergy, remained the chief arbiter and customer of art. By the end of the period the artistic, clerical, and exclusively national spirit of Muscovy had assumed its final form. It remained practically unchanged for another hundred years; even the terrible ordeal of the "Time of Trouble" failed to modify it.

At the turn of the century a brilliant finishing touch was given to the ensemble of the Kremlin's Cathedral Square, by the erection of the huge stone Bell Tower of Ivan the Great (Ivan Veliky). It was remodeled in 1600 under Boris Godunov (Plate 72). The colossal white stone, "column of fame" stands on the brow of the hill to the east of and nearly equidistant from the cathedrals of the Assumption and the Archangel Michael. Situated almost exactly in the center of the Kremlin and rising above the gleaming cupolas, multicolored spires, and shining crosses of the the surrounding cathedrals and palaces, this tower commands the entire scene and consolidates the various groups into one architectural composition. The Ivan Tower, including the cross, is 270 feet high; it rests on a stone foundation, the bottom of which is said to extend down to the level of the Moskva River. The base is of white stone, and the walls are of brick reinforced with iron bars. The lower stories are octagonal in plan, receding progressively in size and height and leading up to a cylindrical drum crowned by a cupola and terminated by a large cross.

The entire composition of the tower is based on the principle of lightening the successive architectural masses as they rise, progressing from the large, heavy, simple elements at the bottom to the smaller, lighter, more complicated at the top—carrying them, as it were, through the cross into space. The effectiveness of this design is largely the result of the subtle transition from the dominant horizontality below to the verticality and broken lines of the architectural elements above. The imposing structure is a definite expression of an age, of a political and social era, reflecting the tastes, material aspirations, and political ambitions of Tsar Boris Godunov, who dreamed of perpetuating his dynasty. It is as though Gudunov felt that by erecting it he had created a symbol of grandeur, a monument dominating everything created before him by the House of Rurik.

The Ivan Tower owes much of its imposing effect to its elevation and singularly conspicuous site. The placing of the huge tower in this spot created a salient vertical axis, commanding the neighboring cathedrals and all the other towers of the Kremlin. This axis of the Kremlin became at the same time the axis of all Moscow.

The Ivan Tower is the dominant element in a group of three contiguous buildings erected at different dates but forming one unit. The central and oldest part of this group is the Bono Tower, begun in 1532 and finished in 1543, antedating the Tower of Ivan by some sixty years. The Bono Tower is a four-story structure from which rises a two-story belfry that houses the principal bell of Moscow. This belfry is surmounted by a cylindrical tower of considerable height crowned by a golden cupola terminating in a cross. The architect used ancient Russian belfries as models but developed a complex architectural composition.

The second building of this group, the Tower of Patriarch Philaret, was built in 1624 during the reign of Philaret's son, Mikhail Feodorovich, the first Romanov. The main tower is four stories high; a fifth story of arches is topped by a central tent-shaped spire surrounded by Gothic turrets. This tower formerly housed the great Patriarchal Sacristy, with its priceless collection of ancient ecclesiastical art.

The sixteenth century produced not only a series of significant works, but perfected new construction methods, types and forms of multi-columned and tent churches, large architectural ensembles of the fortress-monastery type, and formal audience chambers. All this paved the way for formal civil architecture, whose influence on the subsequent development of Russian art is significant. Toward the end of the sixteenth century a special state organization, the Bureau of Masonry Works, was established. The intensive building activities evolved new architectural ideas and types, incorporating and transmuting the attainments of ancient Russian building.

XVI

Seventeenth-Century Architecture

W ITH THE DEATH OF TSAR FEODOR, last of the House of Rurik, his successor, Godunov, found himself unable to maintain as tsar the unquestioned authority he had so skillfully wielded during Feodor's reign. The country became a prey to political disorder and social revolution, aggravated by the invasions of the Poles, Tatars, and Swedes, who used this opportunity for attack upon a once-powerful neighbor. Moscow fell into the hands of the Poles, and the rest of the country was laid waste by rebellious peasants or bands of foreign adventurers. This period, *Smutnoye vremya* (not quite correctly translated as the "Time of Trouble"), ended with the election in 1613 of Mikhail Romanov, the founder of the new dynasty.

A new Russia emerged with the advent of the Romanov dynasty. The power of the princes and the aristocracy was gone and a new social class had taken its place—a class of service aristocracy, consisting mostly of self-made men with a sprinkling of descendants of the former aristocracy, which accepted the principle of service as the sole basis for its rights. This class had decidedly Western leanings and was interested in commercial expansion. The rise of the new social group and the expansion of cultural and trade relations with the West contributed very largely toward bringing about a secularization of culture in the Muscovite state, first in the realm of purely practical affairs, then in the realm of art. Ecclesiastical control of the arts was weakened, giving way to a secular element, now largely imported from the West, chiefly through Poland and the Ukraine.

By the middle of the seventeenth century Russian art turned decisively toward new directions and new ideas. This turn is so marked that it would be quite correct to move back the commonly accepted date for the beginning of the modern period in Russian art (the post-Petrine period) a full half-century, that is, from the founding of St. Petersburg to the first years of the reign of Tsar Aleksei Mikhailovich (1645–76). The turn began with the appearance of foreign artists and craftsmen in Moscow, who, in larger and larger numbers, found employment at the Oruzheinaya Palata (roughly the equivalent of a combination of academy of fine and applied arts and state ministry in charge of military and civil engineering). Here, in this first Russian "academy," the soil was prepared and the seeds of the new aesthetics were sown.

Western influences invaded Moscow via two routes: one from the southwest, Poland and the Ukraine; the other from the foreign colony in the city, the so-called "German Suburb" (*Nemetskaya Sloboda*), northeast of the Kremlin.

Ukrainian and Polish influences gradually transformed the whole fabric of ecclesiastical civilization. In 1685 an academy on the Western model, teaching Greek and Latin, was established in Moscow. A new current of ideas and art forms entered the stream of Russian painting, architecture, literature, and music, influencing and modifying the established traditions. Toward the end of the seventeenth century a whole new generation of Russian artists was reared and educated on new principles.

As a result we notice in the Russian art of that epoch two tendencies running concurrently: the old tendency prevalent in the provincial centers and the hinterland of that day, still vigorously developing the art forms bequeathed by the Moscow period; the other, the pro-Western tendency, adopting, assimilating, and refashioning the forms of the late Italian Renaissance, a movement that took strong roots and became the vogue at the tsar's court and at the capital.

Secular Architecture

The Time of Trouble, the Civil War, and the social upheavals that marked the beginning of the seventeenth century put a stop to Moscow's intense building activities for a few years. The city was plundered and almost razed to the ground, but despite the terrible devastation, Moscow began to build itself anew with surprising rapidity. The old tradition of putting up ready-hewn log houses very quickly eliminated the housing shortage. After they had finished the necessary repairs of the Kremlin walls and cathedrals, the Moscow rulers began to think of more serious work. It is significant that one of their first undertakings was the remodeling and ornamentation of the towers and main gates to the Kremlin.

It was during this period that the extensive reconstruction and enlargements of the old Terem Palace (Teremnoi Dvorets) took place (Plates 107–112). The foundation for the old palace was laid in 1499; the work was supervised by the architect Alevisio Novyi, who had previously demonstrated his abilities in the construction of religious edifices. These living quarters, constituting the lower floors of the still-existing Terem Palace, were finished in 1508 after the death of Ivan III. During its construction, work also proceeded on a masonry wall to protect the palace from the constantly menacing Tatars.

The new palace is a brick structure; the window architraves, portals, entablatures, and parapets are of white stone covered with carved strapwork, foliage, and figures of beasts and birds painted in bright colors. The ornamentation dates from the sixteenth and seventeenth centuries; it was renovated in the early nineteenth century. The apartments, contained within a five-story structure (now forming the north side of the Kremlin Grand Palace), are a series of small, low, generally vaulted rooms decorated with polychrome ornaments and images painted on gold or other backgrounds.

In the reign of Tsar Aleksei Mikhailovich (1645–76) the old palace attained its most beautiful and luxurious aspect. The five apartments of the fourth story were renovated and refurnished as his private quarters. The first room functioned as a waiting room for the boyars seeking audience with the tsar. The second room, the Room of the Cross, served as a reception room for the tsar and occasionally for boyar councils. The third room, sometimes called the Golden Room, was the Tsar's study, where the high officials of state were received. It contained a dais for the throne and some benches along the walls, where the boyars were seated according to seniority. The center window of the Golden Room, known as the Petitioners' Window, had a device for raising and lowering a small box between the room and the ground. Into this box the poor and the wronged could place their petitions and complaints addressed directly to the tsar. The next room, the tsar's bedroom, has a carved four-poster with curtains of brocade and silk. Along its walls are benches upholstered in Venetian velvet. The fifth room was the tsar's private chapel or oratory, which has a pulpit with a fourteenth-century illuminated manuscript of the Book of the Gospels.

Outstanding as decorative features in all these rooms are the great faïence-tile stoves. The stoves in the tsar's study and in the chapel are especially noteworthy as monuments of the great skill and artistry of the seventeenth-century Russian craftsmen in producing colored and glazed tiles and pottery.

The fifth floor or "penthouse" apartment has heavily ornamented vault webbing, pendant keys, door entablatures, window frames, and colored-tile stoves.

This remnant of the past is a labyrinth of low corridors and vaulted chambers adorned with barbaric magnificence. The few extant architectural and decorative elements are truly authentic remains of medieval Russian art. Except for a few modern details and perhaps well-meant but unfortunate restorations, these chambers offer a complete picture of the art and environmental culture of the royal court of the late seventeenth century.

The furnishings and accessories remained practically unchanged from the death of Tsar Feodor in 1682 until the restoration of 1830. Then much of the feeling of antiquity was destroyed, giving these chambers a somewhat artificial toy-like appearance, but there is still a strong seventeenth-century aura about them.

The decoration of the exterior of the Terem Palace is in some ways even more striking than the interior. Alongside the Western classical decorative elements are ornamental motifs of a decidedly Russian folk character, especially in the windows and the entrance portals, that are the most interesting decorative details of the Terem façades. The builders of the palace embellished the windows and doors with luxurious carving—the motifs borrowed from the wooden *khoromy* of tht tsar—and thus transformed them into highly individual creations.

Among the seventeenth-century palaces in the Kremlin is the one that belonged to the boyar Ilia Miloslavsky, who first occupied it in 1651. When Miloslavsky died, Tsar Aleksei Mikhailovich remodeled it into a theater. Known as Poteshnyi Dvorets (Amusement Palace), it still exists, though it has been considerably changed. Its projecting cantilevered balcony, constructed to support a house chapel, is particularly interesting.

Between 1680 and 1690 many gardens, balconies, and stairways were added to the Kremlin. Near the Church of the Saviour Behind the Golden Grille, stone passageways, covered and open arcades, hanging gardens, and cupolas crowning the roofs of various chapels were built—the passages and galleries permitting the tsar to communicate with the patriarch without having to leave cover. During these years, when the ancient and traditional forms merged harmoniously with the elements of the early Moscow baroque, the Kremlin reached its mature beauty.

Following the example of the tsar, who had reconstructed the Terem and Poteshnyi palaces in the Kremlin, the nobility, the important officials, and the rich merchants also began to build for themselves masonry mansions and chapels. These structures show the gradual evolution of the style of the earlier wooden palaces and churches.

The basic structural forms of the Moscow churches were fully developed in the sixteenth century. It remained for the next century to concentrate its efforts on the refinement of these forms and on the embellishment of the façades with opulent ornamentation. We see the "tent" spires degenerate into mere decoration; they are used as exterior ornamented features and are set loosely in numbers over gabled roofs and on top of roof vaulting. This decorative use of the formerly functional element is combined with the liberal employment of the other sixteenth-century structural device—the kokoshniki. These, in retreating and ascending tiers, are used as a decorative screen for the drum-like bases of the spires, and sometimes as parapets over the cornices.

Church building had settled down to a tacit acceptance of the pentacupolar church as dictated by Patriarch Nikon,[1] but it never relinquished the pyramidal tent form. The architects of Moscow resorted to some ruses in order to circumvent the clerical ban on this favorite roof form. They made clever use of the permission granted by the clergy to erect tents over church annexes, that is, over porches and bell towers. These tent roofs over the bell towers present the final and perfected stage in the development of this national roof feature. The variety of forms and the manner with which the Russian builders played with retreating and overlapping kokoshniki, and with arrangement and grouping of cupolas and tents during the sixteenth and seventeenth centuries,

---

[1] Nikon, patriarch of Moscow, born Nikita of peasant origin, began his clerical career as a parish priest, took the orders and assumed the name of Nikon, nominated in 1648 metropolitan of Novgorod, elevated in 1652 by Tsar Aleksei Mikhailovich to the patriarchate, effected reforms in ecclesiastical ritual which caused a schism (raskol) in the Orthodox church, quarreled with the tsar and deposed by a church council (1666–67). While endorsing Nikon's reforms, the council, attended by the four Eastern patriarchs either in person or by proxy, asserted supremacy of tsar over patriarch.

make up one of the enchanting chapters in the history of Russian architecture.

The Church of the Georgian Virgin is a good example of the change to the new official style. It was begun in 1628, but enlarged in 1653 (Plate 92). The wealthy merchants of Kitai-Gorod (Moscow) lavished much money on its decoration. Its architecture is typical of the period. Here we find the change to the new official style fully developed. The transition from the walls through several tiers of ogee *kokoshniki* to the slender drums of the traditional five cupolas is effected beautifully.

The pyramidal spires, forbidden by Patriarch Nikon, are absent from the main body of the church. Only a single spire remains over the entrance porch. The five cupolas rest on slender lantern-like drums. The recessed *kokoshniki*, masking the vaults of the roof, are used merely as decoration, and the cornices are richly adorned.

To the more complicated tent groups belongs the Church of the Nativity of the Virgin of Putinki (Moscow), built at the expense of Tsar Aleksei Mikhailovich. It is an example of the use of pyramidal tents, and one in which the tents were considerably modified. The church is essentially a typical triple-tent rectangular structure complicated by the addition to its west side of a single-tent chapel dedicated to the Burning Bush (*Pridel Neopalimoi Kupiny*). The two structures are united by a single-tent belfry. The towers are blind (*glukhiye shatry*)[2] and purely ornamental, being set on the extrados of the vaults. The lively groups of the various tents are arranged without symmetry and add much to the whimsicality and picturesqueness of the ensemble. The church is the last of the tent churches, having been built in 1652 almost contemporaneously with the Nikonian reforms.

The predominant decorative quality of seventeenth-century

[2] Literally deaf tents; an idiomatic Russian expression for a "blind" building element.

Moscow architecture is fully reflected in this structure. The roofs of the belfry and the Chapel of the Burning Bush are decorated with a pyramidal series of recessed *koskoshniki*. The annexes have all the devices worked out by Moscow architecture for the treatment of the decorative areas. Of special interest is the lengthening of the drum-like base under the tent.

The most elaborate of the later Moscow churches is the Church of the Trinity in Ostankino near Moscow, (Plate 94) built in 1668. The five closely spaced cupolas over the main church are supported on slender drums which rest on a common base rising out of two retreating and overlapping rows of *kokoshniki*. The cornices, the elaborate window architraves, and the portals are in the Russified baroque taste. The window pediments of the apses are especially notable since the combination of the classic crown and the Russian *kokoshniki* produces an unique star-shaped form.

Other churches appeared in rapid succession, but the structural quality, simplicity, and structural logic with which the first churches were endowed soon gave way to an architecture which stressed decorative quality rather than structural considerations. The tent spire began to lose its essentially structural and functional significance, and acquired a purely decorative value. It became smaller and slenderer. The efforts of the architect were concentrated on refining existing forms or developing new patterns and new proportions, and proved to be a very potent stimulant for the architecture of Moscow and the neighboring provinces.

In the details and ornamentation of the Muscovite churches, Byzantine elements began to give way to a less severe and more picturesque style. The façades began to be treated with a view primarily to pictorial effect. Ornament became profuse, varied, and independent of structural logic. By the last third of the seventeenth century the vogue for rich embellishment reached its zenith. Polychromy asserted itself; colored and glazed tile and carved stone ornament used in combination with brick patterns were employed extensively. Some of the wall panels of that period are so intricately and beautifully carved as to produce the effect of exquisite stone lacework.

Muscovite architecture became what Western critics like to describe as exotic and what the Russian art historians of today prefer to designate as "Moscow or Naryshkin Baroque." Baroque ideas found a fertile soil in Moscow and gave fresh vigor to its architecture. They strengthened the existing decorative tendencies, but also quickened the constructive imagination and gave new life to the spirit that had evolved the tent form. The last remains of the severe Byzantine style went overboard, and Muscovite architecture was free to revel in constructive and pictorial freedom.

Moscow or Naryshkin Baroque

The Italian Renaissance at its height overflowed to other lands, but missed Russia. Its impact on Russian architecture took place mainly in its very early and very late (baroque) phases. The first phase of the Renaissance reflected itself primarily in various architectural details and techniques, changing and improving the methods of construction. It hardly touched the building forms then strongly in favor. On the other hand, the late phase of the Renaissance had an enormous influence and brought about the creation of entirely new building types. This influence, manifesting itself as a new power to mold space and to produce a unified whole from the most diverse elements, resulted in what was probably the most international of all styles. Its expression in some countries revealed itself in almost an absence of specific regional characteristics; everywhere there was a uniformity in architectural devices and details.

Russia, however, was able to assimilate and refashion this style into types entirely individual to herself. One reason for this, Grabar' points out, is that the baroque appeared on the Russian scene suddenly, as it were, and not as the result of a protracted process of evolution. Further, Moscow received the motifs of the new style not in their pristine forms, directly from the West, but in a roundabout way, from the South, from the Ukraine, which in turn received them from Poland and Lithuania. The baroque of the Ukraine, though undoubtedly a provincialized version of the universal style, has many local peculiarities, and even its brash pomposity is infused with a distinctly indigenous flavor.

Russia also received from the Ukraine the type of peculiar wooden tent church in which the tent pyramid consists not of one continuous octagonal cone, gradually narrowing to a point, but is a structure composed of a series of octagonal prisms gradually diminishing in size and culminating in small cupolas. This type was translated from wood into stone, and out of its elements a new unique style was evolved and became known as the "Moscow or Naryshkin Baroque."[3] In some ways this mode, though short lived, is one of the brightest phenomena of Russian architecture.

Its outstanding characteristics are a unique application of brick and white stone in the decoration of façades, an extraordinary felicity and nobility of architectural ornament, and a classic simplicity and clarity of composition, with an almost fairy-tale wealth of detail, often a foreign derivation but imaginatively transformed into a clearly expressed national style. In a little over twenty-five years this style developed, grew to maturity, and achieved a finish and a distinct flavor which is still the marvel and pride of Muscovy.

One of the most delightful examples of this style is the Church of the Intercession of the Holy Virgin at Fili, the estate of the boyar Naryshkin in Moscow (Plate 95). This graceful structure was conceived and executed in 1693 with such perfection that few other churches (the church at Nerl near Vladimir and some of the churches and belfries in Novgorod) can be mentioned as its rivals. To quote Grabar', "Everything about this church, from top to bottom, is matchless; its plan, the very enticing idea of the

[3] Boyar Naryshkin was the maternal uncle of Peter I.

sweep of its widely extended grand stairways leading to large terraces out of which rises the body of the church, its finely perceived, carefully studied, elegant, and well-proportioned silhouette, and the lacy belts that crown its walls; everywhere and in everything there is the hand of a great poet and an architect-magician."[4] The church is placed on an elevated terrace-like substructure. An open gallery served by three monumental stairways surrounds the four-lobed base. Over the base rises a series of octagonal prisms, diminishing in size and leading up to a small terminal cupola. The central element is surrounded by semicircular appurtenances, one of which serves as a sanctuary, the others as vestibules or narthexes. The general silhouette is reminiscent of the stately Church of the Ascension at Kolomenskoye (Plate 73).

The style was mainly patronized by the Naryshkins. They were well acquainted with the various manifestations of the baroque and contributed much to its cultivation—hence the name, "Naryshkin Baroque." The church embodies many baroque elements in its interior, which is almost as rich in ornament as the exterior. The iconostasis and the pulpit are finely carved and brilliantly decorated.

It is interesting to contrast the delightful church of Fili (Plate 95) with another church built in the same decade, the Church of the Miracle of the Virgin at Dubrovitsy near Moscow (Plate 98), built in 1690–1704 by Prince Vasili Golitsyn.[5] It is a white stone structure on a four-lobed base. The tower, which is completely covered with elaborate carving, looks like a piece of sculptured ivory. The architecture of the church typifies the state of mind of many of the Europe-oriented members of the nobility at the time Peter the Great came to the throne.

The striking interior and exterior opulence of this church, where formal religious sculpture appears for the first time in a

[4] *Istoriya russkago iskusstva* (1909), I, 20.

[5] Prince Golitsyn was mentor of Peter the Great, later became chief adviser, lover, and confederate of Peter's half-sister Sophia during her regency, 1682–89.

Russian church, is explained by the whimsy of an impetuous and self-indulging Europe-worshiping prince, who, probably abetted by the tsar himself, dared to introduce such innovations and break the centuries-long traditions of Russian church architecture. Its lavish and meticulously carved decorations, in their novelty and sumptuousness, are reminiscent of the French decorative devices of the sixteenth century. French mannerisms are especially noticeable in the rusticated monumental substructure and in the playfully worked architraves and settings of the dormer windows. It was an extremely expensive, striking, and daring structure, and, in its day, created much heated discussion and aroused the sullen, if silent, resentment of the clergy. Yet every nobleman of the period was envious and eager to adorn his estate with a church of somewhat the same style.

PLATE 96: *Church of the Holy Trinity*, Troitzkoye-Lykovo, near Moscow, *ca.* 1700.

PLATE 95: *Church of the Holy Virgin*, Fili, Moscow, 1693.

PLATE 97: *Novodevichei Monastery*, Moscow, sixteenth-seventeenth centuries: panoramic view (below), the Church of the Transfiguration over the entrance gate, 1687–89 (above), and the Bell Tower, 1690 (left).

PLATE 98: *Church of the Miracle of the Virgin,* Dubrovitsy, near Moscow, 1690–1704, and floor plan (right).

PLATE 99: *Church of the Archangel Gabriel* (Menshikov Tower), Moscow, main entrance, 1705–1707.

PLATE 100: *Moscow Kremlin,* modern times.

PLATE 101: *Red Square,* modern times.

PLATE 103: *Trinity Tower*, Kremlin, Moscow, substructure late fifteenth century, superstructure, 1672–88.

PLATE 102: *Kremlin Wall*, Moscow: the Tsar's Tower, 1680 (left); the Beklemishev Tower, seventeenth century (right).

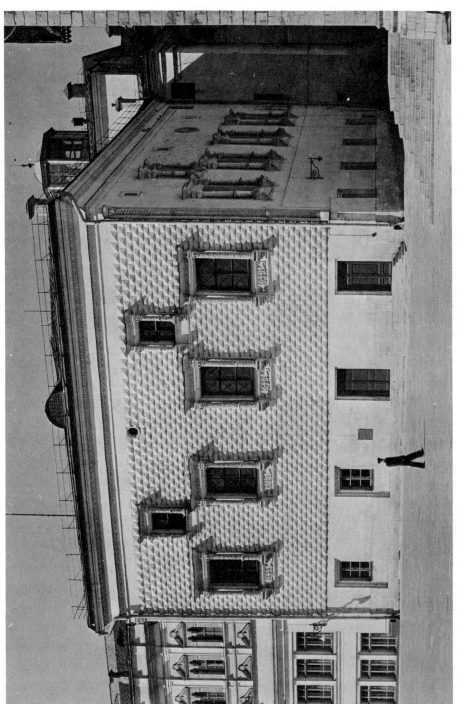

PLATE 104: *Granovitaya Palata*, Kremlin, Moscow, 1487–91.

PLATE 105: *Vaulted Hall*, the Granovitaya Palata, in modern times.

PLATE 106: *Window*, with carved stone ornament, the Granovitaya Palata.

PLATE 107: *Terem Palace*, Kremlin, Moscow, 1636.

PLATE 108: *Terem Palace*, Kremlin, Moscow: side elevation of upper stories and cross section of lower (left), 1635–36; Golden Tsaritsa Chamber, latter sixteenth century (right).

PLATE 109: *Terem Palace*, Kremlin, Moscow: entrance door, facing the Church of the Saviour Behind the Golden Grille (left); window, opposite the Church of the Saviour Behind the Golden Grille (above); window, facing the Armory Museum (right).

PLATE 110: *Corridor*, Terem Palace, Kremlin, Moscow, 1635.

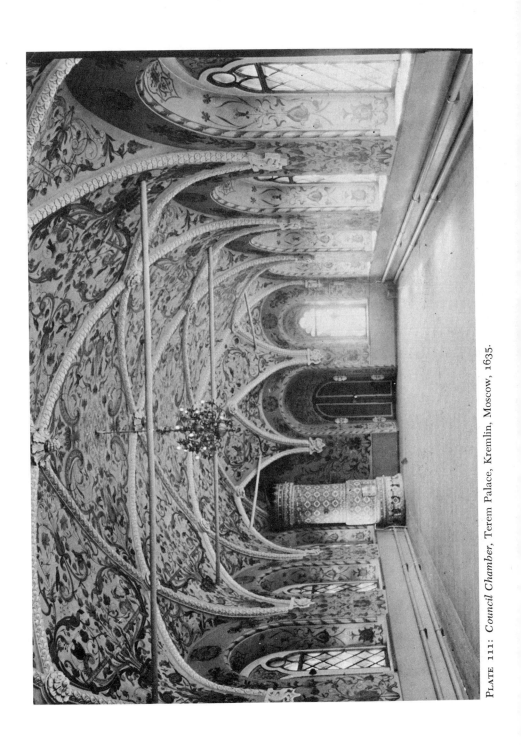

PLATE 111: *Council Chamber*, Terem Palace, Kremlin, Moscow, 1635.

PLATE 112: *Stairway*, Terem Palace, Kremlin, Moscow, 1635.

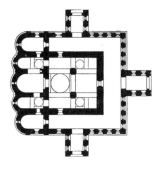

PLATE 113: *Church of St. John the Precursor,* Tolchkovo, Yaroslavl, 1671–87: view from the northeast (right); floor plan (above); detail of porch interior (bottom).

PLATE 114: *Belfry,* Church of the Nativity of Christ, Yaroslavl, seventeenth century.

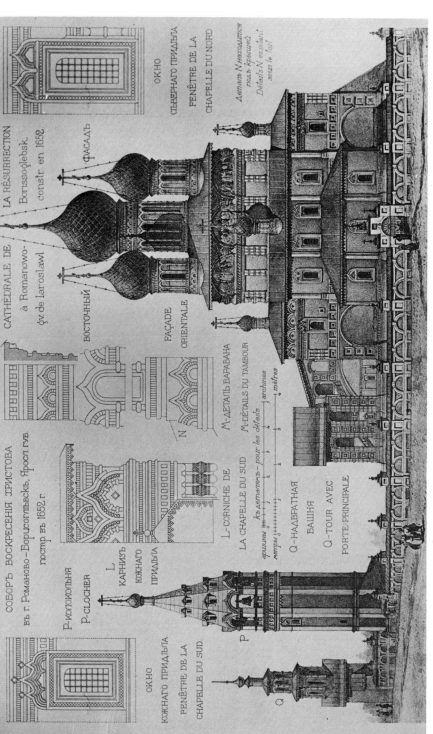

СОБОРЪ ВОСКРЕСЕНIЯ ХРИСТОВА
Въ г. Романово-Борисоглѣбскъ, Яросл губ.
постр въ 1652 г.

CATHÉDRALE DE LA RÉSURRECTION
Borissoglebsk,
à Romanowo-
gv. de Iaroslawl
constr. en 1652.

Р-КОЛОКОЛЬНЯ
P-CLOCHER

L-КАРНИЗЪ ЮЖНАГО ПРИДѢЛА
L-CORNICHE DE LA CHAPELLE DU SUD

ОКНО ЮЖНАГО ПРИДѢЛА
FENÊTRE DE LA CHAPELLE DU SUD

Q-НАДВРАТНАЯ БАШНЯ
Q-TOUR AVEC PORTE PRINCIPALE

ВОСТОЧНЫЙ ФАСАДЪ
FAÇADE ORIENTALE

М-ДЕТАЛЬ БАРАБАНА
M-DÉTAILS DU TAMBOUR

Детали N находятся под крышей!
Détails N existant sous le toit!

ФАСАДЪ

ОКНО СѢВЕРНАГО ПРИДѢЛА
FENÊTRE DE LA CHAPELLE DU NORD

Из деталяхъ—pour les details   3 archines
аршины   4 metres

PLATE 115: *Cathedral of the Resurrection*, east façade, Romanov-Borisoglebsk, Yaroslavl province, 1652–70. Legend: L. detail of cornice of the South Chapel, M. detail of the drum, P. Belfry, Q. Tower over the main entrance. Upper-left corner: window of the South Chapel. Upper-right corner: window of the North Chapel.

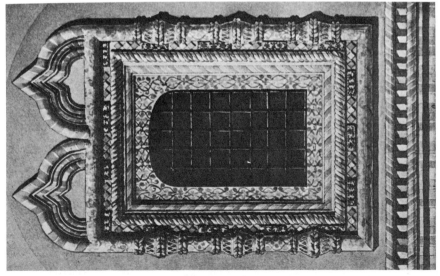

PLATE 116: *Cathedral of the Resurrection*, Romanov-Borisoglebsk: detail of gallery window in the South Chapel (left); enclosed porch (above).

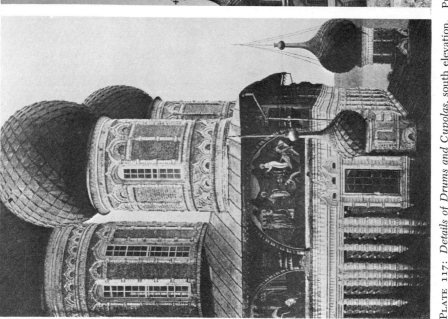

PLATE 117: *Details of Drums and Cupolas*, south elevation, Cathedral of the Resurrection, Romanov-Borisoglebsk.

PLATE 118: *Church of St. John Chrysostom, Korovniki, Yaroslavl, 1649–54*: view of Church and Bell Tower from southwest (left); window frame on east wall (right).

PLATE 120: *The Annunciation,* Moscow School (?), late fourteenth century.

PLATE 119: *Saints Boris and Gleb on Horseback,* Moscow School, 1340.

PLATE 121: *Apostle Paul*, attributed to Rublev, Moscow School, *ca.* 1407.

PLATE 122: *Old Testament Trinity*, by Rublev, Moscow School, *ca.* 1411 (?).

PLATE 123: *Old Testament Trinity*, angel at left, detail from Plate 122.

PLATE 124: *Old Testament Trinity,* angel in middle, detail from Plate 122.

PLATE 125: *Old Testament Trinity,* angel at right, detail from Plate 122.

PLATE 126: *Head of Christ,* attributed to Rublev, Moscow School, *ca.* 1409

PLATE 127: *The Saviour in Glory,* attributed to Rublev, *ca.* 1420.

PLATE 128: *The Zvenigorod Nativity*, Moscow School, early fifteenth century.

PLATE 129: *Aleksei, the Moscow Metropolitan,* attributed to Dionysius, sixteenth century.

PLATE 130: *The Obnorskoye Crucifixion*, by Dionysius, 1500.

PLATE 131: *John the Theologian in Meditation*, Moscow School, sixteenth century.

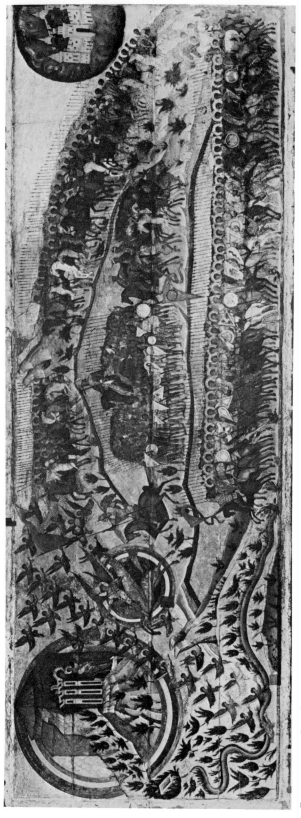

PLATE 132: *The Church Militant*, Moscow School, sixteenth century.

PLATE 133: *The Image of Our Lady Odigitriya*, Moscow School, sixteenth century.

PLATE 134: *The Virgin and Child,* Stroganov School, sixteenth century.

PLATE 135: *Head of Archangel Michael*, from a triptych by a pupil of Prokopius Chirin, Stroganov School, first half of the seventeenth century.

PLATE 136: *St. John the Warrior,* by Prokopius Chirin, Stroganov School, early seventeenth century.

PLATE 138: *Prince Skopin-Shuisky,* Moscow School, early seventeenth century.

PLATE 137: *The Mandilion Portrait of Christ,* Northern Provincial School, seventeenth century.

PLATE 139: *The Annunciation with the Acathist*, by Ushakov, Kazanets, and Kondratyev, Moscow School, 1659.

PLATE 140: *The Traveling Magi,* detail from Plate 139.

PLATE 141: *The Vernicle, or the Holy Mandilion of Edessa,* by Ushakov, Moscow School, 1657.

PLATE 142: *Christ, the Great Archbishop,* by Ushakov, Moscow School, last quarter of the seventeenth century.

PLATE 143: *Iconostasis*, Uspensky Cathedral, Kremlin, Moscow.

PLATE 144: *The Shroud of Christ*, detail, 1555.

PLATE 146: *Sakkos of Patriarch Adrian, 1691.*

PLATE 145: *Sakkos of Patriarch Nikon, 1654.*

PLATE 148: *Book of the Gospels*, gift of Boyarin B. M. Morozov, 1669.

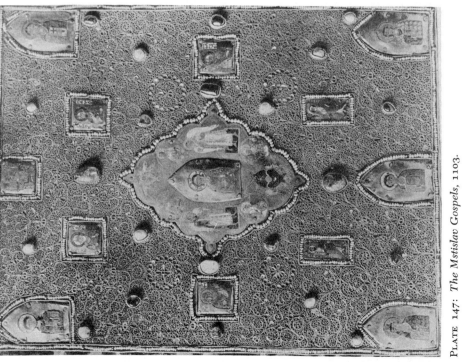

PLATE 147: *The Mstislav Gospels*, 1103.

PLATE 149: *Book of the Gospels*, 1499.

PLATE 150: *Crown of Patriarch Nikon.*

PLATE 151: *Silver Ciborium*, from the Cathedral of St. Sophia, Novgorod, eleventh-twelfth century.

PLATE 152: *Tabernacle Called "Jerusalem,"* 1486.

PLATE 153: *Silver Gilt Vase*, from the Cathedral of St. Sophia, Novgorod, twelfth century.

PLATE 154: *Holy Water Container*, copper, from the Epiphany Monastery, Rostov, 1553.

PLATE 155: *Silver Panagiyarion, 1436.*

PLATE 156: *Chalice*, of Boyarin D. I. Godunov, 1599.

PLATE 157: *Panagiya of Patriarch Philaret.*

PLATE 158: *Silver Panagiya*, with applied gilt ornament, fifteenth century.

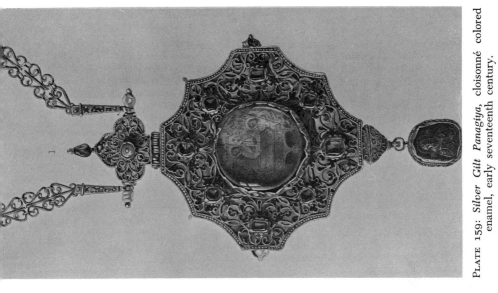

PLATE 159: *Silver Gilt Panagiya*, cloisonné colored enamel, early seventeenth century.

PLATE 160: *Pastoral Staff of Archbishop Dmitri,* seventeenth century.

PLATE 161: *Pectoral Cross of Tsar Mikhail Feodorovich.*

PLATE 162: *Ancient Embroidered* Barmy *(Imperial Collar).*

PLATE 163: *Crown of St. Vladimir,* "the Cap of Monomakh," with (above) detail of filigree work, thirteenth century.

PLATE 164: *Orb of Monomakh.*

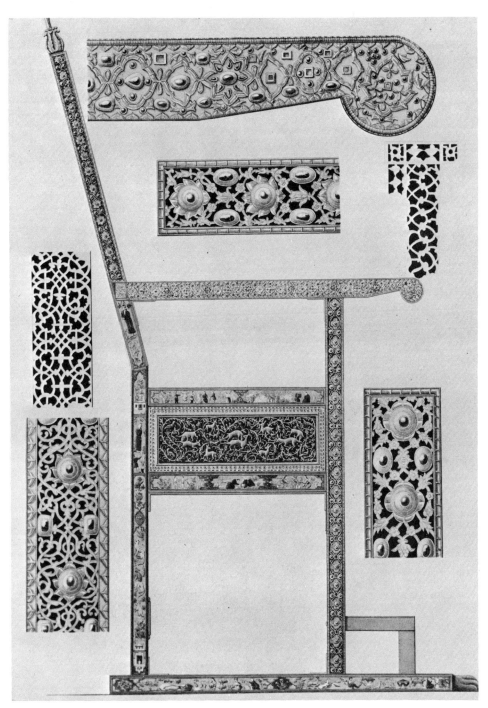

PLATE 165: *Diamond Throne of Tsar Aleksei Mikhailovich.*

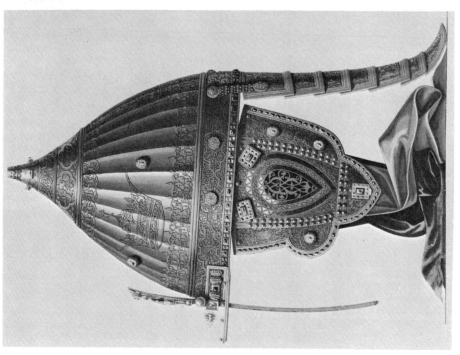

PLATE 166: *Helmet of Tsar Mikhail Feodorovich, and* (right) *detail of ear-guard.*

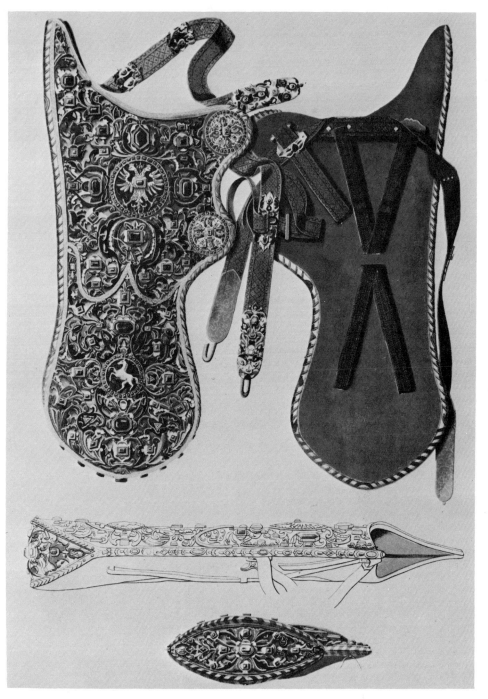

PLATE 167: Saadak (Quiver) of Tsar Mikhail Feodorovich.

PLATE 168: *Gunpowder Flask, seventeenth century.*

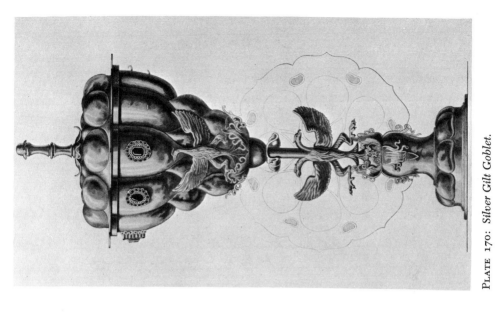

PLATE 170: *Silver Gilt Goblet.*

PLATE 169: *Gold Plate of Tsar Aleksei Mikhailovich.*

PLATE 171: *Gold-lidded Cup*, late seventeenth century.

PLATE 172: *Silver* Bratina, of Councilor M. Danilov, 1627–30.

PLATE 173: *Memorial Silver Gilt* Bratina *of Tsar Mikhail Feodorovich.*

PLATE 174: *Casket,* Usol'sk enamel, second half of the seventeenth century.

PLATE 175: *Repository of the Robe of Our Lord*, seventeenth century.

PLATE 176: *Church Chandelier*, thirteenth century.

PLATE 177: *The "Golden" Grille,* Terem Palace, Kremlin, Moscow, seventeenth century, and (left) detail from grille.

PLATE 179: *Copper Jug* (Kungan).

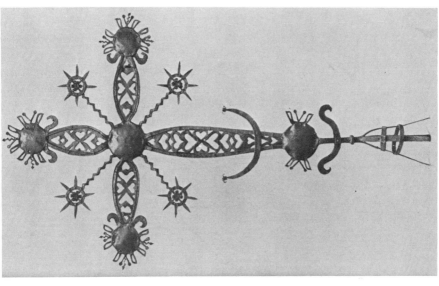

PLATE 178: *Wrought Iron Cross,* dome of the Trinity
Church, Tikhvin Monastery.

PLATE 181: *Throne of Ivan the Terrible, detail of canopy.*

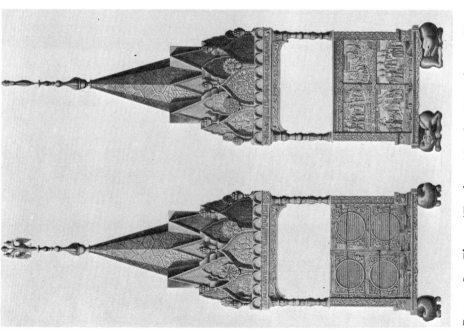

PLATE 180: *Throne (Tsarskoye Mesto) of Ivan the Terrible.*

PLATE 182: *Throne of Ivan the Terrible,* details of carved panels.

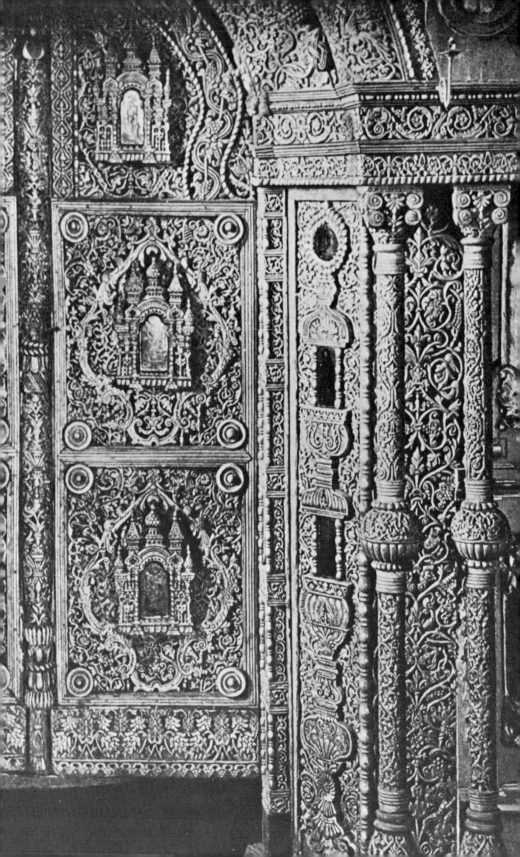

PLATE 184: *Door Panel and Icon Frame*, detail from Plate 183.

PLATE 183: *Detail of the Royal Doors*, of the iconostasis in the Church of St. John the Precursor, Tolchkovo, Yaroslavl.

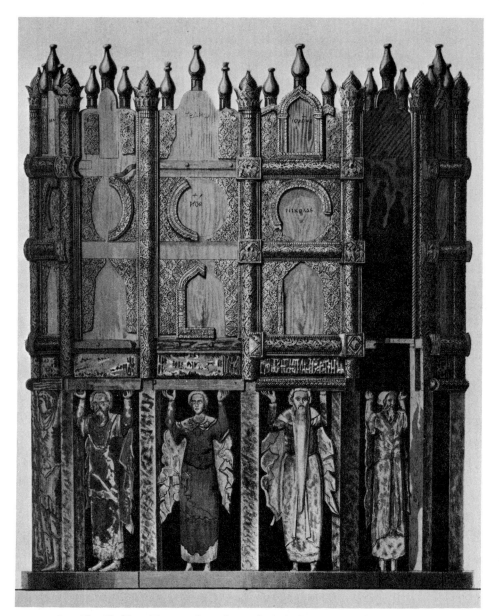

PLATE 185: *The Chaldean Furnace,* from the Cathedral of St. Sophia, Novgorod.

PLATE 186: *Head of St. John the Precursor, seventeenth-century woodcarving.*

PLATE 188: *Glazed Clay Pitcher*, seventeenth century.

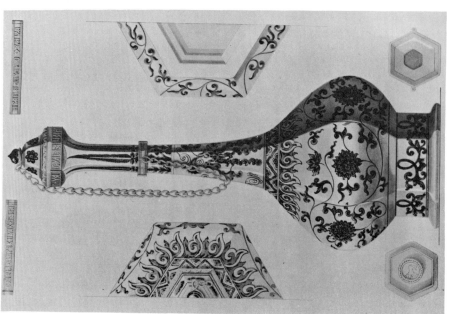

PLATE 187: *Porcelain Flagon of Tsarevitch Ivan Ivanovich*, sixteenth century.

The Moscow School of Painting

M oscow, which had appeared on the historical scene relatively late, did not have her own original artistic culture
in the twelfth century. She had to make use of the accumulated
heritage of the older Russian cities, and it was only natural that
she would first adhere to the traditions of the Vladimir-Suzdal
principality to which she had long been closely tied. The absence
of early monuments prevents us from tracing the first independent steps in the development of the Moscow School of painting.
The frequent raids of the Tatars had systematically destroyed
much that was of cultural value. The oldest archives of the principality, the rare manuscripts, icons, and the costly liturgical
furnishings that, in the words of the chronicler, "filled the Moscow churches to the rafters" were all put to the torch in 1382
by the Tatar General Tokhtamysh.

But late in the fourteenth century came a change that was the
beginning of the flowering of Moscow art. Moscow emissaries
visited Constantinople frequently, and a wave of Greek and
southern Slavonic influence came over Russia. That wave of influence was due in part to the immigration of many Serbian and
Bulgarian clerics fleeing the Turks, who had just put an end to
the independence of their countries. Many Greek artists settled
in Novgorod and Moscow, and a number of Byzantine works of
the Palaeologue Renaissance were brought into Russia.

Moscow icon painting was developing under the best conditions and auspices. To begin with, it derived from the Vladimir-

Suzdal School, which for the early period stood highest in artistic skill, traditions, and aims. Later, when icon painting in Russia began really to flourish, Moscow benefited by having the best artists and the best models from the developed schools of Novgorod and Pskov. Novgorod and Moscow experienced the influence of the final brilliant stage of the Palaeologue Renaissance, reaching its highest point in the last quarter of the fourteenth century. This is particularly reflected in the works of the celebrated Theophanes the Greek, who established his reputation as a great icon painter in Novgorod in the 1370's. In the middle of the 1390's he was invited to Moscow, where he and his Russian assistants decorated the interior of the Church of the Nativity of the Virgin. In 1399 he was working again with his pupils in the old Cathedral of Archangel Michael. In 1405, assisted by the Elder Prokhor from Gorodets and by Andrei Rublev, he executed the iconostasis for the Cathedral of the Annunciation in the Moscow Kremlin.

To Theophanes himself may be ascribed the most important tier of the iconostasis—the enthroned Christ flanked by the Virgin and John the Precursor, and the figures of archangels, apostles, and other saints. The figures are tall, somewhat severe, with dark faces and long thin arms, sustained in rich contrasting tones, full of subdued pathos. These paintings are marked by a close adherence to Byzantine standards of the fourteenth century, but their highly original style places them beyond the bounds of Byzantine art.

The artistic interests of late fourteenth-century Moscow were not limited exclusively to Byzantine art. Her artists became familiar with the works of the southern Slavs. Moreover, by this time Moscow had its own well-established tradition and its cadre of artists who approached problems in their own way. The Byzantine tradition underwent its first vital transformation on Russian soil. In Moscow this movement culminated in that great artist Andrei Rublev.

Rublev (*ca.* 1360–1430), the most significant figure among

Russian icon painters, was a monk of the Trinity and St. Sergius Monastery near Moscow, where he probably received his artistic training. Later he was transferred to the Spas Andronikov Monastery (now the Rublev Museum) in Moscow, where he spent the rest of his life. It was the time when Moscow, rapidly forging ahead to the very front of the disunited and feuding Russian principalities, took the lead in the struggle against the Tatars. The Mongol defeat on the field of Kulikovo resulted in an upsurge in national consciousness and vastly increased the political importance of the Moscow principality.

The decisive years in Rublev's creative growth were the 1390's, when Moscow was fast becoming a major cultural center exposed to all the latest trends of Byzantine and Serbian art. It is highly probable that Rublev had the opportunity to study the work of Theophanes, the leading figure in Moscow art circles. Although Rublev's aesthetic ideals were entirely different from those of the Greek master, the impassioned images of Theophanes' saints must have made a deep impression on the younger artist. It was probably Theophanes who introduced him to the latest trends in Byzantine art, enlarged his color range, taught him new composition devices, and prepared him for the creation of the classic form of the Russian iconostasis.

Traces of his first activities as a mature artist can be seen in Zvenigorod. Here are his early works (the frescoes of the Assumption Cathedral and the icons of the iconostasis in the Cathedral of the Nativity) which throw light on his creative development. Most of his later artistic activities are closely connected with Moscow and its nearby cities and monasteries. He decorated the walls of the cathedrals of the Annunciation at Moscow (1405) and the Assumption at Vladimir (1408) with frescoes.

The best known of his paintings is the icon, *The Old Testament Trinity* (Plates 122–25), painted about 1411 for the iconostasis of the Trinity and St. Sergius Monastery. The subject— the visit of the three angels to Abraham and Sarah—was popular in Byzantine art. In this icon the severe symbolism of the Byzantine tradition has been transformed into something more intimately human. The angels acquire an aspect of gentle grace and supernatural luminosity. In the beauty of the colors, the spirituality of the faces, and the quiet concentration expressed in the three figures we can observe a distinct non-Byzantine feeling, but even more important is the novel, peculiarly Russian mood of dreamy sublimation. Rublev's *Trinity* is one of the great creations of medieval Russian painting. In it we have the unearthliness that is the icon's highest merit.

The icons of the festival tier from the Annunciation Cathedral, the *Last Judgment,* and a few other works are attributed to Rublev. A great similarity to his style appears also in the big half-figure paintings of a *deësis* (the image of the Saviour between the Virgin Mary and John the Precursor) discovered by chance in a half-destroyed state in a storehouse of the Zvenigorod Cathedral. The few authentic works of Rublev (Plates 121–27) help one to realize the degree of independence attained by fifteenth-century Russian art. Before Rublev, Moscow painting was devoid of a clearly defined individuality. It expressed a struggle between two sharply differing trends. The Byzantine current was stubbornly resisting the native Russian. Rublev was the very first to change this condition. While using the Byzantine legacy, he transformed it. To quote V. N. Lazarev:

> Rublev definitely broke with the Byzantine severity and asceticism. From the Byzantine legacy he extracted its antique Hellenistic core and freed it from all the later ascetic stratifications. His art is gentler, more poetic, and more luminous than that of his predecessors. The pigments of his palette are derived not from the traditional color canons, but from his native landscape. His wonderful blues are suggested by the blue of the spring sky; his whites are reminiscent of the whites of the Russian birch trees; his green color is close to the color of unripe rye; his golden ochre recalls the colors of fallen autumn leaves; and in his dark green colors

there is something of the duskiness of the Russian coniferous forest.[1]

He is justly considered the founder of the Moscow School of painting, whose influence ranged far afield; it was powerful with his contemporaries and endured long after his death, making the fifteenth century the golden age of the Russian icon. Rublev was beatified by the Russian Orthodox church, one of the very few artists ever to be numbered among the saints.

It was during Rublev's time that the peculiarly Russian decorative ensemble of icons known as the iconostasis was formulated and became characteristic of the Muscovite church. Novgorod, Pskov, and Vladimir-Suzdal all contributed, in various degrees, to the development of the iconostasis, but it was at Moscow, in the works of Theophanes the Greek, Prokhor of Gorodets, Andrei Rublev, and Daniil Chernyi, that its classical form was evolved and perfected.

The inconostasis is the screen or partition separating the sanctuary, where the sacrament of the Eucharist is celebrated, from the nave, where the congregation stands. It serves as a frame and background for the many icons which are arranged in tiers in a traditionally prescribed manner. Iconostases in the form of a barrier between the sanctuary and the rest of the church existed in Byzantine churches from ancient times. The form and height of these barriers varied. Sometimes they were solid low marble walls or balustrades; at other times they were high latticed screens or arcades. The sanctuary barrier of the Justinian era (527–65), a colonnade surmounted by an architrave, began to grow more complex very early. At first, the architrave was embellished by carved symbols—usually a cross. Towards the end of the ninth century, half-length figures of Christ flanked by saints began to be put upon the architrave. These icons were usually painted on a wooden panel, which the Greeks called *templon*. This Byzantine form of the sanctuary barrier was

[1] In Grabar', *Istoriya russkogo iskusstva* (1953), III, 184.

adopted by the Russians from the Greeks, but the Russians gradually transformed it by increasing the number of icons and tiers. The ancient *templon*, the triptych containing the figure of Christ, was renamed *deisus* (a corruption of the Greek word *deësis*, meaning prayer or supplication). This composition came to embody the idea of intercession by the Virgin and John the Precursor beseeching the Saviour to forgive the sins of humanity.

The gradual evolution and enrichment of the iconostasis took place in the Vladimir-Suzdal and Novgorod regions during the thirteenth and fourteenth centuries. In Moscow, by the fifteenth century, it had reached an impressive multi-tiered height, each tier containing a specified assortment of icons. Its form was to become classic for many generations. Definite positions were assigned to certain iconic subjects, and the icons were arranged in five (occasionally seven) tiers. Their disposition was indicated by the church fathers, primarily with an eye to the inherent symbolic significance of the various subjects and their visual storytelling impact upon the worshipers. The complex iconography of the church dogma—the Revelation, Incarnation, and Redemption—formerly depicted by the mosaics of the central dome and apse drum and by the wall frescoes was gradually incorporated in the iconostasis and its central doors. The Pantocrator, the prophets, and forefathers were transferred from the dome to the prophets' and forefathers' tiers; the church festivals, from the vaults and walls to the holiday tiers; the *deësis* from the central apse to the *deësis* tier; the evangelists from the pendentives to the central or royal doors through which only the officiating priest and tsar might enter the sanctuary.

As an ensemble, the iconostasis provided a visual record of church history, moving from the Old Testament patriarchs and prophets in the upper tier to the local saints in the lowest tier. Most interesting is the way in which the Muscovite artists united the symbolic theme of the iconostasis with a purely decorative function. They developed and expanded the traditional Byzantine image of the *deësis*, placing these three panels in the center above the royal doors and treating them as the nucleus of the composition. On the right and left, they added two archangels, two apostles, two fathers of the church, and two martyrs, a sequence of majestic figures forming the *chin* (the range of archangels, saints, and church fathers flanking the central *deësis*) converging towards the center of the iconostasis and detaching themselves as slender silhouettes on a golden or bright-colored background. The surviving iconostasis of the Cathedral of the Annunciation in the Moscow Kremlin—with its huge figures of the *chin* (forty by eighty inches) and the extensive cycle of the church festivals—marked the birth of the classical form of the Russian iconostasis and prepared the ground for those of the Assumption Cathedral in Vladimir and in the Trinity and St. Sergius Monastery. Their richness of color and beauty of composition are superb examples of pre-Petrine art.

The iconostasis was addressed to a large, mixed, mostly illiterate congregation. It demanded the development of a special art form which would provide a thorough integration of a large number of figures, each preserving its individuality but all woven into a single unit. The height of the structure prompted the artist to outline the figures, other than the representation of the festivals, in a monumental style with a clear-cut silhouette. This vigorous portrayal of figures influenced the treatment of smaller icons—preserving the elongated proportion of the figures, the simplification of the color scheme, and the general pattern. The design of the iconostasis, together with the number and disposition of its various elements, remained for a long time the principal theme of the Moscow School of painting. It created a vogue for complex icons whose composition contained crowds resembling an iconostasis. The complex type of icon with its conventional hieratic images had to relate graphically episodes from the Holy Scriptures, the lives of the saints, the meaning of holidays; in fact, all that might interest the pious but illiterate man in the domain of religion. Thus the icon became the Bible for the masses.

Icon painting continued to flourish throughout the fifteenth century. There was, moreover, an ever increasing demand for icons, especially small ones, from the Moscow nobility and the wealthy merchants, for use in private chapels. The common people were also aspiring to have icons in their homes, several if possible, since each image of the Virgin or of some particularly revered saint was believed to possess its own supernatural powers and protection. One could hardly have too many. The icon became an inseparable companion of the Orthodox Russian from birth to death, and it was used to impart blessings on all significant events. It was transmitted as a family heirloom through generations or presented as a precious gift to the church. It became usual then to place an icon in the far right-hand corner of each room, as well as at the head of each bed in the house.

The outstanding icon painter of the second half of the fifteenth century was Dionysius (Dionisi, *ca.* 1440–1508). His artistic activities coincide with the period of centralization of the Russian state, when Moscow experienced a great political and cultural upsurge and her art began to acquire an all-Russian character. It was during this time that the numerous Russian monasteries became centers of commerce and industry, possessors of vast lands and great wealth. Thus the entire mode of monastic life acquired a more worldly character, which is reflected in the ecclesiastical art of the period.

Dionysius' paintings are marked by the extreme, elongated stylizing of his figures combined with a subtle design. His manner of presentation reveals the interest he felt in the technical aspects of painting, especially composition. In 1480, with three of his co-workers (Pope Timothy, Yarets, and Kon), he was invited to Moscow to execute an iconostasis for the Cathedral of the Assumption, just completed by Fioravanti. In 1484, Paisi the Elder and Dionysius, with his sons Theodosius (Feodor) and Vladimir, painted an extensive series of icons for the Monastery of Volokolamsk. In 1500–1502 he was working with his sons in the Monastery of St. Therapont on the White Lake. The frescoes of the Church of the Nativity of the Virgin in this monastery, executed late in his life, are unquestionably his greatest achievement—truly superb monuments of Russian pre-Petrine art.

Like that of the icon painters of the Rublev period, Dionysius' work was done in collaboration with a team of co-workers. The chroniclers, in recording certain works, usually mention his name with the names of several others. We have only three specimens of easel painting which can be with almost certainty ascribed to his brush: two large icons of the Moscow metropolitans, St. Peter and St. Aleksei (Plate 129), an icon of St. Cyril of Byeloozersk, and an icon of the Crucifixion (Plate 130). These have all the earmarks of the famous master, who loved tall, slender figures with small heads, rhythmic lines, and delicate coloring.

The work of Dionysius represents the creative searchings of the fifteenth century at their height, and at the same time opens up a new era. There is much in his work that is closely related to the classic period of Russian icon painting, but there is in it also a foreshadowing of the beginning of the crisis in the artistic ideals of the Rublev era. Dionysius played an important role in the history of medieval Russian art. By following the path indicated by Rublev but at the same time exercising his own genius, he immortalized the art of his predecessor and made it the common property of all the Russian people. With Dionysius the splendorous, festive, exultant art of Moscow became the leading trend in Russia. It began to be accepted as a standard by provincial art schools and imitated everywhere.

The Sixteenth Century

By the middle of the sixteenth century the Tatar yoke had been cast off, and the last remnants of independence of the various detached principalities had gradually come to an end. The Moscow Kremlin became the center of the artistic life of the country. Here, at the tsar's court, the activities of the state's best architects, painters, designers, scribes, engravers, and craftsmen were concentrated. Work was carried on directly under the supervision of the metropolitan and the tsar. Icon painters were first summoned to Moscow to participate in the unprecedented building and decorating of cathedrals and churches. Scribes, illuminators, and engravers were gathered to compile and illustrate the huge folios of the Nikonian Chronicles and other literary works. These artists, writers, and craftsmen brought with them their individual tastes and their local traditions. The stronger and more individualistic masters combined the principles inherited from Byzantium and those surviving from Novgorod with purely decorative and graphic principles whose roots lay in Russian peasant art. Especially during the second half of the sixteenth century, icon painting is found more and more to contain characteristics of rustic art and themes from real life.

This evolution first became noticeable in the gradual elimination of the Hellenistic setting of the icon—landscape and architecture. Greek basilicas with their porticoes and atria were replaced by the tent-shaped roofs and onion-bulb cupolas of Russian churches. The white walls of these churches and their architectural forms furnished a new ornamental motif. Moreover, many icons now began to represent native Russian saints and episodes in their lives; St. Sergius of Radonezh, St. Cyril of Byeloozersk, and renowned "miracle workers" furnished subjects not derived from Byzantine art. In depicting the life of a saint, the artist found it necessary to reproduce also all that surrounded him, so that types, clothing, churches, landscape, all had to be Russian. Some of these icons, dating from the time of the death of the saint, were no doubt efforts to show him as he actually looked.

The period was marked by the development of literary taste influenced by the large diffusion of ecclesiastical literature, as well as by moral, biographical, and historical works. Side by side with tracts dealing with problems of church doctrine appeared mystical interpretations of various passages of Holy Writ and the Apocrypha. Painting, therefore, was faced with the task of expressing this new interest in its own terms, and the illustrative element clearly begins to appear in the art of this century. The icon ceased to be merely the symbolic representation of the other world. New iconographic subjects appeared: some illustrate the mystical interpretation of the church dogmas; others represent parables and legends and are therefore imbued with a didactic, moral aim. Characteristics of the Byzantine and Novgorodian traditions were interwoven with the Moscow trend, as well as with certain elements of the Renaissance from the West.

There was a notable intensification of the struggle for overcoming the conventional form of iconography, for the right of the artist to greater freedom of creation and for self-expression. At the Church Assembly of 1551, Tsar Ivan IV raised the question: was it permissible to depict in icons people who are still alive? He received the reply that in certain circumstances it was.

The long period of consistent development was, however, marked, throughout its course, by certain changes in direction. The most important of these came in the middle of the sixteenth century, when a radical transformation began to take place, its main factors being the introduction of stronger Western influences and the weakening of the Byzantine traditions. New formulas for icon painting were adopted by the Church Council of 1554 and later codified. The practice of the art was, to some extent, transferred from the monks to lay artists, who at the bidding of rulers or private patrons went from one place to another. The local icon-painting schools became fused into a single national school or were replaced by a series of private workshops.

The impact of new ideas was expressed in icon painting by innovation in composition in the so-called mystico-didactic style, the introduction of which was in part the direct result of Western (Roman Catholic) influence. Previously, religious art had been almost exclusively confined to simple subjects: portraits of Christ, the Blessed Virgin, the apostles and saints, or scenes from the Gospels. But in the sixteenth century, artists began "theological philosophizing"; some compositions were so complex that they required an explanatory commentary. Artists developed liturgical themes and created entirely original cycles of frescoes, new in content and in technique of painting. In reply to a question about one of these icons, the leading authority of the period, Maxim the Greek, replied that such icons "are not painted anywhere but in Russia."[2] At the end of the fifteenth century and during the sixteenth century, Russian icon painting was indeed uniquely innovatory in content and made interesting and important advances in the techniques necessary for more complex and more detailed, frequently multifigured compositions. This was a new chapter not only in the history of Russian religious art but also in the history of thought in Muscovite Russia, in which original and more speculative concepts struggle for expression in new compositions and techniques.

After the great fire of 1547, which nearly destroyed Moscow, it was necessary to paint new icons for the Cathedral of the Annunciation. Artists were brought from Pskov and Novgorod to do the work, and some of the new icons were painted in a manner contrary to the traditions of the old masters. This and a number of other related social and religious tendencies had a disturbing effect. The tsar found it necessary to convene a council of the wisest clergy, bring before it a list of all the various abuses visible in church and state, and devise means of reforming them.

The council, which became known as the Council of One Hundred Chapters (Stoglav Sobor), undertook a number of measures to establish orthodoxy in art and ritual. It published a series of general regulations dealing with icon paintings: icon painters "should be humble and mild men, not given to vain words, live

2 Maxim the Greek, theologian and philologist (1480–1556), was educated in Italy, where he was closely associated with prominent humanists of the period of the Renaissance. At the invitation of Grand Prince Vasili he came to Moscow in 1518 as translator and editor, translating a number of ecclesiastical books and undertaking the work of correcting the Russian theological books. He became involved in the ecclesiastical and political disputes that were raging at this time in Muscovy for which he was condemned to imprisonment in the Volokolam Monastery (1525–51).

piously, not indulge in quarrels or drink, keep their souls pure, and live under the supervision of their spiritual guides." The painters were formed into something like a guild subordinate to the ecclesiastical authorities; the bishops of every district were directed to "insist relentlessly that the master painters, all craftsmen, and their pupils should copy ancient patterns and not paint the Deity out of their own inventions." In the direction of idealization of types, the most they were allowed was to copy Rublev's style, which thus was perpetuated throughout the sixteenth century. In exercising the power of a centralizing state, then, Moscow subordinated to its authority and its tradition both the artists and the art of the Novgorod and Pskov schools.

The fire of 1547 caused enormous damage to the Kremlin palace; roofs were burned out and the gilded *terem* chambers were gutted. By order of the tsar the palace was rebuilt, and its exterior was decorated with carvings and statuary. Barberini, a traveler who visited Moscow in 1565, states that the roof of Ivan's palace was gilt. Another traveler, Mikhalon Litvin, writes that the palace was adorned with Greek statues in the manner of Phidias. The walls and vaulting of this palace, known as the Middle Golden, were frescoed in 1553 under the direction of Sylvester, the priest who was influential in the religious and moral upbringing of the boy Ivan.

The Russian historian P. Miliukov points out that at this time the state, to its own glorification, was collecting Russian Orthodox relics from every part of the country.[3] The Metropolitan Makari ordered all icon painters to be brought from Novgorod and Pskov to Moscow. These painters, working in the shops of the Oruzheinaya Palata ("academy" of art and engineering), under the general supervision of the tsar and his close advisers, developed their own school of painting. They introduced a series of allegorical and historical themes, glorifying the power and wisdom of the tsar, teaching obedience and humility, and bringing

[3] *Outlines of Russian Culture*, III, 38.

225

into Russian art an element of worldliness that clashed with the sacred quality. This opened new horizons for individual creation, freed art from the chains of ecclesiastical tradition, and made it more national and essentially much more Russian in feeling.

The frescoes and ornamentation of the Golden Chamber (Zolotaya Palata) are of special interest. These decorations show a change not only in direction, turning the Byzantine iconographic tradition towards feeling and expression, but in the very types, from Greek to Russian. Most strikingly, these decorations exemplify the characteristic trait of the epoch—the subservience of painting to the general directives of the central government. Here for the first time secular subjects appear in paintings having a definite program character and literary content.

The celebrated icon painter Simon Ushakov and another court official left a detailed description of the frescoes as they existed at the end of the seventeenth century.[4] Sacred and profane subjects were intermingled in the wall paintings of the chamber. They depicted scenes from the Bible as well as the earth with its waters and winds; the fiery circle of the sun and the circle of the moon; the air in the shape of a maiden; time winged with the four seasons; the circle of the creation; the sainted Russian princes; the baptism of St. Vladimir and Russia; events in the life of Vladimir Monomakh; the story of princes Boris and Gleb; and the edifying figures of Chastity, Reason, Purity, and Righteousness.

The corridor frescoes contain an entire theory of government. The tsar, youthful in appearance, is extolled as a righteous judge and fearless warrior; he distributes alms to the poor; from his hands flows water that sanctifies the people; he vanquishes impious foes. The inspirer of this series of pictures (thought to have been the priest Sylvester) for molding the mind and heart of

[4] For Ushakov's detailed description (1672) of the frescoes, see Bartenev, *Moskovsky Kreml'*, II, pp. 183–93, also Grabar'-Muratov, in Grabar', in *Istoriya russkogo iskusstva* (1953), VI, 320. The original manuscript was deposited in the Imperial Public Library, Petersburg in 1867.

the tsar is depicted in the guise of a wise hermit who acts as the young ruler's mentor.[5]

These allegorical frescoes were a distinct innovation, and many persons were offended, particularly by the nude and semi-nude figures. One "wench with naked arms, dancing with abandon," intended to represent "Lust," caused a storm. Viskovaty, Ivan's IV's state secretary, indignantly expressed to the tsar his doubts concerning the merits of the new trend in icon painting in general and of the frescoes in particular.[6] He resented the artists' painting "according to their own understanding and not according to sacred writings." However, Viskovaty dwelled only on minor details, his criticism evidently being aimed at annoying his rival, Sylvester. In 1554 an ecclesiastical council was convened to settle the matter, and the Metropolitan Makari succeeded in having Viskovaty's objections withdrawn.

The frescoes of Ivan's Golden Chamber reveal the influence of German and Italian-Flemish engravings. From this time on the influence of Western engraving on Russian painting grew steadily. These frescoes were in effect the precursors of those that appeared a century later on the walls of the Yaroslavl churches.

Ivan's successor, his son Feodor, exhibited no less taste for the arts and zeal for their development. The number of painters, workers in mosaics and gold, embroiderers, lapidaries, and enameler increased rapidly. The historian Karamzin writes that the Greek Archbishop Arsenius, who accompanied the Constantinople Patriarch Jeremiah on his visit to the court of the tsar in 1558, was amazed to see the exquisite mosaics on the walls of the Irene Palace (also known as the Small Golden Tsaritsa Palace) and the many enormous gold and silver vases,

[5] Sylvester (d. *ca.* 1566), archpriest and dean of the Annunciation Cathedral, was Ivan IV's mentor and exercised considerable influence over him. His political career was cut short because of his opposition to the Livonian war undertaken by the tsar.

[6] For the "Affair Viskovaty" see N. V. Pokrovsky, *Pamyatniki Khristyanskoi ikonographii i iskusstva*, 335ff.; also I. E. Zabelin, *Domashnei byt russkikh tsarei*, Pt. I, 149.

some in the shape of animals such as unicorns, lions, bears, stags, pelicans, swans, pheasants, and peacocks. These vases, so heavy that twelve men could carry them only with difficulty, were manufactured in Moscow.[7]

During the reign of Feodor Ivanovich and the regency of Boris Godunov, the chamber of the Granovitaya Palata (Palace of Facets) was decorated with frescoes similar to those in the Golden Palace. According to Ushakov, who restored the paintings in 1663, these frescoes also contained a mélange of biblical and quasi-historical subjects, edifying parables, and allegorical figures. Legendary scenes linking the Muscovite rulers with a representative of the world's oldest monarchy, Augustus Caesar, were alloted even more space, and political significance was stressed. One scene shows the aging Augustus Caesar "organizing the world" and sending his own brother Prus to the banks of the Vistula—the country that was thereafter called "Prus." Rurik, supposedly a fourteenth-generation descendant of the Roman Prus, was invited to be prince of Rus'; hence Ivan the Terrible's claim that his family was descended from Augustus Caesar.

Another scene depicts the Byzantine Emperor Constantine Monomakh sending the imperial regalia to the Kievan Prince Vladimir. Tsar Feodor Ivanovich, wearing his crown and dressed in imperial robes, is seated on his throne; at the right stands Boris Godunov magnificently attired. They are flanked by many boyars in their colorful *kaftans* and caps. The innovation is characteristic of the Moscow School, which from that time became more and more independent of the Novgorod School, setting itself to the study of nature and the human form. While Novgorod, imbued with the old traditions, was adhering to dark flesh tints, idealization of expression, simplicity of composition, and close harmony between its figures and background, Moscow strove for picturesqueness, used warmer colors, more accurately

[7] Bartenev, *Moskovsky Kreml'*, II, 234.

portrayed human forms, and endowed human features with a certain grace and worldly expression.

The Ushakov frescoes remained on the walls of the Grano-vitaya Palata for more than two centuries. But the years and the elements took their toll, and in 1881 the faded and damaged frescoes were repainted by the brothers V. and I. Belousov of the Palekh Sofonov Studio.

The conditions of the tense and stormy life of sixteenth-century Russia—the acute struggle of monarchical power with reactionary boyardom, the increasing demands of the peasants and townspeople for their rights, the rise of opposition to the claims of the monastic clergy to ownership of serfs, lands, and others forms of property—were reflected in the literature of the times. Contemporary publicists were earnestly discussing the difficulties that plagued Muscovite Russia. The best minds of those days, the men endowed with a social consciousness, hoped that, by pointing out the ailments torturing the long-suffering Russian society, they could somehow alleviate the prevailing miseries and hardships.

Much of the literature—the didactic, moral, biographical, and historical works of the period—was devoted to the various painful problems of the time. Generally, these works were written in the form of an epistle addressed to some important living or imaginary person. Most often they were in the form of a parable. This was a time when allegory was greatly in vogue; speaking openly was not very healthy.

One of the besetting evils of the times was the great wealth and growing power of the church: her outrageous claims and demands, and her efforts to dominate the affairs of state. The priests and the monks—the white and the black clergy—while preaching love of truth, temperance, continence, and unselfishness were themselves, with rare exceptions, indulging in heavy drinking, gluttony, and sodomy. The hypocrisy, debauchery, and avarice of the monastic clergy were proverbial and became the burning issues of the age, reflected not only in literature but also in iconography. This can especially be seen in a few icons of that period.

Among the icons which best reflect the mood and aspirations of that period are *The Parable of the Halt and the Blind, The Vision of the Stairway*, and *The Vision of Evlogi.*

The Parable of the Halt and the Blind[8] tells the story of a man who hired a blind man and a cripple to guard his orchard. He thought that neither of them would rob him since the blind man would not be able to see the fruit and the cripple would not be able to get them. However, his watchmen outsmarted him. The cripple sat on the back of the blind man and directed him; in this way they both managed to rob the orchard. For this their employer flung them into a dark dungeon. In the upper part of the icon are shown the lame man with his withered legs and the blind man in a dark cavern signifying the pit of Hell. In the middle we see the orchard, the watchmen stealing the apples. Below we see a depiction of the Last Judgment. The parable is aimed at the rapacious and cunning churchman, who styled themselves as guardians "of the garden of Christ," but rob it themselves.

The Vision of the Stairway[9] graphically depicts how, instead of mounting the stairway of spiritual perfection, the monks who have given vent to temptation fall into the pit of Hell. This icon is connected with the name of the learned Byzantine monk of the sixth century, John Climacus of Sinai (Ioann Lestvichnik), known for his work, the *Ladder*, a kind of a code of regulations aimed at strengthening the spiritual aspirations and moral standards for guidance of the monks. On the left side of this icon, we see the saintly author reading his book to his monastery brethren. To the right, there is an illustration for his sermon: a ladder leading from earth to heaven—to the very portals of paradise. The gates are open, and in the archway stand Christ, the Virgin, John the Baptist, and Archangel Michael; somewhat to the left, in the clouds, are the souls of the righteous and the saints. On

[8] Reproduced in K. Kornilovich, *Iz letopisi Russkogo iskusstva*, 159.
[9] Reproduced in Kornilovich, *Ibid.*, 157.

the ladder are shown several monks anxious to get to the top, looking forward to a blissful life in the garden of paradise. But only one of them has succeeded in reaching the last few rungs of the ladder; Christ is shown stretching out His arm in welcoming him. The others are depicted as barely able to hold on to the lower rungs, or having reached the middle of the ladder they are hurled downward and thrown right into the mouth of Hell, where the Devil and his cohorts are waiting.

The most notable of the three icons is *The Vision of Evlogi*,[10] one of the finest examples extant of Russian sixteenth century painting. Against the background of a shapely church with snow-white walls and a red roof is depicted a triangular-shaped group of angels, bishops, and monks crowned by an angel's fiery wing resembling a tongue of flame. There is an edifying scene showing some angels distributing gold, silver, and bread to the poor—a symbol of monastic care for the needy; but there is also another scene showing some angels refusing to admit greedy monks to paradise.

About the end of the sixteenth century came another renaissance, a school of artists arose which, though its work was highly decorative and full of elaborate ornament, nevertheless produced paintings of inimitable beauty. This was the so-called Stroganov School, bearing the name of a wealthy Novgorodian family which acquired unique economic and political significance in Russia at this time.[11] The Stroganovs were liberal pa-

---

[10] Reproduced in Grabar', *Istoriya russkogo iskusstva* (1953), III, 567.

[11] The great and influential house of merchant princes (originally from Novgorod) that accumulated much wealth in the sixteenth century by exploiting the region of the river Kama and the northern Urals. It was Anika Feodorovich Stroganov (1498–1570) who laid the foundation of the family fortunes by establishing the great salt works, engaging in fur trading and building cities and monasteries in the Perm province. The family contributed greatly to the conquest of Siberia (1584) and its branches were established in Sol'vychegodsk, Ustiug, and Perm. The early Stroganovs were keen patrons of art, maintained icon studios, and collected around them a number of painters and craftsmen. Their name is associated with that of the seventeenth-century School of Icon Painting, also with the School of Applied Art established in St. Petersburg about the middle of the nineteenth century.

trons of religious art. These merchant princes, aptly called Russian Medicis, encouraged a particular manner of icon painting in diminutive size and with an elaborate execution of details, in the spirit of Persian miniatures. Undoubtedly, examples of Oriental art in various media had captured the eye of these broad-minded lovers of art.

The principal innovations introduced by the Stroganov School were a lavish use of gold in the rendering of vestments and accessories. Outstanding features of the school are the elegant attitudes of the figures and the Eastern flavor of the colors. The pigments in common use are vermilion, brown-red, buff-green, brownish yellow, pale pink, orange pink, and gold. Common to the whole school are certain peculiarities of racial type, type of buildings, hills, and vegetation, and the introduction of purely Russian, highly fanciful architectural motifs. Whenever animals appear in the composition, their treatment is Oriental. Like the Moscow painters, the Stroganov masters drew heavily upon the legacy bequeathed by Dionysius. Their art has much in common with that of his sixteenth-century followers and is thus related to the Moscow School of icon painting. The icons are small, of great technical skill, and, as a rule, depict personal rather than formal religious feelings.

The main tendency of this school, which arose in a period when artisans' methods were increasingly invading the domain of icon painting, was to retain art on the level and in the channel of the old traditions. This was also rendered necessary by the growing influx of Western innovations.

The combination of the Stroganov technique and the Moscow thematic material produced a characteristic and easily recognizable style of icon. For a better understanding of the confluence of these two currents, it is necessary to keep in mind the extensive range of subjects treated by the Moscow painters. A definite cycle of subjects was centered on the Apocalypse. Storytelling was a favorite motif of the Moscow artist, and the striking visions of the Relevations lent themselves excellently to a pictorial narrative.

The Beginning of Modern Painting

At the beginning of the seventeenth century, Russia was passing through a crucial period, the Time of Trouble (*Smutnoye Vremya*).[12] The years of strife and devastation ended with the election of Mikhail Romanov in 1613 to start a new dynasty. With the consolidation of Russia under a new ruler, the political role of the Stroganovs came to an end. While members of this family continued to be interested in ecclesiastical art, many of the Stroganov artists joined the ranks of the special studios created in Moscow by the tsar for maintaining the painting of icons on the highest possible level.

During the reign of Tsar Mikhail there appeared at the court of Moscow some foreign masters, Poles and Germans, who were commissioned to paint both pictures and portraits. After the 1640's there was a continuous influx of foreign masters, whose many Russian pupils introduced Western standards into icon painting.

Although the representational art of the seventeenth century continued to be mainly religious, it was undergoing an internal process of secularizing subject matter, turning to scenes from everyday life, to landscape, and to portraiture. The latter was the the first genre that established itself independently, and became known as *parsunnoye pismo*.[13] Such paintings were at first painted in the icon painters' technique of tempera on wood as, for example, the portrait of *Prince Skopin-Shuisky* (Plate

---

[12] See chapter XIII, note 14.

[13] *Parsunnoye*, from persona, person; *pis'mo*, literally letter, also writing, but used here in the sense of painting. Hence *parsunnoye pis'mo* means portrait painting. The Russian word *pisat'* (from which *pis'mo* is derived) means "write" as well as "paint," and the word *pis'mo* is specially used to indicate the "style or school" of icon painting; for example, *Novgorodskoye pis'mo* (the Novgorod School), *Moskovskoye pis'mo* (the Moscow School), and so on.

138). Later in the second half of the seventeenth century, portraits began to be painted in oil on canvas and from life.

These inroads of Western ways of painting into the world of the icon were made by the followers of the so-called "Friaz" (Slavic corruption of "Frank") style. The timid experimentation with the art of the Fraiz was probably a bold adventure for young artists who had never dared, theretofore, to approach such innovations. Friaz art was the abomination of the conservative Orthodox, who saw in the new manner a heretical desecration of holy standards.

In the second half of the seventeenth century, when the extensive works of restoring the frescoes in the Cathedral of the Assumption and those of the Archangel Michael were undertaken (1653, 1657, 1660), the tsar issued a strict decree ordering the artists who still remained in the northwest to be sent to Moscow. Skilled icon painters received steady work and yearly salaries, and became the accredited icon and picture painters (*izografi*) of the tsar. They were subordinated to the Oruzheinaya Palata, which had control of everything relative to the tsar's household. A number of young people were apprenticed to these artists, and thus towards the second half of the seventeenth century the Tsar's Icon Painting School was born.

A state art policy was inaugurated, and a special department of arts was set up, forming an annex to the Oruzheinaya Palata. In this department worked the tsar's official masters and those who were employed by wealthy persons such as the Stroganovs. Serious discussions were held on such subjects as what should art be, what are its ideals, and what are the means of achieving them? The painters employed in this department worked out a new aesthetic and constituted a new school styled the "Tsar's School." They searched for a fresh way of expressing the old traditional ideals of religious painting. They were intrigued with the realistic representation of things and interested in rendering the palpable, in both volume and color.

A typical representative of the Tsar's School was Simon Ushakov (1626–86), deemed by some nineteenth-century Russian art historians a Slavic Raphael. He was appointed court painter at the early age of twenty-one and soon was put in charge of the icon painting studios at the Oruzheinaya Palata—the organization that directed all official art work in the state.

A man of many talents and a wide understanding of art, a master of icon painting, of draftsmanship, and of engraving, Ushakov took part in theoretical art discussions. However, Ushakov the author of *Words to the Lovers of Icon Painting*—a work containing advanced views on painting and appealing for a natural manner of representation—was a different man when he came to paint himself. Brought up in the school of ancient tradition, he adopted the new outlook, and by fusing it with the tradition, had succeeded in creating his own style. Fascinated by Western religious art, he attempted to produce naturalistic illustrations of the Bible. The best known of the latter, his woodcut depicting *Man's Seven Deadly Sins*,[14] is remarkable for its vigor and conviction.

Among his icons the best known are *The Annunciation with the Acathist* (Plates 139, 140), *The Vernicle* (Plate 141), *Christ, the Great Archbishop* (Plate 142), and *The Trinity*.

In *The Vernicle* and *Christ, the Great Archbishop*, the head of Christ is depicted in a manner quite close to nature; the artist employed skillful shading to model volume and he worked out in detail every feature of the face, the hair, and even the folds of the cloth in the background. In this work the conventional flatness of icon painting decisively yields to a new manner of painting.

In *The Trinity*[15] (1671), Ushakov used the old Rublev composition of the three angels seated at a table, leaning toward each other as if conversing. In his coloring he seems to have gone back to a period before the color schemes of the fifteenth and sixteenth centuries, showing an inclination for general dark tones

---

[14] Reproduced in Grabar', *Istoriya russkogo iskusstva* (1953), IV, 499.
[15] Reproduced in *Ibid.*, 382.

and for the archaic convention of outlining the garments with gold. Yet we may detect in his icon a number of quite new methods not found in ancient Russian icon painting. Instead of the conventional mountains and palm trees, we find a realistically rendered tree with a rounded trunk and densely leafed crown, and instead of the conventional tent we find a building presented with due regard to linear and spatial perspective. The angels have bright, rosy-cheeked faces and natural human expressions.

Another outstanding artist of the period was Emelian Moskvitin, especially known for the richness and harmony of his palette, original tastes, and freedom of technique. The term "Emelian manner" was applied not only to his works but also to icons executed in a similar spirit. In his art is a belated echo of the Dionysius murals of St. Therapont.

The art of Stroganov and the Tsar's painting schools found its highest expression in the works of Procopius Chirin, a member of a family of many artists. He was active in Moscow from 1620 to about 1642 and achieved great fame for his purity of tones, smooth shading in the treatment of facial features, and sumptuous richness in the depiction of patterned garments. His work exemplifies some of the characteristic traits of the translation period between the old styles of Novgorod and Moscow and the new painting of the Tsar's School (Plate 136).

The simplicity and moderation which had endured through centuries began to be lost. The broad planes and the monumental feeling of the image, the classical rhythm, and the antique purity and strength of color disappear in a passion for complexity and abundance of details. Excessive attention to the rich brocades in which the images are clothed reflects the growth of a more worldly and materialistic spirit, while the ornate detail and rich color schemes suggest the affinity to Oriental, especially Persian, painting. This period is a turning point in Russian iconography. The treatment rather than the religious meaning of the icon assumes the dominant role.

These icons are distinguished by a profusion of detail in their elaborate settings and exceedingly decorative backgrounds. The abundance of architectural features representing the churches and new buildings of Moscow is especially evident. On the other hand, landscapes are handled decoratively instead of naturalistically. Cities are represented as bundles of bulbous domes and sharp church spires, pale blue stripes stand for clouds, brown streaks represent the earth, and fire is depicted as a red mass with tongues of flame. The saints have the ruddy, strong-boned faces of the Muscovites, and the colors range from blood-reds to browns with black shadows. Paul Muratov points out that "in such icons the main thing is no longer in what is represented, but in the enrichments and patterns, the elaborate shale of the ground and the excessively detailed drawing of star-like flowers upon their stalks, in curls, and tiny clouds filling the grey-blue vault of heaven."

This process of secularization continued throughout the seventeenth century, gaining particular impetus from the great schism (*raskol*) which split the Russian church into two irreconcilable camps.[16] It was connected with the movement in the higher ranks of the clergy to draw Russian Orthodoxy into closer unity with the Greek church as a whole, and in particular to revise the liturgies in use, which had been corrupted in the past by copyists' errors, and bring them into conformity with Greek usage. The movement came to a head in 1652 with the consecration of Nikon as Russian patriarch, the most striking figure of the whole Russian hierarchy. A strong-willed man, intensely pious yet arrogant, he changed the whole course of Russian church history, and his place in the life of the country can only be compared to that of another ardent reformer, Peter the Great.

The changes Nikon introduced in 1653 might elsewhere have appeared trivial. The most notable required that communicants making the sign of the cross should join three fingers symbolizing the Trinity, not two fingers symbolizing the dual nature of

[16] For a discussion of the origin of the schism see Miliukov, *Outlines of Russian Culture*, Part I, pp. 27–39.

Christ, which was the ancient custom in Russia. But change in any form flouted the theory of Moscow as the Third Rome— the old conviction that Russian Orthodoxy alone was the True Faith, and that not a single iota of its dogma and ritual might be changed.

The patriarch favored a mild form of modernism in the painting of icons, while Tsar Aleksei, father of the great innovator Peter I, strove helplessly to keep a middle course between his own personal sympathies for a more life-like treatment of the saints and a loyal devotion to strict Orthodoxy. The very first deviations from the traditional in icon painting and in minor religious observances prompted conservatives to reject all innovations of this kind.

Both tsar and patriarch wanted reform, each for reasons of his own, but the first advocated going about it quietly, without unnecessarily enraging the Old Believers. The patriarch, on the other hand, wanted to crush the schism and eradicate everything connected with it, including the old uncorrected religious texts and the icons painted not in accordance with the Greek models.

The Archdeacon Paul of Aleppo, who accompanied Macarius, patriarch of Antioch, on his travels in Russia (1654–57) provides us with an eye-witness account of Nikon's attack upon "new icons drawn after the fashion of Frankish and Polish pictures."[17] He says that Nikon ordered all new-fangled icons to be collected and brought to him, even from the houses of high officials. He put out the eyes of the icons, and the *streltsy* (tsar's musketeers) bore them round the town proclaiming that anyone who painted such icons thereafter would be severely punished. Paul further remarks: "When the Muscovites saw how the patriarch was treating the icons, they were offended and disturbed and regarded him as an iconoclast . . . . The patriarch anathematized and excommunicated all who should make or

[17] Archdeacon Paul, who accompanied Macarius on his visit to Russia (1654), left a copious diary of all that occurred. It is particularly valuable as a record of the experiences and the impressions of a Syrian Orthodox Christian observing the Russian church and its clergy during the great schism.

keep such icons. He took one icon after another in his right hand, showed it to the people, and dashed it down to shatter it upon the iron floorslabs; then ordered that they should be burnt. The tsar was standing close to us with bared head, silently listening to the sermon, but as he was very pious he quietly begged the patriarch, 'No, Father, do not burn them. Let them be buried in the ground.' And this was done."

To justify his iconoclasm, Nikon afterwards told the people of Moscow that the style of the destroyed icons was "imported by Germans from the German land." It is clear that Nikon was attacking what to him was a new and dangerous departure in icon painting. The objections of Nikon as well as those of the leader of the Old Believers, Archpriest Avvakum, were directed against the wave of naturalism.[18] But Avvakum especially denounced the realistic treatment of saintly personages in icons. To him the whole matter of venerating the icons was at stake, and he accused Nikon of heresy. In one of his epistles he wrote: "God hath allowed the wrong makers of icons to multiply in our land. They paint the images of Immanuel the Saviour with plump face, red lips, dimpled fingers, and large, fat legs and thighs, and altogether make Him look like a German, fat-bellied and corpulent, only omitting to paint a sword at His side. . . . And all this was invented by the dirty cur, Nikon, who contrived to represent holy figures on the icons in the Friaz or German manner."

Avvakum even went so far as to invent various extravagancies, such as Our Lord with a beard at His Nativity, Our Lady pregnant at the Annunciation, Our Lord with full draperies upon the cross, as being found among the pagan Franks. He used these

[18] Avvakum (Habakkuk, 1620–81), archpriest, was leader of the Old Believers (*Starovery*) opposition, a talented and prolific writer produced by the schism. For a most interesting sketch of the life and works of this extraordinary man, see N. K. Gudzii, *History of Early Russian Literature*, S. W. Jones tr., New York, 1949. pp. 378–96; see also *Avvakum, Archpriest, the Life of, by Himself*, translated by Jane Harrison and Hope Mirrlees from the seventeenth-century text, published by Leonard and Virginia Woolf at the Hegarth Press, London, 1924.

means to rouse his followers and dissuade them from having anything to do with the heretical icons.

As a result, there was a violent reaction to the change in ritual. It became a burning issue within the church and was more important to the people than the reforms of the service books carried through by Nikon. In 1654 a church council called in Moscow approved the reforms of Nikon in service books and ritual. In 1665 further regulations were published instituting a strict watch against novelties in icon painting.

A bitter opponent of religious innovation and a staunch defender of the old ritual and of iconography in the old tradition, Avvakum refused all compromise and denounced Nikon as a heretic and a tool of Satan. He was exiled to Siberia, where he remained for nine years, dragged about from place to place and mercilessly persecuted. In 1664 he was brought back to Moscow, where considerable changes had taken place. Nikon had fallen and a synod was to judge both Avvakum and Nikon. The synod condemned Avvakum's tenets, and thus the schism became final. Avvakum was exiled to Pustozerk in the far northeast of Russia. There he became an even more active and daring leader than before. He kept on preaching and writing his eloquent epistles to his followers, urging them to defy their persecutors and seek martyrdom. He himself won a martyr's crown in April, 1682; he was burned at the stake, thus inspiring among his followers a renewed passion of self-destruction before the coming of Antichrist.

The movement for a return to the old ritual gathered momentum, and not all the repressive measures launched by the government could stop it. The persecution of the Old Believers by the government was ruthless, but it only heightened their fanaticism. They came to believe that the apostasy of the official church from true Orthodoxy signalized the coming of Antichrist and sought martyrdom at the hands of the triumphant Nikonians. Large groups sought sanctuary in the forests of the north and beyond the Urals. They endured unspeakable hardships, or burned themselves, locked in their churches, rather than be made to accept what seemed to them to be the ritual of the Antichrist.

Thus it was mainly within the communities of the Old Believers, who zealously clung to every iota of their ancestral cult, that the ancient icon paintings were not only reverently guarded but continued.

Tsar Aleksei stood between the old and new worlds. Desiring to pursue a progressive course in artistic matters, he invited many foreign artists and craftsmen to Russia. These artists, quite naturally, brought along with them their own art concepts, methods, and techniques, and thus were instrumental in spreading contemporary Western ideas among their Russian colleagues. Toward the end of the seventeenth century, a whole new generation of Russian artists was being educated on new principles.

With the gradual disappearance of Byzantine traditions, popular art remained the only living source of inspiration for church decoration. But by the end of the seventeenth century, this art also came to an end, and with the reign of Peter the Great, Russian art entered upon a new historical period and began to take its place in European development.

XVIII

The Art and Architecture of the Upper Volga Region

THE UPPER VOLGA REGION deserves attention not only for its numerous monuments but because of the striking originality of its architecture and art. This art, like the art of all Russian provincial schools, was essentially conservative and showed itself less hospitable to the influence of the Polish and Ukrainian baroque which had begun to invade Moscow. Yaroslavl and Rostov, seats of the traditions of the past, could be likened to great strongholds, the last line of defense, to which medieval Russia retreated in order to give battle to the steadily advancing alien modernity of the West.

The national traits in ecclesiastical architecture and decorative art shared the same fate as the traditional ritual of the Russian church. During the sixteenth century both flourished and played a prominent part, but in the second half of the seventeenth century they were condemned by the reforms of Patriarch Nikon as heretical and unbecoming to the traditions of the Byzantine Mother Church. Opposition to the Moscow decrees, though sternly suppressed, was strong and bitter, and it manifested itself in many ways and in many parts of the country, especially in the North and in the upper Volga region.

During the middle of the seventeenth century the architectural activities of Moscow were extended to the region of the upper Volga, especially to Yaroslavl, which was steadily growing in importance as a commercial center, and to Rostov Veliki, which was an old metropolitan see of the church.

The Art and Architecture of the Upper Volga Region

The Churches of Yaroslavl

Yaroslavl, next to Moscow, is the richest in architectural monuments of the second half of the seventeenth century; its churches are even larger and vastly richer in decoration than those of the capital. The city, founded in the eleventh (*ca.* 1026–36) century by Prince Yaroslav the Wise, had been a center of culture since medieval times. The opening of the northern trade route and the founding of the city of Archangel (Arkhangelsk) in 1584 brought Yaroslavl to the very forefront of the important commercial centers in seventeenth-century Russia. Its merchants carried on extensive trading with Persia and the Near East via the Volga and the Caspian. They also maintained lucrative commercial relations with Europe via Vologda and Archangel. This prosperity explains the large construction activities of the wealthy merchants. The history of many of the Yaroslavl architectural monuments is closely bound with the names of the local "Medicis," especially the Scripin brothers, the jewel merchants (formerly of Novgorod), who carried on a large business not only with Moscow but with the West.[1]

A disastrous fire ravaged the city in 1658. It destroyed most of the city's churches and houses, but at the same time served as an incentive for reconstruction and brought about more homogeneity to the new buildings. Almost all the new churches were constructed between 1660 and 1690, all are stamped with the characteristic style of local architecture. The rich and pious Yaroslavl merchants, wanting to assure for themselves a place in heaven, vied with each other in gifts for erecting magnificent churches. Although their architects did not dare dispense with the models prescribed by the Moscow ecclesiastical authorities (the five-dome type), they managed to introduce their own favorite features; they built around the central quadrangle of the church spacious galleries and porches with magnificent portals;

[1] For the history of architecture in the Yaroslavl and Rostov regions, see A. Pavlinov, *Drevnosti Yaroslavskiye i Rostovskiye;* Yu. Shamurin, *Kul'turnyia sokrovishcha Rossii,* I (*Yaroslavl', Romanov-Borisoglebsk, Uglich*).

they erected tent-shaped bell towers (Plate 114); and they decorated the exterior walls with ornamental brick and tiles and the interior with frescoes. The Yaroslavl style was also adopted in Rostov, Romanov-Borisoglebsk, and Uglich. Altogether these regional patterns form a separate chapter in the history of Russian Art. Outstanding are the churches of St. John the Precursor (Ioann Predtecha) in the suburb of Tolchkovo (Plate 113) and St. John Chrysostom (Ioann Zlatoust) in the Korovniki district.[2]

Many influences contributed to the development of the local style. The architectural principles of Byzantium are clearly visible in the basic plans and structural modes of the local churches. But there is also an unmistakable reflection of the wooden architecture of northern Russia tinged with the Norman, which is especially noticeable in the linear and geometrical character of the decoration and in the embellishment of the entrances. And, finally, there are greatly in evidence many elements borrowed from the East—from central Asia and from distant India. Such are the brick patterns, the lay and bond; the colored tiles of the revetments and paneling; the fine, close, flat carving; and the foliage and animal forms of the tropics, the fairytale dragons and monsters, and even Chinese ornamental motifs. All these elements were modified and transfigured by the Russian builders wittingly and unwittingly, creating an art sharply differing from that of the West and producing a style distinctly Russian with specifically regional, Yaroslavlian overtones.

Though building in masonry, the architects of Yaroslavl did not forget the forms of wood architecture. The Nikonian reforms, aiming to channel the national creative impulses along Byzantine lines, forbade the construction of tent roofs over the churches, permitting them, as we have already mentioned, only over belfries and entrance porches. But the Yaroslavl builders stubbornly erected them also over chapels. Other distinctive features of the

[2] For plan, elevation, and details of this church, see Grabar', *Istoriya russkogo iskusstva* (1953), IV, 202–209; and M. I. Rzyanin, *Pamyatniki russkogo zodchestva*, plate 48.

Yaroslavl churches are the bulbous scaly cupolas, again very close in texture and silhouette to the cupolas of the northern wooden churches. The fine-proportioned quality of these bulbs is due, in large measure, to their sensitively designed supporting necks or drums. With their svelte silhouettes and general masses soaring upwards they are more reminiscent of the forbidden tents than of the Byzantine domes. The arrangement and grouping of the cupolas and tent spires, the decoration of the walls, the sumptuous finish of the portals and window architraves, and the variegated tiles heighten and deepen the effect of radiant picturesqueness.

The churches of Yaroslavl constitute a special group in the general seventeenth-century architecture of Moscow. They retain on the whole the basic plan of the newer Moscow churches—that is, a central rectangle with the chapels arranged on the sides and surrounded by a gallery—but, at the same time, retain the older scheme of introducing columns to break up the central space, into several bays, permitting the construction of five light-admitting cupolas. In other words, the Yaroslavl churches are of the type in which the central area can be covered by several vaults instead of one. This resulted in the Yaroslavl churches becoming twice as large as those of Moscow. The expanse of the walls provided large surfaces for decoration, and the builder, disregarding the Moscow custom of dividing the walls into three parts (*trekhdol'noye deleniye*), gave free reign to his imagination and embellished them with polychrome tile paneling and painting.

One of the best examples of the Yaroslavl monuments is the Tolchkovo Church of John the Precursor, built in 1671–87 under the supervision of Priest Abrosium and Deacon Rodion (Plate 113). It is square in plan and has three semi-circular apses, widely extended spacious galleries, and three porches of beautifully detailed finish. Its galleries and staircases are decorated with figured brick and tile paneling, and the soft red of its brick walls is enriched with bands of moulded light-blue tiling. The walls of the apses are faceted like the Granovitaya Palata in the Moscow Kremlin, and the wall spaces over and between the windows, the cupola drums, and many other elements are bejeweled with tiles, dazzling in the interplay of their colors. The size of its chapels permitted the placing of five cupolas over each of them, and the combined effect of the fifteen heavily gilded cupolas, with the soft red hues of the brick walls brightened by the bluish areas of glazed tiles, is unforgettable. The faceted walls of the apses are uniquely beautiful, and no photograph could possibly convey the effect produced by the general ensemble of cupolas, galleries, porches, and the free-standing, multi-storied belfry.

The interior decoration and furnishings of the church—its unique brick benches, magnificent portals, wrought-iron doors, carved iconostases, and icons—present some of the finest examples of seventeenth-century Russian decorative art.

The next in wealth of tile decoration is the Church of St. John Chrysostom in Korovniki, at the confluence of the Kotorosl and Volga rivers near Yaroslavl, built in 1654 at the expense of the wealthy merchants, the brothers Nezhdanovsky. This is also an assemblage of spacious porches, galleries, chapels, and bell towers surrounding a cube-shaped church with five cupolas—all commingled with a beautiful sense of relationship. One of its outstanding details is the altar-apse window (Plate 118). Its architrave of colored glazed tile, wide and deeply splayed, consists of several small profiled members—a typical decorative device widely used in Russian brick architecture of the seventeenth century. The colonnettes actually consist of two equal, slender elements joined by tiny balusters and terminating at the top and bottom with small square caps and molded drops.

Rostov, its Kremlin and the Belaya Palata

Rostov Veliki (the Great) is one of the oldest cities of Russia, but unfortunately very little of its medieval grandeur, except the frequently reconstructed Uspensky Cathedral, has survived.

Only its magnificent seventeenth-century Kremlin, located on the shore of Lake Nero, is still in a good state of preservation.

Almost all the buildings of the Rostov Kremlin, as well as the monasteries of Borisoglebsk and Uglich, were erected by Iona Sysoevich, a man of humble origin, who became metropolitan of Rostov in 1652. He and his contemporary, Patriarch Nikon, with whom he saw eye to eye in matters of church reforms, were perhaps the most prolific ecclesiastical builders of the second half of the seventeenth century.

All these buildings have the characteristic elements of religious, civil, and military architecture combined. The metropolitan set out to erect veritable fortress-monasteries, citadels of the church, protected by massive crenelated walls and watch towers. Like most of the great monasteries of Russia—the Troitse-Sergieva Lavra, the Novodevichei Convent in Moscow, the Solovetsky Island Monastery—the Rostov Kremlin was designed to withstand possible attack and siege, and it has all the robust features of a powerful fortress. Though it was erected nearly two centuries later than the Moscow Kremlin, it is much more medieval in appearance. The churches, instead of being grouped in the interior of the fortress, are located along its periphery perched above the several entrance gates, each one flanked by two massive towers. Interconnected by a protected walk running along the wall ramparts, these churches could easily be converted into bulwarks of defense.[3]

Inside the fortress, sheltered by this ring of church bastions, stands the Bishop's Palace, the Belaya Palata (the White Palace). Its grand chamber, its vaulting supported by a single massive pier (somewhat analogous to the Granovitaya Palata in the Moscow Kremlin), now serves as a museum. The palace is surrounded by eleven towers and five churches.

[3] For a reproduction of the Church of the Resurrection on the north wall of the Rostov Kremlin, see Grabar', *Istoriya russkogo iskusstva* (1953), IV, plate facing p. 86.

Romanov-Borisoglebsk

The building activities of the upper Volga region were not confined to Yaroslavl and Rostov. We find several interesting architectural examples in the small cities of the region not far from Yaroslavl.

Romanov-Borisoglebsk is a twin city astride the Volga. On the left bank is Romanov, founded by Prince Roman in the middle of the fourteenth century, and on the right the somewhat older, sleepy town of Borisoglebsk with its tiny cottages and a few old churches surrounded by gardens and orchards. Dominating all is the Resurrection Cathedral (Voskresenky sobor)— a remarkable seventeenth-century architectural monument that surpasses the Yaroslavl churches not only in size but in the prodigality and beauty of its decorations (Plates 115–17).

The cathedral, consecrated in 1652, was enlarged in 1670 by Metropolitan Iona. He added a second story, spacious galleries, monumental porches, and a belfry. The building covers a large area and has many of the characteristics of the Yaroslavl churches of that time, but it was conceived and executed with more perception and finish. It is an almost ideal example of Russian regional architecture, radiating a warm spirit, sweep of imagination, and creative enthusiasm. The general silhouette is simple and its straight lines harmonize beautifully with the calm landscape of the Volga. A magnificent two-story, arcaded gallery surrounds the cube-shaped five-domed church on its three sides. Three portals with hanging keys lead into these light-flooded galleries whose walls are entirely covered by frescoes.

There are many other outstanding monuments in the region of Yaroslavl, admirable for their harmonious forms and wealth of ornamentation. Their style spread far into northern and eastern Russia and left its imprint upon such widely scattered cities, to name only a few, as Murom (the Monastery of the Trinity), Solikamsk in the region of Perm, and Kargopol on the Onega.

At Solikamsk there is a very beautiful "Cold Church" surrounded by a gallery, with pot-bellied (*puzatyie*), baluster-shaped columns, magnificent windows architraves, and portal settings. The play of the brick patterns in the interior produces the effect of rich woven textiles, and the columns are covered with most delicate lacy carving.[4]

The churches of Kargopol combine the austerity of Novgorod architecture with a feeling for grace, rhythm, and the opulent decorativeness of Moscow. At the Church of the Vladimir Virgin, the window architraves reveal a great variety of design.[5] The decoration of the Church of the Annunciation is even more remarkable for its finely worked details, the delightful grouping and spotting of the windows, and the discreet ornamentation of the altar apses with meticulous and exquisite "pearly" carving *(bisernaia rez'ba).*[6]

With a few rather simple but imaginative devices—the play of brick and the sensitive employment of colored tile—Russian architecture, of the end of the seventeenth century, achieved some highly original and delightful effects. The half-century that gave us the church at Fili, the churches and belfries of Yaroslavl, the Kremlin at Rostov, and the Resurrection Cathedral at Borisoglebsk is surely one of the great epochs of Russian architecture.

The Murals of the Yaroslavl Region Churches

The mural paintings of the Yaroslavl and neighboring churches are in some ways even more striking than their architecture. Although these murals do not reach the level of the fifteenth-century Novgorod frescoes, they do reveal the strength and poetic nature of their regional creators. The art of the Yaroslavl frescoes was more virile than the art of the Moscow School of icon painting and displayed more resistance to the inroads of decadence. Even in its decline we can still detect the afterglow of a grand style.

The number of frescoes painted in the cities of the upper Volga

[4] Reproduced, *ibid.*, II, 139.
[5] Reproduced, *ibid.*, 142.
[6] Reproduced, *ibid.*, 143.

between 1670 and 1695 is prodigious. All the walls and vaults of the great churches, the galleries, porches, altar apses, and even the window embrasures present a solid tapestry of painting, unique in its state of preservation and overwhelming in wealth of subject variety, color, and charm of decorative effect. To cover tens of thousands of square feet with frescoes, some new and abundant iconographic thematic material was needed. The Byzantine patterns, the standard iconographic subjects contained in the official icon painting manuals (podlinniki), were not sufficient. The painters had to look for fresh and more copious sources even if they were not strictly orthodox. Here, as in Moscow, they began to examine the engravings coming from "beyond the sea" (zamorskiye kunshty), principally those from Holland and Germany. The illustrated editions of the Bible depicting scenes from the Old and New Testaments and the Apocalypse, became immensely popular and a source of fresh subject matter. The Bible, or rather the huge album of Bible illustrations (Theatrum Biblicum), of Jan Vissher, better known under his latinized name of Piscator, became the most important source of material for the frescoes in the churches of Yaroslavl, Romanov-Borisoglebsk, Kostroma, Rostov, and other towns.

The first edition of Johannes Piscator's Theatrum Biblicum appeared in Amsterdam in 1650, but his work circulated long before that in the form of an album of 277 engravings illustrating the Old and New Testaments, the Acts of the Apostles, and the Apocalypse. One copy of the Bible of Piscator was found in Vologda. Another copy (probably the Amsterdam edition of either 1650 or 1676) was acquired in 1677 by Bezmin, one of the tsar's artists, for the personal use of Tsar Feodor Alekseevich. When it reached Russia the Bible of Piscator was many decades behind the times, for it reproduced chiefly the works of the sixteenth and early seventeenth-centuries Dutch and Flemish masters. In this way the Italian influence came to Russia as modified by the Dutch artists. Although the Yaroslavl and Kostroma painters drew their material from Piscator, it never occurred to them to reproduce his engravings in their original form. They transformed his scenes into essentially Russian compositions painted in vivid colors, converting the foreign "heretical" religious pictures into Orthodox icons, extracting from those examples everything they needed, and disregarding all the elements unbecoming to a Russian Temple of the Lord.

Like the earlier Muscovite icons, these wall paintings abound in elaborate architectural backgrounds featuring buildings in the national style. They are imbued with naive religious nationalism. The saints have round, Great Russian faces, and their robes as well as the backgrounds are brilliantly and gaily colored. In the Church of St. Elijah at Yaroslavl there is a mural depicting the scene of the Four Horsemen of the Apocalypse (borrowed from Dürer). The horror-stricken fugitives, trampled under the horses' hoofs, are clad in characteristic Tatar caps. The sinners and the unbelievers, gathered at the awesome mouth of Hell, are divided into three groups, their nationality designated by their characteristic headgear. The virtuous, the elect, those who are shown entering the gates of paradise, are dressed in Russian costumes and presumably all Orthodox.[7]

The frescoes are arranged in seven or eight tiers divided into innumerable little panels forming a chaos of disparate scenes in bright colors. According to Kondakov, the walls of St. John the Precursor at Tolchkovo are covered with 3,724 figures. The variety of subjects surpasses the Greeks, and in St. John's there is no surface at all without painting; even the doors and the splays of the windows are covered with figures. These frescoes executed in 1694–95 represent the ultimate creative effort of Russian painting of the pre-Petrine period. Sixteen artists *(izografi)* worked steadily for two years, and since it was physically impossible for only sixteen men to accomplish so much work in so short a time, they were compelled to employ as many helpers as they could

[7] For a discussion of the frescoes in the Church of St. Elijah, see N. Pervukhin, *Tserkov' Il'i Proroka v Yaroslavle,* Moscow, 1915; for reproductions and comments by I. E. Danilova and N. E. Mneva, see Grabar', *Istoriya russkogo iskusstva* (1953), IV, 417–27

obtain. The master painter and guiding spirit was Dmitri Grigoriev, a native of Pereyaslavl-Zalieski, who worked at the Oruzheinaya Palata in Moscow. Almost the same type of frescoes, evidently executed under the same conditions, are found at Rostov, Kostroma, Vologda, and other towns on a smaller scale. Many inexperienced hands were employed; whole teams (*arteli*) of apprentices and novices worked hastily under the direction of some master painter, and it goes without saying that the result was not always happy and, as in all collective works, of unequal value.[8]

In the frescoes of the Resurrection Cathedral at Borisoglebsk, blues and yellows predominate. The colors are not as intense and not as variegated as those of John the Precursor, and the decorative effect is quieter and much more harmonious. The frescoes that cover the walls of the galleries illustrate almost the entire Old Testament. There are scenes from the Creation, the Earthly Paradise, the Story of Noah, the building of the Ark, the Deluge, and the gigantic Tower of Babel, its top lost in the clouds, and its audacious builders plunging earthwards—all treated with great realism. The most remarkable part of the decoration of the interior of the cathedral proper is the vast composition of the Last Judgment swarming with hundreds of figures covering the west wall. This scene is found in almost all of the churches of the Yaroslavl region, but none of them attains the grandiose sweep of composition, the nightmarish quality of religious mysticism, and the primative fantasy of the Borisoglebsk cathedral.[9]

The sanctuary and the interior of the church were generally painted with more care than the galleries or the porches, but the most interesting element of these great complexes of frescoes is not the important part within the body of the church itself, but

[8] For a discussion of the frescoes in the Church of St. John the Precursor, see Pervukhin, *Tserkov' Ioanna Predtechi v Yaroslavle*, Moscow, 1913; for reproductions and comments by I. E. Danilova and N. E. Mneva, see Grabar', *Istoriya russkogo iskusstva* (1953), IV, 429–37.

[9] For a discussion of the frescoes in the Resurrection Cathedral at Borisoglebsk, see Pervukhin, *Stenopisniye kompozitsii v tserkovnykh galereiyakh goroda Yaroslavlya i Borisoglebskogo sobora*, Tver, 1905.

the painting of the porches and passages leading to it. It was here that the Russian painters felt themselves under the least surveillance, least bound to dogma, and therefore allowed themselves the most freedom. In the porches, corridors, and galleries there is a sudden change to absolute freedom of symbolic representation, and the appearance of allegorical subjects completely alien to the Byzantine tradition. In monasteries in southern Russia, canvases with subjects painted in oil were hung or nailed to the walls of such passages. In northern Russia, compositions explaining the liturgy, scenes depicting the Old Testament stories, legends from the lives of the saints and the eastern anchorites, stories from the Apocalypse, the Last Judgment, Our Lord's Passion, and the Acathist of Our Lady were painted directly on the walls.

Here the painter, not restrained by tradition in depicting man and beast, let his fancy loose. He treated his angels and the apocalyptic living creatures in a free manner. But the most fantastic treatment was reserved for Satan and the denizens of Hell. Some of them have long and snaky tails, some are short and squat, and some appear as many-headed hydras—all painted in a wonderful blaze of color.

These prodigious cycles of frescoes—a mixture of Byzantine and Novgorodian traditions perpetuated by the obligatory use of the official pattern-books but greatly modified by the novelties borrowed from Western engravings—are the swan song of ancient Russian painting. Although there is much repetition of stock motifs both in composition and background, and a notable lack of subtlety in drawing and color, the Yaroslavl frescoes offer many examples of the vitality and validity of the old icon-painting traditions. The creators of these cycles compensated for their technical shortcomings by the fresh, sure intuition with which they approached their subjects. Above all, there is no denying the decorative instinct of the artists and their uncanny facility for exploiting the opportunities offered by the large wall surfaces for the deployment of the most complicated compositions.

Part Four

The Decorative Arts and Crafts

XIX

Religious and Secular Objects

THE DECORATIVE ARTS and crafts of medieval Russia constitute one of the most varied and extensive categories of the art of that period. The demand for objects of symbolic and utilitarian value was at its height during the sixteenth and seventeenth centuries; and it was the employment of such objects by the church that brought about the creation of some of the finest examples in the arts of gold and silver work, enameling, book illumination, embroidery, and carving. It is known that many such objects of great intrinsic value, highly venerated for their religious association, have been destroyed or melted down for the sake of the precious metals used in making them. However, the number of these objects still in existence is very great, enabling us to infer a vast production of first-rate works, especially during the reigns of Ivan IV, Boris Godunov, and Aleksei Mikhailovich Romanov.

The role that the church played in fostering the decorative arts was highly important. Icons and iconostases were commonly decorated with frames and encasements of precious metals. The wood frames of the iconostases and their royal doors were richly carved or, when made of bronze, gold plated. Altars were covered or enclosed with lavishly ornamented panels of gold and silver. Relics of saints were enshrined in sumptuous caskets of enameled gold or carved ivory. Gospels and prayer books used for the liturgical services in the cathedrals or the private chapels of the tsar and the great nobles were bound in elaborately tooled leather covers decorated with ivory plaques, filigree work of gold, silver, and precious stones. The vestments of the patriarchs, metropolitans, and officiating priests were richly embroidered, and among the altar cloths, icon covers, and the shrouds of Christ are many superb pieces of the art of needlework. Every great cathedral possessed magnificent thrones of carved wood or gilded bronze in which the patriarch and the tsar sat during the service. The divine liturgy was celebrated in the sumptuous setting of the gilded iconostases, the shimmering silver lamps and flickering candles, the gold and jewels of the altar, and the gorgeous vestments of the clergy.

Goldsmith and Enamelwork

Metalwork and enameling were for centuries the glory of Russian craftsmanship. Copper, brass, bronze, steel, and the precious metals, singly or combined, were used for a variety of objects, ranging in size from huge bells and monumental vases to minute gold beads and delicate filigree work. Russian craftsmen were particularly sensitive to the intrinsic beauty of the materials they handled, precious metals, polished marbles, and gems; and they delighted in the colorful effects obtained by juxtaposing them. The decorative techniques included open work, embossed and solid reliefs, engraving, chiseling, damascening and inlay, enamel, filigree, and niello work.

Not unlike the Persians and the Greeks, the Russians have shown a marked predilection for the limpid or opalescent colors of enamel *(finift'* or *emal'*). Everything from simple costume accessories and jewelry to monumental architectural decoration, including the production of tile and faience, was enriched by this dazzling art of earth and fire. The fine examples of Greek, Greco-Scythian, and Sarmatian work found in the tumuli of South Russia are sufficient evidence of the art's antiquity, and their presence refutes the assumption of some art historians that Russia was chiefly indebted to Byzantium for its knowledge of enameling.

Although a discussion of the origin and development of Russian enamel work lies beyond the scope of this book, it is important that we take a look at the most widely practiced techniques of enamel work and its use in combination with precious stones, filigree, and niello work.

Cloisonné enamel *(Peregorodchataya emal')* is one of the most outstanding genres in the art of medieval Russian jewelry. It derives from Byzantium, but was brought to a high level of development in Kievan Russia. Briefly, cloisonné enamel is like inlay work in that it was devised to produce polychrome jewelry, and is technically somewhat similar. The foundation of both is a metal plate, and on this the contours of the figure or pattern and the color areas required by the design are defined by tiny bars soldered on their edges to the metal ground. The height of the bars in the finest examples of old Russian cloisonné enamel work, according to the art historian Kondakov, does not exceed half a millimeter, while in the cruder examples it is as much as two millimeters. Whereas in inlay these units are filled with different stones, in the cloisonné work each cell is filled with a mixture, in fine granular form, of pulverized glass and the material that gives the color, and the whole thing is then heated white hot, so that the mixture is fused and fixed as enamel.

In the cloisonné technique, *cloisons* of twisted wire, minute corded filigree patterns, and borders edged with fine chain work are frequently found. In most examples, it will be noted that the enamel does not present a level surface but sinks toward the middle of the compartments. The filigree (*skan'*) technique in its simplest forms was known in Russian folk art from time immemorial, but it achieved great refinement and perfection in the eleventh and twelfth centuries and continued to be a source of potent influence, especially in the production of religious objects. *Skan'* is mostly found on smaller pieces and on jewelry.

There are two main types of filigree work. The first is the work employing granulous metal fillets or threads made up of small grain-like particles, bent with nippers to form borders, edges, and open-work designs. This is the type properly called filigree. The second type consists of the use of drawn gold or silver wire, or thread, either for winding around the articles to be decorated, or to form various ornamental designs to be applied to the surfaces of the article. This is perhaps the oldest known type of filigree work. Around the ninth century this second type became dominant and resulted in truly artistic works. In Russia of the ninth to twelfth centuries we find some of the finest examples of this art.

One of the great monuments of Russian historical and artistic antiquity is the crown of St. Vladimir, with which the Russian tsars and emperors were crowned. This crown (Plate 163) has also been known as the cap of Monomakh (*Shapka Monomakha*). Here the filigree is in its rarest manifestation—the "ribbon" type made of very thin sheet ribbons bent and soldered to the ground, forming *cloisons* but without enamel.

Other fine examples of ancient filigree work are the cover of the Mstislav Gospels (Plate 147) and the medallions of the Ryazan treasure.[1]

The finest kind of Russian enamel work dates from the sixteenth century. It is mostly cloisonné, the enamel being incrusted in cavities in such a way that it is not brought to the surface and to the same polished level. The ornament consists generally of tracery and arabesques of floral derivation with sharply pointed leaves and pearled borders, and it has a distinct, easily recognizable character of its own. The colors are often sober and harmonious; certain combinations, such as dark green, dead whites, and a peculiar pink, were frequently used.

Many of the samples show two kinds of enamel work—that which is painted and that which is incrusted in cavities formed by the smooth or filigreed bands constituting the designs. Such designs were probably first completed and then applied to the piece to be decorated. In some work we find both incrusted and painted enamels on the same piece. These seem to have been in vogue in the seventeenth century. The flower designs, in which

---

[1] Reproduced in G. A. Boguslavsky, *Gosudarstvennaya oruzheinaya palata Moskovskogo Kremlya,* plates 123–28.

tulips predominate, probably of Persian origin, are often mingled with birds, scenes from Russian folk tales, figures, or portraits.

Niello is a branch of the arts of engraving and enameling. It is a method of producing delicate and minute decoration on a polished metal surface by incised lines filled in with a black metallic amalgam, *nigellus* (Latin, black), from which the Italian name *niello* appears to be derived. The art was introduced into Russia, probably by the Greek craftsmen of Crimea, two or three centuries B.C. (fine fibulas of nielloed silver were discovered in the tombs of Panticapaeum). Perfected techniques were introduced in the early part of the sixteenth century when numbers of Italian artists and craftsmen were employed by Ivan III and his son, Vasili III. Executed in the manner it acquired in Russia, niello demanded experts in draftsmanship and engraving. The niello, a compound of silver, copper, lead, sulphur, and borax, was mixed, and fused, and afterwards reduced to a powder. This was spread over the engraved parts, and then again fused by blowing the flame of a clear fire over it. The melted niello, in cooling, attached itself firmly to the roughened parts of the engraved silver and, when cold, was rubbed smooth with a pumice stone, so that the niello in the engraved lines or in the decorative lettering was all that remained. The whole was then polished with leather.

Church Furnishings, Vessels, and Jewelry

In the history of the development of ideas and forms of Russian art, objects of religious cult predominate. Therefore, in any survey of Russian decorative art, especially that of the pre-Petrine period, we are faced with the arts and crafts fostered by the church: iconography, the illumination of manuscripts, and the production of church furnishings. It was a particular system of representing certain forms and symbols which gave the art of Orthodox Christianity its distinctive character. Essentially an art reflecting the thought of the medieval Russian religious mind, it was enabled by the wealth, prestige, and support of the church to maintain a position of lasting influence.

Art for the church was primarily a medium for conveying the doctrines of its theologians to the minds of the common people. The church, therefore, organized art as she organized dogma and developed a special system for the representation of sacred subjects and the dramatization of symbols. However, the artists and craftsmen whom she employed did not always follow her dictates and often managed to produce works of strong emotional appeal. They were largely influenced by Eastern art and so, wittingly or unwittingly, introduced a new appreciation of decorative design.

Ecclesiastical jewelry is frankly designed for richness of effect; extensive surfaces of precious metals are displayed, and the gems are large and of dazzling color (Plates 150–64). The designs are well executed, and the color effects produced by the precious stones and enamels are harmonious. The decoration is based on the principles of flat design in sharply contrasted colors and is infused with the spirit of the Orient. The human figure is freely used in the representation of religious subjects. Ornament consists largely of foliate designs and scrolls; a relation with similar designs in textiles or decorative sculpture is apparent. Gems and pearls enrich the more precious objects; the gems in box settings or gold cells, the pearls threaded on gold wire to form borders around medallions or compartments or as frame edgings.

One of the unique and interesting specialties of the art of the Moscow goldsmiths—a specialty which became highly developed at the beginning of the seventeenth century—was the decorative encasement (oklad) of the icons. This custom of enriching the painted image with gold and jewels, thus forming a magnificent and dazzling piece of ornamented metalwork, became a thoroughly established tradition. Spurred on by the pious zeal of the donors and yielding to the general taste for opulent backgrounds, the goldsmiths began adorning the icons with precious metal plaques, embossed, chiseled, or engraved with arabesques, nielloed or enameled in color on a silver or gold background, and studded with precious stones and pearls. The borders of the frames were covered with similar strips of silver sometimes set with jewels. The flat golden nimbus of early times was given relief as a halo adorned with *repoussé* or with filigree or twisted gold wire sometimes picked out with enamel; later the halo became an actual crown. But the zeal of the donors did not stop at these symbolic adornments. The artists began to decorate icons with silver-gilt collars in the symbolic form of crescents, with pendants attached to them. To the halos they began to add earrings and strings of pearls or diamonds, sapphires, rubies, and emeralds to hang along the forehead. The passion for magnificence and opulence in the design of religious objects became truly extravagant. (See, for example, the encasement of *Our Lady Odigitriya*, Plate 133.)

As early as the fourteenth century, under Greek influence, the Russians began to cover even the figures with plates of silver, showing in relief, more or less, the outlines and folds of the clothes and vestments. Such a plate is called a *riza*, properly speaking, a religious vestment, especially a chasuble or alb. It was first applied to the large stationary icons and later to those which individuals received as gifts at baptism or on special occasions. The masses of gold, diamonds, and pearls produce a striking effect. This is how Paul of Aleppo describes the look of the icons in the Uspensky Cathedral in Moscow:

All around the church and about the four piers are set great icons of which you can see nothing but the hands and faces. Hardly any of the clothing (that is, the painting) can be distinguished; the rest is thick *repoussé* silver and niello. . . . Even more opulent were the trappings of the icons in the Cathedral of the Annunciation (the favorite church of the wives and daughters of the tsars). No goldsmith, however skilled, could evaluate the great stones, diamonds, rubies, and emeralds, set upon the icons and halos of Our Savior and Our Lady; the jewels glow in the darkness like burning coals. The gilding of the icons with pure gold, the many-hued enamel executed with the finest art, all arouses the admiration of the discerning observer. The value of the icons in this church would fill several treasuries.[2]

It should be noted in this connection that the Western notion that one species of art is inherently superior to another meant little to the Russians. They had a scale of values of their own, in which the costliness and rarity of the materials employed and the difficulties in manipulating them ranked high. This particular approach to decoration of ecclesiastical furnishings was clearly bound up with polychromy in general, and above all with a prevailing taste for polychrome decoration employing several techniques simultaneously. By a judicious use of enamels for figures and ornamental details, together with inlays of gold and precious stones, the artist achieved a highly effective over-all integration of the composition.

The icons enriched with goldsmith's work, cabochons, and enamels are good examples of this taste. Here not merely symbols are involved: the purely aesthetic effects produced by the use of these glowing, highly ornamented surfaces cannot be wholly dissociated from the observer's consciousness of their costliness and rarity. These opulent trappings were the means of rendering more tangible to the spectator's imagination the supramondane reality he was invited to contemplate—an initiation, as it were, into a celestial world. And inevitably, these sumptuous adornments conjured up thoughts of Heaven and its glories.

The outstanding examples of ecclesiastical metal craftsmanship are the various articles and vessels used in the preparation and celebration of the Holy Eucharist, as prescribed by the Orthodox church: the chalice, the paten, the spear, the astericos used to cover the paten, a star-shaped object with rays bent to form feet, and the spoon used with the chalice—all of chiseled or enameled gold. There are also the *panagiae*, pectoral crosses, and symbols of office, worn by bishops, and a host of other objects

[2] Minns, *The Russian Icon*, 37.

used during the liturgical services, or great ceremonial processions: censers, ciboria, reliquaries, crucifixes, croziers, processional lanterns, and staffs (Plate 160). These were all given special attention in careful workmanship and lavish decoration.

The *panagiya (panhagiya)* is a peculiar ornament or sacred vessel of the Russo-Greek church. The word *panagiya* (most holy) refers figuratively to the Holy Virgin and by extension to the triangular communion wafers and to their containers, which are of two kinds: the pectoral *panagiya* is a jewel worn suspended from the neck by the high dignitaries of the church as a symbol of office, an object on which much care and rich decoration are lavished; the portable or travel *panagiya,* usually in the form of a circular or elliptical locket, made of two hinged, concave pieces, is worn by priests in the same way, and used for carrying the communion wafers on a journey or when visiting the sick. The *panagiyar* is a small round plate decorated with the image of the Virgin, on which the communion bread is placed for the rite of Elevation.

Many of the *panagiyas* in the Armory Museum of the Kremlin are fine specimens of craftsmanship; they are of gold or silver, enameled and set with precious stones and, some of them, with remarkable cameos (Plates 157–59).

Several types of crosses are used on different occasions. These crosses vary in size, design, material, and richness of decoration—from the simple, rudely stamped brass crosses of the poor peasantry to the enameled and bejeweled crosses of the patriarchs, metropolitans, tsars, and wealthy nobles (Plate 161). Very often a plain cross is set in the center of another, more elaborate or conventional, and nearly always sacred monograms and inscriptions in Slavonic characters are engraved on the field.

The small pectoral cross *(tel'nik* from the Russian word *telo,* meaning "body") is the most common, and is worn directly on the body.

Crosses, somewhat larger than the pectoral, worn by the members of the clergy over their vestments usually have an image of the Crucifixion on them; these are called bosom crosses (*naperstnyie kresty*).

Encolpion crosses consist of two crosses joined together one over the other by a hinge. They were mostly used for relics. Usually this type of cross has on one side the Crucifixion, on the reverse side images of saints.

The large wood, ivory, or metal altar crosses (*naprestol'nyie kresty*) are used by the priest for blessing the worshipers and also at various other ceremonies.

The censer, the use of which seems to have derived from the ancient Hebrew ceremonial, is one of the most important sacred utensils, and is in constant use in the Russo-Greek church.[3]

As in the West, certain architectural forms were used in church vessels (Plates 151, 152), and it is not surprising that certain features of Russian ecclesiastical architecture and ornament are prominent, especially the bulbous cupola (*lukovitsa*). A square or hexagon-shaped body with a cover is often used, suggesting a series of *Kokoshniki* supporting one or several drums that bear cupolas, each surmounted with a cross (Plate 152).

Representations of the Saviour and of the saints are usually arranged on the sides of the principal element in *repoussé* and chased niches. The hieratic characteristics of Byzantine iconography have been preserved, but Russia's distinctive treatment of the figures of saints and groups is manifest. The foot is often ornamented with niello tracery and with decorative inscriptions of interlaced Slavonic letters in compartments. The chains are of simple oval links, with now and then a small cross; the thumb pieces are similar to the cover in style, and are highly decorated.

The tabernacle or ciborium, the vessel for Eucharistic wafers (*darokhranitel'nitsa*)—often called "Zion" or "Jerusalem"—is usually in the form of a church or shrine with domes or cupolas surmounted by a cross (Plates 151, 152). The "Jerusalem" taber-

---

[3] For a fifteenth-century chased silver censer reproduced in color, see Rybakov, *Treasures in the Kremlin*, plate 49.

nacle (Plate 152) made during the reign of Ivan III for the sacristy of the Uspensky Cathedral is now in the Armory Museum of the Moscow Kremlin. It is built in the form of a cupola church, and is a characteristic specimen of Russian art of that period.

The prayer books, the gospels, and the psalters were of exceptional magnificence. Their design was an art and a handicraft which involved the services of calligraphers, printers, illuminators, miniaturists, jewelers, leatherworkers, and bookbinders who worked in the Oruzheinaya Palata. The book covers are usually of precious metals enriched with filigree or *repoussé* ornament and gems. Pearls often serve to form borders around Biblical scenes and figures of saints executed in enamels or in embossed work. Smaller scenes of figures are usually arranged along the margins and at the corners. The Mstislav Gospels, 1103–1551, the Book of Gospels presented to the Uspensky Cathedral by Ivan III in 1499, and the Book of Gospels of Boyarin B.M. Morozov, 1699, are but three of the outstanding examples of the art of the book and its covering (Plates 147–49).

In the ornamentation of sacred books a great deal of freedom and originality was shown. Russian illuminators borrowed from many sources, but in adapting diverse foreign elements, they transformed them and stamped them with their own national genius.

The earliest Slavonic ornamental motifs are characterized by arabesques of pointed ivy-shaped leaves with curled-in edges, in greens, blues, and reds on a gold ground, heightened with white for the reds and blues, yellow for the greens, and combined with thin stalks in blue, forming a flowery geometrical combination. The ornaments consist of initial letters, head- and tail-pieces and borders often bearing on the upper part figures of birds or grotesques.

To the end of the fourteenth century belong two remarkable manuscripts—the "Evangel (Gospels) of the Boyar Koshka" and the "Evangel of the Boyar Khitrovo." Both are beautifully executed and ornamented on parchment. (They are at present in the

Lenin Library, Moscow.) Lazarev ventures the opinion that both of them came from the Moscow studio of Theophanes the Greek.

The Koshka Evangel has no miniatures. It is decorated with chapter heads and initials in which foliage is skillfully combined with fantastic animal bodies. Dragons, birds, dolphins, and snakes are vividly and realistically rendered. The initials have a jewel-like finish; their pure bright colors—golden, blue, green, and red —are remarkable for their brilliancy. The volume has gorgeous silver covers richly decorated with *repoussé* work, filigree, and enamels.[4] It is one of the great fourteenth-century masterpieces of the art of book designing and bookbinding.

No less great is the Khitrovo Evangel—the gift of Tsar Feodor Alekseevich to the boyar Khitrovo (superintendent of the Oruz-heinaya Palata, 1654–80). We do not know who were its creators, but its design, craftsmanship, and style of decoration all point to Theophanes the Greek. There are, however, a number of Russian art historians—among them Alpatov—who think that some of the miniatures were painted by Rublev.

The Khitrovo Evangel differs from the Koshka; it is decorated not only with chapter heads and initials but also with miniatures representing the four evangelists and their symbols (the eagle, the angel, the bull, and the lion). The capital letters are drawn in the form of birds, dolphins, and snakes. Especially finely rendered is the drawing of a blue heron standing on a snake and staring at it.

The finest miniature in the Khitrovo Evangel is the figure of a curly-haired angel with a book in his hand, symbolizing the Apostle Matthew.[5] It is a figure of youthful charm and grace in motion. Book in hand, he is shown moving swiftly over the edge of the frame, his broad wing lightly spread out behind him, so that he seems to be soaring. The figure is fitted into the round frame with a subtle sense of proportion; and the flowing lines

[4] Reproduced in Grabar', *Istoriya russkogo Iskusstva* (1953), III, 221.
[5] Reproduced in color, *ibid.*, plate 89.

of the folds in the robe complement the round frame. This miniature seems to have all the earmarks or Rublev's genius. Another miniature in this manuscript is that of an eagle symbolizing the Apostle John. The bird, however, looks more like a gentle dove than an eagle, the only acquiline feature being its curved beak. Its wings are slightly lifted, in its claws it holds a book, and, poised within the round frame, it appears in flight. Thus the legendary symbol of John came to appear in this manuscript as a prophetic bird.

The close of the fifteenth century and the century following are the richest periods of Russian illuminated manuscripts. They show a creative vitality and a fertile inventiveness in a great variety of ornamented motifs. Persian, Arabic, Indian—all the splendor of the Eastern styles mingled with much that was borrowed from Western sources. All that was combined, transformed, and resolved into something quite original and unique, something that had a flavor all its own.

Embroidery

The elaborately embroidered vestments of the clergy, the altar cloths and icon covers, and the palls and shrouds of Christ used on specific occasions are a further illustration of the practice established by the church in educating the masses by means of pictorial representation (Plates 144–46, 162). The composition subjects, largely from Byzantine tradition, include religious scenes such as the Annunciation and the Lamentation. Although the message is conveyed in the language of the art of Byzantium, the accent is decidedly Russian. The solemnity and beauty of the Byzantine models must have captured the imagination of the Russian artist, and he was quick to recognize their artistic merit and accept their underlying principles and techniques. But here again, as in the other branches of art, he set out to assimilate and transform the Byzantine models and imbue them with his own spirit.

To students of Muscovite culture, old Russian embroidery has an additional and very special interest because it is the creation of feminine hands of old Russia, a profoundly revealing expression of the spiritual and emotional nature of the Russian woman secluded in her convent or *terem;* it demonstrates the zeal, taste, and skill not only of the convent-trained nun, but also of the staff embroiderers in the workshops of the princely courts.

The many technical problems encountered in embroidery make it one of the most difficult of arts. It was the icon painter who usually outlined the general composition of the picture, but it was the woman needleworker who did the embroidery. From the moment she took over the design, she had to have a full appreciation of the problems involved—technical as well as artistic; and at the very first threading of her needle it was necessary for her to visualize fully the finished product as it might be affected by the combined result of texture, thread, stitch, hue, and sheen of her media. Many of the extant needlework pictures rival in conception, beauty, and technique the paintings which adorned the iconostases and walls of the churches.

An outstanding example of historical and artistic interest is the icon cover used to decorate the Rublev icon of *The Trinity.* This cloth, now kept in the Zagorsk Historical Museum, was designed and embroidered in 1499 by order of the Tsargrad (Constantinople) Tsaritsa, Grand Princess of Moscow Sophia (Zoë Palaeologue).[6] A large cross with Slavonic inscriptions fills the central area of the cloth. The panels bordering the central area depict several scenes from the Gospels (Annunciation, Ascension, Descent of the Holy Spirit, and the Trinity) and scenes from the lives of various saints. This work has one peculiar feature not found in other monuments of Russian embroidery— the surfaces of the vestments, of the architectural elements, and of the trees are covered with varicolored specks. The Russian art historian A. N. Svirin ventures the opinion that this feature was borrowed from samples of Western textiles. In all probability, the Palaeologue princess was anxious to incorporate in the deco-

[6] Reproduced in *ibid.,* 532.

ration of this icon cover certain well-remembered Italian motifs.

More complex in composition than the icon covers are the shrouds of Christ *(plashchanitsy)*. They are oblong panels of fairly large dimensions (seven to eight feet long), having a border of geometrical design or conventionalized Slavonic lettering. The shrouds are used in Orthodox churches on Good Friday as coverings for the ceremonial bier of Christ; the principal subject is the dead Christ mourned by the Virgin, the angels, and the saints. One of the finest shrouds in existence is the so-called *Puchezhskaya Plashchanitsa* (1441).[7] The artist resorted to extreme elongation in the portrayal of Christ's body on the shroud, although the figures of the Virgin, St. John, and the angels are of normal proportions. The device of distortion was evidently used as a means of heightening expression. The embroidery is on a background of silk; the needlework is exceptionally fine, of great simplicity, and shows exquisite taste in the choice of color. Experts consider it a superlative example of embroidery.

Another beautiful example of an embroidered shroud, rivaling that of the Puchezh, is one made in the shops of Princess Evfrosiniya Staritskaya and presented by her about 1562 to the Kirillo-Byelozersk Monastery. In the technique of its needlework, richness of ornament, and masterly blending of gold, silver, and pastel threads, this shroud is one of the outstanding productions of the period (Plate 144).

Secular Gold and Silver Work

The church was the principal but not the sole patron of the decorative arts and crafts. Russia's goldsmiths and other craftsmen were set a number of new tasks of a secular nature by the rising, wealthy upper layer of the urban population. Most important, life at the tsar's court and in the households of the great nobles was becoming more and more ostentatious, demanding magnificence, luxury, and color in surroundings, appointments, and personal apparel. The walls and ceilings of the palaces were

[7] Reproduced in color in Rybakov, *Treasures in the Kremlin*, plates 86, 87.

covered with brilliant frescoes, and the furniture and furnishings were richly ornamented in the spirit of the time, in keeping with the decorative vogues of church furnishings and the architecture of the Muscovite state (Plates 64–78, 92–97, 145–60, 175–82).

The tsar and the patriarch maintained their own workshops in the Oruzheinaya Palata staffed with native and foreign artists and craftsmen skilled in the production of luxury articles. Many craftsmen working privately with a few helpers supplied the ever-growing demands of the nobles and rich merchants for jewelry and other luxury wares.

We have eye-witness accounts of the splendor of the court, the prodigious wealth, and the treasures of gold and silver plate of the Moscow tsars of the sixteenth and seventeenth centuries (Plates 169–74). English travelers of that period, especially those who had an eye for precious metals and gems, described Moscow as another Peru. Richard Chancellor left us a vivid description of a royal banquet given by Ivan the Terrible in 1553:

> The Emperor sitting upon a high and stately seat, apparelled with a robe of silver and with another diadem on his head; our men, being placed over against him, sit down. In the midst of the room stood a mighty cupboard upon a square foot, whereupon stood also a round board, in manner of a diamond, broad beneath, and towards the top narrow, and every step rose up more narrow than the other. Upon this cupboard was placed the Emperor's plate, which was so much that the very cupboard itself was scant able to sustain the weight of it. The better part of all the vessels and goblets was made of very fine gold; and amongst the rest, there were four pots of very large bigness, which did adorn the rest of the plate in great measure, for they were so high, that they thought them at the least five feet long. There also upon this cupboard certain silver casks, not much differing from the quantity of our firkins, wherein was reserved the Emperor's drink . . .
>
> On Christmas day we were all willed to dine with the Emperor's Majesty, where for bread, meat, and drink we were served as at other times before. But for goodly and rich plate we never saw the like or so much before. There dined that day in the Emperor's

presence above 500 strangers and 200 Russians, and they all were served in vessels of gold, and that as much as could stand one by another upon the tables. Besides this there were four cupboards garnished with goodly plate, both of gold and silver. Among the which there were twelve barrels of silver containing about twelve gallons apiece and at each end of every barrel were six hoops of fine gold. This dinner continued about six hours.[8]

Another striking picture of the great collection of gold and silver plate and jeweled cups, as it existed before the Polish occupation of 1612, is presented by the Burgundian captain Jacques Margeret, who served under Boris Godunov and Dmitri the Pretender:

> The treasury of the tsars is filled with all sorts of jewels. . . . There is a large number of gold and silver vessels of various sizes. Besides this there is an infinite number of gilt and non-gilt silver plate. I have seen a half dozen huge casks made of silver and a large number of enormous and very heavy bowls with ring-shaped handles attached to each side, so that when filled with meal they could be conveniently carried. These vessels require the services of four attendants each to carry and distribute them among the guests, usually one bowl per table. With each bowl there were provided a number of large, boat-shaped ladles *(kovshi)* used for dipping into the contents of the bowl. All those vessels are of Russian work. Besides those, there were a large number of silver vessels of German, English, and Polish make—either gifts of various kings and princes, sent through their ambassadors, or items acquired by the Russian tsars because of the beauty of their workmanship.[9]

Among the representative examples of secular gold and silver work are the drinking vessels used at the princely courts and the households of the great nobles on ceremonial and festive occa-

[8] These descriptions by Richard Chancellor are given in the voluminous *Principal Navigations and Voyages* of Richard Hakluyt.

[9] Jacques Margeret's description of the tsar's treasury is quoted in A. Maskell's *Russian Art*, 119–20, from J. Margeret's *Estat de l'empire de Russie*.

sions or at private family affairs. There is variety in these drinking vessels, but some of them are peculiar to Russia, especially the loving cup *(bratina)*, the ladle *(kovsh)*, and the small cup *(charka)* used for strong liquors (Plates 172–73).

Tall beakers with flaring silhouettes are also favorite forms, but the bulbous shape is the most common. It is evident that the bulb-form, which is such a distinctive feature of the Russian church cupola, was adapted for these drinking vessels. We find a semblance of this form in the old crowns of the patriarchs and metropolitans of the church and in the decorative elements of the censers, ciboria, and vases. In the *bratina* and in some vases, the bulging body, the coving up of the bottom of the bowls, and the use of convex lobes suggesting strength are quite common.

The name *bratina* (from *brat,* brother) was given to a peculiar sort of bowl or loving cup which was passed around the table during feasts and customarily used for drinking to the health of the guests or the hosts. The drink was consumed as a token and a promise of lasting brotherhood. The form and ornament were confined within certain traditional conventions. Nearly all these cups are of a globular shape resting on a low base or on animal feet. Their lips as a rule bear an inscription. Some are provided with handles and covers.

The *bratina* is usually of silver gilt—in accord with the sentiment expressed in an old Russian adage: "Love is like a golden vessel; though it bends it can never be broken." The body was usually decorated with *repoussé* flower ornament or foliage on a matted ground, with fruit and fretwork, or with medallions depicting hunting scenes or animals of the chase. The bottom of the bowl was often decorated with a convex and nearly hemispherical chased or engraved medallion. An almost invariable ornament was the inscription around the rim or lip, engraved or nielloed in the interlaced Slavonic lettering that so often contributed a distinctive feature to the Russian decorative arts. The inscription recorded the name of the owner or a toast or a sentimental motto, such as "Drink to our health" or "Praising God and wishing long life and good health to the tsar."

Herberstein, in describing the drinking customs of the Russians and their manner of proposing toasts, was evidently referring to the *bratina* in his travel notes of 1549:

> Silver goblets and various other vessels containing liquor are produced, and all strive to make each other drunk; and very clever they are in finding excuses for inviting men to drink, and when they are at a loss for a toast to propose, they begin at last to drink to the health of the emperor and the prince, his brother, and after that to the welfare of any others whom they believe to hold any position of dignity and honor. They think that no one ought or can refuse the cup when these names are proposed. The drinking is done in this fashion. He who proposes the toast takes his cup and goes into the middle of the room and, standing with his head uncovered, pronounces in a festive speech the name of him whose health he wishes to drink, and what he has to say in his behalf. Then after emptying the cup, he turns it upside down over his head, so that all may see that he has emptied it, and that he sincerely gave the health of the person in honor of whom the toast was drunk. He then goes to the top of the table and orders many cups to be filled, and then hands each man his cup, pronouncing the name of the party whose health is to be drunk, on which each is obliged to go into the middle of the room, and, after emptying his cup, to return to his place. He who wishes to escape too long a drinking bout must pretend that he is drunk or sleepy, or at least declare that, having already emptied many cups, he cannot drink any more; for they do not think that their guests are well received, or hospitably treated, unless they are sent home drunk.[10]

Most persons of eminence and wealth had their own particular family *bratina*, which was especially valued as a gift. This fact explains why so much care was lavished upon the design, and

[10] Sigmund von Herberstein was ambassador from Vienna to the Court of the Grand Prince Vasili Ivanovich in 1517 and again in 1526. (See his travel notes, *Commentaries on Muscovite Affairs*, I, 95–96, 105–106; II 131–32.)

why these cups were among the best examples of Russian crafts-manship.

An interesting example is the *bratina* of Peter Alekseevich Tretyakov, who was a secretary of the State Council under Mikhail Feodorovich about 1618. It is of silver, partly gilt, weighs about three pounds, and stands eleven and four-tenth inches high. The bowl is of the conventional form, but around the base are several figures of men in doublet and hose supporting the bowl in their upstretched arms. The cover is coved, and from it rises a silver flower on a long stem. Most of the surface of the bowl and cover is embossed with foliage and flowers. Four attached gilt plaques are decorated with similar *repoussé* ornament and with shields flanked respectively by a heraldic lion and unicorn, two fishes, two pages, and two eagles. Beneath each plaque the same design is engraved on the plain surface. The form and floral decoration of these plaques recall the jeweled pendants (*tsaty*) hanging from the necks of icons. At the bottom of the bowl is the usual convex medallion engraved with the question: "Man, who art thou who looketh at me, dost thou perchance desire to swallow me?" The inscription on the rim, freely translated, reads: "Know thou man, as arms are necessary to a warrior on the day of battle, so is rain in time of drought; even as the comfort of consolation from a true friend in time of misfortune and sorrow, so is the need for moderation, understanding, and companion-ship for all those who would partake of the sweetness. The *bratina* of Peter Alekseevich Tretyakov."[11]

The *kovsh* is a kind of boat-shaped bowl with a long handle. It is used for ladling out such common beverages as *kvas* (a sour-sweet drink made of water and rye bread) or beer. These bowls are of different sizes, some quite large; most of them are elon-gated, with the front turned up to a point. They were used in the homes of the peasantry, in monastery refectories, in army mess halls, and in many other places. The Russian museums con-tain examples dating from the fourteenth and fifteenth centuries

[11] Bartenev, *Moskovsky Kreml'*, II, p. 324.

which have been studiously imitated until comparatively recent times.[12]

The *kovsh* and the *bratina* derived from old models fashioned in wood by the early Slavs. Gradually they lost their original practical function and became symbols of honor conferred by the tsar on members of his court or on his ambassadors and generals as an award for some exceptional service to the state. The design and ornamentation of the early examples of these traditional vessels were relatively simple, but in the eighteenth century, under the influence of Western fashions, they became highly ornate. The late nineteenth century introduced a fresh, more cosmopolitan conception of decorative art, which led Karl Fabergé and other adherents of the new trend to produce some beautiful ceremonial *kovshi* and *bratinas* inspired by early seventeenth-century styles.

The *charka*, a kind of a small cup used for strong liquors, is usually hemispherical, sometimes on small animal feet, and nearly always with one flat open-worked handle. The lip is usually engraved with Slavonic inscriptions or mottoes similar to those on the *bratina*. The *charka* was usually made of two shells decorated with lobsters, sea horses, men-swallowing fish, mermaids, or other fantastic sea creatures; some were made of semiprecious stones mounted with bands of gold.[13]

Arms and Armor

Quite understandably, a people so persistently engaged in warfare and so imbued with love of colorful ornamentation attached much importance to the decoration of arms and armor. In the Oruzheinaya Palata and the Moscow Historical Museum are many splendid examples of the varied forms and ornaments of sixteenth- and seventeenth-century helmets, shields, maces, halberds, pikes, sabres, saddlery, and harness richly decorated with

[12] For typical, highly decorated examples of the *kovsh*, see Rybakov, *Treasures in the Kremlin*, plates 51, 52.

[13] For a typical example of the *charka*, see Boguslavsky, *Gosudarstvennaya, oruzheinaya palata Moskovskogo Kremlya*, plate 166.

niello, enameling, damascening, and incrustation with varicolored gems (Plates 166–68).

Richard Chancellor offers us a glimpse of the military trappings of the army of Ivan the Terrible in 1553.

> All his men are horsemen. The horsemen are all archers with such bows as the Turks have, and they ride short as do the Turks. Their armor is a coate of plate, with a skull on their heads. Some of their coates are covered with velvet or cloth of gold; their desire is to be sumptuous in the field, and especially the nobles and gentlemen; as I have heard their trimming is very costly, and partly I have seene it, or else I would scarcely have believed it; but the Duke himselfe is richly attired above all measure: his pavilion is covered either with cloth of gold or silver, and so set with stones that it is wonderful to see it. I have seene the King's Majesties of England and the French King's pavilions, which are fayre, yet not like unto his. And when they bee sent into farre or strange countreys, or that strangers come to them, they be very gorgeous. Els the Duke himselfe goeth but menaly in apparrell; and when he goeth betwixt one place and another hee is but reasonably apparrelled over other times. In the while that I was in Moscow the Duke sent two ambassadors to the King of Poleland, which had at the lest five hundred horses; their sumptuousness was above measure, not onely in themselves, but also in their horses, as velvet, cloth of golds, and cloth of silver set with pearles and not scant. What shall I farther say? I never heard of nor saw men so sumptuous.[14]

Moscow armorers became renowned for their skill in preparation of steel as well as for their artistry in damascening, nielloing, enameling, and gem encrusting. The registers of the Oruzheinaya Palata mention blades, coats of mail, and helmets made in Moscow, Circasian, Turkish, Persian, and German styles.

The helmets were usually hemispherical or conical, with backpieces, earpieces, and a guard for the face in the form of a movable arrow-shaped piece or nosepiece damascened with gold—a type common in the East (Plates 166).

[14] Hakluyt, *Principal Navigations*, II, 229, 230.

Several varieties of maces, adapted either for use in war or as scepters, are preserved in the Oruzheinaya Palata. Some are provided at the top with six wings or projections that served as cutting edges; others have handles that are richly damascened, nielloed, enameled, or studded with jewels and were used only at important state affairs.

The battle-axes are of various shapes; some were used by the tsar's bodyguards on ceremonial occasions. They are of silver-gilt, with crescent-shaped steel blades damascened with gold and handles decorated with arabesque designs.

Breastplates and other parts of the body armor and the large round shields or bucklers were covered with elaborate designs in *repoussé* work. Color effects were obtained by the gold inlay of damascening. Niello, enamel work, and jewels used in profusion heightened the richness.

It is particularly during the reign of Aleksei Mikhailovich, from whose time we have so many richly ornamented monuments, that we find arms of great magnificence. Outstanding are a bow-case and a quiver (Plate 167) used by the tsar on gala occasions. They are of the same character and workmanship as the scepter and globe (Plate 164). The work is ascribed to Ivan Yuriev. There are several other bow-and-arrow cases, recalling the ancient Scythian form, made of various precious materials and elaborately enameled and jeweled.

A fine example of *repoussé* and chased work is a powder flask or priming-horn (Plate 168). It is a circular silver-gilt box, *repoussé* and chased in high relief on both sides; the design on one side represents the so-called "Tsar's vision" (*Tsarskoe videnie*), that is, an eagle attacking a dragon; round these is a border of leaves interspersed with birds and animals, all on a matted ground. On the other side is a figure of St. George striking a dragon surrounded by a border of foliage. An inscription in Russian running round the edge records that the flask belonged to A. I. Nesterov.[15]

[15] A. I. Nesterov was assistant (in 1660) to Khitrovo, superintendent of the Oruzheinaya Palata.

The Oruzheinaya Palata

In the preceding pages we referred to the Oruzheinaya Palata and its contribution to the arts and crafts of Muscovite Russia. Its role in the design and manufacture of arms and armor was great, but no less great was its role as a training center of generations of icon painters, manuscript calligraphers, illuminators, miniaturists, jewelers, and many other craftsmen in the field of the decorative arts.

It does not come within the scope of this book to present a detailed history of this unique institution. However, a few of the more important events in its long life, its manifold activities, and its significant personalities, so far as they have influenced Russian decorative arts and crafts, must be singled out.[16]

This institution, which is the oldest and richest museum of decorative art in Russia, was created in the first years of the sixteenth century as an arsenal. It became successively a technical, scientific, pedagogical, and art institute, and contained shops and studios of icon and portrait painting and gold and silver work, keeping at the same time its original purpose—the manufacture of arms. By 1628 some of its artifacts were already worthy of being museum pieces.

The office in charge of the tsar's treasure, organized during the reign of Ivan III and mentioned for the first time in 1494, consisted of three sections: the Grand Treasury, which contained the tsar's regalia; the Armory (Oruzheinaya Palata), which housed shops for the manufacture of the tsar's arms; and the storehouse or depot that contained the imperial robes, uniforms, arms, and armor for the tsar, his bodyguards, and his most trusted military units.

Even among the first employees of the shops there were not only craftsmen skilled in arms manufacture, but also artists who

[16] For a detailed, richly illustrated study of the Moscow Kremlin Armory and its museum, see S. K. Bogoyavlensky, *Gosudarstvennaya Oruzheinaya Palata*; Boguslavsky, *Gosudarstvennaya Oruzheinaya Palata*. For good color illustrations of some of the outstanding objects in the Armory museum, see Rybakov, *Treasures in the Kremlin.*

specialized in the embellishment of the tsar's weapons, armor, trappings, and the imperial household vessels and plate.

In the icon-painting chamber (Ikonnaya Palata), which was somewhat like the Italian l'Opera del Duomo, were artists who designed the tsar's emblems and standards and other decorative items for the tsar's immediate family. These artists also painted the frescoes in the tsar's apartments.

The manufacture of arms was at an especially high level during the reign of Aleksei Mikhailovich. The Russian craftsmen either followed the models of foreign masters or used the old Russian models as their inspiration, perfecting and elaborating them or inventing new models and decorating them in the "Moscow Style," in keeping with the rich national costumes of the period.

In Muscovite Russia the Oruzheinaya Palata, with its closely integrated gold and silversmith workshops and the private shops of the tsar and tsaritsa, was the very fountainhead of Russian national art. It was a kind of central station, where nearly everything pertaining to the arts and crafts largely originated, and from which its various products spread all over the land. Although the Oruzheinaya Palata was not exactly a stronghold of tradition —more of the latest innovations, local and foreign, could be found there than anywhere else—still its products must be considered as the "work of Moscow" (*Moskovskoye delo*), art largely influenced by the spirit of medieval Russia.

The particular style—often of monumental character and imposing magnificence—developed by the Oruzheinaya Palata was the result of its craftsmen's study of the arts of the times of Ivan the Terrible and his predecessors. Ivan was especially influential in developing the artistic activities of the Oruzheinaya Palata. He bought stocks of precious metals and gold and silver vessels in Germany and commandeered artists and artisans skilled in embellishing icon encasements from Novgorod. He also imported craftsmen specializing in religious vessels from Riga. These craftsmen became members of the staff of the Oruzheinaya Palata, contributing their knowledge and skill to the development of the

arts and crafts as well as to the further growth of weapon manufacturing. The bureau grew in importance and became firmly
established as an industrial, scientific, and artistic center.

During the Time of Trouble the administration of the Oruzheinaya Palata ceased to function, and many of its artists and
craftsmen deserted to the provinces. Much of the gold and silver
plate was melted down and minted into coin for payment to the
Polish and Swedish invaders. The succession of false pretenders
to the throne and upstart rulers plundered and sold the great
collections of jewelry accumulated by generations of grand
princes and tsars. With the accession of Tsar Mikhail Feodorovich the scattered Palata staff returned to Moscow and resumed
work. Moscow came to life again, ushering in a strong revival of
cultural and artistic activities.

Tsar Mikhail re-established the Oruzheinaya Palata, but concentrated mainly on the purely technical side of arms manufacturing because he felt that decoration and embellishment could
wait. He imported mining engineers and technicians and built
powder and firearms plants; he invited the best native and foreign
specialists to his service. The bureau in charge of arms manufacturing became the most important section of the Armory. The
goldsmithing and silversmithing sections were detached from
arms manufacturing and functioned as separate bureaus subordinated to the arms office, in which all the industrial and artistic
activities were centered—mining, smelting, and casting; painting
of icons, portraits, designing of emblems, blazonry, military standards, government documents, charters, and citations; and miniature painting, manuscript illuminating, and bookbinding. The
administration of each one of these activities, headed by a special
functionary, was housed in a separate building or buildings. The
buildings were close to the palace and functioned as branches of
the court household.

An important period in the artistic activities of the Oruzheinaya
Palata began with the appointment of boyar Bogdan Matveevich
Khitrovo (1616–80) to the office of armorer. His appointment, by

Tsar Aleksei Mikhailovich in 1654, to this high post coincided with the initiation of the Nikonian reforms, which had far-reaching effects on Russian history and art. The figure of Khitrovo, as an administrator and enlightened progressive, is so important that it is necessary to consider both the man and the historical setting in which he moved.[17]

Both Patriarch Nikon and Tsar Aleksei Mikhailovich wanted to introduce into the art of icon painting a current of new ideas and to bring it in line with the reforms. They also decided to reintroduce the outer and inner features of the Greek church: the basic plan, cupolas, furnishings, vessels, ambos, bishops' crosses, vestments, and cowls. For that purpose it was necessary that the head of the icon and goldsmith chambers should be a man who could see eye to eye with the tsar and the patriarch and act in agreement with them in all matters related to the Nikonian reforms.

Khitrovo happened to be the ideal man for the position. He had already distinguished himself as soldier, diplomat, judge, administrator, and builder. He was not creative, but he had a gift of sensing the problems of his artists and craftsmen. Above all, he had a knack of combining the management and co-ordination of things purely technical with those that belong to the spiritual and creative world. Although he had the greatest respect for the past, he encouraged any new expression that fitted the temper of an age when Western art was becoming firmly established in Russia.

The thorniest problem facing Khitrovo was to determine the line of demarcation between Orthodoxy and heresy in icon painting—to reconcile his own artistic judgment with the often-divergent preferences of the tsar and the patriarch. On the one hand, he had to take into consideration many hallowed traditions in the treatment of religious subjects; on the other, he had to struggle

[17] For an analysis of Khitrovo's activities in the Oruzheinaya Palata, see V. K. Trutovsky, "Boyarin i oruzhnichii Bogdan Matveevich Khitrovo i Moskovskaya Oruzheinaya Palata," *Staryie Gody* (July, 1909), 366ff.

with the technical difficulties peculiar to Russian religious painting, with the fact that the icon was not a creation of a single artist but the collective work of a number of specialists. Then, too, the Western influences in icon painting were antithetical to the very spirit of Russian icon painting—a folk creation, its content representing the confession of faith, its techniques the ways of the people.

Khitrovo undertook the job with energy and boldness. In spite of the sharp protest of Nikon and the tirades of the fanatical Archpriest Avvakum, he welcomed Western influences. The works of art produced during the twenty-six years of his tenure clearly indicate that he was a man of great culture who appreciated talent and individuality in artists, giving his greatest encouragement and support to those who could value foreign models, adapt them to the needs of Russia, and imbue the finished product with the Russian spirit.

The activities of the icon chamber were not limited strictly to sacred painting. Its artists also painted portraits and miniatures, illuminated manuscripts, made maps and charts, designed furniture and furnishings, created frescoes and objects of gold, designed textiles for vestments. They did everything and anything that required creative power, imagination, and ability.

The celebrated Ushakov prepared designs for a number of gold and enamel vessels in the ateliers of the Oruzheinaya Palata and also decorated arms and drew maps. His chief work at the Palata was designing church vessels to be executed in precious metals and enamels; he is thought to have been the designer of Patriarch Nikon's miter, which has some noteworthy enameling, especially in the upper part (Plate 150).

During the second half of the seventeenth century the ornamental patterns of a secular nature gradually underwent a change, away from the Russian and Byzantine models toward those of Western Europe. However, the floral ornamentation of manuscripts and icons was still in the ancient Russian style, featuring extensive application of gold and silver backgrounds. "Frankish" or Western ornament—the motifs and style of the baroque—was used rarely and timidly. The craft of embossing and chasing reached a high level of excellence in this period, and the objects from the tsars' and patriarchs' treasures, both religious and secular, are all outstanding examples.

The principal business of the Oruzheinaya Palata, the purely technical and industrial phase of arms manufacturing, reached a high level of competence. Along with the technical improvements in ceremonial arms, their embellishment was also greatly perfected. Here we see decorative art come to the fore. Among the artists and the craftsmen we often find the personalities already familiar to us as icon painters, book designers, illuminators, and illustrators.

During Khitrovo's tenure the arts of enameling, niello, and filigree were even more cultivated than those of gold and silver *repoussé*. They achieved a style all their own and acquired unique distinguishing characteristics of refinement and elegance—novelties in design and technique, new fashions in the application of gold and silver, and unique and entirely different color schemes, all of which was reflected in the other arts and crafts of that period. The activities and innovations in this field were largely due to Tsar Aleksei Mikhailovich and express his personal tastes. His influence is especially revealed in two fields, gold sheet stamping and enameling. Aleksei was favorably disposed toward the Orthodox East and its representative arts. As a result, a number of jeweled articles appeared in the Tsargrad (Constantinople) style—a combination of the art of the Turkish Mussulman East with that of the Greeks and Mount Athos. The style of the Western jewelers, so much in vogue during the reign of his father, receded into the background.

The Tsargrad style in jewelry was distinctive in its extensive use of thin gold plaques and sheathing decorated with stamped Greek-Byzantine designs and enriched with emeralds, rubies, diamonds, and enamels of the same shades as the gems. This style, in great favor throughout Aleksei's reign, seems to have been peculiar to his epoch.

In the art of enameling, the influence of Aleksei's tastes reveals itself in his partiality toward the colors green, blue, and white, with the frequent addition of yellow and sometimes of red shades. During his reign pink Turkish foliage designs and flowers also appeared in the enamel ornamentation. These same pink flowers can be seen in the illuminations and page borders of manuscripts and in the design of chapter heads, citations, charters, and patents of nobility. Aleksei's preference for green tints was so strong as to influence even the architectural decoration of his day—for example, the exterior wall murals of the Poteshnyi Palace.

Partly under the influence of Mount Athos and with the help of Greek craftsmen, niello work reached a high level of development. This art was long known in Russia, but it was rarely used except for very fine lines in ornament and inscriptions. During the reign of Tsar Aleksei it was more frequently and widely applied in gold and silver work. Niello was often used to cover the entire background and thus became the forerunner of the niello ground that was so much in vogue during the Moscow period of Peter the Great's reign.

The Oruzheinaya Palata with its many shops continued to develop and prosper until 1707. The last armorer was Prince Peter Ivanovich Prozorovsky. In 1711, Peter I ordered the personnel of the Oruzheinaya Palata transferred from Moscow to the newly established armory in St. Petersburg. All the designers and craftsmen in any way connected with the arts went along. The year 1711 is considered by many historians as the darkest year in the history of Russian national Art. The Russian art historian V. K. Trutovsky writes:

> The most remarkable artistic institution, the only one of its kind, in the truest sense of the word, an institution, the like of which never existed anywhere or at any time, was destroyed with a single

stroke of the pen, with the scribble of five letters (Peter). With it died the very heart of national Russian art. It never beat again and there was never a true renaissance. It carried with it to its grave the old traditions, originality, and uniqueness which so powerfully and brilliantly informed all its creations, subjugating everything foreign and external: the art of the Franks *(friaz-heskoye)*, of Byzantium (Tsargrad or Constantinople), Persia, and Venice. It carried with it to the grave the very spirit and sensitivity of the Russian artistic soul."[18]

Trutovsky's estimate of this "most remarkable institution" is quite correct, but his gloomy comments on the results of its destruction have no basis in fact. The very heart of national Russian art "did not die." Its heart beats could still be felt, and more and more so as time passed.

Towards the end of the eighteenth century, and more markedly in the first three quarters of the nineteenth, the Western styles which dominated Russia for over a century, began to seem foreign, imported, and dry. Official nationalism and the growing tide of Slavophilism—two currents running parallel but issuing from different political and social sources—were instrumental in arresting the tide of Western classicism and turning the aspirations of the Russian intelligentsia toward the interrupted development of national art.

Russian goldsmiths and jewelers returned increasingly for inspiration to Byzantine Muscovite shapes and motifs. Old forms and the old techniques of filigree, niello, and *cloisonné* enamels were revived and adapted to the taste and demands of the Slavophil movement. Teapots and trays, cups, saucers, and cigarette boxes were shaped and decorated in mixed European and Muscovite Russian styles.

The design of the tea-glass holders, tumblers, tankards, and *charkas* was derived from the seventeenth-century Russian models. Some enameled silver-gilt objects, made in the 1870's by the

18 Trutovsky, *ibid.*, 348.

Moscow silversmiths, Paul Ovchinikov, Ivan Khlebnikov, Pavel Sazykov,[19] and many others, prove how viable were the artistic techniques and imaginative folklore ornament of seventeenth-century Russia.

Interest in old Russia artistic silver plate and jewelry was greatly heightened by the work of Karl Fabergé (1846–1920), the court-jeweler of the late nineteenth and early twentieth centuries. He was the last in a long line of gifted craftsmen to devote themselves to fashioning objects of the highest artistry. Fabergé is best known for the beautiful Easter Eggs made for the Imperial Family and many objects of fantasy fashioned by the master craftsmen of his establishment in St. Petersburg (Leningrad).[20] Most of his work was influenced by the *Mir Iskusstva* (*World of Art*) movement which flourished in Russia during the late nineteenth and early twentieth centuries. It ushered in some fresh ideas, a broader cosmopolitan conception of art, and, at the same time, a better understanding of the Russian national past.

It was in this spirit that most of the Fabergé creations were fashioned. They derive from the old Muscovite tradition and have the unmistakable Russian characteristics—the Slavic folklore motifs, filigree spirals, and massive bosses executed with great skill and restraint in the classical manner of eighteenth-century French art.

[19] For illustrations of their works, see Marvin C. Ross, *The Art of Karl Fabergé and His Contemporaries.*
[20] For the life and works of Karl Fabergé, see Ross, *ibid.*; H. C. Bainbridge, *Peter Carl Fabergé*; A. K. Snowman, *The Art of Carl Fabergé.*

XX

Woodwork and Carving

WOODCARVING IN RELIEF and in the round has been practiced in Russia for centuries. Long before the introduction of Christianity, many of Russia's artists and craftsmen were engaged in carving wooden statues of the various deities worshiped by the pagan Slavic tribes. The ancient chronicles of Russia contain descriptions of huge, elaborately carved and gilded statues of Perun, god of thunder and disaster; Lada, goddess of love and mercy; and Volos, god of trade and agriculture.

With the introduction of Christianity, it was quite natural that the art of woodcarving would be employed to serve the requirements of the new religion. The sculptors and carvers in wood were given the task of producing the many religious vessels and furnishings used for the elaborate rites of the new faith. The very first art forms introduced to the Russian craftsmen were the formal symbols and furnishings of the new faith: the crosses, crucifixes, ciboriums, tabernacles, and altars that the Byzantine priests brought with them.

The more important church furnishings were modeled after Byzantine examples, but there is strong evidence that the Russian carvers consistently adhered to their own inherited practices and favorite patterns. Moreover, as in architecture and other arts, they transformed the imported art elements into something intrinsically Russian.

By the end of the sixteenth century several schools of carving had developed, namely, those of Novgorod, Moscow, the Volga

289

region, and the northern provinces. Differences in local racial stocks, in history, and in contacts with foreign lands account for the variety of styles and techniques. Roughly speaking, the style of Moscow was that of the Great Russia; Novgorod was affected by the West; the Volga region was leavened by the Orient; while the style of the northern provinces was influenced by Scandinavia. Naturally, these styles merge into one another, and as a result certain works display a variety of art elements.

The churches of the Far North, Novgorod, and the Moscow and upper-Volga regions contain a number of interesting collections of church and secular wooden vessels and furnishings. Especially rich are the collections of carved articles in the churches of Yaroslavl and in the Belaya Palata Museum of Rostov. There are chalices and wedding crowns, crucifixes, carved images, iconostases and royal doors, elaborate four-tiered chandeliers with as many as twenty-four branches, candlesticks and candle chests, holy water vases, and a host of other articles all made of wood and most of them beautifully carved. These objects eloquently tell the story of woodwork and carving in rural Russia from the fifteenth to the eighteenth century. They afford us a glimpse into the truly "wooden age" of Russia and reveal the freshness, simplicity, and picturesqueness of a "primitive" art that has been developing through many centuries in the isolated quietness of the village, and in the calm of the limitless dense forests.

Ecclesiastical Woodwork

The ecclesiastical woodwork of Medieval Russia is best represented in the design and decoration of the various interior elements of the church: the iconostases, the baldachins or canopies over the altars, and those over the seats of the patriarchs and the tsars, the pulpits, the candle chests.

The beginning of the fifteenth century saw the development of elaborate iconostases which greatly affected the internal appearance of the Russian church. Credit for the innovation is due to the Novgorodians who introduced it near the end of the fourteenth century, and to the Muscovites who developed it into a feature rivaling the screens and roods of the Western churches.

The present grandiose and richly decorated screens date from the middle of the sixteenth century, for it was then that the screens began to assume the aspect of highly elaborate architectural compositions. They grew in height and in number of tiers until they became the present magnificent, lavishly decorated, veritable curtain-walls of gold, extending from the north wall to the south and from floor to ceiling. The part of the iconostases which usually received the greatest attention, and upon which were concentrated all the ornamental ingenuity and skill of the designers, were the royal portals (*tsarskiye vrata*) or, as they are more often called, the royal doors through which, according to the rites of the Greek Orthodox church, none may pass but the celebrating priest and tsar.

These doors, usually quite small and low, set in finely worked architraves, and pivoting on delicately profiled jambs, are paneled and adorned with icons. Each panel holds a small niche-like frame (*kiot*)—generally in the form of a miniature church—and each frame contains an icon of the Saviour, the Virgin, the Annunciation, and so forth, all (usually six) arranged in accordance with the rules of the church. The casements, arches, and door leaves are covered with a network of foliated appliqued or pierced ornament, the whole effect enhanced by brilliant multicolored backgrounds and the gold and jewels of the icons.

Nowhere in Russia did the art of ecclesiastical woodcarving reach such a high state of beauty and degree of technical perfection as in the province of Yaroslavl. In the churches and monasteries of that province are preserved many truly wonderful examples of that art: carved iconostases, royal doors, thrones of the tsars and patriarchs, altars, canopies, and lecterns. Many of these objects are elaborate and beautiful in composition, matchless in the skill of their execution, and marvelous in the apparently inexhaustible inventiveness of their decorative patterns.

The carving is of great variety. Open-work and appliqué ornaments are found next to chiseled or chipped designs. Some parts are heavily gilded or silvered, others painted red or blue. What most impresses the beholder is not so much the virtuosity and delicacy of craftsmanship as the endless variety of patterns, the verve and charm of the linear rhythms. The design is fantastically rich and intricate. The sinuous lines undulate and surge, weave in and out. They interlace, tangle, and merge forming mysterious knots, and then cunningly disentangle, continue their flow, and reach out in bold curves. The effect is hypnotizing, yet the general impression is that of unity, of well-conceived, carefully studied, disciplined design, above all, of great beauty.

All this carving reveals a kinship with the Mohammedan art of the East. There is the astonishingly complicated design found in ancient Persian textiles and especially in chased and filigreed metal objects. Undoubtedly samples of Mohammedan art had reached Yaroslavl via the trade routes of the Volga and fired the imagination of the Russian craftsmen with their beauty and splendor, for nowhere does the spirit of Oriental art reflect itself so clearly as in these examples of ecclesiastical woodwork.

The Russian craftsman used conventionalized motifs for his ornament, but he developed them into a system of highly decorative forms. Two principal elements appear in this decoration: floral forms, as the basis of a whole series of carved motifs, and symbolic figures represented principally by what are technically termed "grotesques"—incongruous combinations of natural forms, as when a human or a beast's body terminates in a bunch of foliage. Only to a limited extent do we find sculpture in the round employed as decoration.

The mouldings and borders are elaborately carved but usually treated more boldly than the panel surfaces, thus establishing two scales of carving and heightening the effect of contrast. Friezes and bands are commonly ornamented with a foliated scroll. The surfaces of the capitals, the column shafts, and the bases are covered with pierced and incised carving of foliage or basketwork. Occasionally one finds rudimentary volutes recalling classic tradition. A derived and enriched form of the anthemion appears in the bands and coronas, while legendary beasts and birds-griffins, unicorns, *sirins, alconosts,*[1] and double-headed eagles are common features of panel carving. The motifs, floral and animal, though based on classical prototypes, are given a wholly new aspect, and every surface is adorned with designs of extreme complexity and intricacy. It seems as if the Russian artist was dominated by a feeling which could not tolerate a plain surface.

Color was essential to the decorative scheme and was used effectively. In the dim interiors mere sculpture or relief would have been wasted. The most appropriate treatment possible was the application of brilliant color to pictorial forms cut in low relief or outlined by deep incision with the edges of the figures delicately rounded.

The Russian artist-carvers of the sixteenth and seventeenth centuries who created this strange decorative art were Christians with something of the old vague paganism of the Slav tribes and the orientalism of Persia and India still clinging to them. The monsters, beasts and birds, exotic trees and flowers of a far-away dreamland lurked in the depths of their consciousness, and their carving tools brought back to life images of ancient mythology depicted on the panels of the royal doors and the spandrels of their arches.

Royal Doors

Among the remarkable examples of Russian medieval woodwork and carving are the royal doors in the iconostasis of the wooden church of St. John the Evangelist in the village of Bogoslovo on the Ishna River near Rostov.

The decoration of the church interior is in keeping with the village simplicity and the peasant artlessness of the exterior architecture. The icons are arranged on wooden shelves along the walls. None of them is encased in an expensive frame or adorned with precious stones. The iconostasis is four-storied, extremely simple, devoid of carving and bright gilt. Around the icons are

[1] See Chapter I, note 9.

hung pieces of cloth, bits of brocaded silk—modest decorations that are in the spirit of this village church. Only the royal doors with their gilt ornament, bright against the red background, stand out sharply among the church furnishings. The doors with their wondrous, crisp carving amidst the surrounding simplicity look royal, indeed.

The decorative scheme of these doors was conceived in two different scales, somewhat similar to the decorative treatment of the ambo at the St. Sophia Cathedral at Novgorod (the so-called Chaldean furnace, Plate 185). The members of the door frame—the half-round stiles, the mullions, the semicircular bands of the arch, and the corona—are embellished by bold, large-scale carving, while the surface of the panels is covered with an over-all design of incredibly complicated, minute, lace-like patterns. The panel pattern fields are broken in the center by icon niches and the strong color of the images. The flatness of the principal door members accentuates the beauty of the ornamental patterns. One may miss the rhythmic quality and the play of light and shade so characteristic of seventeenth-century Russian carving, but the effect of the subtle distribution of the decorative elements, the marked contrast in scale values, and the freshness and crispness of the carving is admirable. These doors were carved by Brother Isaiah. The inscription on them reads: "In the year 7070 [1562] on the 29th day of the month of August, in commemoration of the beheading of St. John the Precursor, these doors were done in the reign of the most pious Tsar and Grand Prince Ioann Vasilievich (Ivan the Terrible) of all the Russias . . . Brother Isaiah."

The personality of Brother Isaiah remains an enigma and it is interesting to speculate on the artistic influences to which his creative consciousness was subjected. Perhaps we shall never know their exact origin, or the route of their travel, but it is reasonable to infer that the endless variety of patterns, the verve and charm of the rhythms, the strange wildness and mysterious richness of Russian art of that period was derived from Eastern sources. We do know that this influence was potent during the life of Brother Isaiah. It was in the sixteenth century, during the reign of Ivan the Terrible, that Russia entered upon a period of great distinction in all phases of artistic activity, notably in architecture and the decorative arts—woodcarving, gold and silver work, enameling and embroidery. And it was especially in the decorative arts that Russian craftsmen demonstrated a marked predilection for the forms and patterns, methods, and workmanship of the Orient.

Another outstanding example of the woodworking craft is the portal and royal doors in the Chapel of St. Gurii, Church of St. John the Precursor at Tolchkovo, Yaroslavl (Plates 183–84). The church was completed in 1687 (Plate 113), but the royal doors are probably older than the church by several decades. Tradition claims that they were brought over from Kazan long before the construction of the church began, and were donated to the chapel.

These doors and their magnificent portal-like setting are a singularly fine example of the craftsmanship of that age. The door leaves are divided into three panels, covered with pierced carving of an intricate floral design applied against an azure background. The contours of the upper panels conform to the semicircular arch of the doorway. They are housed in wide gilt bands of carving on a green field. The lower rectangular portion of each door leaf consists of two identical square panels edged by narrow gilt baguettes. In the center of each panel there is a small, delicately carved niche-like icon frame in the form of a miniature seventeenth-century five-cupola church. The surrounding field is of perforated ornament applied against a red background. Additional decorative prominence is given to each of the six icon niches by curving mouldings, rising slightly above the center of the floral field, and serving as a second frame and setting for the icons.

The doors are set within a deeply recessed portal, whose architectural and decorative elements—the piers, jambs, architraves, imposts, and archivolts—are also outstanding examples of Russian seventeenth-century carving.

Though broadly modeled after the portal of the Cathedral of the Annunciation in Moscow (which is of Italian Renaissance derivation), the doorway has the aspects of a distinctly native work of art. It integrates the separate strains of Russian art—Eastern, Western, and Byzantine—and fuses the various elements into a harmonious whole. The motifs which were originally conceived in stone are adapted to wood. The scale of the ornament and its very proportions are altered. The shafts of the colonnettes become slender and delicate. The surfaces of the archivolts, piers, and doors are covered with relief and perforated, carved ornament—gilded, silvered, or polychromed—applied against vari-colored backgrounds, in some places painted, at others covered with gold or silver leaf.

The motifs based on Eastern and Western prototypes are thus given a wholly new aspect. The shapes of the leaves are modified; they are made sharp and crowded. Local floral motifs are introduced in a seemingly endless variety of lace-like patterns. In a word, everything is changed or modified, so much so that we can truthfully claim this work to be genuinely Russian.

Church Thrones and Their Canopies

The canopied thrones and chairs of carved and gilded wood which adorn the Russian churches of the sixteenth and seventeenth centuries are masterpieces of wood sculpture fully comparable to the choir stalls of the great Western cathedrals. One of the oldest examples of this art is the canopied throne *(Tsarskoye mesto)* of Vladimir Monomakh at the Uspensky Cathedral in Moscow (described in chapter XIII).

Some sumptuous examples of these canopies are found in Yaroslavl. In the Church of St. Nicholas Mokrinsky there are two very interesting canopied thrones, one at each of the western pillars of the church. Although there is no documented information on their designers, carvers, or the time of their installation, tradition has it one of them was made especially for Tsar Aleksei Mikhailovich and the other for Patriarch Nikon. The Russian architecture historian A. M. Pavlinov describes them as rare and grand examples of old Russian woodwork, outstanding for their state of preservation, the height of their canopies, and the freedom and beauty of their composition.

They are richly carved and painted and almost identical in appearance. The difference is apparent only in the decoration of the canopies and in the carving of certain details. The tsar's throne is square in plan, with a low, paneled railing around the seat, which consists of a simple wooden bench covered with a pillow. Four turned and richly carved posts support the canopy. The carving of the spandrels is of the pierced variety, the ornament consisting of floral and bird motifs. The square stage of the throne terminates in a cornice. Four ogee *(bochka)* pediments and pinnacles partly screen the octagonal second stage, which serves as a base for the tent-shaped canopy. The canopy, highly attenuated, is composed of five tiers of *kokoshniki* receding in steps and diminishing in size, as they range upward. Each *kokoshnik* is embellished with relief ornament applied against a blue, green, or red background, and is surmounted by a seraph spreading his wings. The canopy terminates in a slender drum and richly carved, graceful cupola.

The same decorative scheme is found in the splendid altar canopy of the Church of St. Elijah at Yaroslavl. According to the inscription on the cornice, the canopy dates from the year 7165 (1657) and was erected in the reign of Tsar Aleksei Mikhailovich and Patriarch Nikon.[2]

The side of its square base measures more than seven feet. Its height from the spring of its arch to the cross is over twenty-three feet. Its architectural composition is distinctly Russian, inspired by the tent-shaped roofs of the wooden churches of the North, but the elaborate, highly sophisticated, cunningly intertwined ornamental patterns bring to mind the spice and splendor of the Orient. The gilt ornaments, composed of foliage, flowers and fruit,

[2] For a reproduction of the seventeenth-century throne canopy in the Church of St. Elijah in Yaroslavl, see Grabar', *Istoriya russkogo iskusstva* (1953), IV, 323.

parakeets, doves, and a double-headed eagle with spread wings, are arranged on varicolored backgrounds. From a picturesque grouping of *kokoshniki* springs an octagonal pyramid surmounted by a long slender drum and terminated by a bulbous cupola. On the canopy ceiling there is a painting of the Saviour surrounded by gilded seraphs on a blue background.

The carving in relief is gilded and silvered. In those portions where the ornament is applied (that is, not open work) the background—or, to use the terminology of the seventeenth century, the "ground" *(zemlya)*—is painted blue or red.

In general, the tendency that prevailed during the medieval ages in the arts of the gold and silversmiths—when their works reproduced, in miniature forms, the silhouettes of cathedrals—is strongly noticeable in the general composition of Russian ecclesiastical woodwork. The altar and seat canopies and the icon settings on the royal doors reflect the architectural forms of the churches with their tent-shaped roofs and cupolas and thus become miniature reproductions of favorite building elements.

Ambos and Pulpits

This so-called "Chaldean furnace" (Plate 185) is one of the most interesting relics of the sixteenth-century Novgorod school of carving. Its decorative scheme is characteristic of the contemporary tendency to employ the human figure and floral motifs together as ornamental elements in the same composition.

The wooden "furnace" is a hollow, three-tiered, cylindrical structure, about seven and one-half feet high and a little under six and one-half feet in diameter. It is built up of ornately carved, slender colonnettes and horizontal bands, forming a series of panels. The lower tier is open and is decorated with a row of carved and painted caryatid-like figures—eleven venerable prophets, saints, and youths supporting an ornately carved superstructure. Window-like spaces in the upper section evidently once served as frames for images, as on them are partly obliterated inscriptions which read "Gedin" (Gideon), "Solomon," "Iliya,"

"Ioann," and "Nikolae." An inscription on the lower part is illegible.[3]

A sixteenth-century Novgorod chronicle contains a description of this "furnace" and indicates the time of its installation. Freely translated and briefly quoted, the chronicle reads:

> In the year 7041 [1533], during the reign of the Orthodox Grand Prince Vasili Ivanovich, Autocrat of all the Russias, and the God-loving Archbishop of Novgorod and Pskov, Makari, this ambo was installed in the Cathedral of St. Sophia. It is of marvelous appearance and hath many sculptured figures; saints there are thirty, arranged in three rows at the top; and the entire ambo is embellished with carving and various colored figures and gilt foliage, all most wonderfully executed; near the ground the ambo hath twelve little wooden men-like figures bedecked in fine raiment; and, lo, there is much fear in their faces, for on their heads they support this most sacred structure . . ."[4]

The chronicler, as noted, speaks of it as an ambo (pulpit), but tradition holds that this ambo was used for more than a century as a piece of stage property for the then-customary pre-Christmas performances of the ancient miracle play "The Three Hebrew Youths," with Shadrach, Meshach, and Abednego cast into the midst of the fiery furnace by order of the Babylonian King Nebuchadnezzar and delivered from the flames by the Lord's angel. The design of the ambo and the treatment of its decorative details suggest the Biblical "Chaldean Furnace," and give rise to the conjecture that in the sixteenth century it contained some implements for the enactment of the miracle play, which took place annually at the St. Sophia Cathedral, and later at the Uspensky Cathedral in Moscow. These performances ceased during the reign of Tsar Aleksei Mikhailovich, and the "furnace" was removed from the cathedral and put into a storehouse for safe-

[3] According to Father I. Arsenev the inscription read: "The Chaldean furnace is made exceedingly hot by fire but the Spirit cooleth it." Notes on the Chaldean Furnace, *Iskusstvo i khudozhestvennaya promyshlennost'* (St. Petersburg, Sept. 1901).

[4] Excerpts from the Russian Chronicles, Vol. VI, p. 299.

keeping. Later, it was transferred to the Museum of Aleksander III in St. Petersburg (now the Russian Museum in Leningrad).

According to Kondakov, the name "Chaldeans" was attached, at the beginning of the seventeenth century, to bands of jesters or mummers who wandered through the streets of Moscow at Christmas time, putting on shows for the purpose of advertising their forthcoming miracle play.[5] They would sometimes run in bands through the streets with burning pine torches, indulging in all sorts of pranks and rough horseplay at the cost of the populace. These Chaldeans wore tall, painted wooden hats suggesting that they were the Babylonian slaves of King Nebuchadnezzar, getting ready to make the furnace "exceedingly hot" for the "Three Hebrew Youths." It is quite possible that the portrayal of the Chaldeans was inspired by the attitudes and robes of the prophets, saints, and youths supporting the superstructure of the "furnace."

Carved Images

It would be sheer speculation to state the exact origin, date, or manner of appearance of religious sculpture in Russia. More than one route and more than one version of the manner of appearance may be noted, and we see in the sculptured images of the simultaneous penetration of Western realism and the formalized representational reliefs in low salience which are of Eastern origin.

Although very few sculptured images exist today, it is the concensus of Russian historians that, in the sixteenth and seventeenth centuries, there were many such images in the churches and chapels of Russia and that they were venerated in the same way as the painted icons. Few of them have survived the ravages of time and fire, and especially the stubborn hostility of the upper ranks of the Church hierarchy—a hostility which resulted in the edict (1722) of Peter I forbidding the veneration of carved and cast images and ordering their removal from the churches.

[5] Tolstoi and Kondakov, *Russkiya drevnosti*, IV, 156.

The first recorded examples, dating from the 1530's, are the eleven biblical prophets, saints, and youths supporting the superstructure of the ambo (Plate 185) of the St. Sophia Cathedral in Novgorod. The appearance of this sort of religious sculpture in the sixteenth century is quite understandable in the light of the changes that Russian religious thought had been undergoing. It was an age in which old customs and traditions were gradually giving way to new ones, thus preparing the ground for the creation of a new and unique Russian religious culture.

This was the century in which the masonry tent-shaped church towers, the magnificent multi-tiered iconostases, and the carved royal doors made their appearance. It is quite reasonable to suppose that, in the prevailing spirit of the times, the experimenting with new architectural forms and techniques also spread to the pictorial and plastic arts, and that a few of the more daring souls had the courage to introduce sculptured images into iconography. These statuettes were at first timidly brought as an offering to the village and small-town churches and gradually won the favor of the populace and the approbation, first, of the lower ranks of the church hierarchy and, later and more grudgingly, of the higher authorities.

The statuettes were carved of lime-tree blocks and painted. At a later date, some of them were gilded. The nature of the material put certain limitations upon the artist, and, as the figures are fairly large (about three-quarters life size), it was practically impossible to present them with extended arms and thus attain a measure of freedom and plasticity. However, the aim of the artist was not natural appearance; he had the same disdain for the naturalistic school of iconography as his contemporary brothers, the icon painters, and he was seeking to convey the inner meaning of the message behind the appearance.

The Pskov Chronicles of 1540 contain a curious item pertaining to sculptured icons: "Certain elders who have made a pilgrimage to foreign lands have brought into Pskov two images of St. Nicholas and St. Paraskeva fashioned in carving and encased in small temples." It is known that, up to that time, the burghers of Pskov did not possess any such icons.

In the seventeenth century carved images were accepted, though grudgingly, by the church authorities, and carving became a legitimate medium of religious iconographic art. On the strictly forbidden list there remained only hollow-blown or soldered statues, or any hollow figures. (It seems that the authorities were of the opinion that the ancient Greek idols were fashioned in that way).

An outstanding example of seventeenth-century carving is the statuette of St. Paraskeva in the Bryansk Petropavlovsk Monastery.[6] She is depicted standing in a somewhat stiff ritualistic attitude, her arms half outstretched. The modeling of her face is handled in large planes, the folds of her robes and the forms of her body are stiff and rigid.

Two other notably beautiful creations of religious sculpture— the heads of St. John the Baptist (Plate 186)—testify to the high degree of perfection that the Russian master carvers attained in expression of their spiritual emotions through their art.[7] The hard, precise, somewhat stiff carving technique heightens the impression of tragedy and horror hovering over the severed head. The general effect certainly justified the opinion that there is a close affinity between works of this type and the best examples of seventeenth-century icon painting.

Too few works of sixteenth- and seventeenth-century sculpture by Russian masters remain for us to reach a definite conclusion on the state of the plastic arts in those centuries. However, the

[6] For a reproduction of the wooden statue ot St. Paraskeva, see Grabar', *Istoriya russkogo iskusstva* (1953), IV, 330. St. Paraskeva (Friday) is, according to G. Fedotov, a mythical rather than a hagiological figure, and was considered to be the giver of fertility to praying wives. Unmistakably pagan reminiscences were attached to the Russian cult of St. Paraskeva which played a great role in medieval Russia. George P. Fedotov, *The Russian Religious Mind*, 389.

[7] The subject of rendering St. John's head on a platter, as thematic material for Russian iconography, made its appearance early in the seventeenth century. Such statues, often naturalistically colored, were usually placed at church and chapel entrances for veneration by the faithful.

few that have survived fire, vandalism, and the hostility of the church demonstrate that the predilection of the Russian people for sculpture was very strong, and that numerous examples of this art must have existed.

After the edict of Peter many of the carved statues were removed from the churches and destroyed or stored in various cellars, attics, or barns to rot away. But even the tsar's edict could not entirely eradicate the love of the masses for sculptured images. Stealthily but stubbornly various forms of this art infiltrated into the Russian church, and under the influence of Roman Catholicism, the Jesuits, and the spread of baroque, there began to appear on the iconostases and their icon niches carved figures of angels and the instruments of the passion. Above the iconostases and on the walls were installed carved and painted crucifixes with figures of the Virgin, John the Baptist, and other saints. The church authorities tried again and again to remove these carved figures and put them out of sight, but apparently it was not easy to remove them from the affections of the people.

XXI

Ceramics

THE POTTER'S ART in Russia passed through many stages of evolution from the pre-Christian era, through the long course of the Byzantine and Moscow epochs (plates 187, 188), to modern times. The marked revivals of native designs at various periods have been due to the craftsmen who kept alive an earlier tradition and gradually transformed designs left by the Scythians, Sarmatians, and Greeks of South Russia, by the Tatars, Persians, and West Europeans, into something characteristically their own.

Like most other crafts, that of the potter had a humble origin in satisfying purely utilitarian needs, but from the first it was potentially a means of aesthetic self-expression. The rudiments of the craft had been acquired long before the formation of the Kievan state. Primitive earthenware was roughly shaped by the hands alone, unaided by any mechanical contrivance and lightly baked over an open fire. Glaze was a refinement that developed gradually; with its introduction, earthenware became impermeable and much easier to manufacture. Its wide adaptability of form made it the essential material for domestic vessels.

In his survey of crafts of ancient Russia, B. A. Rybakov notes that in the Russian cities of the tenth to the thirteenth centuries the art of the potter was widely developed.[1] It is commonly known that the ancient cities of Novgorod and Moscow had special potter's quarters (*Goncharskiya slobody*). The households of

[1] *Remeslo, Istoriya kul'tury drevnei Rusi; Domongol'sky period,* 139–44.

the princes and the wealthy aristocracy preferred to use gold and silverplate and looked with disdain upon the use of clay vessels. Nevertheless, large quantities of earthenware were used by the princely households and especially by city dwellers. The products of the city potters naturally differed from those of the village in finish and in greater variety of forms. The city craftsman perfected the technique of clay grinding and removing the impurities from it and thus produced a material of better texture. He also improved the art of clay firing, if we are to judge by the pottery kiln discovered in a tumulus near the Kremlin of the old city of Belgorod (near Kiev).

It is quite possible that pedal-driven potters' wheels and some primitive kind of kiln were in use as early as the eleventh century. The typical and most widespread ornamentation of ancient Slavic ceramics were designs consisting of horizontal bands of parallel wavy or zigzag lines made with a simple stick. There was also ornamental scoring fashioned on the surface of the clay by a wide-spaced comb. Occasionally the city potters used special stamping devices producing rhomboid grilled patterns.

The old southern cities (Kiev, Chernigov, Vyshgorod) present a larger variety of pottery than do the northern. Archaeological excavations brought to light many types of clay vessels, beginning with the simple cooking pot and culminating in the graceful amphora. The pots usually have one or two handles at the top. There are tall jugs, barrel-shaped jars, bowls, plates, casseroles, cylindrical candle holders and candlesticks, and many kinds of toys.

According to Rybakov, many slender-necked and narrow-bottomed amphoras were found in the tumuli around Kiev and other cities of the Dnieper basin.[2] One can easily trace on these vessels the ribbon technique of modeling. The assumption that they are of Khersonesus origin must be rejected, as many of these vessels have Russian inscriptions that were made on the clay before firing. It is quite possible that the old chronicles referred to these

[2] *Ibid.*, 142.

amphora-like vessels as *korchaga*. One of these inscriptions taken from several extant fragments and written in old Slavonic contained a motto of good wishes that could be rendered as follows: "Blessed be this *korchaga* with abundance . . ."

Pottery was intimately associated with the daily life of the people for it fulfilled many practical and aesthetic needs. Moreover, the art and skill of the potter invaded the field of architectural decoration, not only supplying elements of cornices, wall panels, and door and window architraves, but providing a special type of resonating vessels, *golosniki* (from *golos*, voice, and by extension, resonators or acoustical devices), intended for insertion into the walls and vaulting of a structure for the purpose of improving the acoustical qualities of the chamber and, at the same time, lightening the dead weight of masonry.

For the decoration of walls and floors and other architectural elements small tiles were interspersed among the square flat bricks used in Kievan Russia. These tiles were covered with complicated enamel designs. The enamel was vitrified in special double crucibles, each compartment holding enamel of a different color. The contents of the crucible were alternately poured on the red-hot clay plate forming rich polychrome designs. Often the design was in the form of stylized foliage; occasionally it consisted of birds (as at Bogoliubovo). Sometimes small particles of hard enamel were thrown into the molten mass; the bits of enamel affected by the heat would melt slightly but, at the same time, would keep the full brilliance of their colors and create the impression of miniature mosaics.[3]

Again, Rybakov points out that not only were tiles covered with this kind of enamel, but all sorts of toys—egg-shaped rattles, human statuettes (idols), and dishes.[4] (Excavation in Novgorod uncovered a shop where glazed-clay toys were manufactured.) In Kiev and the surrounding cities, side-by-side with the glazed wares of Khersonesus, there were locally produced wares. The

[3] *Ibid.*, 143.
[4] *Ibid.*, 144.

color of the glaze was usually green. Kiev also manufactured large quantities of clay toys, often colored and occasionally glazed. In subject matter and treatment these toys are very close to the ritual designs of the Scythian-Sarmatian period.

Decoration evolved concurrently with form and technique. The softness of the clay before firing would naturally suggest thumb marks, channels or ridges impressed by the hand, or lines scratched with a pointed stick as the most obvious form of decoration. Some of these devices served to impart texture to the surface, making it of equal interest with ornament. Observation of the varied colors assumed by different clays in firing would suggest the possibility of polychromatic decoration; clay of a lighter color would be applied to the body of the vessel, either as a coating which could be carved into a pattern against the darker body beneath or moulded in the form of a decorative device.

Tile in Architectural Decoration

The centuries that elapsed between the decline and fall of Kievan Russia and the revival of the potter's art in the sixteenth-century Moscow state may well be called the dark ages of Russian ceramic history. The scarcity of surviving examples makes it almost impossible to establish any historical continuity for the wares of that period.

Some students, among them I. Sakharov, are of the opinion that the art of ceramics was well developed in the early Kievan period.[5] Zabelin is a little more cautious and not as positive as Sakharov. In his opinion the art of earthenware glazing, though undoubtedly much older than enameling, reached Russia from the East, possibly via Byzantium. Later it was influenced by the Tatars who, judging from recent excavations on the site of the Golden Horde, used large quantities of glazed pottery. Floor tiles

[5] Sakharov, I. (as quoted by I. Sultanov) in "Obozreniye russkoi arkheologii," *Izraztsi v drevne russkom iskusstve (Materialy po istorii russkikh odezhd i obstanovki zhizni narodnoi*, L. Prokhorov, ed.), St. Petersburg, 1885.

found in some of the oldest Kiev churches (the Desiatinnaya, 980–96, and Irininskaya, *ca.* 1040) indicate that glazed tiles were used architecturally in Russia as early as the tenth century.[6]

The sixteenth and seventeenth centuries were the periods of greatest development in Russia of the manufacture of ceramics and, also, enamels. The production of tiles and the art of glazing and coloring them were known in Medieval Russia as *tseninnoye delo.* Under the general term *tsenina* were included all descriptions of enameled and glazed pottery. The term probably was limited to the actual technique of enameling or glazing and the processes of applying it to pottery products.

From tradition and the study of ancient buildings and works in which the faïence products were used, we gather that at one time every town in which a faïence factory existed had its favorite colors. Thus Rostov was remarkable for its blues and greens, Moscow for greens and light blue, and Vladimir excelled in painting of figures and plants. The manufacture of faïence, originally influenced by alien sources, soon became adapted to Russian tastes and acquired a distinctive character.

The real development and widespread use of tiles in Russia occurred in the seventeenth century. The center of this industry was the city and region of Moscow. From there it spread to other regions. We find tiles on many of the seventeenth-century buildings in all of the principal Russian cities of that period, beginning with Suzdal and extending to Rostov. But especially rich in tile work were the Resurrection Monastery (New Jerusalem) near Moscow and the churches of Yaroslavl.

The initiative in developing this craft must be credited to Patriarch Nikon, under whom much was done in this field, first at the Iversky Valdaisky Monastery (founded by him in 1653), and then, on a much larger scale, at his new brain child, the Resurrection Monastery begun by him in 1656 (Plate 93).

[6] Zabelin, I., (as quoted by Sultanov) in "Istoricheskoye obozreniye finiftyanago i tseninnago dela v Rossii," *Zapiski (Journal of the Imperial Archaeological Society,* Vol. VI. St. Petersburg, 1893.)

The most opulent and profuse tile ornamentation was lavished on the principal church of the monastery, the Resurrection Cathedral. Both exterior and interior are decorated with tiles. Especially rich in tile ornamentation is the east façade, the cornice of the cupola drum, the double windows of the second floor, and the frieze above the windows of the altar apse. Inside the cathedral many of its elements are also embellished with tiles; but what is especially notable are the tile iconostases of which there are seven in the cathedral and the various chapels—a very rare example of medieval Russian decorative art. The tiles are varicolored and strikingly brilliant but harmoniously blended. The colors are blue, azure, soft red, yellow, white, and green, the blues and greens predominating.

Another Moscow example of tile decoration is the Terem Palace in the Moscow Kremlin. The palace consists of several units built, altered, or rebuilt at various times. The interesting unit is the penthouse built over the central area of the fourth floor in 1635–36 by Tsar Mikhail Feodorovich for the two young tsarevichi, Aleksei and Ivan. The cornices of both stories of this terem are decorated with tiles covering the entire frieze. The ornament consists of polychrome foliage—green leaves, white flowers, and yellow stems and buds—over a blue field.

Of the buildings beyond the walls of the Kremlin, the best preserved and most abundantly decorated is the Krutitsky Teremok built in 1674–76 over the double-arched entrance gate to the Krutitsky Monastery. Its second-floor street façade, cornices, columns, consoles, window pediments and sills, niches, and the very wall surface are all of tile. The basic and dominant color scheme, a warm sparkling green with deep yellow tinges, is wonderfully conceived and forms a most appropriate decorative spot against the background of the superb gardens of the monastery.[7]

This rich ornamentation of the façade tiles is indubitably one of the best examples of Russian workmanship. The colonnettes decorated with winding garlands of green foliage and clusters

[7] Reproduced in Rzyanin, *Pamyatniki russkogo zodchestva*, plate 62.

of berries were favorite ornamental motifs of that period. Here the foliage and the clusters are not only magnificently modeled, but sharply accentuated with open work and deeply incised veins. The tiles on the flat surfaces are decorated with relief ornament as delicate in modeling as if wrought in silver. The motifs are budding flowers partly stylized, often drawn from the rich textiles of the period. The richness of ornamentation recalls the carving of ecclesiastical woodwork. Columns covered with winding stems and leaves are often found in the portals and the royal doors of the iconostases.

In this wealth of ornament and seeming extravagance there is nevertheless a harmoniousness all of its own. We find a large assortment of various tile designs: profiled shapes, cylindrical forms, moulded consoles, bosses, finials and many other members of the terracotta and majolica architectural ornamental family. All these elements were introduced and bountifully applied by the potter craftsmen who lived nearby in the pottery quarter of Moscow.[8]

Tiles had many and various applications; they were used for facing walls and cupola drums, for cornices, arcatures, niches, and door and window architraves. They were also used for the embellishment of circular and square piers, pilasters, and floors. In ecclesiastical architecture the favorite areas to be decorated were the friezes under the main cornices. A popular device of embellishment was the solid facing of the frieze with tile, without any breaks. The tiles as a rule were arranged in two rows, one over the other in order to cover the entire width of the frieze. The effect thus obtained is very rich, because at a distance the joints can hardly be seen and the frieze looks as though it were made of one solid piece.

Among the outstanding examples are the Palace of the Tsar[9] (1664–69) in the Troitse-Sergieva Lavra (Monastery of the

---

[8] Seventeenth-century Moscow had an extensive pottery manufacturing quarter known as *Goncharskaya sloboda*.

[9] Reproduced in Grabar', *Istoriya russkogo iskusstva* (1953), IV, 237, 287.

Trinity and St. Sergius), which has windows set in a field highly decorated with colored tiles, and the Church of St. Gregory the Neo-Cesarian, built about 1674–79 at the expense of Tsar Aleksei Mikhailovich. Its cornice is decorated by S. I. Polubes with a magnificent frieze in ceramics rivaling that of the Krutitsky Teremok.

The relatively small churches of Moscow did not offer a favorable field for this medium of decoration. The Moscow decorative tile elements are insignificant in comparison with those of the churches of the upper Volga region. It is in the vast churches of Yaroslavl that these colored tile revetments receive their most varied and most happy applications; they are used either to cover the façades of the lower stories or to frame and outline entire bays. These ceramics fulfill the same role in the exterior decoration of the brick façades as frescoes in the decoration of church interiors. The rich decorative faïence in the apse of the Church of St. John Chrysostom at Korovniki (Plate 118) and that of the Yaroslavl churches of Saints Peter and Paul, and Nikolai Mokrinsky, show what can be accomplished with these brilliant multicolored architraves standing out vividly against the surfaces of the brick walls.

Tile decorative elements of those churches alternate with those of brick insets and projections, effectively breaking the monotone wall surfaces. This is an especially prominent feature of the walls of the apses, usually the most decorated elements in Orthodox churches. The tile patterns, with their Eastern character of design and complex entanglement of composition, merge and blend the disparate forms into a single decorative scheme, very similar in concept to that of the carved wooden baldachins and royal doors of those churches. Just as in the baldachins, in which the patterns of Eastern character blend harmoniously with the forms of wooden Russian architecture, so there is in the tile decorations with their fields of warm blue, green, and yellow a complete congruence with the general design of the church and the ornamentation concepts of Russian seventeenth-century art.

Tiles in the Decoration of Heating Stoves

A favorite application of the faïence tile was in the decoration of heating stoves. There are many examples existing in museums, in the apartments of the ancient palaces of the Kremlin,[10] and in various monasteries and churches. The town of Yaroslavl has a particularly large collection of those stoves. The tiles are blue and green, either plain or figured. The decorations are in colored designs; sometimes they are composed of figures in low relief or of inscriptions. These stoves are rectangular or circular and often resemble miniature storied buildings complete with classic bases, niches, arches, columns, and cornices. They are often decorated with amusing allegorical designs and bands or friezes carrying humorous mottoes.

The Russian stoves are mountainous masonry fire boxes, many of which were constructed to provide sleeping space (*lezhanki*) on their tops. They are usually built of ordinary clay or of brick, but when used for warming purposes and not for cooking, they are generally faced with tiles. The tiles were sometimes unglazed and ornamented with low-relief designs (plants, birds, human figures, and many different combinations of geometrical ornament similar to that used in carving). Some were covered with glazes of various colors; others were made with a smooth surface, ornamented with designs in enamel, designs similar to those found on plates, jugs, and vases. We also find tiles with a general luster ornamentation over the object, the elements of which are arabesques interspersed with birds, usually drawn with extreme simplicity, but the few lines employed adequately expressing their forms.

The stove maintained a picturesque and definitely Russian character down to the times of Catherine II. With the appearance of Western neoclassicism, polychromy began to disappear. The stoves assume the forms of temples and other artificialities, with decoration derived from antique reliefs. Native art in the design and ornamentation of stoves lingered only in out-of-the-

[10] Reproduced, A. M. Andreev, ed., *Moskovsky Kreml'*, plates 119, 120.

way districts, in the houses of wealthy merchants and prosperous farmers.

One of the interesting speculations in the history of Russian decorative tile concerns the place of origin of the decorative methods so eagerly adopted by the Moscow and Yaroslavl architects. Here again we find the working of two combined influences. Some archaeologists explain the resemblance of the bluish tiles of Yaroslavl to the faïence tiles of Delft by assuming that some Dutch masters participated in the construction and decoration of Yaroslavl churches. This is a fairly credible hypothesis when we consider the close commercial relations that existed after the opening of the Archangel route between the merchants of Yaroslavl and Holland. On the other hand, we know that Moscow and Yaroslavl were in constant and close touch with Persia, via the Volga River and the Caspian Sea. It may well have been that the Russians borrowed the idea of tile revetments from the architects of Persia, who employed them so successfully in the decoration of their mosques and palaces. The natural predilection of the Russians for polychrome ornament explains the rapid success of this innovation. Furthermore, this similarity in decorative elements can be ascribed to elements naturally evolved wherever materials come into the hands of craftsmen competent to use them.

Description of Plates

INCLUDED in the information on the plates are the present location of each item, given in parentheses in the first sentence of each description, and the source from which the illustration was obtained, given in parentheses at the end of each description.

1: Sitting Stag, from the Kostromskaya Tumulus, seventh-sixth century B.C. (Hermitage Museum, Leningrad). This solid-gold plaque probably served as an emblemating decoration of an iron shield. It is one of the outstanding examples of the animal style, illustrating the characteristic peculiarities in the portrayal of animals by Scythian artists. The stag is shown with his legs bent under and tightly pressed to its belly; his body stylized, the size of his antlers greatly exaggerated and represented as a series of ornamental waves in the form of bent, rhythmically repeated hooks.

2: Dying Stag, from the Kul-Oba Tumulus, fourth century B.C. (Hermitage Museum, Leningrad). An electrum plaque with *repoussé* ornament depicts a dying stag in his last agonies. There are figures of various wild animals placed on different parts of the stag's body as if ready to devour it. The plaque is thought to have been executed by a Greek artist who tried to emulate the Scythian example found at the Kostromskaya Tumulus in the Kuban district.

3: Gold Gorytus (Bow-and-arrows case), from the Chertomlyk Tumulus, fourth century B.C. (Hermitage Museum Leningrad). The gold plaque which ornamented the gorytus of the buried king belongs to the finest epoch of Greco-Scythian art.

4: Electrum Vase, from the Kul-Oba Tumulus, fourth century B.C. (Hermitage Museum, Leningrad). The ornamental scheme of the lower portion of the vase consists of simple fluting and a band of guilloche. The upper portion consists of a frieze decorated with scenes from Scythian military life. Notable are the expressions of attention, pain, and comradely solicitude, all beautifully rendered. (Detail of frieze from Tolstoi-Kondakov, *Russkiya drevnosti*, II, 142.)

5: Gold Earring, from the Kul-Oba Tumulus, fourth century B.C. (Hermitage Museum, Leningrad). The earring medallion contains a relief figure of a woman modeled after a statue by Phydias.

6: Gold Helmet, from the Seven Brothers Tumulus, fourth century B.C. (Hermitage Museum, Leningrad). The helmet, discovered in 1875, is of pure gold weighing nearly two pounds avoirdupois. It is a demi-ovoid in shape, and the ornament is of *repoussé* and pierced work. The design is undoubtedly of Greek inspiration, but the whole was transformed by the Scythian craftsman into an object truly representative of Scythian art.

7: The Nikopol Vase, from the Chertomlyk Tumulus, fourth-third century B.C. (Hermitage Museum, Leningrad). This vase is unique in the style of its *repoussé* work and in the design of its frieze which, in a sequence of several beautifully executed reliefs, portrays the most important part of the daily occupation of the nomadic Scythians—the breaking and training of the wild horses of the steppes. The figures on the frieze, the bearded men and the young boys, are evidently Scythians, the same type shown on the

Kul-Oba electrum vase (Plate 4). Their facial features, hair cuts, costumes, and implements have many of the characteristics found among their descendants, now living in that region.

8: Diadem from the Treasure of Novocherkask, first century B.C.–third century A.D. (Hermitage Museum, Leningrad). The diadem, of pure gold, is set with large pearls, amethysts, and garnets, and ornamented with a large carved amethyst stone representing a bust of a woman. Under the band are pendants, over a row of figures representing three sacred trees, flanked by goats and deer. The treasure was found in 1864 near Novocherkask on the lower Don.

9: Lion-Griffin Attacking a Horse, one of a pair of cast gold belt buckles, with stone insets, from western Siberia (Hermitage, Museum, Leningrad). The buckle is from Peter the Great's Siberian collection. Date indefinite.

10: Hunting Scene, a Siberian belt buckle in the shape of a horizontal B, with pierced gold plaque inlaid with blue paste, pink coral, and black enamel, from western Siberia (Hermitage Museum, Leningrad). The plaque portrays two Sarmatian horsemen and their dog hunting a boar. Rostovtzeff assigns it to the Sarmatian period in South Russia, (second century B.C.–third century A.D.).

11: Scene from the Life of the Early Siberian Nomads, of openwork gold plaque, from western Siberia (Hermitage Museum, Leningrad). The scene, in the opinion of some archaeologists, depicts a midday halt beneath the shelter of a tree. The leader of the group is seen reclining on the ground, his head on the lap of a woman who sits resting against the trunk of the tree, while an attendant holds the reins of two saddled horses. A quiver is hanging on the tree.

12: Dragon Engaged in a Fight with a Tiger, of gold plaque with turquoise inlay, from western Siberia (Hermitage Museum, Leningrad). The dragon has the typical upturned nose and a crest which consists of four eagle-griffin heads. The same kind of head forms the extremity of its tail. The work is probably of the fifth century B.C.

13: Figure of a Lion, from a felt saddlecloth, from Mound 1, Pazyryk, eastern Altai (Hermitage Museum, Leningrad). The silhouette of a lion, cut from leather and covered with tinfoil, was found on one of the bright-red saddlecloths which came from the Pazyryk Tumulus. (From Rudenko, *Kul'tura, naseleniya Gornogo Altaya*).

14: Eagle-Griffin and Lion-Griffin in Combat, from a leather cutout appliqué ornament on a saddlecloth, from Mound 1, Pazyryk, eastern Altai (Hermitage Museum, Leningrad). Both mythical beasts have the body of the lion, but the feet of the eagle-griffin are those of a bird. (From Rudenko, *Kul'tura naseleniya Gornogo Altaya.*)

15: Pole Top, with head of a stag in the beak of a griffin, of wood and leather, Mound 2, Pazyryk, eastern Altai (Hermitage Museum, Leningrad). A favorite motif, used for the decoration of the Pazyryk pole tops, was the head of some herbivorous animal —ram or stag—in the beak of a fantastic bird. Various materials were used; for example, the small decorative details of the wooden pole top were made of thick, hard leather. (From Gryaznov, *Drevnee iskusstvo Altaya.*)

16: Swans, decorative figures on a felt tent cover, from Mound 5, Pazyryk, eastern Altai. Felt was skillfully and effectively used by the Scythian nomads for decoration of many objects. The swans, which decorate the top of the tent cover, were made of soft, colored felt. (From Gryaznov, *Drevnee iskusstvo Altaya.*)

17: Early Slavic Stone Idol, from the tumulus near the Village of Akulinnino, Moscow region (Historical Museum, Moscow). The idol is without any sign of a cap, beard, or mustache and most likely represents a female diety. The nose and mouth are barely indicated by slightly incised lines and cannot be seen in profile. (From Grabar', *Istoriya russkogo iskusstra*, 1953.)

18. Figure of a Man, cast silver from the Martynovka Tumulus, near Kiev, sixth century A.D. (Kiev Historical Museum). The figure is one of four identical male figures found, among many other silver objects, in the Martynovka Tumulus. The men have shoulder-length hair and are dressed in long-sleeved, belted shirts and ankle-length trousers. Their bent legs and the position of their arms seem to indicate that they are dancing. An important detail of their costumes, which permits us to determine their ethnic origin, is the wide embroidered inset in the front of their shirts. Such shirts are still popular and considered to be a necessary part of the present-day Ukrainian and Byelorussian men's apparel. (From Grabar', *Istoriya russkogo iskusstva*, 1953.)

19: Figure of a horse, cast silver from the Martynovka Tumulus, near Kiev, sixth century A.D. (Kiev Historical Museum). Several of these figurines were found in the Martynovka Tumulus. They were probably used as amulets. The manner of representation is rather curious. The treatment of the horse's muzzle is quite realistic, but the body, as a whole, is highly stylized. (From Grabar', *Istoriya russkogo iskusstva*, 1953).

20–22: Cathedral of St. Sophia, Kiev, 1037. The Cathedral—the Mother Church of Russia in the Mother City of ancient Rus'—was founded by Yaroslav the Wise. It is the only Kievan structure of the grand-princes' period which still stands and retains, at least in the interior, any approach to its original form. Repeatedly damaged and looted by the feuding Russian princes, wrecked and plundered by the Tatars (in 1240, 1416, and 1482), it lay in ruins with gaping holes in its walls and roof for almost four centuries. Not only were most of its sculptured decorations and antique furnishings pillaged, but many of its wonderful mosaics and frescoes were severely damaged, and some had all but disappeared. Yet the beauty of Yaroslav's cathedral is eloquently manifested in the few remaining original bays and decorations.

The most extensive remodeling of this Russified Byzantine monument took place during the rule of the legendary Hetman Ivan Mazeppa and Metropolitan Varlaam Yasynsky (1690–1707) when the vogue of the Ukrainian, or so-called Cossack, baroque style was at its height. Mazeppa's alterations and decorations seriously changed the primitive aspect of Yaroslav's edifice. The original plan and silhouette of the church are now obscured by additional bays and stories to its lateral galleries, a new tower, and many bizarre baroque cupolas. Only the central portion survives from the eleventh century, and even this has been tampered with. (Photographs of façade and plan from Rzyanin, *Pamyatniki Russkogo zodchestva;* nave from Union of Architects Library, Moscow.)

23: Cathedral of St. Sophia, Novgorod, 1045–52. The cathedral, built by Vladimir, son of Prince Yaroslav of Kiev, replaced a wooden thirteen-dome church of the same name. Although the new cathedral followed its Kievan namesake in plan, its divergencies from the Byzantine pattern are quite apparent: it has five aisles but only three apses; externally, where the church differs even more from its southern prototype, it has only five cupolas, its walls are austere, the buttresses are flat and bare, and the windows are small and narrow. There is something genuinely Russian in the silhouette of its helmeted cupolas and in the vigor and verticality of its masses. (From *Rzyanin, Pamyatniki Russkogo zodchestva.*)

24: The Korsun' Gates, twelfth century, Cathedral of St. Sophia, Novgorod. The gates, eleven feet eight inches high, are of bronze mounted on wood, and are located on the west side of the cathedral. The two leaves, each a little over four feet wide, contain twenty-six plaques in chased frames. The subjects depicted in relief are taken from the Old and New Testaments, the history of the church, general history, mythology, and allegory, (From Solntsev, *Drevnosti Rossiiskago gosudarstva.*)

25: The Sigtuna Gates, eleventh century, Cathedral of St. Sophia, Novgorod. The gates, about eight feet nine inches high, are of cast light-yellow bronze. The metal, about one-fourth inch thick, is mounted on wood, and the ornament is in very light relief. Each leaf, a little over three feet wide, has three panels containing a cross. The borders are ornamented with rosettes and arabesques. The name is of Swedish origin. (From Solntsev, *Drevnosti Rossiiskago gosudarstva.*)

26: Cathedral of the Assumption, Vladimir, 1185. The present cathedral is the result of reconstruction and enlargement of the original cathedral built by Prince Andrei Bogoliubsky in 1158 and seriously damaged by the fire of 1183. The restorer, Prince Vsevolod expanded it by adding an arcade on the north, south, and west sides. He also added four corner cupolas, thus creating a five-domed arrangement which, three centuries later, served as a model for the Cathedral of the Assumption in the Moscow Kremlin and for many other Russian churches. (From Rzyanin, *Pamiatniki Russkago zodchestva* and, panoramic view, from Shchusev Museum of Architecture, Moscow.)

27: Church of the Intercession of the Virgin on the River Nerl, near Vladimir, 1165. The church is a replica in miniature of the original (1158) Cathedral of the Assumption in Vladimir and the finest surviving example of the Vladimir-Suzdal style of architecture. (From Grabar', *Istoriya Russkago iskusstva,* 1909.)

28: Tower of Palace at Bogoliubovo, near Vladimir, 1160. This

stair tower is the only surviving part of the magnificent Bogoliubovo palace complex built by Prince Andrei Bogoliubsky. It
served as an entrance to the palace and to the galleries of the
palace cathedral. The structural forms and the decorative details,
such as the blind arcades on the northeast walls and the deeply
set triple window of the second story, suggest a Romanesque
influence. (From Rzyanin, *Pamyatniki Russkogo zodchestva.*)

29: Cathedral of St. Dmitri, Vladimir, 1193–97. This cathedral,
dedicated to St. Dmitri of Salonica, was the central element of
the now-vanished sumptuous architectural ensemble of Prince
Vsevolod's palace. In plan and general distribution of its masses,
it recalls the Church of the Intercession of the Virgin on the river
Nerl (Plate 27). Its most striking features are the elaborately
carved stone reliefs on the walls and on the drum of the dome.
(From Rzyanin, *Pamyatniki Russkogo zodchestva.*)

30: Church of the Transfiguration, Novgorod, 1374. This characteristically Novgorod church still has its original high-ridged,
eight-sloped roof surmounted by a central drum and helmeted
cupola. The single apse is decorated by a blind arcade at the
middle and a series of niches above. (From Rzyanin, *Pamyatniki
Russkogo zodchestva.*)

31: Cathedral of St. George, Yuriev-Polsky 1230–34. The Cathedral was built by Prince Svyatoslav Vsevolodovich in the capital
of his appanage. It collapsed in 1471 and was rebuilt at the order
of Ivan III by the Moscow architect V. D. Yermolin. The cathedral is a four-columned, single-cupola structure with three apses
and three porches. The walls are entirely covered with low reliefs.
The principal elements of the decoration consist of arabesques
formed of creeping vines and of designs of a very pronounced
Oriental character. (From Shchusev Museum of Architecture,
Moscow.)

32: The Virgin of Vladimir, Greek, early twelfth century (Tret-yakov Gallery, Moscow). This icon, known in Russia as the *Vladimir Mother of God (Vladimirskaya Bogomater')*, is one of the oldest surviving in Russia. It was brought to Kiev in the first half of the twelfth century. After a short stay in the south of Russia it was transferred to the north in 1155 by Prince Andrei Bogo-liubsky and installed in the Uspensky Cathedral at Vladimir where, as the miraculous *Virgin of Vladimir,* it became the most venerated of all the ancient icons. In 1395 it was transferred to Moscow, and though it was at times taken to various other places for short intervals, its home was established there in the Uspensky Cathedral until 1919. The icon has been subjected to repeated repaintings in the thirteenth, fifteenth, sixteenth, seventeenth, eighteenth, and nineteenth centuries. A careful cleaning under-taken in 1919 showed that only the faces of the Mother and Child and part of the Child's shoulder belonged to the original painting.

The distinctive feature of this icon is the posture of the Virgin and the Child whom she holds in her right arm. She is bending her head towards Him, and her left hand is prayerfully extended to Him and at the same time directs the spectator's attention to Him. The Child has His arms around His mother's neck, His face pressed against her cheek.

Icons, such as this, depicting the mutual gestures of affection between the Mother and the Child are called "Our Lady of Ten-derness" *(Umileniye).* In contrast to the solemn and severe majesty of the icons of the Mother of God as *Hodigitriya (Odigi-triya),* which emphasize the divinity of the Child-Christ, icons of Our Lady of Tenderness convey the natural human feeling of mother love and tenderness. Here, more than in the *Hodigitriya,* is expressed the human aspect of Divine Motherhood and In-carnation.

The warmth and deeply moving quality of this icon account for the profound affection with which it was regarded by the Russian people. It may also be considered as a prototype of a new iconographic theme which, in various versions, constantly reappears in later Russian religious painting. (See also Plate 44.)

33: Saint Dmitri of Salonica, portable mosaic, eleventh century (Tretyakov Gallery, Moscow). The mosaic is one of the very few medieval decorations to survive from the series of mosaics which adorned the destroyed Church of St. Michael with the Golden Roof in the Monastery of the same name in Kiev (often referred to as the Monastery of St. Dmitri).

34: The Virgin Orans, twelfth-thirteenth century, Yaroslavl School (Tretyakov Gallery, Moscow). The iconographic type represented by this icon was known in Russia as "Our Lady of the Sign" *(Znameniye)* or as the "Great Panagiya"—one of the most revered icons of the Mother of God. The Virgin is shown standing in a frontal position, her arms raised in the gesture of prayer, and bearing on her breast a medallion image of Christ Emmanuel. The Infant's arms are outstretched, His hands in a gesture of blessing. On each side of the Virgin's head is a medallion half-length painting of an archangel. The icon comes from the Monastery of the Saviour at Yaroslavl. Its prototype was the celebrated mosaic image of the Virgin Orans in the Church of Blachernae in Constantinople.

35: St. George the Victorious (Georgi Pobedonosets), twelfth century, Novgorod School (Cathedral of the Annunciation, Kremlin, Moscow). The icon came from the Monastery of St. George in Novgorod. It is one of the best-preserved examples of early Russian iconography. It is believed that the icon was painted for the youngest son of Andrei Bogoliubsky, Georgi Andreevich, prince of Novgorod. St. George appears in this icon as the patron of the prince, his namesake. He is depicted as a young brawny knight wearing a red cloak covered by a brown coat of mail. In his right hand he is holding a spear, in his left a sword. His head is crowned with golden curls. The figure is half-length painted on wood (*ca.* 1170). On the reverse side of the panel is a fourteenth-century icon of the Virgin, also believed to have been brought to Moscow from Novgorod. (From Alpatov, *Khudozhestvennyie pamyatniki Moskovskogo Kremlya.*)

36: Mandilion Portrait of Christ, twelfth century, Novgorod School (Tretyakov Gallery, Moscow). This icon is known in Russia as *Spas Nerukotvorny (The Image of the Saviour Not Made with Human Hands)*. It is the oldest known Russian rendering of the Vernicle (Veronica). The image is painted on the front of a large processional icon. (On the reverse side of the Vernicle is the *Adoration of the Cross,* a work by another contemporary painter.) The portrait has all the formal individual features of the Byzantine Mandilion: only the head alone is shown, with neither the neck nor the shoulders visible; the halves of the face are symmetrical. This applies to the plaited hair which falls in locks on either side, as well as to the ends of the beard; golden threads run through the hair. The large eyes are wide open, and one eyebrow is drawn slightly higher up than the other. In the nimbus is inscribed the sign of the cross. This cruciferous nimbus will be found on all the representations of Christ. Lazarev ventures the opinion that this painting is the work of a Novgorod artist.

37: The Annunciation of Ustiug, twelfth century, Novgorod School (Tretyakov Gallery, Moscow). The icon represents an original achievement of the Novgorod School. The Virgin is shown standing alongside Archangel Gabriel—a composition differing from the usual rendering of the scene in which the Virgin is shown sitting. The representation of the Child is also unusual. The contours of His figure shine through the garments of the Mother.

38: Archangel Gabriel (Angel with the Golden Hair), twelfth

century, Novgorod School (Russian Museum, Leningrad). This icon, generally known as the *Golden-hair Angel,* was probably a part of a *deësis.* The anchangel has a young oval face with a small crimson-lipped mouth and abundant curly hair. The bright yellow of the face, the touches of crimson on the cheeks, the use of light and shade to express volume indicate that the painter's skill was based on observation of life. The Novgorod artist was evidently trying to express himself in a style which was Oriental rather than Byzantine. We see this endeavor in the singular beauty of the angel with his huge velvety eyes, strikingly marked eyebrows, and in his neatly arranged hair with gold outlines stressing its rhythmical, decorative coils. In Russian folk poetry and literature the description "golden haired" is sometimes used to denote special beauty. (From Grabar', *Istoriya Russkago iskusstva,* 1953).

39–40: Dormition of the Virgin, thirteenth century, Novgorod School (Tretyakov Gallery, Moscow). The composition of this icon closely follows the scheme used in Byzantium for depicting the legend of the Dormition. It shows the apostles assembled around the bier: St. Paul to the right and St. Peter at the head of the bier. Christ is shown standing between two candlesticks and holding the soul of the Virgin in His hands; above Him two angels carry it up to Heaven. The upper part of the icon depicts the flight of the apostles who, according to the legend, were brought on clouds to Jerusalem by angels from all parts of the world.

41: St. Demetrius of Thessalonica, fourteenth century (?), Novgorod School (Likhachev Collection, Russian Museum, Leningrad). A detail from an old icon of Russian origin. The coloring is somber but intense. The dark face of the saint is enlivened by strong white highlights. (From *Russkaya ikona,* a short-lived periodical published in 1914.)

42: The Dormition of the Virgin, Novgorod School, *ca.* 1380

(Tretyakov Gallery, Moscow). The icon is probably the work of a Novgorod follower of Theophanes the Greek. Here the specific Novgorod characteristics (peasant types of face, geometrical simplicity of composition, sharpness of outline) are particularly prominent. For the dramatic quality of its conception and the directness of expression, this icon ranks among the masterpieces of medieval Russian painting. The icon comes from the Cathedral of the Annunciation, Kremlin, Moscow.

43: The Prophet Elijah, Novgorod School, late fourteenth century (Tretyakov Gallery, Moscow). The image of the Prophet Elijah was identified in the mind of the rural population with that of Perun, the ancient Slav god of storm, thunder, and fire. The attributes of the pagan deity were passed on to the Old Testament prophet who was believed to have power over the elements, particularly over fire. It was for this reason that he was venerated by husbandmen as the rainbearer and the protector of their homes from fire.

The biblical legend of his ascent to heaven in a chariot of fire drawn by fiery horses led by an angel emphasizes the connection of Elijah with fire. His role was especially important in the latter capacity, for fire was one of the direct calamities which medieval Russia had to contend with.

The Novgorodian painters usually depicted him as an ascetic with shaggy hair falling down to his shoulders, a long beard spreading out on both sides, and a sun-burned face, with his figure placed against a background of flaming vermilion.

44: The Virgin of the Don, attributed to Theophanes the Greek, late fourteenth century (Tretyakov Gallery, Moscow). This icon represents the same subjects as those shown in *The Virgin of Vladimir* (Plate 31), but here the artist's conception of the relationship between Mother and Child has a distinctly idyllic quality. The Virgin plays with the Child; she is shown with her arm around Him and, bending her head, lovingly turns her face to Him. The prominent nose, full lips, and lovely hands and face lightly touched with pale pink, all mark the painting as the work of Theophanes.

45–47: The Transfiguration of Christ, by Theophanes the Greek, fourteenth century (Tretyakov Gallery, Moscow). Christ transfigured is represented standing on the summit of a mountain, conversing with Moses and Elijah. Clad in a shining white garment, He is shown against an irregular white hexagon inscribed in a large *mandorla*. Moses, holding a book, stands on His left. Elijah, an old man with long hair, is on His right. At the foot of the mountain can be seen the Apostles Peter, James, and John in different attitudes of astonishment. The violent movement of the Apostles, reeling back from the blinding supernatural light, is conveyed with great power. Lazarev describes this icon as one combining Byzantine-type coloring with the dynamic and expressive manner of Russian work.

48: Christ with the Angry Eye, fifteenth century, Novgorod School (Russian Museum), Leningrad). The very name and character of this image reflects the medieval conception of the Pantocrator as a stern supreme judge, meting out punishment to all transgressors. One is impressed with the overpowering strength of this image: the large head, the powerful neck, the gaunt face with its rugged features, and the large wide-open eyes with their steady piercing gaze. (From *Russkaya ikona.*)

49: The Miracle of Saints Florus and Laurus, fifteenth century, Novgorod School (Tretyakov Gallery, Moscow). The cult of Florus and Laurus, patron saints of horse breeders and grooms, was widespread in Novgorod. The two saints, in this icon, are depicted standing at the sides of Archangel Michael who is handing them the reins of the two saddled black and white steeds at the right and left of his feet, signifying that he is entrusting their care to the saints. Below we see a herd of horses driven by three holy grooms.

Florus and Laurus appear in this icon not in the role of heavenly appointed guardians of herdsmen but rather as intercessors on behalf of poor peasants who lost, or are afraid that they might lose, the most important object of their worldly goods, the horse. The carefully balanced symmetry in the composition of this picture suggests that it was conceived as a heraldic pattern. The design and draftsmanship reveal the great mastery of line attained by the Novgorodian icon painters.

50: The Nativity of Christ, Novgorod School, fourteenth to fifteenth century (Tretyakov Gallery, Moscow). The Virgin is shown lying pensively on a mattress in the center of the picture. The Child in swaddling clothes lies behind her in a crib, the ox and the ass standing by. Grouped around are a number of subsidiary compositions depicting several related events: At the left are shown the three magi bearing gifts. At the top right the angel of the annunciation is handing on the Christmas message to a young shepherd, who stands in the middle tier playing his horn. Below we see the bathing of the Child by the attending women, and the stooping figure of the devil in the guise of an old shepherd, who tries to raise doubts in the mind of St. Joseph. Three half-length figures at the very top are Saint Eudokia, Saint John Climacus, and Saint Juliana.

51: The Miracle of St. George the Victorious, Novgorod School, first half of the fifteenth century (Tretyakov Gallery, Moscow). The fight of Saint George with the dragon was one of the favorite subjects of the Novgorod icon painters, for whom this saintly knight represented the incarnation of courage, of forces of light and righteousness engaged in struggle with forces of darkness and evil. He was also regarded as the protector of cattle and guardian of flocks. The hand of God, shown in the upper right-hand corner, blesses the knight from above and directs his efforts. The decoration of the saint's shield consists of the pagan emblem of the sun. Sun worship had been widespread in pre-Christian Russia, and pagan emblems and symbols survived for several centuries as decorative devices in peasant art.

52–53: The Battle between the Suzdalians and Novgorodians, late fifteenth century, Novgorod School (State Art History Museum, Novgorod). The subject matter of this icon (discussed in Chapter XII) is treated in the free and generalized Novgorodian manner. Though limited by the conventional methods of icon painting, the artist succeeded in presenting an account of an important historical episode in a clear and easily understandable pictorial language.

54: Entry into Jerusalem, early sixteenth century, Novgorod School (Tretyakov Galley, Moscow). The icon has a decorative and festive quality, in keeping with the character of the festival itself. There is a strong sense of decorative design in the sculptured terraces of the mountain and in the roofs and towers of the city gate. Christ is depicted riding sideways on a donkey. His head slightly turned towards the apostles walking behind Him. He is being welcomed by the people with palm branches in their hands, while children spread garments along His way.

55: The Forty Martyrs of Sebastiya, early sixteenth century, Novgorod School (Tretyakov Gallery, Moscow). This scene as depicted in this icon is based on the story of the martyrdom of forty Christian soldiers which took place at a lake near the town of Sebastiya in A.D. 320. It is recorded that Emperor Licinius ordered the soldiers to stand seminaked, during the entire night before their execution, in the ice-cold waters of the lake.

We see the huddled men, shivering with cold, steadfastly awaiting death. Only one of them, unable to stand the torture any longer, is shown entering the warm bathhouse nearby. The man in charge of the execution, impressed by the unwavering faith of the remaining soldiers, removes his own shirt and takes the place of the apostate. His eyes are lifted heavenward, where a number of crowns can be seen floating, symbolizing a crown of martyrdom for every one in the group.

The artist skillfully used inverted perspective to show the various reactions of almost every one of the tormented martyrs.

56: The Saviour with the Wet Beard, sixteenth century. Novgorod School (Ostroukhov Collection, Tretyakov Gallery, Moscow). This icon is one of the several versions of the type called the Saviour Painted without Human Hands. The pointed beard with its two ends is firmly drawn downwards, which led to the name *The Saviour with the Wet Beard*. The treatment of the face is basically graphic, the symmetry of the moustache, beard, and hair is marked.

57–58: Four Saints, late fourteenth century, Pskov School (Tretyakov Gallery, Moscow). The saints represented are St. Anastasiya (?), who holds a cross in her right hand; St. Gregory the Theologian with a square beard; St. John Chrysostom, clean shaven; and St. Basil the Great, with a long black beard. The three male saints hold in their right hands Gospels, which they support with their left hands on the folds of their pallia.

Outstanding is the figure of St. John Chrysostom (Plate 58). There is almost spectral quality in this portrait: the vast dome of his forehead, the jet-black eyes and their far-away gaze suggest that the artist aimed at depicting the great fourth-century orator, writer, theologian as an ascetic visionary.

The geometrical treatment of the saints' garments, the crosses, the Gospels in their hands, and the thin red outlines of the nimbuses produce the effect of vigorous expressionism.

59: St. Nicholas, early fourteenth century, Pskov School (Tretyakov Gallery, Moscow). This icon comes from the *deësis* tier of the iconostasis in the Pskov Church of Saint Nicholas. The *deësis* as a whole was executed in the Byzantine traditions of the twelfth and early thirteenth centuries, but the icon of Saint Nicholas has marked Russian characteristics. His face is rendered in dark flesh tints typical of the work of Pskov. Some of the features, such as the deeply furrowed face and the hair at the temples, are suggestive of the Byzantine representation of Saint Nicholas, yet the general impression of this ascetic figure is distinctly that of a kindly father, rather than a stern judge. The lines are softer and more supple, and fine gold threads run through the omophorion. The saint holds in his left hand the Gospel, open to show the text from the St. Nicholas liturgy of December 6. At the sides of his head are shown two tiny half-length figures of Christ and the Virgin extending to him the book and omophorion.

60: Dormition of the Virgin, first half of the fifteenth century, Tver School (Tretyakov Gallery, Moscow). The icon is known as the *Blue Dormition (Goluboye Uspeniye)* because of the wonderfully vibrant blue tones which predominate in it. In the lower part of the picture Christ is shown, standing among the apostles, holding the Virgin's soul (in the form of a swathed child) in His hands. In the upper part the Virgin is depicted as being carried bodily by two angels in an aureole to heaven; the apostles surrounding her are borne on clouds supported by angels.

61: Entombment, last quarter of the fifteenth century, North Russian School (Tretyakov Gallery, Moscow). This icon was at one time attributed to the Novgorod School. It is now known that it comes from the iconostasis of the cathedral in the town of Kargopol (on the river Onega, Archangel region), so it must be considered as the work of what is known as the Northern School. Although this school was in many respects dependent upon Novgorod, it developed along lines of its own, and it occupies a prominent place in the history of medieval Russian painting.

62: Descent from the Cross, fifteenth century, Northern School (Tretyakov Gallery, Moscow). The icon comes from a festival tier of an iconostasis in a Kargopol church. It is notable for the simplicity of presentation and the absence of extraneous detail. In the general compositional structure of the icon, one is impressed by the artist's sensitive feeling for linear rhythm, and by his exquisite adaptation of the other figures in this icon to the curvature of Christ's body. The Kargopol artist must have possessed a knowledge not only of Novgorodian painting, but also of the art of Moscow.

63: Trinity-Sergius Monastery (Troitse-Sergieva Lavra) at Zagorsk; the Assumption Cathedral and the Church of the Trinity. The Assumption Cathedral was modeled after its namesake in the Moscow Kremlin. It is a massive six-columned, five-apsed structure crowned with five cupolas. Its construction was begun in 1554 by Ivan the Terrible, finished in 1585 by Boris Godunov. The interior was decorated with frescoes in 1684.

The Church of the Trinity (Dukhovskaya tserkov') was built in 1476–77 by Pskov architects. It is a small well-proportioned, three-apsed, single-cupola brick building. Its white stone substructure is decorated with carved trefoil figures. The walls are vertically divided into three arched panels by slender pilasters. A chapel was added in 1593 to the north façade. It stands over the grave of Maxim the Greek (see chap. XVII. n.2.). (From Shchusev Museum of Architecture, Moscow.)

64–66: Cathedral of the Assumption, Kremlin, Moscow, 1475–79. The edifice, the largest cathedral in the Moscow Kremlin, designed by Fioravanti, was modeled after the Cathedral of the Assumption in Vladimir, which since the twelfth century was considered the exemplar of Russian ecclesiastical architecture.

The plan, with minor exceptions, resembles the original (1158) Assumption in Vladimir, rather than the present cathedral with Prince Vsevolod's additions (1185–89). By suppressing the galleries Fioravanti gained the effect of spaciousness. By deepening the foundations and connecting the walls and arches with iron tie rods, he gained stability and strength.

The basic forms of this cathedral served for centuries for the design of innumerable Russian churches. (Photographs for Plates 64 and 66 from Union of Architects Library, Moscow; floor plan from Rzyanin. *Pamyatniki Russkogo zodchestva;* portals and longitudinal section from Rikhter, *Pamiatniki drevnyago Russkago zodchestva.*)

67–68: Cathedral of the Annunciation, Kremlin, Moscow, 1482–90. This little cathedral, where the tsars were christened and married, was built on the site of an earlier church by architects from Pskov. Though the smallest, it is the most picturesque of the three cathedrals in the Kremlin. Here we find the encorbelled arches (*kokoshniki*) evolved by Pskovian architects and the ogee barrel-like *(bochka)* roof sections used with great decorative success. (Floor plan from Rzyanin, *Pamyatniki Russkogo zodchestva;* photograph from Union of Architects Library, Moscow.)

69: Cathedral of Archangel Michael, Kremlin, Moscow, 1505–1509. The cathedral was destined to serve as a burial place of the tsars of the Rurik dynasty and of the early Romanovs. In plan and the use of five cupolas, the architect followed the traditions of Vladimir, but in the decoration of the façades the architect introduced a number of features derived from the Italian Renaissance style, used for the first time in Russia. (Floor plan from Rzyanin, *Pamyatniki Russkogo zodchestva;* photograph from Union of Architects Library, Moscow.)

70: Church of the Consecration of the Chasuble, Kremlin, Moscow, 1484–85. This small, single-cupola church was built by Pskovian architects, probably by the same that built the Cathedral of the Annunciation. Here we find most of the characteristic structural and decorative features developed by the

Pskovians: The ogee-shaped roof sections and arcatures, the deeply recessed portal with its ogee-shaped arch, and engaged columns. (From Union of Architects Library, Moscow.)

71: Drum and Cupola Detail: Church of the Virgin's Nativity, Kremlin, Moscow, late fourteenth century. This church, built by Russian architects, was originally designed as a private chapel for a Russian princess. An outstanding feature of this little church is the brickwork ornamentation of its beautifully proportioned drum and cupola. (From Andreev, *Moskovsky Kreml'.*)

Small Cathedral, Donskoy Monastery, Moscow, 1593. The cathedral, dedicated to the Virgin of the Don, is a columnless, single-cupola, brick structure. The slender drum, supporting the cupola, is surrounded by three tiers of superimposed, semicircular *kokoshniki*. The exterior decoration is quite simple, consisting only of mouldings and a brick entablature. The added lateral chapels and refectory date from the middle of the seventeenth century. (Photograph from the Shchusev Museum of Architecture, Moscow.)

72: The Belfry of Ivan Veliky, Kremlin, Moscow, 1532–1624. This imposing tower, whose upper stories were rebuilt, increased in height, and decorated during the reign of Boris Godunov, is a definite expression of a political and social era, reflecting the political ambitions of the tsar who dreamed of perpetuating his dynasty. Godunov envisaged it as a triumphal "column of fame," rising way above the Kremlin and dominating everything created before him by the House of Rurik. (From Union of Architects Library, Moscow.)

73: Church of the Ascension, Kolomenskoye, near Moscow, 1532. The church, erected by Vasili III, presents a decisive step in the process of transition from alien to national form. It ushered in a new era in Russian architecture. Here the most characteristic and expressive of national wooden architectural form—the "tent"—

was successfully incorporated, for the first time, into ecclesiastical masonry architecture.

The superstructure rests on an extensive cruciform base and is surrounded by covered arcades reached by three stairways. The transition from the cruciform substructure to the octagonal base of the pyramidal tower is skillfully accomplished by the application of the Pskovian method of the recessive, tapering-off arches arranged in tiers.

Situated in most picturesque surroundings, on a high bluff overlooking the Moscow River, the church is like the northern wooden churches, an integral part of the landscape—nature and building blending into an architectural whole. It is one of the most beautiful in the entire Moscow region. (Photograph from Martynov, *Environs de Moscou;* cross section from Rzyanin, *Pamyatniki Russkogo zodchestva.*)

74: Church of the Transfiguration, Ostrovo, near Moscow, 1550. This is another pyramidal church. Its central conical tower resembles that of the Kolomenskoye church, but the multitude of *kokoshniki* that adorn its base are purely decorative. (From Grabar', *Istoriya Russkago iskusstva,* 1909.)

75: Church of St. John the Precursor, Dyakovo, near Moscow, 1553–54. The plan is basically a square containing the central octagon-shaped church flanked by four smaller octagonal chapels, all connected by galleries. The transition from each of these elements to the cupola drums is accomplished by recessive tiers of *kokoshniki.* The central and the four lesser elements are crowned by flat domes, thus the church remains pentacupolar as tradition demanded, but its actual silhouette is that of the pyramidal spire. (From Martynov, *Environs de Moscou.*)

76–78: Church of St. Basil, Moscow, 1555–60. This church is the most original creation of Russian architecture built by two Russian architects, Barma and Posnik Yakovlev, who, in the words of the contemporary chronicles, were "wise and eminently fit for this wondrous work."

The building is of stone and brick, both thickly covered with stucco and paint. The predominant colors are mellow brick red and green. The eight chapels, grouped about the central church, are connected by low vaulted passages in the thickness of the walls.

Saint Basil the Blessed, for whom this church was named, was a popular mendicant preacher about four centuries ago. He claimed, as his distinctive glory, that he was idiotic "for Christ's sake." It should be noted that idiocy was a form of religious mendicancy very common in medieval Russia and that saintly idiots (*urodivyie*) were treated with reverence. (Photograph for Plate 76 from *Moskva, Sobory, monastyri i tserkvi;* for Plate 77, west elevation, from Rikhter, *Pamyatniki drevnyago Russkago zodchestva* and plan and section, Rzyanin, *Pamyatniki Russkogo zodchestva;* for Plate 78, drawings, Viollet-Le-Duc, *L'Art Russe,* and photograph, Shchusev Museum of Architecture, Moscow.)

79: Nikolskaya Church, Panilovo, Archangel province, 1600. This is one of the oldest surviving, austere and majestic, tent-type, wooden churches of northern Russia. Its central element is a tall octagon adjoined by a square apse and vestibule, which is reached by a double-covered stairway. Both the apse and the vestibule have *bochka*-shaped roofs. (From Rzyanin, *Pamyatniki Russkogo zodchestva.*)

80: Church of St. Paraskeva, Shuya, Archangel province, 1666. The main body of the church is rectangular and is capped by a "cube" roof; the sanctuary is covered by a *bochka*, while the rest of the structure has a gable roof. Such combination roofs were extensively used, often producing delightful effects. (From Suslov, *Pamyatniki drevnyago Russkago zodchestva.*)

81: Uspensky Church, Varzug, Archangel province, 1674. This

wooden church is one of the best examples of the octagonal tent-type church on the cruciform plan. The central rectangle is adjoined by square projections on all four sides, thus forming a cross. The transition from the cruciform substructure to the octagonal base of the tent is managed by the use of three recessive, *koko-shnik*-like-tiers of *bochka*-shaped roofs over the projections. (From Grabar', *Istoriya Russkago iskusstva*, 1909.)

82: Church of the Resurrection, Ust-Padenga, Archangel province, 1675. This church represents an important step in the development of *izba*-type rectangular tradition. The three block-work units, the narthex, nave, and sanctuary, are juxtaposed in a straight line. The central unit has a sharp-pitched wedge-type roof, but the apse and the narthex are covered with *bochka* roofs. (From *Mir Iskusstva*, 1904, No. 11.)

83: Window frame, Church of the Assumption, Village of Cherevkovo, Vologda province, 1683–91. The setting and ornamentation of this window is an eloquent example of the innate taste and consummate skill of the Russian carpenter. (From Suslov, *Pamyatniki drevnyago Russkago zodchestva.*)

84: Cathedral of the Assumption of the Holy Virgin, Kem, Archangel province, 1714. This is a triple-tented church. The central element is flanked by two similar but smaller ones, all combined in a single building. The transition from the square elements of the substructure to the octagons supporting the tents and their cupolas was achieved by cross-beams cutting off the square's corners. Small *kokoshniki* were put up against the alternate sides at the base of the emerging octagons. The framing and fitting of the logs at the corners produce the effect of great strength and stability. (From Suslov, *Pamyatniki drevnyago Russkago zodchestva.*)

85: Church of Saints Florus and Laurus, Rostovsk Village, Archangel Province, 1755. Although this church was built rather late, it is quite apparent that its construction was influenced by earlier and no-longer-existent wooden churches. This is a single-tent church. Its central element is a square adjoining by a semi-octagonal apse and a rectangular vestibule. It has only one lateral chapel, thus its plan is not of the traditional cruciform type. Most attractive are its massive tent and the bochka-shaped roofs over the chapel, and vestibule, and over the double stairway. (From Shchusev Museum of Architecture, Moscow.)

86: The Twenty-Two-Cupola Church of the Transfiguration at Kizhi Island, early eighteenth century. Among the many and various creations of early eighteenth-century ecclesiastical architecture, the most remarkable of all is the multi-cupola church at Kizhi Island on Lake Onega. It is perhaps as unique in the field of wood architecture as is the Church of St. Basil in the field of masonry.

The central element of this church is an octagon to which, on every other side, were added square projections forming the arms of a cross. Externally the arms are roofed over, not by the usual tent, but by four flights of recessive *bochki,* each carrying a bulbous cupola.

The result of this dexterous combination of traditional and revolutionary elements, coupled with the mass of rhythmically upsurging cupolas, is a picturesque, fairy-like pyramidal structure expressing the genius of the Russian builders in the Far North. (From Rzyanin, *Pamyatniki Russkogo zodchestva* and *Mir Iskusstva,* 1904, No. 11.)

87: Church of the Intercession, Kizhi Island, corner cupola and central cupola. This nine-cupola church, built in 1764, is a part of the Kizhi churchyard complex. It is one of the last churches built in the tradition of ancient Russian wooden architecture. Most attractive is the pyramid-shaped cluster of drums and cupolas covered with silvery aspen shingles. (From Opolovnikov, *Pamyatniki Derevyannogo zodchestva.*)

88: The Palace at Kolomenskoye, Moscow suburb, seventeenth century. The village of Kolomenskoye near Moscow had been a favorite country residence of the grand princes and tsars—a kind of a "Russian Versailles." Construction was begun by Ivan Kalita, but the palace was remodeled and expanded by his successors, repeatedly destroyed by fire and rebuilt during the second half of the sixteenth century. It was radically reconstructed and greatly enlarged during the reigns of Tsar Aleksei Mikhailovich and his son Feodor. Construction was carried on by a group of Russian carpenters headed by Elder Semyon Petrov and Chief Carpenter Ivan Mikhailov. Its lavish interior decoration was supervised by Simon Ushakov, the famous artist. Russian contemporaries regarded this palace as the "eighth wonder of the world." (From Solntsev, *Drevnosti Rossiiskago gosudarstva.*)

89: Roof construction details, *izba* in the Vologda province. A measured drawing by V. V. Suslov showing roof construction methods and characteristic details of its important elements. (From Suslov, *Pamyatniki drevnyago Russkago zodchestva.*)

90: The Horse-head motif, in the decoration of the ridge pole of peasant cottages in western Siberia. Skulls of horses were regarded by the ancient Slavs as potent charms for warding off evil spirits. This belief lingered on for centuries, and, to this day, we find carved wooden heads of horses decorating the ridge poles of many peasant houses and huts throughout Russia. (From Ashchepkov.)

91: Teremok, inn and pub, on the highway between Kostroma and Yaroslavl, eighteenth century, from a lithograph by André Durand. The lithograph is from an album of Russian architectural plates published in the 1840's by Count Anatoli Demidov. The drawings were made by André Durand, the French artist who accompanied Demidov on his travels throughout Russia in 1839. The originality of the basic architectural forms, the wealth and variety of details, faithfully reproduced in these plates, gives an idea of the vitality of the native wooden architecture which flourished in Russia up to the middle of the eighteenth century. (From Grabar', *Istoriya Russkago iskusstva*, 1909.)

92: Church of the Georgian Virgin, Moscow, 1653. This is one of the best examples of seventeenth-century Moscow ecclesiastical architecture. Erected in 1628, in the Nikitinsky Alley on the site of a previous wooden church, it was greatly enlarged in 1634–35 and finished in 1653, when its interior was decorated with frescoes attributed to Simon Ushakov.

The builder was the adventuresome and wealthy merchant Gregori Nikitinkov (hence the name of the alley), who lavished money on its construction. Nikitinkov's own mansion adjoined the church, and this might help to explain the assymetry of the plan of the church and the somewhat peculiar distribution of its elements. Apart from two independent chapels north and south of the main five-cupola church, there are two refectories, a long gallery-type narthex, and several storage rooms. There is also a belfry and a magnificent entrance porch, with double arches and pendants, covered by an octagonal tent spire—a modified element of the nobleman's wooden mansion *(khoromi)*. The group of buildings rests on a tall substructure and is mainly of brick; the first floors and some details are of white stone. The church, which dominates the entire group, is decorated with engaged double columns, ogee-shaped window frames, and an elaborately ornamented cornice.

The juxtaposition of the several buildings and the intermingling of domestic and ecclesiastical, structural and decorative elements resulted in an unusually picturesque composition, lending the church a rather strong worldly and homey aspect. This type of church became extremely popular, and it strongly influenced the design of many subsequent ecclesiastical buildings. (From Suslov, *Pamiatniki drevnyago Russkago zodchestva.*)

93: Cathedral and Belfry, the New Jerusalem Monastery on the Istra, 1656–85. The New Jerusalem Monastery was founded by Patriarch Nikon in 1656. The Church of the Resurrection in this monastery was modeled on the Church of the Holy Sepulchre at Jerusalem, thereby constituting a departure from the traditional Russian pattern of five cupolas. The original dome collapsed in the eighteenth century, and a new one was built, possibly after designs by B. Rastrelli. The monastery was totally destroyed during the Second World War. (From Rzyanin, *Pamyatniki Russkogo zodchestva.*)

94: Church of the Holy Trinity, Ostankino, near Moscow, 1668. This elaborately decorated church is on the estate of Count F. I. Sheremetev. Its architect, Pavel Potekhin, a serf of Count Ya. K. Cherkasky, was a gifted master decorator with a special predilection for jagged silhouette, verticality, and richness of ornamentation.

Brick was his favorite medium for wall surface decoration: bricks of every imaginable size, shape, and color, laid in various fanciful ways; bricks cut, carved and molded in the manner of a sculptor working with pliable clay. He used this material for his window frames, their jambs and architraves, for portals, panels, cornices, and other details with great effect, producing a pictorial richness seldom found anywhere else. (From Rzyanin, *Pamyatniki Russkogo zodchestva.*)

95: Church of the Holy Virgin, Fili, Moscow, 1693. This church represents the crystallized form of the late seventeenth-century ecclesiastical architecture. It combines the traditional features of the sixteenth-century churches—the Ascension at Kolomenskoye, the Transfiguration at Ostrovo, and St. Basil in Moscow—with

some innovations in the baroque spirit. In some ways it antici-
pated the work of Russia's most famous baroque architect, B. B.
Rastrelli (1700–1771). (From Rzyanin, *Pamyatniki Russkogo
zodchestva.*)

96: Church of the Holy Trinity, *ca.* 1700, Troitzkoye-Lykovo,
near Moscow. The architect was Yakov Bukhvostov, a serf of
M. U. Tatishchev. He was the designer of several outstanding
ecclesiastical structures, among them the Church of the Saviour
at Ubory and the Cathedral at Ryazan.

The Holy Trinity Church is on an elevated terrace and surrounded by a gallery reached by three wide stairways. The central element is a square structure surmounted by three receding
tiers of octagons culminating in a cupola. The sanctuary and the
vestibule (rounded appurtenances) are symmetrically arranged
east and west of the central mass, each one crowned with a
small cupola.

The architectural forms and the decorative features are those
developed by the Moscow baroque (Naryshkin phase) of the
late seventeenth century, and the church possesses the characteristic flavor of that period. The decorative scheme consists of a
unique amalgamation of Italian Renaissance motifs with the traditional ornament of Russian architecture. There are oddly
shaped parapets adorned with cockscombs, curiously curved pediments, carved finials and corbels, and many other details directly derived from the national forms of wood architecture.
(From Rzyanin, *Pamyatniki Russkogo zodchestva.*)

97: Novodevichei Monastery, Moscow, sixteenth-seventeenth
centuries. This picturesque fortress-monastery, on the banks of
the Moskva River, was founded by Basil III in 1525. Construction was carried on during the sixteenth and seventeenth centuries.

The oldest monument is the five-domed Smolensk Cathedral
built by Ivan the Terrible in 1550. The fortified walls and towers

and the Palace of Tsaritsa Irina were built during the reign of Boris Godunov.

Tsarevna Sophia, half sister of Peter the Great, made it her residence, and during the last decade of the seventeenth century rebuilt it in the style of Moscow baroque. It was during her reign that the great Bell Tower, the huge refectory, the five-domed Church of the Transfiguration, and the three-domed Church of the Intercession were erected. (From Shchusev Museum of Architecture, Moscow.)

98: Church of the Miracle of the Virgin, Dubrovitsy, near Moscow, 1690–1704. This is a unique example of a centralized tower-type church resting on a cruciform base. The plan is similar to that of the Intercession at Fili, but the appurtenances adjoining the main element are trefoil instead of semicircular. The three-storied octagonal tower, rising from the center, is topped with a cupola above which is an open-gilt metal crown. (From Rzyanin, *Pamyatniki Russkogo zodchestva.*)

99: Church of the Archangel Gabriel (Menshikov Tower), Moscow, main entrance, 1705–1707. The church, built at the expense of Prince Menshikov and designed by Ivan Zarudnyi, is one of the last works of the period of the Moscow baroque. Its tall, tiered tower is composed of octagons rising from superimposed cubic substructures and is tastefully decorated with early baroque elements. Its upper octagons were damaged by fire in 1723, and the church was rebuilt some fifty years later. (From Rzyanin, *Pamyatniki Russkogo zodchestva.*)

100: Moscow Kremlin, modern times. The view is from Moskvoretsky Bridge. Left to right: the Grand Kremlin Palace, group of the principal cathedrals, and the Belfry of Ivan the Great. (From Rzyanin, *Pamyatniki Russkogo zodchestva.*)

101: Red Square, in modern times. Red (or Beautiful) Square

343

(Krasnaya Ploshchad')—the center of political and social life of medieval Moscow—is a large oblong rectangle bounded on the west by the battlemented wall of the Kremlin, in front of which stands the Lenin Mausoleum; on the east by the grand façade of the commercial arcades (GUM); on the north by the Historical Museum; and on the south by the Church of St. Basil. (From Rzyanin, *Pamyatniki Russkogo zodchestva*.)

102: Kremlin Wall, Moscow: The Tsar's Tower, 1680, is located between the Nabatnaya and Spasskaya towers of the Moscow Kremlin, and rests directly on the wall ramparts. Before 1680 it was a wooden structure in the form of a pavilion, where, it is said, Ivan the Terrible loved to sit and watch the crowds on the Red Square. It was torn down and in its place was erected the present brick tower. Its lower tier is supported on arches; the superstructure, an octagonal tent with four finials at the corners, is carried by four baluster-shaped bellied columns. This decorative column motif became very popular in the seventeenth century and, later, was reintroduced to the architecture of the eighteenth century by the Russian architect Kazakov. (From Andreev, *Moskovsky Kreml'*.)

The Beklemishev Tower of the Kremlin Wall, Moscow, late seventeenth century, one of the three corner-towers of the Kremlin, is at the southeast corner. The substructure was built by the Italian architect, Marco Ruffo, in 1487; the tent-shaped superstructure was added in the second half of the seventeenth century. (From Andreev, *Moskovsky Kreml'*.)

103: Trinity Tower, Kremlin, Moscow, substructure late fifteenth century, superstructure 1672–88. The architecture and the decorative elements of the tower have a pseudo Gothic flavor. The interior of the tower and its front-protecting barbican, the so-called Kutafya Tower, were considerably altered and disfigured in the nineteenth century. The upper decorative elements of the Kutafya Tower were done in the so-called "Naryshkin"

344

style, very much in vogue towards the end of the seventeenth century. Its ornamental motifs have exercised an influence on the work of the Moscow architects of the second half of the eighteenth century. (From the Shchusev Museum of Architecture, Moscow.)

104–106: The Granovitaya Palata (Palace of Facets), Kremlin, Moscow, was built in 1487–91 by the Italian architects Marco Ruffo and Pietro Solario. It was specially designed to serve as a throne room for the reception of foreign ambassadors; it was also the scene of great banquets and of many notable events in medieval Russian history. (Plate 104 from Union of Architects Library, Moscow; Plate 105 from Rzyanin, *Pamyatniki Russkogo zodchestva;* Plate 106 from Grabar', *Istoriya Russkago iskusstva,* 1909).

107: The foundation for the Terem Palace, Kremlin, Moscow, 1636, was laid in 1499; the work was supervised by the Italian architect, Alevisio Novyi. These living quarters, constituting the lower floors of the present five-story structure (now forming the north wing of the Grand Kremlin Palace) were finished in 1508.

The reconstruction and enlargement of the old quarters took place during the reign of Tsar Aleksei Mikhailovich, under the supervision of the Russian master-stonemasons B. Ogurtsov, A. Konstantinov, T. Sharutin, and L. Ushakov. (From Rzyanin, *Pamyatniki Russkogo zodchestva.*)

108: The Golden Tsaritsa Chamber (Zolotaya Tsaritsyna Palata), Terem Palace, Kremlin, Moscow, second half of the sixteenth century. The chamber is about thirty-three feet square. The two intersecting arches which support the vaulting are reinforced by gilded iron tie-bars arranged crosswise. There are seven arched, deeply splayed windows with built-in seats, and on the walls and vaults are a series of frescoes, on legendary ecclesiastical and historical themes, painted on a gold background (from which the name "Golden Chamber" is derived). The chamber served as a reception room for the tsaritsa where, on great holidays and special occasions, she received congratulations and offerings from the clergy, members of the court, and the nobility. During the reign of Peter I, the chamber was neglected and served as a storeroom; by order of Nicholas I, it was renovated and restored to its original state. (Cross section from Rikhter, *Pamiatniki drevnyago Russkago zodchestva*; Golden Chamber from Solntsev, *Drevnosti Rossiiskago gosudarstva*.)

109: Entrance door, Terem Palace, Kremlin, Moscow, facing the Church of the Saviour Behind the Golden Grille. The upper chamber was built on the roof by order of Tsar Mikhail Feodorovich for his two boys, Tsarevichi Aleksei and Ivan. The entrance door architrave is of white stone and decorated with richly carved and varicolored designs of stylized flowers, birds, beasts, and hunters.

The windows are of various forms and are remarkable for their ornamentation as well as for the meticulous quality of workmanship; they differ from one another in the design of their arches, architraves, entablatures, and sills. The ornamentation consists of griffins and dragons, double-headed eagles, pigeons, and birds of paradise with crowns and necklaces, foliage, flowers, and arabesques. The carving on the window architraves is in high relief. (From Solntsev, *Drevnosti Rossiiskago gosudarstva*.)

110: The corridor in the Terem Palace, Kremlin, Moscow, 1635, leading from the Terem chambers to the Church of the Crucifixion is long and narrow. The floor of the corridor is covered with stone plates carved in ancient patterns. The corridor windows face the Palace Court, while the opposite windows face the Verkhospasskaya platform.

Tradition has it that this corridor served as the place of inspection for the girls eligible to become the tsar's bride. On appointed days the most beautiful daughters of the best families of the land would be lined up in this corridor; the tsar, walking slowly up and down, would look them over thrice, and when his eyes fell upon the most desirable, he would present her with a specially embroidered kerchief *(shirinka)* as a token of his favor. (From Bartenev, *Moskovsky Kreml'*.)

111: Council Chamber, Terem Palace, Kremlin, Moscow, 1635. The chamber—the third room on the palace fourth floor—was the tsar's study, where the high officials of state were received. This chamber contained a dais for the throne and some benches along the walls, where the boyars were seated according to seniority. (From Union of Architects Library, Moscow.)

112: The stairway in the Terem Palace, Kremlin, Moscow, 1635, with its fronting double arch, was designed by Bazhen Ogurtsov. (From Rzyanin, *Pamyatniki Russkogo zodchestva.*)

113: The Church of St. John the Precursor, Tolchkovo, Yaroslavl, 1671–87, is of the square four-columned type with three apses, surrounded on three sides with a wide vaulted, richly frescoed gallery. At a short distance from the church with its gilt cupolas rises a free-standing octagonal multi-storied belfry. (From Rzyanin, *Pamyatniki Russkogo zodchestva,* and, interior, from Shchusev Museum of Architecture, Moscow.)

114: Belfry, Church of the Nativity of Christ, Yaroslavl, seventeenth century. This brick pyramidal belfry is built up in a series of receding tiers with variously shaped openings supporting a blind tent crowned with a cupola. (From Suslov, *Pamyatniki drevnyago Russkago zodchestva.*)

115–17: Cathedral of the Resurrection, Romanov-Borisoglebsk, Yaroslavl province, 1652–70. The cathedral at Romanov-Borisoglebsk (at present Tutayev) is a five-domed church of the four-column type with three apses, surrounded on three sides by a wide gallery terminating at the lateral apses and approached by two covered stairways. By its vast dimensions and luxurious decoration it surpasses all the churches of Yaroslavl and is justly considered to be the outstanding architectural monument of this epoch. (Plates 115 and 116, window, from Suslov, *Pamyatniki drevnyago Russkago zodchestva;* Plates 116, porch, and 117 from *Khudozhestvennyia sokrovishcha Rossii.*)

118: Church of St. John Chrysostom, Korovniki, Yaroslavl, 1649: The wide and deeply splayed architrave of the window in the east wall consists of several small delicately profiled members set in a wide bluish-green tile frame—a typical decorative device widely used in Russian brick architecture of the seventeenth century. The colonnettes are formed of two equal slender elements joined end to end by tiny balusters and terminating at the top and bottom by small square caps and moulded drops. (From Grabar', *Istoriya Russkago iskusstva,* 1909, and view from southwest from Shchusev Museum of Architecture, Moscow.)

119: Saints Boris and Gleb on Horseback, 1340, Moscow School (Tretyakov Gallery, Moscow). The saints Boris and Gleb, assassinated by their brother Svyatopolk, were symbols of princely power of Moscow. The doctrine of the right of the grand princes of Moscow to the whole of Russia and of divine character of the power entrusted to them was busily propagated, especially after the Kulikovo battle (1380). The two brothers are shown on horseback, their lances in hand, against a background of an abstract rocky landscape, hovering, as it were, in the air. At the right hand top corner of the painting Our Lord is depicted raising His right hand in blessing.

120: The Annunciation, late fourteenth century, Moscow School (?) (Tretyakov Gallery, Moscow). The Virgin is depicted sitting on a throne, her head inclined toward the angel approaching her with vigorous strides. The sumptuous architectural background of the Palaeologian Renaissance is effectively used by the artist

348

to dramatize the emotions and tensions created by this event. The contour of the portico with its awning seems to echo that of Mary's head, bent in meditation, while the tower to the left of the angel strengthens the illusion of grace and vigor of the heavenly messenger.

The Russian art historian Lazarev is inclined to think that the icon might have been painted by a Greek artist—a long-time resident of Moscow.

121: Apostle Paul, early fifteenth century, Moscow School (Tretyakov Gallery, Moscow). The representation of St. Paul with his high forehead and slightly curled beard is somewhat similar to the early Christian prototypes. The style of this icon is close to that of the St. Paul of the iconostasis in the Trinity Cathedral at Zagorsk, near Moscow. Lazarev attributes it to Rublev.

122–25: Old Testament Trinity, by Andrei Rublev, early fifteenth century, Moscow School (Tretyakov Gallery, Moscow). In icon painting the theme of this icon is usually referred to as the "Old Testament Trinity," to distinguish it from the "New Testament Trinity," or the "Paternity." This type of icon is sometimes also called "Hospitality," referring to the hospitality shown by Abraham to the three strangers. The icon was painted by Rublev for the Trinity Cathedral of the Troitse-Sergieva Lavra, *ca.* 1411.

In this *Old Testament Trinity.* Rublev depicts three angels seated at a table, each holding a pilgrim's staff in his left hand. On the table stands the sacrificial bowl referred to in ancient Russian poetry as "the bowl of mortality"—the pledge of eternal life. The bowl contains a calf head, a reminder to the spectator that though Abraham and Sarah are not shown in the picture, they are represented as hosts to the visitors. In the background is a tree, representing presumably the Oak of Mamre. The turret is in the Byzantine style.

Although the actual forms of Rublev's *Trinity* may be all derived from Byzantine originals, they have taken on a quite new meaning. The painting shows, perhaps more clearly than any other, the concentrated religious emotion which is characteristic of Rublev. The severe symbolism of the old Byzantine tradition has been transformed into something new, more humanistic, more intimate. Even more important is the novel, peculiarly Russian mood of dreamy sublimation.

126: Head of Christ, attributed to Andrei Rublev, early fifteenth century, Moscow School (Tretyakov Gallery, Moscow). The picture of the Saviour belongs to a poorly preserved *deësis* discovered in a storeroom of the Uspensky Cathedral at Zvenigorod near Moscow. It is one of the first of the large Russian *deësis* icons of an iconostasis. There is a strong resemblance between the features of Christ here and those of the *deësis* mosaics in the Kahrieh-Djami in Constantinople. However, there are deviations from the original, the painter transforming the severe majesty of the Greek original into a gentler Russian concept.

127: The Saviour in Glory, attributed to Andrei Rublev, *ca.* 1420 (Tretyakov Gallery, Moscow). The icon depicts the Saviour as the King of Glory, surrounded by the heavenly powers. Sitting on a magnificent carved throne the Saviour blesses with the right hand, while with the left He supports the open Gospels resting on His knee. He is surrounded by an oval *mandorla* and by two curved squares forming an octagonal star. Here the first square embraces only the majestic figure of the Pantacrator. This square is enclosed in a *mandorla* which contains seraphim surrounding the throne. In the corners of the second square, traced back of the *mandorla,* are placed the symbols of the evangelists. On the left of the spectator, above, is the symbol of the Evangelist Mark, a lion. On the right is an eagle, symbol of John, and a bull, symbol of Luke. Despite the emphasis on linear pattern, there is far more here than mere calligraphy.

128: The Zvenigorod Nativity, early fifteenth century, Moscow School (Tretyakov Gallery, Moscow). Our Lady is represented clad in a dark robe and hood and reclining at full length, with her face turned to the side, on a mattress. She is in a meditative mood. Behind her in a cave, clad in swaddling clothes and reposing in a manger, can be seen the Child. An ox and an ass are standing near Him; and the rays of the star in the east, visible at the top of the icon are directed upon Him. On the top left corner are the three kings or wise men on horseback and wondering at the appearance of the star. Below them are three angels adoring the Child. At the bottom left corner is Saint Joseph confronted by the hunchback Firsus, who symbolizes the spirit of temptation. At the top right corner two angels are gazing at the rays of the star. A third is stooping to talk to two of the shepherds who stand below. At the bottom right corner are shown two women washing the newborn Child. The whole scene is set against a rocky background overgrown with shrubs and small trees.

129: Aleksei, the Moscow Metropolitan, attributed to Dionysius, sixteenth century (Tretyakov Gallery, Moscow). This icon comes from the Cathedral of the Assumption in the Moscow Kremlin. The figure of the saintly Metropolitan represented in this picture forms the central part of a large hagiographical icon. The miniature scenes surrounding the central figure depict the most important events in the life of this outstanding religious and political leader.

130: The Obnorskoye Crucifixion, by Dionysius, 1500 (Tretyakov Gallery, Moscow). This icon originally formed a part of the festival tier of an iconostasis in the Obnorsky Monastery in the province of Vologda. On the left stand the Virgin, shown in a state of shock, and the three Marys, one of whom supports her. On the right can be seen St. John the Baptist and Longinus, the centurion.

The tall, elongated figures, the delicate highlights of their costumes and the underlying modeling recall the Byzantine tradition, but the faces are distinctly Russian, and the figure of Christ, with its thin arms and gently curving body, is quite foreign to anything that one would find in the contemporary Greek world.

131: John the Theologian in Meditation, sixteenth century, Moscow School (Tretyakov Gallery, Moscow). St. John is depicted in a state of solemn meditation. The fingers of his left hand are pressed to his lips in a gesture of silence. The linear treatment of the picture shows mastery of the medium, and, while the representation of some features—the knuckles and ear—is rather primitive, the artist succeeded in conveying a sense of depth, volume, and a mood of contemplation.

132: The Church Militant, second half of the sixteenth century, Moscow School (Tretyakov Gallery, Moscow). This huge (13′ 2″ x 4′ 9″) horizontal icon was originally intended to serve as a decoration for the walls of Ivan the Terrible's palace. It remained there for some time, and was then transferred to the incense-manufacturing chamber at the Kremlin. At present it is in the Tretyakov Gallery.

Its central theme—the triumph of the Cross over the Crescent—is closely related to the religious and political climate of the 1550's. Essentially, it is a historical picture depicting the final phase of the war with the Moslem Khanate of Kazan′: The flame-enveloped "heathen" city, the homeward-bound march of the victorious troops, and the apotheosis of Ivan. The story is told in a language of symbols and allegories reminiscent of the frescoes of the Golden Chamber described by Ushakov in Chapter XVII. The composition is divided horizontally into three sections formed by three columns of the army marching along the banks of a meandering river. The cavalry units are shown in the upper and lower sections. They are headed by the reincarnated spirits of the Russian Warrior Princes Alexander Nevsky and Dmitri

Donskoy. The middle section of the composition depicts a column of foot soldiers surrounding the Roman Emperor Constantine I on horseback with a cross held aloft (thus echoing the legend, *in hoc signo vinces*). This is followed by another infantry column led by sainted Princes believed to be Vladimir, Boris, and Gleb.

In his desire to glorify this campaign, to lend it an aura of holiness, and to point out the heavenly rewards awaiting the crusaders, the painter strongly dramatized the approach of the procession to Holy Moscow (personifying the Celestial City): At the gates, the enthroned Virgin and Child are waiting. Overhead a host of angels bearing crowns of glory are flying toward the marchers. Most conspicuous are the figures of Archangel Michael and Tsar Ivan the Terrible. The Archangel—the Chief of heavenly hosts—is presented astride a winged red horse galloping at the head of the procession. Back of him is Ivan on horseback marshaling his troops. He is depicted as a young handsome knight in shining armor, waving a red banner. Above him hover three angels, each holding a golden crown of glory as his reward for defending the Orthodox Faith.

133: The Image of Our Lady Odigitriya, sixteenth century, Moscow School (Armory Museum, Kremlin, Moscow). The *Odigitriya* (*Hodigitriya*) is one of the Russian iconographical types of the Virgin. She is usually represented holding the Child on her left arm, the right arm lifted as though guiding souls toward her Divine Son. The type of the *Odigitriya* has given rise to several iconographic variants. The most venerated in Russia are the icons of Smolensk, Tikhvin, and Kazan.

The icon reproduced here comes from the Cathedral of Archangel Michael in the Moscow Kremlin. In the solemnity of expression, manner of highlighting (*ozhivki*), and symbolic representation it shows some relation to the Byzantine prototypes. Yet the modeling of the faces, the precise, delicate drawing, and the fluent blending of the pigments reveal that it is a product of a new age in Russian icon painting.

The face is somewhat oval and modeled with hardly any suggestion of bone structure. The nose is thin and slightly prominent, the hands supple and refined. The soft flesh coloring, tone, and quality, all identify the painting as belonging in sentiment to the work of Rublev or one of his closest followers. The composition reflects a new kind of rhythm; the angularity and rigidity of the Greek painters are gone, and the style is distinguished by an aristocratic subtlety, a soft poetic quality informed by a new spiritual significance.

The embellishment of the gold encasement in filigree and enamel is remarkable for its artistry and richness. The crown or the halo *(venchik)* is of gold and cloisonné enamel. To it are attached a collar *(grivna)* in the form of a crescent and three pendants *(tsaty)*. They are all heavily encrusted with precious stones, mostly uncut. The image of the Child is embellished in the same way. On the golden medallions around the pearl-bordered frame are niello engravings of the saints whose name days correspond with the Christian names of the owner and members of his family.

Of the ten medallions, seven are inscribed with the names of the saints whose name days correspond with the Christian names of Ivan the Terrible's family, before the death of his first wife Anastasiya, thus establishing not only the ownership of the icon, but also the approximate date of ordering the encasement as *ca.* 1557–60. (From Solntsev, *Drevnosti Rossiiskago gosudarstva.*)

134: The Virgin and Child, sixteenth century, Stroganov School (Ostroukhov Collection, Tretyakov Gallery, Moscow). This icon represents the same subject as the Vladimir Virgin, known as *Umileniye*. The Mother, clad in a dark brown maphorion, is tenderly bending her head toward the Child. (From *Russkaya ikona.*)

135: Head of Archangel Michael, from a triptych by a pupil of Prokopius Chirin, Stroganov School, first half of the seventeenth century (Russian Museum, Leningrad). In this icon the head of the archangel is rendered in the *friaz* manner. It is thickly covered with fluffy curls falling in waves along the temples and cheeks right down to the neck. The ribbons of the head-band twist down his ear, thus giving him the appearance of a fifteenth-century young Italian court dandy. (From Kondakov, *Russkaya ikona.*)

136: Saint John the Warrior, by Prokopius Chirin, Stroganov School, early seventeenth century (Russian Museum, Leningrad). The saint is depicted as if he were going to meet the heavenly vision of the Virgin with the Child upon a throne surrounded by angels; his face resembles that of Ivan Stroganov of whom he was the patron saint and to whom the icon was given by his father. (From Kondakov, *Russkaya ikona.*)

137: The Mandilion Portrait of Christ, seventeenth century, Northern Provincial School (State Art History Museum, Novgorod). The picture of the Saviour by this anonymous painter shows an attempt to render the ancient iconographic type of the Mandilion in a naturalistic manner.

138: Prince Skopin-Shuisky, Moscow School, early seventeenth century (Tretyakov Gallery, Moscow). Prince Skopin-Shuisky was one of the outstanding young officers in the Russian army during the Time of Trouble. He died in 1610 at the age of 24. There are both old and new stylistic characteristics in this portrait. The conventional method of icon painting is here combined with a realistic treatment of the prince's facial features. One may detect in this picture some definite signs of a new trend in Russian art: the secularization of subject matter and the turning toward naturalistic portrait painting.

139–40: The Annunciation with the Acathist, by Ushakov, Kazanets, and Kondratyev, Moscow School, 1659 (Historical Museum, Moscow). This icon was painted for the Church of the

Georgian Virgin in Nikitinki (Plate 92). The picture of the Annunciation which is the largest and most important element in this icon is surrounded by twelve subsidiary scenes, illustrating the hymns of the Acathist. The Annunciation proper is credited to Simon Ushakov; the background and figures of the surrounding scenes to Yakov Kazanets; their details to Gavrilo Kondratyev.

The three-dimensional figures of the Annunciation and its Italian Renaissance architectural forms are undoubtedly the work of Ushakov. But the surrounding scenes with their tiny, finely rendered, elegant figures scattered among the architectural details of the landscape have little in common with Ushakov's style. It seems to indicate that in Moscow of the 1650's there existed several competing trends in painting, and that Ushakov—the supposed head of the group—was either unable or unwilling to exercise his authority over his collaborators.

141: The Vernicle, or the Holy Mandilion of Edessa, by Simon Ushakov, Moscow School, 1657 (Tretyakov Gallery, Moscow). This is one of a series of icons of the Mandilion painted by Ushakov. The artist seems to have been fascinated by the theme of this subject. He worked on it for years trying to break away from the old conventional scheme and to find new means for creating an image that would retain the essence of the old type of *The Saviour Not Made with Hands* (see Plate 36) but at the same time give it an illusionistic representation. Gone is the stern look and the flatness of the old images. Instead we have an earthly human head and face masterly modeled in chiaroscuro.

142: Christ, the Great Archbishop, by Simon Ushakov, Moscow School, last quarter of the seventeenth century (Tretyakov Gallery, Moscow). The naturalistic rendering of Christ's head has the quality of a European painting rather than of an icon. However, the artist succeeded in expressing a strong religious feeling combined with human greatness and dignity.

143: Iconostasis, Uspensky Cathedral, Kremlin, Moscow. The iconostasis is a high wall of burnished vermeil, with five rows of icons set in richly ornamented encasements of embossed metal that leave visible only the faces and hands of the saints. The iconographic material illustrates two themes: religion and the state. The religious theme stresses the idea of the Universal Church—the union of the Old Testament with the New. The state theme dwells on the importance of the unification of all the Russian states by Moscow.

The top row—the Forefathers'—symbolizes the Church of the Old Testament: the Lord of Sabaoth, seated upon a throne, with Christ and the Dove in the midst of the twelve Patriarchs. The second row—the Prophets'—symbolizes the Church from Moses to Jesus Christ: the Mother of God holding Emmanuel upon her lap, flanked by David and Solomon and the Prophets. The third row—the Festivals—depicts the Church festivals: the Birth of the Virgin, the Presentation in the Temple, Baptism, Raising of Lazarus, Entry into Jerusalem, Transfiguration, Crucifixion, Descent from the Cross, Entombment, Ascension, the Descent of the Holy Spirit, and the Dormition. The fourth row—Prayer or Intercession—is given to the *Deësis:* the Saviour flanked by the Mother of God and St. John the Baptist, the Archangels Michael and Gabriel, St. Peter, St. Paul, and the other apostles. In the bottom row are the icons of the locally revered Festivals and Saints and the Royal Doors with the Annunciation and the Four Evangelists on the door leaves. To the left of the Royal Doors is a copy of the icon of *Our Lady of Vladimir.* Next follow the icons of *Our Lord,* adored by Varlaam Khutynsky (brought from Novgorod in 1476) and of *Our Lady of Smolensk.* To the right of the Royal Doors is the icon of *Our Most Merciful Lord* (also brought from Novgorod) and next to it is the icon of the *Dormition or Repose of the Mother of God*—the dedication feast of the cathedral. This icon is traditionally attributed to the Metropolitan Peter and is a good example of the thirteenth- and fourteenth-century Russian icon painting. (From Solntsev, *Drevnosti Rossiiskago gosudarstva.*)

144: Shroud of Christ, *ca.* 1562 (Kirillo-Byelozersk Monastery). This is one of the many shrouds and icon covers designed and embroidered in the private needlework shops maintained in Moscow by Princess Evfrosiniya Staritskaya. Other examples of embroidered shrouds, produced in her shops and dated 1558–61 are preserved in the Monasteries of Volokolamsk, Trinity-Sergiev, and in the Museum of Smolensk. (From Grabar', *Istoriya Russkogo iskusstva,* 1955.)

145: Sakkos of Patriarch Nikon, 1654 (Armory Museum, Kremlin, Moscow). The sakkos (saccos) is shaped as a Western dalmatic, that is, slit up the sides and with short sleeves. Originally limited to the patriarch, it is now worn by all bishops. This sakkos was made, during the reign of Ivan IV, for the Metropolitan Dionisi and altered in the seventeenth century to be worn by Patriarch Nikon. The vestment is made of Italian double-looped velvet, and adorned with Russian sixteenth-century embroidery, large pearls, gems, gold spangles, and superb niello miniatures. (From *Mir iskusstva,* 1904.)

146: Sakkos of Patriarch Adrian, 1691 (Armory Museum, Kremlin, Moscow). The vestment is made of Italian golden-green velvet decorated with orange-colored vegetation shoots. Its outstanding feature is the superb ornamentation of the sides and hem composed of double-headed eagles and unicorns outlined in fresh-water pearls. The work was done by the embroiderers in the shops of the tsaritsa. (From Boguslavsky, *Gosudarstvennaya oruzheinaya palata.*)

147: Front cover of the Book of the Mstislav Gospels, 1103 (Historical Museum, Moscow). Written and illuminated on parchment about 1103, this book derives its name from its first owner,

Prince Mstislav Vladimirovich of Novgorod. The scribe is identified by Russian historians as Aleksei Lazarev, the son of a Novgorod priest. According to tradition, the prince sent the finished manuscript to Tsargrad (Constantinople), celebrated then for its jeweled and enameled metals, to be bound and embellished with enameled gold covers. The book remained for several centuries in the Church of the Annunciation at Novgorod. In 1551, by order of Ivan Grozny, its cover was renovated and the book removed to the Cathedral of the Archangel Michael in the Moscow Kremlin. The present enamel decorations (the images of the saints) on its silver-gilt filigree cover are the products of different periods varying in styles and techniques. (From *Mir iskusstva,* 1904).

148: Cover of the Book of the Gospels, gift of Boyarin B. M. Morozov, 1669 (Armory Museum, Kremlin, Moscow). The Gospels appear in Slavonic on parchment, two columns on a page, according to fifteenth-century regulations. The front cover is of gold embellished with filigree patterns and colored enamel plaques. In the center are representations of the Resurrection of Christ and of the Evangelists. Above, below, and on the sides are the Twelve Apostles and the archangels. In the corners are Saints Basil the Great, Gregorius the Theologian, John the Golden-Mouthed, Nicholas, and four cherubims. (From *Mir iskusstva,* 1904.)

149: Silver cover for a manuscript of the Book of the Gospels, 1499 (Armory Museum, Kremlin, Moscow). The cover for the book was made by Moscow craftsmen at the behest of Ivan III who presented it to the Cathedral of the Assumption in the Moscow Kremlin.

The filigree work of the "ribbon" type covers the surface with a luxuriant network of lace, and forms a frame for five cast and chased icon shrines. Within these shrines, against a limpid green enameled background, are the images of the Crucifixion (center) and of the four Evangelists (corners). (From Boguslavsky, *Gosudarstrennaya oruzheinaya palata.*)

150: The Crown (Miter) of Patriarch Nikon (Armory Museum, Kremlin, Moscow). The crown is encrusted with pearls and precious stones; it has some noteworthy enameling, especially in the upper part. Its design is attributed to Simon Ushakov. (From *Mir iskusstva*, 1904.)

151: Large silver Zion (Ciborium), eleventh-twelfth century, from the Cathedral of St. Sophia, Novgorod (Hall of Facets, Novgorod Kremlin). Ciboriums of this kind, generally built in the form of a church, were often called Zions or Jerusalems. Neither the cathedral inventory lists nor oral traditions mention the origin of this ciborium. On its flat dome is embossed the *Deisus*, that is, the Saviour and the Intercessor Saints. On the panels of the main body are the Twelve Apostles. The rendering of the faces is in the Byzantine manner. The inscriptions are a mixture of Greek and Slavonic characters. The engaged colonnettes and other decorative elements have many characteristics of the Byzantine style and resemble the fifteenth- and sixteenth-century vessels of this type. (From the State Art History Museum, Novgorod.)

152: Ciborium or tabernacle called "Jerusalem," 1486 (Armory Museum, Kremlin, Moscow). The ciborium is of silver-gilt and embellished with niello. It is built in the form of a five-cupola church surrounded by embossed, high-relief figures of the twelve Apostles. On the sloping walls of the superstructure are the figures of four prophets surrounded by winged beasts. The inscription in Slavonic on the inside of the door indicates that it was built by order of Ivan III for the Cathedral of the Assumption in the Kremlin. The style of the decorations and the inscription suggests that the ciborium is of Moscow workmanship. (From Solntsev, *Drevnosti Rossiiskago gosudarstva.*)

153: Silver vase *(Kratir)* for communion wine by Master Bratilo, twelfth century, from the Cathedral of St. Sophia, Novgorod (Hall of Facets, Novgorod Kremlin). The vase is an outstanding piece of decorative art remarkable for the beauty of its workmanship. On one of its panels Christ is represented, one hand raised in blessing, the other holding the gospels; on another panel is the Virgin Orans. St. Peter is shown with his staff and scroll, and St. Barbara and St. Anastasiya appear with crosses in their hands. Surrounding the figures are chased designs of birds and interlacing foliate motifs. The inscription at the bottom, freely translated, reads: "Lord, help thy slave, Florovi (Flor). Made by Bratilo." (From the State Art History Museum, Novgorod.)

154: Copper holy water container, 1553, from the Epiphany Monastery (Belaya Palata Museum, Rustov). (From *Obraztsy dekorativnago iskusstva.*)

155: Silver Panagiyarion, by Master Ivan, 1436, from the Cathedral of St. Sophia, Novgorod (Hall of Facets, Novgorod Kremlin). This panagiyarion (panagiyar) consists of a saucer-shaped plate, a cover plate of the same shape, and a pedestal. The upper surface of the cover is embellished with a miniature low-relief image of the Ascension signed by Master Ivan. The pedestal is surrounded by four angels supporting the plates with their uplifted arms. At the foot of the pedestal are four lions encircled by a border of shrubbery. The figures of the angels and the beasts are sculptured in the round. (From the State Art History Museum, Novgorod.)

156: Chalice, of Boyarin D. I. Godunov, 1599 (Armory Museum, Kremlin, Moscow). This golden chalice is richly adorned with large gems and niello ornamentation. (From Boguslavsky, *Gosudarstvennaya oruzheinaya palata.*)

157: The Panagiya of Patriarch Philaret (Armory Museum,

Kremlin, Moscow). This *panagiya* is an elliptical medallion. Its gold frame, set with precious stones and two rows of pearls, contains a four-ply agate on which is carved the image of the Virgin. On the back of the *panagiya* is an engraved representation of the Epiphany. At the top there is a very large amethyst. The workmanship is by Russian craftsmen of the Patriarch's shops. (From Solntsev, *Drevnosti Rossiiskago gosudarstva.*)

158: Silver panagiya, with applied gilt ornament, fifteenth century (Armory Museum, Kremlin, Moscow). (From Simakov, *Russky ornament.*)

159: Silver gilt panagiya, cloisonné colored enamel, early seventeenth century (Sacristy of the Trinity Cathedral, Pskov). (From *Obraztsy dekorativnago.*)

160: Pastoral staff of Archbishop Dmitri, seventeenth century (Belaya Palata Museum, Rostov). (From *Obraztsy dekorativnago iskusstva.*)

161: Pectoral cross of Tsar Mikhail Feodorovich (Armory Museum, Kremlin, Moscow). According to the Armory Museum inventory of 1835, the cross is made of gold, enriched with precious stones and ornamented with foliate motifs of varicolored enamels. In the center are ten emeralds surrounded by diamonds. An image of St. Peter is on the reverse side of the cross. (From Solntsev, *Drevnosti Rossiiskago gosudarstva.*)

162: Ancient embroidered *Barmy* or Imperial Collar (Armory Museum, Kremlin, Moscow). These peculiarly shaped regalia collars or capes *(barmy)* are traditional emblems of imperial authority worn during the coronation investiture and other solemn occasions by the Russian tsars and emperors. Together with the golden bonnet or Cap of Monomakh *(Shapka Monomakha),* they are said to be fashioned in the style of ancient Byzantine imperial regalia. The inventory of the "Large Treasury" *(Bol'shaya Kazna)* of 1642 describes the *barmy* illustrated here as embroidered in spun gold on dark-violet satin. The borders between the figures are of strung pearls. (From Solntsev, *Drevnosti Rossiiskago gosudarstva*.)

163: The Crown of St. Vladimir (The Cap of Monomakh *(Shapka Monomakha)*, thirteenth century (Armory Museum, Kremlin, Moscow), has for centuries been the symbol of power in Russia. Its significance, and the implied heavy burden upon the head of its wearer, was best epitomized by Pushkin in *Boris Godunov: "Tyazhela ty shapka Monomakha"* ("Heavy art thou, Cap of Monomakh"). The exact origin of the crown is debatable, but tradition claims that it was sent as a gift by the Byzantine Emperor Constantine Monomachus to Grand Prince Vladimir in 1116. It is the oldest of the imperial caps. Some Russian historians speculate on the possibility that it is the very same "Golden Cap" *(Zolotaya Shapka)* mentioned in all the last wills and testaments of the Moscow princes, beginning with Ivan Kalita *(d.* 1341). Actual records show that the Cap of Monomakh was first used in the coronation (1498) of Dmitri Ivanovich, a grandson of Ivan III. The last tsar to be crowned with it, in 1682, was Ivan Alekseevich V, a brother of Peter the Great. All succeeding emperors had the Cap paraded in their coronation processions to symbolize their inheritance of the throne.

Aside from the historical, sentimental, and intrinsic values attached to it, it is a work of exquisite taste and craftsmanship. On a foundation of eight triangular gold filigree panels, forming the body of the crown, are incrusted pearls and other jewels of great value, arranged with admirable understanding of the art of ornamentation. The 1696 inventory of the treasury says: "The Tsar's cap, called Monomakh, is of gold filigree work. It is surmounted by a plain gold cross having four pearls at the extremities. On the base of the cross (the dome or the "apple") are three large stones—a topaz, a sapphire, and a ruby. Between them are three large pearls, all in gold settings. Upon the crown itself are four emeralds, four rubies set in gold, and twenty-five pearls of Ormuz in gold settings. The cap is bordered with sable fur and lined with red satin." (From Bartenev, *Moskovsky Kreml'*.)

164: The Orb of Monomakh (Armory Museum, Kremlin, Moscow), surmounted by a cross, is the symbol of the sanctified rule of religion over the earth. In the age of Augustus Caesar the idea of imperial might was symbolically represented by a figure of a victory on top of a globe. With the establishment of Christianity in Constantinople, the symbol of world rule became the Cross overshadowing the universe. The 1642 inventory of the Treasury of Tsar Mikhail Feodorovich says that the orb is of "Frankish" work *(Friazheskoye delo)*—that is, made in the Italian or French style. The "apple" or the globe *(Yabloko Velikoderzhavnoye)* of this symbol of power is of chased gold embellished with enamel and precious stones. It is studded with 58 diamonds, 89 amethysts, 23 sapphires, 50 emeralds, and 37 pearls set in enameled gold frames. In the four triangular sectors of the globe are depicted: the annointment of David by Samuel; the victory of David over Goliath; David's victorious return from the fight; the banishment of David by King Saul. (From Solntsev, *Drevnosti Rossiiskago gosudarstva*.)

165: The Diamond throne of Tsar Aleksei Mikhailovich (Armory Museum, Kremlin, Moscow) is one of the most luxurious and resplendent Russian thrones. It was made by special order and presented in 1660 to Tsar Aleksei Mikhailovich by an Armenian trading company in Persia, with an eye on obtaining special commercial privileges in Russia.

The throne is lavishly covered with gold ornament and jewels of beautiful workmanship and is embellished on its front, sides, and rear with carved ivory panels containing figures of animals, birds, and flowers. The ivory carvings, of undoubtedly Eastern origin, are in light relief against a tinted background. The metal ornaments, as well as the miniature paintings that decorate the vertical and horizontal members of the chair, are of Russian workmanship; they harmonize beautifully with the foreign elements. The Oruzheinaya Palata (Armory) inventory of 1676, in a detailed listing of the gems on the various parts, describes the chair as studded with 876 diamonds of various sizes and 1,223 amethysts, in addition to rubies, turquoises, and three strands of pearls running around an inscription in Latin, which reads in part: *"Potentissimo et Invictissimo Moscovitarum Imperatori Alexio . . ."* (From Solntsev, *Drevnosti Rossiiskago gosudarstva.*)

166: The helmet of Tsar Mikhail Feodorovich (Armory Museum, Kremlin, Moscow). This helmet or Cap of Jericho *(Shapka Yerikhonskaya)* is claimed by tradition to have belonged to Grand Prince Alexander Nevsky (1246–63), celebrated for his victories over the Swedish and German knights (the subject of Prokofiev's cantata). It is made of a high-quality Damask steel encrusted with gold ornament. Its name (The Cap of Jericho), its shape, simplicity of line, and its Arabic inscription quoting the Koran ("Help from God, victory is drawing nigh . . .") suggest the possibility that it was made in Palestine for some knight, probably during the Crusades, and that it somehow found its way into Russia, finally turning up in the Kremlin Armory.

By order of Tsar Mikhail Feodorovich this helmet was remodeled and redecorated for his own use. According to the Kremlin Armory inventory of 1621, the ornamentation, the embellishment in precious stones, and the enamel image of the Archangel Michael above the nose protector were made by Master Nikita Davydov, a Russian craftsman, employed at the Armory during the reign of Tsar Mikhail Feodorovich. (Helmet from Solntsev, *Drevnosti Rossiiskago gosudarstva;* detail of ear-guard from Boguslavsky, *Gosudarstvennaya oruzheinaya palata.*)

167: *Saadak* (Quiver) of Tsar Mikhail Feodorovich (Armory Museum, Kremlin, Moscow). This quiver is of the same character and workmanship as the scepter and orb (Plate 164). Like a number of other extant magnificent bow-and-arrow cases, this seventeenth-century quiver recalls the ancient Scythian form. They are all made of various precious materials and elaborately decorated with enamel and enriched with jewels.

The quiver was made by craftsmen of the Armory (Oruzhe-inaya Palata) and was ornamented with a pierced-gold pattern of multicolored enamel and diamonds, rubies, and emeralds. Special interest attaches to the heraldic figures of the eagle, lion, griffin, unicorn, and so forth. All are covered with a transparent colored enamel. At royal processions, noblemen walked in front of the tsar carrying the *saadak*, together with other articles of the "great regalia," the crown, scepter, and mound. (From Solntsev, *Drevnosti Rossiiskago gosudarstva*.)

168: Seventeenth-century gunpowder flask (Armory Museum, Kremlin, Moscow). This gunpowder flask (or priming-horn) is of chased silver and is three and one-half inches in diameter. According to the inscription running round the edge between the two plaques, it belonged to Chamberlain *(Stol'nik)* A. I. Nesterov, the assistant to Boyarin Khitrovo, superintendent of the Armory (Oruzheinaya Palata).

Both sides of the flask are decorated with symbolic scenes: on one side is St. George striking a dragon; on the other, a combat between an eagle and a dragon. Round these is a border of foliate design interspersed with birds and beasts, all on a matted ground. This flask is the work of the craftsmen of the Armory, who frequently used these symbolic motifs (borrowed from Byzantium) for the decoration of the Tsar's arms. (From *Khudozhestvennyia, sokrovishcha Rossii*, 1902.)

169: The gold plate of Tsar Aleksei Mikhailovich (Armory Museum, Kremlin, Moscow), is fairly representative of the artistry and skill attained in the shops of the Armory in the seventeenth century. It was made in 1667 by Master L. Konstantinov and is fully equal to the art of the East. The borders of the plate are decorated with a band of flowers and foliate designs in green, blue, red, and azure enamels. The edges are scalloped and studded with sixteen rubies. In the center, surrounded by eight roses, on a green star-spangled field, is the Russian imperial seal —the double-headed eagle with three crowns. The inscription reads: "Tsar, Sovereign and Grand Prince Aleksei Mikhailovich, Autocrat of all Great, Little and White Russia." (From Solntsev, *Drevnosti Rossiiskago gosudarstva.*)

170: Silver-gilt goblet (Armory Museum, Kremlin, Moscow). According to the Armory inventory, each of the convex facets of the goblet is adorned with amethysts and diamonds. The big amethysts are surrounded by small ones, and so are the diamonds. (From Solntsev, *Drevnosti Rossiiskago gosudarstva.*)

171: Gold-lidded cup, late seventeenth century (Armory Museum, Kremlin, Moscow), is adorned with colored enamel and gems. In 1694, it was presented by Peter the Great to his son Prince Aleksei. (From Boguslavsky, *Gosudarstvennaya oruzheinaya palata.*)

172: Silver *bratina* (loving cup), of Councilor M. Danilov (Armory Museum, Kremlin, Moscow), dates from the first half of the seventeenth century. It was awarded to the Councilor (*Dyak*) for his long (1613–43) service to the tsar. The surface of the *bratina* is beautifully chased with a freely weaving foliate design. Inside of it, at the bottom, is a circular medallion embossed with a figure of Samson and the Lion. (From Boguslavsky, *Gosudarstvennaya oruzheinaya palata.*)

173: The memorial silver-gilt *bratina* of Tsar Mikhail Feodorovich (Armory Museum, Kremlin, Moscow) is adorned with engraved nielloed ornaments. Around the lip, interspersed among the foliate designs, are nielloed inscriptions indicating that the *bratina* was made by order of Tsar Mikhail Feodorovich to be placed on the bier of Tsarevich Ivan Ivanovich, to commemorate the murder of the Tsarevich by his father, Ivan the Terrible. (From Solntsev, *Drevnosti Rossiiskago gosudarstva.*)

174: Casket, Usol'sk enamel, second half of the seventeenth century (Armory Museum, Kremlin, Moscow). The Usol'sk (*Usol'ye*) type of enamel work was developed, in the later part of the seventeenth century, in the Solvychegodsk icon-painting, embroidery, and goldsmith shops maintained by the eminent Stroganov family. A characteristic feature of the Usol'sk enameling is the peculiar choice and arrangement of colors—bright yellow, blue, green, and brick red—on shiny, pure white backgrounds, and the use of crosshatching to show shading. The favorite ornamental motifs are large tulips with long stems and lush leaves, sunflowers, poppies, birds, and scenes from Russian folktales. (From Boguslavsky, *Gosudarstvennaya oruzheinaya palata.*)

175: The repository of the robe of Our Lord, first quarter of the seventeenth century (Cathedral of the Assumption, Kremlin, Moscow), stands in the southwestern corner of the cathedral, among the sarcophagi of the patriarchs. It was erected by order of Patriarch Philaret in 1625 to house the robe of Christ sent to Moscow by the Shah Abbas of Persia. The robe, according to an ancient legend, was brought to Georgia by one of the Roman soldiers stationed at the foot of the cross, and was preserved for many centuries in the Cathedral of Mtschet. The structure, of chiseled gilded bronze decorated with *kokoshniki* running around the base of its roof, is ten feet, six inches square, by twenty-four feet high. It was built by Master Dmitri Sverchkov. (From Snegirev, *Uspensky Sobor.*)

176: Thirteenth-century church chandelier (Historical Museum, Moscow). (From Barshchevsky, *Russkiya drevnosti.*)

177: The "golden" grille *(zolotaya reshotka)*, seventeenth century, Terem Palace, Kremlin, Moscow, was cast in 1670 from the copper coins that, because of their decrease in value, caused the bloody uprising in 1662 (The Copper Revolt), and were therefore withdrawn from circulation. (From Solntsev, *Drevnosti Rossiiskago gosudarstva.*)

178: Wrought iron cross, from dome of the Trinity Church, Tikhvin Monastery. (From Barshchevsky, *Russkiya drevnosti.*)

179: Copper jug *(kungan)*, Historical Museum, Moscow. (From Barshchevsky *Russkiya drevnosti.*)

180–82: Throne *(Tsarskoye mesto)* of Ivan the Terrible, Cathedral of the Assumption, Kremlin, Moscow. For a description of this throne, see Chapter XX. (Plates 180 and 182 from Solntsev, *Drevnosti Rossiiskago;* Plate 181 from Andreev, *Moskovsky Kreml'.*)

183–84: Detail of the seventeenth-century royal doors of the iconostasis in the Church of St. John the Precursor, Tolchkovo, Yaroslavl. For a description of these royal doors, see Chapter XX. (From *Khudozhestvennyia sokrovishcha Rossii.*)

185: The Chaldean furnace, from the Cathedral of St. Sophia, Novgorod (Russian Museum, Leningrad). For a description of this ambo, the so-called "Chaldean furnace," see Chapter XX. (From Solntsev, *Drevnosti Rossiiskago gosudarstva.*)

186: Head of St. John the Precursor (the Baptist), seventeenth-century woodcarving (Russian Museum, Leningrad). For comment, see Chapter XX. (From *Khudozhestrennyia sokrovishcha Rossii.*)

187: Porcelain flagon of Tsarevich Ivan Ivanovich, sixteenth century (Armory Museum, Kremlin, Moscow). The flagon *(suleiya)* is of Chinese porcelain; its top section is adorned with silver gilt and fastened to the body with a finely wrought chain. Around the neck runs an inscription in Slavonic: "Suleiya of Tsarevich, Prince Ivan Ivanovich." (From Solntsev, *Drevnosti Rossiiskago gosudarstva.*)

188: Glazed clay pitcher, seventeenth century (Belaya Palata Museum, Rostov). The general form has an oriental character, but the ornamentation is wholly the product of the Russian craftsman's fantasy. Such pitchers, and also *kvas* containers *(kvasniki)*, were often given fanciful shapes. Especially popular were vessels made in the shape of double-headed eagles, or formed as thick-bodied hoops, in the center of which were scenes depicting centaurs, birds, lions, bears, and other animals. The glaze is usually brown or green, less often yellow or violet. (From *Khudozhestvennyia sokrovishcha Rossii.*)

Chronological Table

Important Events and Dates in
Russian Ancient and Medieval Art History

VII–III B.C.
Rule of the Scythians in the steppes of the Black Sea region

VII–VI B.C.
The establishment of Greek colonies along the Black Sea littoral

IV B.C.–III A.D.
The Sarmatians in the steppes along the Black Sea

ca. 400
Khersonesus (Korsun') founded

ca. 500
Panticapaeum (Kerch) founded

825
Establishment of the Russian Principality of Tmutorokan

862–879
Rurik, a Varangian, establishes his power at Novgorod, marking the traditional beginning of the Russian nation (the Varangian-Rus' of Rurik)

882–915
Oleg, Rurik's successor, conquers Kiev and establishes himself in that city, proclaiming it the "Mother of Russian cities"

915–945
Igor, Grand Prince

957
Olga, widow of Igor, princess regent of Kiev, receives baptism

ca. 988–989
Vladimir Svyatoslavovich, prince of Kiev, takes Khersonesus (Korsun'), the principal Greek city of the Crimea; he is baptized there and brings to Kiev priests, sacred vessels, and icons; married Anna, daughter of the Byzantine emperor, and declares Christianity the official religion of Russia

989
Founding of the *Desiatinnaya Tserkov'*

371

1017–1054
Reign of Yaroslav, "the Wise"

1017–1037
Construction of the St. Sophia Cathedral in Kiev

1045–1052
Construction of the St. Sophia Cathedral in Novgorod

1053–1125
Vladimir Monomakh, prince of Pereyaslavl and Kiev

1108–1114
Period of artistic activities of Alimpi, the first Russian mosaicist and icon painter

1144
Decoration of St. Sophia Cathedral with frescoes finished

1147
Moscow first mentioned

1157–1175
Andrei Bogoliubsky, prince of Suzdal and Vladimir; Vladimir on the River Klyazma becomes the capital of the principality

1158–1161
Construction of the Cathedral of the Assumption in Vladimir

1165
Construction of the Church of the Intercession of the Virgin on the river Nerl

1183–1189
Reconstruction and enlargement of the Cathedral of the Assumption in Vladimir

ca. 1167–1180
The frescoes of the Church of St. George at Staraya Ladoga executed by Novgorodian artists

1193–1197
Construction of the Cathedral of St. Dmitri in Vladimir

1199–1246
The frescoes of the Church of the Saviour at Nereditsa, probably the work of Novgorodian artists

ca. 1220
Prince Yuri, son of Andrei Bogoliubsky, marries Queen Tamara of Georgia

1223
Battle of the Kal'ka; the Tatars defeat the Russian princes

1237–1240
Conquest of Russia by Batu; destruction of Kiev

1243
Beginning of the Mongol period in Russia

1299
Metropolitan Maxim transfers his see from Kiev to Vladimir

1305–1326
Peter, metropolitan of Russia (the first to reside in Moscow, 1309)

1326

The metropolitan see is officially transferred from Vladimir to Moscow

1327–1341

Ivan Kalita (Money Bag), prince of Moscow and Vladimir

1340

Founding of the Troitse-Sergieva Lavra (Trinity-Sergius Monastery) by St. Sergei of Radonezh

1353–1378

St. Aleksei, metropolitan of Russia

1362–1389

Dmitri, "of the Don," grand prince of Vladimir and Moscow

1367

Construction of the first masonry walls and towers around the Kremlin

ca. **1378–1410**

Period of the artistic activities of Theophanes the Greek in Russia

1380

Battle of Kulikovo Pole. Victory by Dmitri stimulates unity among the several Russian principalities

ca **1390–1430**

Period of artistic activities of Andrei Rublev

1439

Council of Florence

1446

Church of Russia declared autocephalous

1450

Rise of the Stroganov family

1453

Fall of Constantinople

1462–1505

Grand Prince Ivan III

1471

Novgorod begins its last decisive struggle with Moscow

1472

Ivan III marries the Byzantine Princess Zoë Paleologue

1474

First mission under Simeon Tolbuzin dispatched by Ivan III to Venice with instructions to hire architects, engineers, and craftsmen

1475–1509

Construction of the Uspensky, Blagoveshchensky, and Arkhangelsky cathedrals in the Moscow Kremlin

1480–1508

Period of artistic activities of Dionysius (Dionisi), icon painter

1484–1493

Missions sent abroad for the purpose of obtaining foreign artistic and technical help

1485–1508
Reconstruction of the masonry walls and watchtowers of the Moscow Kremlin

1487–1491
Construction of the Granovitaya Palata (the palace of Facets) in the Moscow Kremlin

1499–1508
Construction of the Terem Palace

1500–1501
The frescoes at the Kirillo-Ferapontov Monastery by Dionysius

1502
Dissolution of the Golden Horde: end of the Tatar yoke

1511
Establishment of the office of the Armorer (Oruzheinichei) supervising all activities of the Oruzheinaya Palata in the Kremlin

1511–1517
Pskov and Ryazan annexed; northern and central Russia lands united under Moscow

1517–1526
Herberstein in Russia

1518–1556
Maxim the Greek in Russia

1524
Founding of the Novodevichei Convent by Vasili III

1532–1554
Construction of the churches at Kolomenskoye, Ostrovo, and Dyakovo ushering in a new era in Russian architecture

1532–1543
Construction of the Bono Bell Tower in the Kremlin

1533–1584
Grand Prince and Tsar Ivan IV (the Terrible)

1542
Makari, metropolitan of Moscow

1547
Makari transfers icon-painting studios from Novgorod to Moscow

1547–1552
The frescoes in the Golden Chamber of the Kremlin Palace

1551
The Hundred Chapters Ecclesiastical Council (Stoglav Sobor) convenes

1552
Conquest of Kazan

1553
First arrival of a British merchant ship under the command of Captain Chancellor at the Port of Archangelsk; establishment of the Muscovy company

374

1555–1560

Building of the St. Basil Church in Moscow

1556

Conquest of Astrakhan, the last Tatar stronghold on the lower Volga

1560–1570

The Illuminated Nikonian Compilation, The Imperial Book *(Tsarstvennaya Kniga);* the Book of Degrees or Steps of the Imperial Genealogy *(Stepennaya Kniga)*

1563

Establishment of a printing press in Moscow

1564

The first (?) printed book, the *Apostle*

1570

Destruction of Novgorod and Tver

1584

Yermak overthrows khanate of Siberia

1584–1598

Tsar Feodor; Boris Godunov, "Lord-Protector"

1588

Visit of Constantinople Patriarch Jeremiah

1589

See of Moscow raised to patriarchal rank

ca. **1590–1598**

The frescoes of the Granovitaya Palata

1591

Murder of Tsarevich Dmitri, son of Ivan IV

1595–1600

Building of the Smolensk Kremlin

1598

Feodor, Ivan the Terrible's son, dies intestate, and the old dynasty, tracing its descent from Rurik, becomes extinct

1598–1605

Tsar Boris Godunov

1601–1603

Construction and decoration of the upper stories of the Belfry of Ivan Veliki

1604–1613

"Time of Trouble" (Smutnoye Vremya)

1605

Death of Tsar Boris (April, 1605) and accession (two months later) of the Pretender "False Dmitri"

1610–1612

Polish occupation of Moscow

1610–1613

Interregnum

1613

Mikhail Fedorovich Romanov elected tsar by the Zemski Sobor

375

(Consultative Land Assembly); crowned Tsar of All Russia

1620–1642
Period of artistic activities of the icon painter Prokofi Chirin

1624
Initiation of building decorative superstructures over the Kremlin towers

1624
Initiation of building decorative superstructures over the Kremlin towers

1634
Publication of the first printed Russian alphabet

1634–1638
First and second visit of Olearius of Holstein to Moscow

1639
Establishment of the first glass factory

1642–1707
Work of restoring the Cathedral of St. Sophia in Kiev

1645–1676
Tsar Aleksei Mikhailovich

1645–1686
Period of artistic activity of the icon painter Simon Ushakov

1649–1671
Construction of the Palace at Kolomenskoye, the Russian Versailles

1652
Founding of the *Nemetskaya Sloboda* (German Suburb) near Moscow as a residential district for foreign technicians and craftsmen

1652
Consecration of Nikon as patriarch

1652–1670
Construction of the Cathedral of the Resurrection at Romanov-Borisoglebsk

1652–1690
Metropolitan Ioann Sysoevich of Rostov; construction of the Rostov Kremlin

1654
Reforms of the church service books and rites by Nikon leading to the Great Schism *(raskol)*

1654–1657
Paul of Aleppo in Russia

1654–1680
Oruzheinaya Palata under management of Khitrovo

1663
Semyon Polotsky (scholar and poet) arrives in Moscow from Kiev; becomes influential as exponent at Moscow of Renaissance scholarship on a Latin basis

1666–1676
Siisk illuminated icon painting manual

1667

Patriarch Nikon deposed

1672

First theatrical performance at the Court of Moscow

1676– 1682

Tsar Feodor Alekseevich

1680

The cycle of frescoes in the Church of Elijah at Yaroslavl

1680–1690

The cycle of frescoes in the Resurrection Cathedral at Romanov-Borisoglebsk

1682

Founding of the Slavonic-Greek-Latin Ecclesiastical Academy

1682

Accession of Peter the Great and the revolt of the *strel'tsy;* murder of Matveev

1682–1689

Ivan V and Peter, nominal tsars; regency of Tsarevna Sophia

1687

Construction of the Church of St. John the Baptist on the Ishna; Belaya Palata at Rostov Veliki

1689

Attempted *coup d'état* by Sophia against Peter; Sophia immured in a convent

1690–1708

Construction of the churches at Fili, Troitskoye-Lykovo, and Dubrovitsy

1694–1695

The cycle of frescoes in the Church of St. John the Precursor at Tolchkovo, Yaroslavl

1697–1698

First journey of Peter I abroad

1698

Edict ordering the shaving of beards and wearing of Western clothes

1700

Suspension of the patriarchate

1702–1706

First public theater in Moscow

1703

Appearance of the first Russian newspaper *Vedomosti* in Moscow

1703

Founding of St. Petersburg

1712

St. Petersburg formally declared capital of Russia

1714

Edict forbidding construction of masonry buildings anywhere in Russia except St. Petersburg

1721

Abolition of the patriarchate and institution of the holy synod

1725

Death of Peter I

Glossary

Russian Archaeological, Iconographical, Ecclesiastical Architectural, Art, Folklore, and Technical Terms

Akafist (Acathist)—a special form of prayer used in the Orthodox Church to glorify Jesus Christ, the Virgin Mary, or any particular saint; *Akafist Bogoroditsy*—the twenty-four praises sung in honor of the Mother of God on the fifth Saturday in Lent.

Akinak—a Scythian short sword.

Aksamit, Pavoloka—brocade fabrics; a type of costly cloth woven in twisted gold or silver thread on a silk background. If the ornament was done in relief, in the form of loops (stitches), this type of cloth was known as *aksamit petel' chatyi*—stitched *aksamit*.

Amvon—a reading stand, ambo (in a church).

Analoi (Naloi)—lectern, pulpit.

Anastasis—Resurrection. The pictorial representation of this feast is usually the Harrowing of Hell.

Angel khranitel'—Guardian Angel.

Aprakos—the "Aprakos Lections" gospels (those in which readings were arranged by days of the week to fit the church service).

Arkatura—arcature; a nonfunctional closed or false arcade serving as an ornament; a decorative band of blind arches.

Arkhimandrit—father superior of a monastery.

378

Artos—blessed bread distributed at Easter.

Assistka—size for gold, *inokop'*. Gold lines (done with liquid gold), such as are used, for instance, on the Saviour's garments.

Bagor'—dark red, purple.

Bakan'—dark mauve, dark purple-brown, maroon.

Barmy—part of the regalia of the Moscow tsars; a collar of broad form made of black silk overlaid with gold and jewels (Herberstein's description).

Bashnya—a word of Tatar origin, *bash* signifying head or top and, by extension, tower.

Basmenoye delo—gold, silver, or copper sheet stamping; metalwork used in covering icons with an *oklad* or a *riza*. The metal is mechanically stamped with dies that make a repeating pattern; the work, though generally rough, is effective at a distance.

Blagosloveniye—benediction. See also *Dvuperstnoye* and *Triperstnoye*.

Blagoveshcheniye—Annunciation.

Blazhennyi—blessed, beatified.

Bochka, Bochki (pl.)—barrel; roofs with a section like a pointed horseshoe.

Bogomolets—pilgrim.

Bogoroditsa, Bogomater'—Mother of God.

Bogoslov—theologian (epithet applied to St. John, the Evangelist).

Bogosloviye—theology.

Bogoyavleniye—Epiphany. The apparition of Christ to the people on the banks of the Jordan.

Bol'shaia kazna—Grand Treasury of Muscovite princes.

Boyarin, Boyar—member of highest social and political class in Russia until Peter the Great established the "Table of Ranks" (1722), which made rank technically dependent on service position; the boyars descended from Rurik, Gedimin of Lithuania, or other sovereign rulers bore the title of Prince *(kniaz);* the rest were untitled.

Bulava—scepter, a commander's baton used as a symbol of authority by hetmans (chieftains) in the Ukrainian and Polish armies in the seventeenth and eighteenth centuries.

Bylina, byliny (pl.)—Folk song of epic or balladic character.

Catholikon—central nave of a church.

Chasovnya—an isolated chapel.

Chekan'—a form of *repoussé* work, performed with dies, and finished with a graver; *Chekanka*—stamping, coinage; chasing; *Chekannyi*—stamped, chased.

Chernetz—monk.

Chervlen'—crimson.

Cheti Minyeii—lives of the saints, instructing and eulogistic discourses intended for daily reading and having the material arranged by days.

Chin—order, rank; different orders of angels or saints (such as the seven orders of angels, or the order of intercessors on the *Deisus*).

Cinnabar'—red ochre; *cinnabar* (Venetian)—bright red; vermillion.

Darokhranitel'nitsa (Kivorii)—tabernacle or ciborium, a vessel for Eucharistic wafers—often called "Zion" or "Jerusalem"—usually in the form of a church or shrine with domes or cupolas surmounted by a cross.

Deisus, Deisis (Deësis, the Greek form of the word)—an icon or a series of icons (as in an iconostasis) showing Our Lord enthroned with Our Lady on His right and St. John the Baptist on His left. The word *Deisis* means prayer. In the case of an icon it shows those standing in prayer before the Saviour *(predstoyashchiye)*—the Mother of God is always shown on the right, John the Baptist on the left; added are members of various hosts of heavenly and earthly sainthood: angels, apostles, and hierarchs.

Derzhava—imperial globe.

Detinets, Detintsy (pl.)—an archaic Russian word signifying inner fortress; citadel of the reigning prince.

Dolichnik—the artist (helper) who paints the landscape, draperies, and accessories of an icon.

Domostroy—a code of regulations, a house orderer, or a guide for living, to regiment human behavior, providing a religious, moral, and practical life-pattern for the family under the guidance of the master of the house, the father and husband. It determined the usages and customs of the land for generations and was instrumental in excluding women from public life, relegating them to separate quarters in the house, the *terem* (see). The code was compiled about the middle of the sixteenth century by Archpriest Silvester.

Dospekh—armor, suit of armor (knightly armor); *zertsal'nyi dospekh*—armor made up of thin, highly polished narrow steel-plate sections, often chased, embellished with silver and gold ornamentation. The *zertsalo* was usually worn on top of the mail armor.

Druzhina—a retinue of free men serving a prince or other magnate both as an armed force and as companions and advisers; *Druzhinnik,* a member of a *druzhina.*

Dukh—spirit; *Svyatoi Dukh*—Holy Spirit; *Dukhovenstvo*—clergy; *Dukhovnyi*—spiritual; *Dukhovnyi stikh*—spiritual song.

Dvizhka—bright patch of color.

Dvuperstiye—the sign of the cross with two fingers. Formally it stands for, and is understood to be the symbol of, the two hypostases (the unique essence of the Godhead) of Jesus Christ, representing the unity of His divine and human aspects, or, in modernized form, the idea of God-Man *(Bogochelovek).*

Dvuperstnoye blagosloveniye—two-fingered blessing; Greek benediction with two raised fingers. Cf. *Triperstnoye.*

Dyak—secretary, same origin as the English "deacon"; *Dumnyi Dyak*—executive secretary of the Boyars' Council or head of some *prikaz* (bureau); state secretary.
Dyakonik—sacristy.

Edinorodnyi Syn—the Only Begotten Son.
Endova—a large rounded (usually copper) vessel, with a spout (*nosik*), its form somewhat similar to a *bratina*.
Eparkhiya—bishopric, diocese.
Epitrakhil—stole, a long band of embroidered silk, a neckpiece worn by priests.
Etimasiya—altar prepared.
Evkharistii—the Eucharist, Holy Communion; Lord's Supper.

Felon—a chasuble, at first made of soft stuff; when made of stiff material it was for convenience shortened in front. A special variety of felon was entirely covered with a pattern of crosses; this was reserved for bishops.
Fonar'—lantern, the small, many-windowed cupola which took the place of the "eye" of the Roman dome.
Freska—fresco, the technique of painting on a support of moist, freshly spread plaster. The pigments are mixed with water, thus incorporating themselves chemically with the plaster. The term is also applied to any painting or mural so executed.
Fronton—pediment.
Fryazin (Frank)—a generic name by which all Latins of the Mediterranean basin were designated. Their works were called *Fryazheskiya dela* (Frankish Works).

Glikofilusa—*Umileniye*, Our Lady of Tenderness (see *Umileniye*).
Glukhaya glava—blind cupola; *Glukhie shatry*—literally deaf tents; an idiomatic Russian expression for a "blind" building element.
Golosniki (from *golos*, voice)—resonators or sound amplifiers used in Novgorodian and Suzdalian churches. The *Golosniki*

were earthenware pots embedded in the walls, their mouths open to the interior of the church.

Golovnaya ikona—head alone.

Golubets—a pale blue color like modern cobalt.

Golubinaya Kniga—Book of the Dove, a religious poem.

Goluboi—blue, azure.

Gornoye mesto—a special seat occupied by the bishop in the sanctuary behind the altar.

Gospod' Savaoth—God Sabaoth, Lord of Hosts.

Gospodi pomilui—Kyrie eleison, Lord have mercy.

Gospod' v silakh—God among the Powers, Lord Sabaoth.

Gost'—member of the upper ranks of the merchant class, engaged in interstate or foreign trading and endowed with special privileges. The term is derived from the word *gostit'*, which means both to visit and to trade.

Grafya—an outline scratched with a sharp stylus nail into the *levkas* or *gesso* layer below the paint. The *grafya* had the advantage over the drawn outlines in that it was not so easily obliterated by subsequent painting.

Gramota—instruction; charter, record.

Greben'—comb; *Petushinnyi greben'*—cockscomb.

Gridnitsa-Gridnya (archaic)—reception room (in old Russian mansions).

Gusli—an ancient stringed musical instrument, psaltery.

Ikona—icon, from the Greek work *eikon*, originally used both for murals and easel pictures. The Russian religious painting is called *ikona* or *obraz;* pl. *ikony* or *obrazy.* The church attributes to the icon the same dogmatic, liturgic, and educational significance as it does to the Holy Scriptures.

Ikonnaya Palata—the chamber of icon painting (somewhat on the order of the Italian l'Opera del Duomo).

Ikonopisnyi podlinnik—manual of icon painting. The Russian manual is compiled either in alphabetic order, or according to the calendar. It usually includes interpretations of various services, rites, prayers, and hymns; it gives details about the deeds of saints and indicates schemes of compositions.

Ikonostas—iconostasis, a screen, composed of icons, separating the sanctuary, where the sacrament of the Eucharist is celebrated, from the central part, the nave, where the congregation stands.

Inokop'—originally meant damascening, inlaying, or encrusting, for example, bronze with gold, and secondarily painted imitation of this effect; gold hatching.

Iosifskoye ucheniye (Iosifskii dogmat)—the Josephite doctrine, promulgated by Joseph Volotsky (Ivan Sanin, 1440–1515), abbot of the Volokolamsk Monastery, advocated the sanctification of autocracy and the preservation of all the privileges and landed possessions of the church. The abbot, one of the first theorists of absolutism, taught that "the Tsar was similar to humans only by nature, but by the authority of his rank similar to God; he derived his authority directly from God, and his judgment could not be overruled by that of any prelate."

Ipatiyevskaya Letopis'—the Ipatiyev Chronicle, one of the two basic versions of the *Initial Chronicle* written by a continuator at the turn of the fourteenth century, and found in the Ipatiyev Monastery at Kostroma.

Izba—the modern Russian word *izba* is probably derived from the old Slavonic *istuba* and has its counterpart in the German *stube*, or the English "stove." Essentially the *izba* is a warm chamber.

Izograf—artist, icon painter; according to Kondakov, the title *Tsarskii izograf* (the Tsar's painter) was accorded only to outstanding creative artists who did not merely use other men's designs.

Izvayaniye—statue, sculpture.

Kadilo—censer, a piece of church furniture in constant use in the Russian-Greek church.

Kalita—money bag.

Kamennaya baba—stone statue of an idol worshipped by the early pagan Slavs.

Kapishche—pagan temple.

Kazanskaya Bogomater'—Our Lady of Kazan' depicted holding Christ erect on her arm. It is an iconographical type of the Holy Virgin, a variant of the *Hodigitriya*.

Khiton—undergarment.

Khorugv'—banner for church procession, labarum.

Khory—gallery, galleries.

Khozhdenye po mukam—the road to Calvary.

Kinovar'—cinnabar, vermilion, brilliant red, red ochre.

Kiot, kioty, kiotsy (pl.)—a niche, a frame or cupboard in which one or more icons may be housed; it is generally adorned with pediment above and glazed in front. This makes a kind of shrine, or it may form a kind of triptych often with iconic scenes painted upon the doors.

Kirillitsa—Cyrillic alphabet; the Slavic alphabet used in church books and, in a revised form, in the secular literature of the Russians, the Ukrainians, the Bulgars, and the Serbs. The Cyrillic alphabet is based on Greek uncials with the use of some additional characters to denote sounds not covered by the Greek letters. The alphabet was invented in 862 by Constantine the Philosopher, known by his monastic name of St. Cyril.

Kleimo—the original meaning was a "stamp"; in icon painting it denotes marginal scenes painted around the edges of the icon, representing events (relating to the life of the saint) not happening at the same time or at the same place. Each of the scenes is represented in a separate picture; *Kleimo probirnoye* —hallmark, mark of assay.

Kliros—church choir platform.

Klobuk—cloth covering a priest's headdress.

Kokoshnik, Kokoshniki (pl.)—originally a structural feature, a series of corbelled-out, round or pointed arches arranged in receding tiers for the purpose of supporting the elements of the superstructure. Later it developed into a purely decorative feature used as ornament for all kinds of articles.

Kontsovka—tailpiece, colophon, an ornamental device (design) put on the last page of a chapter or a book.

Koromchaya Kniga (The Nomocanon)—a compilation of Byzantine church canons combined with the civil laws governing the church.

Korsun'—the ancient Greek colonial city of Khersonesus Taurica, founded by the Dorians, became the starting point of the Christianization of Russia by Byzantium owing to the fact that St. Vladimir had been baptized and married to one of the Emperor's daughters there in 988. In later times, ancient ritual objects, and especially icons believed to be very old, were described as being from Khersonesus, "Korsun'." The adjective *Korsunskaya*, that is, of Korsun', continued to be attached even to pictures which were mere copies of those venerable originals.

Kovcheg—the original meaning was "ark" or "reliquary"; later it was used to describe the part of the wooden panel onto which the first coat of paint is laid, after it had been covered with a piece of linen, called *povoloka*.

Krasnoye—the word admits of a double interpretation: first and literal meaning is "red," second is "beautiful." *Krasnoye kryltso* signifies "beautiful stairway" or "beautiful entrance." *Krasnaya devitsa* means "beautiful girl."

Krasnyi ugol—corner of the house devoted to the display of icons; place of honor in a house.

Kratir—a vessel used for communion wine.

Kreml'—kremlin; the derivation of the word has long been a subject of debate. Karamzin, the great Russian historian, holds that the word is derived from *kremen'*, signifying flint, and by extension, a flint-like rock fortress difficult to crack. The lexicographers Stroev, Dahl, and Grot hold that *kreml'* is derived from the old Russian word, *krom*, signifying fortress. Modern opinion ascribes its derivation to the word *krem,* which in North Russian provincial dialect signifies large structural timber.

Krest—cross.

Krestets—a gathering place near the Spas Gates in medieval Moscow, a kind of a labor exchange for the unemployed priests offering their services to merchants and boyars who had their private house chapels; they were ready to say mass and to perform whatever rites were demanded of them for a small monetary consideration.

Krestitel'—baptizer.

Krestokupol'nyi—a church with a dome over the crossing.

Krestoobraznyi, Krestovidnyi—cross shaped, cruciform.

Kurgan—conical mound, tumulus; ancient burial mound, barrow.

Kustar'—a craftsman who works on his own, in his own house in a town or village, as opposed to a manufacturer and his employees. The word is probably derived from the German *kunst.*

Lavra—(from the Greek *laure)*—a passage, or street, later a group of shops along a street. In ecclesiastical usage a *lavra* came to mean a series of hermitages around a monastery, and by association an important monastic foundation. Of the many Russian monasteries only four had the rank of *lavra:* the Kievan Pecherskaya, the Trinity-St. Sergius near Moscow, the Alexander Nevsky in St. Petersburg, and the Pochaevskaya in western Russia.

Lazur', Lazor—blue, azure, ultramarine, or its substitutes.

Lemekh—wood shingles.

Levkas—(1) A powder made of gesso or alabaster, mixed with lime and soap and dissolved in warm water. (2) In icon painting, the first coat of paint made of this material and applied to the piece of linen on which the *levkas* is laid. The panel is coated with several consecutive applications of this solution.

Lichnik—painter of faces.

Lik—literally face, visage, figure, but sometimes a group, a choir of angels; an order of saints; *Lik Kliroshan*—order of choristers;

Lik muchenikov—order of martyrs; *Lik svyatitelei*—order of sainted bishops.

Lipa—lime tree, linden.

Litsevaya rukopis'—illuminated manuscript (with miniatures).

Litsevoi podlinnik—illustrated manual of icon painting.

Lobnoye Mesto—a circular stone tribune (on Red Square, near St. Basil's) from which the tsars proclaimed their edicts. Death sentences were also pronounced from it; a tribune, somewhat like the Roman Rostrum or the Novgorod *Veche stepen'* (Assembly Platform).

Lopatka—a vertical projection in the wall, a pilaster without a capital.

Lubok—popular Russian pictures, prints. In them, ornament is combined with representations of incidents from the lives of people. The word is derived from *lub*, bast, inner bark, which was originally used in the fabrication of a cheap cliché for a print.

Lukovitsa—bulb, bulbous cupola.

Lunnitsa—a semicircular pendant.

Makovitsa, Makovka—crown, top, summit, small cupola.

Mandorla—like the nimbus, one of the attributes of Christ. It is an iconographic symbol in the shape of a circle or an oval signifying heaven, Divine Glory.

Maforii, Maphorion—a large shawl covering the head and shoulders. Originally the costume of Palestinian and Syrian women, it was then worn by the early Christian deaconesses. Decorated with the Virgin's star, it forms an essential part of the Virgin's garment in icon painting. The Virgin's star is an emblem which can be traced back to the Spica, the old Oriental virgin's star.

Makovitsa, Makovka—crown, top, small cupola.

Maslenitsa—festivities of the vernal equinox; shrovetide.

Mat' syra zemlya—Mother Moist Earth.

Menologion—menology, saints and religious festivals corresponding to the days of the calendar; a complete encyclopedia of ancient Russian literature; "All the holy books which can be found in Russia" compiled by Metropolitan Makari.

Menologiya, Synaxaria—hagiographical calendars.

Mestnaya ikona—"fixed" or local icon (on the iconostasis bottom row) representing Our Saviour, Our Lady, single saints, or festivals. It bears the monumental character which was proper to it in the pre-Mongolian period when it stood singly on the entablature of the sanctuary screen or was disposed against the walls.

Mironositsy—the Holy Women at the Tomb bringing spices.

Mitra—mitre, headdress of a bishop.

Mladenets—the Infant Jesus.

Mlekopitatel'nitsa—Mother of God nursing Her Child.

Mnogoglaviye tserkvi—multi-cupola churches. The practice of having two, three, five, seven, nine, and thirteen cupolas dates from the eleventh century. The numbers are symbolic: the two signify the two natures of Jesus Christ; three represent the Trinity; five Our Lord and the Four Evangelists; seven the Holy Sacraments or the seven gifts of the Holy Spirit; nine the nine celestial hierarchies; and thirteen Our Lord and the Twelve Apostles.

Mokosh—Mother Earth the Humid; goddess of water and weaving. The image of Mokosh was reflected in Russian art as a representation of a woman, her arms held up high, taking the form of a distaff comb.

Mokraya Brada, Mokraya Boroda—Our Lord of the Wet Beard, the icon of the portrait of Christ "not made with human hands" (the Holy Mandilion or Napkin of Edessa). The type of Our Saviour of the Wet Beard is one most favored in Russia icon painting. It is so called because of the curious form of His pointed beard.

Molennaya ikona—devotional icon.

Monakh—monk.

Monisto—necklace made of gold or silver coins.

Moshchi—uncorrupted body of a saint.

Muchenik—martyr.

Musiya—mosaic, a form of surface decoration in which patterns are composed with small pieces of glass, stone, marble, and so forth, set in a mastic.

Naboika—printed cloth.

Nadgrobiye—epitaph, inscription on a tomb, grave stone, tomb-stone.

Nagornaya propoved'—Sermon on the Mount.

Naloi (Analoi)—pulpit.

Naperstnyi krest—bosom cross.

Naprestol'nyi krest—altar cross.

Ne Dremliushchee Oko—literally "Non-Slumbering Eye" or "Vigilant Eye." Such Russian icons represent Christ as Emmanuel reclining on a couch in the presence of the Virgin and St. Michael.

Neopalimaya Kupina—Our Lady of the Burning Bush; the Bush that is not consumed.

Nerukotvornyi spas—the Mandilion, the "Image of Christ Not Made with Human Hands," referring to a legendary contemporary portrait of Christ supposed to have been painted by Ananias for Abgar IV, King of Edessa.

Nikonovskaya Letopis'—the Nikon Chronicle. Digest of earlier Greek chronographies and Russian chronicles, compiled in the middle of the sixteenth century.

Novgorodskaya letopis'—Novgorodian Chronicle for the years 1016–1471.

Novodevichei Monastyr'—New Nunnery monastery in Moscow, founded in 1524.

Novo-Ierusalimsky Monastyr'—New Jerusalem Monastery, founded by Patriarch Nikon in 1654.

Obednya—mass; *Zaupokoinaya obednya*—special church service for the dead.

Obitel'—convent.

Oblacheniye—priestly vestments.

Oblo, v oblo—in the round, a carpentry method of assembly; the framing and fitting of the logs at the corners. The logs are fitted together and crossed at the corners in such a manner that the ends project on either side, producing the effect of ponderous strength and stability.

Obraz—icon image.

Obraznaya—icon room.

Obrazok—small icon, especially of brass.

Obronno—carving in relief; *obronnaya rabota*—relief work; a special technique of metal carving in which the background of the drawing (around the figure) is lowered with a graver.

Ocherk—outline, essay.

Odigitriya—Hodigitriya, she who guides, leads; one of the Russian symbolic representations (iconographical types) of the Virgin. She is always represented standing, and holds the Child on her left arm, with the right arm lifted as though guiding souls toward her Divine Son. The image of *Our Lady Odigitriya* is known in Russian religious art as *Smolenskaya Bogomater.'* The type of the *Odigitriya* has given rise to several iconographic variants. The most venerated in Russia are the miraculous icons of Smolensk, Tikhvin, and Kazan.

Okhlupen'—ridge beam.

Okhreniye (vokhreniye)—rich dark ochre coat; production of flesh tints.

Olifa—a special kind of varnish applied to the finished icon; a layer of flaxseed or olive oil which temporarily brightens the colors.

Omofor, Omophorion—pallium, band of silk material, generally ornamented with Greek crosses, worn by bishops over the shoulders.

Omoveniye nog—washing of the feet.

Oplechiye—shoulder piece.

Oplechnaya ikona—icon representing the subject to the shoulders.

Oprava—setting (of a stone), rim (of eye glasses), mounting.

Orarion—a band of red velvet embroidery, a part of the *stikharion* (see) used by the deacon during the service.

Otechestvo—the New Testament Holy Trinity.

Otshel'nik—anchorite, hermit, recluse.

Ozherel'ye—necklace.

Ozhivka—from *ozhivat'*, to enliven; enlivening highlight, indicating the brightest touches of light upon the three-dimensional objects represented on the icon.

Palata—mansion, usually a storied masonry structure containing many chambers and halls; by extension, a bureau in charge of production.

Palitsa—part of the vestment of a bishop worn as a symbolic representation of the spiritual sword.

Palomnik—pilgrim.

Panagiarion—consecrated vessel or plate used in the rite of elevating Our Lady's particle of the Host in a sanctified refectory.

Panikadilo—chandelier, lustre in the form of an open-work disk.

Panikhida—a funeral service.

Pantocrator (Vsederzhitel')—the Omnipotent, the symbolic representation of the glory of the risen Christ. The formal type of the risen Christ figure, the Pantocrator, evolved about the ninth century. The Omnipotent is usually represented sitting in a frontal position on a throne or on a rainbow, surrounded by an aureole, or *mandorla*. His right hand is raised in blessing while with His left hand He holds the book of Gospels (the Book of Life) on which the Alpha and Omega is inscribed. The image of the Pantocrator is usually placed in the dome of the churches, set into a medallion in the concave of the main cupola; the medallion is bordered by a number of concentric circles in rainbow colors. The letters IC and XC, that is, Jesus Christ, are arranged on either side of the nimbus. On the iconostasis, the image of the Pantocrator is placed in the center of the prophets' tier.

Papert'—parvis, covered or uncovered gallery circling the church on three sides.

Paraskeva Pyatnitsa (Friday)—an iconographical type representing saintly womanhood; the giver of fertility to praying wives. The cult of St. Paraskeva is associated with the sacred birch.

Parcha—brocade.

Parus—pendentive, the spherical triangle of vaulting springing from the corners of a rectangular area, serving to support a circular or polygonal dome.

Paterik, Pechersky—a thirteenth-century collection of Lives of Saints of the Pechersky Monastery in Kiev.

Paterikon (or Trefologion)—tales about ascetics or hermits living in a given locality or monastery; lives of the fathers.

Patriarshaya Riznitsa—vestry of the patriarchs.

Pelena—veil, altar cloth, pall below icon; swaddling cloth.

Perevod—pattern (for icon painters); stencil for tracing icons.

Perun—the god of thunder (*gromovnik*); the Jupiter of Slavic mythology, who is traditionally considered the main deity in the old Slavic Russian pantheon. In the early Christian period the popular image of Perun was assimilated with that of the prophet Elijah who caused the descent of fire from heaven.

Petushinyi greben'—cockscomb (a popular decorative motif in Russian folk art).

Pis'mo—literally letter, also writing, but often used in the sense of painting, hence *Ikonnoye pis'mo* means icon painting. The Russian word *pisat'* (from which *pis'mo* is derived) means write as well as paint, and the word *pis'mo* is especially used to indicate the style of school of icon painting: *Novgorodskoye pis'mo* (the Novgorod School); *Moskovskoye pis'mo* (the Moscow School), and so on.

Plach—lamentation.

Plashchanitsa—epitaph, an embroidered representation of the dead Christ carried in procession on Good Friday.

Plav—(from the Russian verb *plavit*, to melt; a special technique of icon painting based on the encaustic technique of late antiquity: tempera colors are laid upon the *levkas* (see), whereby the light colors always cover smaller spaces and stand out higher than the dark ones. This produces a flat relief, in which the dark shadows lie lower than the light colors, especially as the latter are further heightened with white lead in the flesh tints.

Podlinnik—the Russsian icon-painting manual. See *Ikonopisnyi podlinnik*.

Podpusk—priming.

Podubornaya ikona—an icon meant to be covered by a metallic *repoussé riza*, so that only the faces, hands and feet need to be executed; generally, an inexpensive icon; a board painted only where the flesh parts showed through the metal *riza*.

Podvizhnik—ardent fighter, zealot, ascetic.

Poganyi—pagan.

Pogost'—parish church yard, church cemetery.

Pogrudnaya ikona—icon representing the subject to the breast.

Pokloneniye volkhvov—adoration of the magi.

Poklonnaya ikona—venerated icon (specially displayed in the church on certain days). *Poklonniya icony* (pl.)—fixed icons; they are so called because when the pious worshipper goes round before service to venerate the fixed icons he bends his knee before them (*poklon* is a deep bow or genuflection).

Pokrov—the Miracle of the Virgin's veil; the intercession of the Virgin. *Pokrov Bogomateri*—the Intercession of the Mother of God; the Veil and Protection; corresponds to the Virgin of the Misericord in Western iconography.

Pominaniye—private family record of the departed.

Ponomar'—sacristan.

Porphyrogenetets—born to the purple; members of the Byzantine imperial house who were considered especially sacred.

Poruchii—liturgical armlettes (manchettes).

Posadnik—chief official of early Russian towns, generally appointed by a prince (who might be non-resident); at Novgorod

in the thirteenth century the *veche* (see) secured the right to
elect the *posadnik*, bishop, and other officials.

Posadskiye liudi—burghers, people engaged in commerce and
industry and living chiefly in urban settlements.

Poslushnik—novice, lay brother.

Posol'sky prikaz—foreign office (in pre-Petrine Russia).

Povoloka—a piece of linen cloth on which the first coat of paint
is applied directly on the icon panel.

Pravda Russkaya—the Old Kievan code of laws known as the
Rus' Law.

Pravoslaviye—orthodoxy; the Greek church; the term "Orthodoxy" designates Eastern Christianity as distinguished from
Roman Catholicism.

Prazdniki (pl.)—Holy Days; the twelve principal holy days celebrated by the Church; the events of the New Testament which
are celebrated by the Church with particular solemnity.

Prazelen'—whitened green color, ochre of various shades, includes not only green but various dark-blue tones and indigo.
It is the chief mark of Novgorod painting in the fifteenth century, being used very freely to take the place of light-blue
Greek draperies. *Zelen'* in Russian is green color; *Pra* is a pre-
fix suggesting antiquity.

Prechistaya Deva—The Immaculate Virgin.

Predstoyashchei—intercessor.

Predtecha—St. John the Baptist or Forerunner, Precursor.

Preobrazheniye—Transfiguration.

Prepodobnyi—literally "very like," a Slavonic church term used
with reference to the monastic type of sanctity.

Prestol—sanctuary table, altar; throne.

Prichastiye—communion.

Pridel—chapel (lateral).

Prikaz—a command or order; the duties or functions a boyar was
ordered to discharge; the administrative organ developed for
the permament discharge of such functions, that is, a bureau;
juridical office of the Muscovite state in charge either of spe-

cial government activities or of governing certain regions. These various offices were established in the last decade of the fifteenth century; they were replaced by the Collegia of Peter the Great.

Prikhod—parish.

Pritvor—narthex; porch of a church.

Probel—highlight or bright plane.

Prodrome—St. John the Baptist. See *Predtecha*.

Proobraz—prototype, pre-figure, symbol.

Proris'—tracing.

Prosvira (prosphora)—bread used in the communion service, wafer.

Prosvirnitsa—the woman who bakes the wafers.

Prothesis—small apse to the left where the bread and wine are prepared.

Protoierei—archpriest.

Protoslavs—the Scythian Aroteres (Plowmen). They lived in the upper Bug region (central Ukraine). Above them (in north-western Ukraine) lived the Neuri whose customs, according to Herodotus were "Scythian." Niederle and Minns identify them as Proto-Slavic tribes.

Psaliya (Trenzel')—parts of a horse bridle fastened on both sides of the bit, and peculiar to Iranian bridles.

Psalter—Psalter, Psalms.

Pushchevik—evil spirit of the dense forests, his arms represented as gnarled tree branches, his hair of a green color.

Pyatochki (little heels)—shaley rocks; the hills with their "heels" or shaley steps along the edges of the horizontal ledges; the Novgorodian icon-painters' manner of indicating hills. In the hands of the seventeenth-century painter the indication of mountains with numerous heels developed into a kind of grove of unknown coral growths or shrubs *(kustiki)*.

Raka—in the Christian church a large box for keeping the remains of saints (see *Moshchi*). The *Raka* is kept in the church on an elevated platform under a baldachin, constructed in the form of a sarcophagus and decorated with various figures and precious stones.

Raskol—schism.

Raspyatiye—Crucifixion.

Ripida—a flabellum or scepter with a hexagon image of a seraph.

Riza—the icon drapery concealed by a *repoussé* plate.

Rusalka, Rusalki (pl.)—river and tree nymphs, women and maidens whose death was "unclean," that is, as a result of violence.

Samoderzhets—the counterpart of the Byzantine Autokratos.

Sandrik—window or door pediment.

Sankir—flesh priming, the base for flesh tints, made with dark ochre.

Sarafan—a sleeveless dress, a kind of a pinafore.

Semik (or *rusaliya*)—festivities of the summer solstice rites; later became merged with Pentecost.

Shablon—template, pattern.

Shchipets—gable.

Sheiya—neck, blind drum supporting a cupola.

Shirinka—large embroidered handkerchief, embroidered short towel; a kind of a pocket-handkerchief made from a square piece of material embroidered either at the corners or all around. They were very popular as wedding presents among not only the peasants but also the noblemen, and even the tsars, for whom the *shirinki* (pl.) were more handsome, being of silk or muslin, richly embroidered in gold, and decorated with fringes and tassels. Sometimes, instead of embroidery, they were embellished with wide gold lace, interwoven with real pearls. The *shirinka* was both an object for display and one of the indispensable adjuncts of the Russian woman's wardrobe, the most obvious and the favorite article; and it was the custom to hold it in the hand when going to church or on visits, or during ceremonies.

Shponki—cleats in an icon board to prevent the latter from warping.

Sion (Zion)—The tabernacle or ciborium, a vessel for eucharistic wafers (*darokhranitel'nitsa*), often called Zion, usually in the form of a church or shrine with cupolas surmounted by a cross.

Skit—a small monastery with regulations stricter than those in an ordinary monastery.

Skladen'—folding frame, diptych, triptych.

Skoropis'—cursive writing.

Sladkopevets—sweet singer, St. Romanus Melodius, deacon of St. Sophia in Constantinople.

Sliuda—mica.

Slovo o polku Igoreve—"Tale of Igor's Expedition" or the "Lay of Igor's Campaign"—a famous epic poem relating the story of a daring raid undertaken in 1185 by Prince Igor of Novgorod-Seversk against the nomads with the object of reaching the Lower Don area. The armor and vestments of the Russians and Cumans are described with a remarkable factual accuracy. The poem contains many references to heathen deities and is strongly suggestive of the persistence of pagan beliefs among the masses of the people.

Sluzhebnik—a book of ritual.

Snyatiye so kresta—Descent from the Cross.

Sobor—an assembly, whether ecclesiastical (synod) or lay; also used for the Russian equivalent of cathedral, or an assembly of churches under one roof. In Russian usage, the *sobor* was not necessarily the seat of a bishop but might be a more important or venerable church.

Sofiya (Sophia) *Premudrost' Bozhiya*—The All-Wisdom of God; the Church of Santa Sophia, the masterpiece of Byzantine architecture, built in Constantinople under Emperor Justinian (A.D. 532–38). Its low-curved dome on pendentives is the most characteristic feature of Byzantine architecture and it furnished the prototype for many of the early Russian churches.

Soleiya—an elevated platform, approached by several steps, at the entrance to the sanctuary.

Solovetsky Monastyr'—one of the greatest monasteries in Russia, on an island in the White Sea.

Somnevaniye apostola Fomy—the incredulity of St. Thomas (cf. *Uvereniye*).

Soshestviye Svyatogo Dukha—Descent of the Holy Spirit.

Soshestviye vo ad—Descent into Hell.

Sreteniye—purification.

Sreteniye Gospodne—Presentation of Jesus at the Temple.

Srub—derived from the Russian verb *rubit*, to cut, to hew with an axe, *srub*, therefore, connotes a structure formed of axe-hewn logs or timber.

Starina—in Russian music, a chanted folk song similar in form and purpose to the *bylina* (see). In substance it concerned itself with the famed *bogatyri*, legendary heroes of the Russians.

Stepennaya Kniga—Book of Degrees of the Imperial Genealogy, which extols and glorifies to the utmost the historic past and the present of Muscovite Rus', primarily by praising and glorifying the rulers as having acted in full accord with the church. It lists the ecclesiastical and civil events of Russian history from a purely religious point of view, and is arranged by the reigns of the grand princes. The beginning of this book is attributed to Metropolitan St. Kiprian, who is said to have brought it to the thirteenth degree (his own times). The Metropolitan Makari continued the work to the seventeenth degree (from Grand Prince Vladimir to Ivan IV); later it was brought up to the eighteenth degree (to the reign of Aleksei Mikhailovich).

Stikharion—dalmatic worn by deacons during the service.

Stoglav Sobor—the "Council of the Hundred Chapters," (so-called from the number of its resolutions), held in Moscow in

1551 to give moral support and ecclesiastical sanction to the reforms of Ivan IV.

Stoyachaya ikona—an icon representing the subject standing, full length.

Stopa—tankard, flagon.

Strastnaya Bogomater'—Our Lady of the Passion.

Strastnoye Blagoveshcheniye—the Annunciation of the Passion.

Strelets—fusilier, musketeer.

Strel'tsy—semiprofessional soldiers living in special quarters with their families and engaged in industry and petty trade; first organized by Ivan the Terrible; most efficient part of the army until importation of foreign officers to train Russian regiments was begun under Tsar Michael Romanov; mutinies in 1682 and 1698 led to their abolition by Peter (1699).

Stribog—an early Slavic deity, god of the winds.

Strigol'nichestvo—shearers, a religious sect associated with the name of a certain Karp, who was apparently a cloth shearer, hence the name of the heresy. The heresy originated in Pskov.

Strochnaya bukva—lower-case letter.

Styazhateli, Iosiflyane—the "Possessors," the followers of Joseph of Volokolamsk, who upheld the right of monasteries to possess lands, as opposed to the *Nestyazhateli, zavolzhskiye startsy* —the "Non-possessors," the "Transvolga Elders," the followers of Nil Sorsky, who denied this right. See *Iosifskoye ucheniye.*

Suleiya—a vessel in the shape of a bottle.

Suzdal—in early times largest town in the northeastern region between upper Volga and Oka; a name loosely used to distinguish this area from older areas of Slavonic settlements in the Dnieper basin and around Lake Ilmen; also called "the Low" because it was downstream for traders from Novgorod.

Suzdal'sky krai—Suzdal region; the Slovenian and Krivichian— the two streams of colonization merged in the Rostov-Suzdal region. In the ninth and tenth centuries there were already numerous Slavic settlements in that area which had been originally inhabited by Finno-Ugrian tribes.

Synodik—an official ecclesiastical record in which are inscribed the names of the departed whom the church desired to commemorate at the liturgy or requiems.

Synodiki—books of pious memories, full of edifying extracts from the fathers of the church, dealing with eschatology and legend.

Tainaya Vecherya—the Last Supper.

Teoriya tret'yago Rima—the theory of Moscow as the Third Rome, first formulated by the monk Filofei (Philotheus) of Pskov (*ca.* 1480). "Two Romes have fallen," wrote Filofei, "and the third stands, while a fourth is not to be." Relevant legends were revived, and an imperial genealogy was later officially devised, according to which the Rurik dynasty of Russia was of Roman imperial origin. Ivan III's marriage to Zoë Palaeologue added no little to the transfer of primacy from the second Rome to the third.

Terem, Teremok, Terema (pl.)—upper-floor apartment, traditionally reserved for the women of the family. It is usually located at the top story of the house and provided with an arcaded open balcony and sometimes with a small observation tower. By extension the word *teremok* (little *terem*) came to signify a dwelling unit built in the style of the ancient *terem*.

Titulyarnik—Book of Genealogy of the tsars.

Tmutorakan'—the Tmutorokanian principality in the Taman peninsula, established *ca.* 825.

Tolkovyi podlinnik—explanatory manual of icon painting; an icon-painter's guide with full descriptions.

Treba (obryad)—ceremony, rite.

Trebnik—missal, a book containing all the prayers necessary for celebrating mass.

Triperstnoye blagosloveniye—Latin benediction with the first three fingers raised, symbolizing the Trinity.

Troitsa vetkhago zaveta—The Old Testament Trinity; the illustration of a theme from the Old Testament, the three angels entertained by the hospitable Abraham and Sarah. These angels who ate at the table of Abraham came conventionally to represent the earthly image of the Divine Trinity and are symbolic of the Christian Trinity itself. Known in Russian as *Otechestvo*, the Trinity personified by God the Father, the Son, and the Holy Ghost.

Troista Monastery—Monastery of the Trinity, better known as Troitsko-Sergievskaya Lavra, strongly fortified monastery about forty miles northeast of Moscow, founded by St. Sergius in the fourteenth century; popular center for pilgrimages.

Tsarskiye znamenshchiki—the tsar's designers.

Tsarskiya vrata—royal gates or royal doors in the iconostasis.

Tsata—a crescent-shaped ornament hanging from the neck of the icon.

Tyablo—cross pieces of an iconostasis forming an icon shelf.

Ubrus—the Holy Napkin (the image of Christ "made without human hands"); the Mandilion portrait of Christ. According to the legend Christ had pressed His face into a kerchief which preserved the image. The *ubrus* differs from the vernicle of Western art, as the crown of thorns is not shown in it. See *Nerukotvornyi*.

Udel—Russian princely appanages. *Udel* signifies portion, share. Hence, *Udelnaya Rus'*, the Russia of small domains, as compared to *Veliko-Knyazheskaya Rus'*, the Russia of the grand principalities.

Umileniye—Our Lady of Tenderness, a Russian development of the Byzantine iconographical type of Eleusa, emphasizing the spirit of maternal love.

Uspeniye, icon of—Assumption, Dormition (the Greek form), showing the body of the Virgin, stretched on a bier and attended by the sorrowing disciples. Behind the bier Christ is shown holding in His arms a small image of the Virgin's soul.

Ustav—uncial script.

Uvereniye Fomy—the assurance of Thomas.

Vayanye—sculpture in the round.

Veche—town assembly in early Russian towns.

Veles (Volos)—god of poetry and oracles, kin to Apollo. He is also considered as protector of cattle and commerce.

Veliki Knyaz—grand prince.

Velikomuchenik—great martyr.

Venchik—small crown, nimbus of an icon.

Venets—crown; carpentry term; each range of logs forms, as the Russians call it, a "crown" *(venets)*, and the entire pile of "crowns," forming the desired height of the structure, is called *srub*. See *Srub*.

Venets, Brachnyi—marriage crown; *Ternovyi venets*—crown of thorns.

Verbnoye Voskreseniye—Palm Sunday.

Videniye—sight: vision, apparition.

Vityaz—knight-errant (in ancient Russia).

Vkhod v Ierusalim—Entry into Jerusalem.

Vladyka—archbishop; lord, sovereign.

Vlasyanitsa—hair shirt, attribute of St. John the Baptist.

Voevoda—a military commander; in the seventeenth century also a provincial governor.

Volkhvy—Finnish magicians or sorcerers; magi, pagan priests.

Voploshcheniye—incarnation.

Votchina—patrimonial estate.

Vozdukh (or *Sudar*)—rectangular altar cloth of airy transparency and lightness, used to cover the chalice during the mass.

Vozneseniye—ascension.

Vsederzhitel'—Pantocrator, or Christ the Almighty.

Yarilo—an early Slavic deity, symbol of sun and fertility.

Yarlyk—charter, patent (Tatar term).

Yaroye Oko—Our Saviour of the Burning Eye; Christ with the Angry Eye. The stern expression recalls the earlier Byzantine conception of the Pantocrator.

Yavleniye—Apparition of an icon, a term current in old Russian chronicles and hagiographies, means a miraculous event by which an icon, hitherto unknown, becomes notable as a new source of the manifestation of grace.

Yel' (el)—fir, spruce.

Zakomara—the parapet over the extrados of the vaulting, conforming in outline to the type and number of vaults, and thus dividing the parapet into several arched sections.

Zavolzhskiye Startsy—"Trans-Volga Hermits," a group of Russian monks supporting the mystical trend in Orthodox spirituality (fifteenth and sixteenth centuries).

Znameniye—Our Lady of the Sign.

Bibliography

General Histories of Russian Art

Ainalov, Dmitry Vlas'evich. *Geschichte der russischen Monumentalkunst.* Berlin, 1932–33.

Alpatov, M. *Russian Impact on Art.* New York, 1950.

Grabar', I. E., ed., *Istoriya russkago iskusstva.* 6 vols. Moscow, from 1909.

———, and others, eds. *Istoriya russkogo iskusstva.* 12 vols. Moscow, from 1953. A monumental, collective, richly illustrated work dealing with the development of the Russian fine and applied arts from antiquity to the present day.

Nikolsky, V. N. *Istoriya russkogo iskusstva.* Moscow, 1923.

Novitsky, A. *Istoriya russkago iskusstva, s drevneishikh vremen.* Moscow, 1903.

Réau, Louis. *L'Art russe.* Paris, 1921–22. Vol. I, edited by Henri Laurens: *L'Art russe des origines á Pierre le Grand;* Vol. II: *L'Art russe de Pierre le Grand á nos jours.*

Tolstoi, I. I., and N. P. Kondakov. *Russkiya drevnosti v pamyatnikakh iskusstva.* 6 vols. St. Petersburg, 1880–89.

Viollet le Duc, E. *L'Art russe, Ses origines, ses elements constitutifs, son apogée, son avenir.* Paris, 1877.

The Greco-Scythian and Early Slavic Periods, 700 B.C.–A.D. 1100

Anichkov, E. *Yazychestvo i drevnyaya Rus'.* St. Petersburg, 1914.

Artamonov, M. I. *Ocherki drevneishei istorii Khazar*. Leningrad, 1936.

Belov, G. *Khersones Tavrichesky (Khersonesus, Taurida)*. Leningrad, 1948.

Blavatsky, V. D. *Iskusstvo severnogo prichernomor'ya antichnoi epokhy*. Moscow, 1947.

Bobrinskoi, A. *Reznoi kamen' v Rossii*. Moscow, 1918.

Borovka, G. *Scythian Art*. London, 1928.

Dintses, L. *Russkaya glinyanaya igrushka*. Moscow, 1936.

Gaidukevich, V. F., ed. *Antichniye goroda severnogo prichernomor'ya*. Moscow, 1955.

———. *Bosporskoye tsarstvo*. Moscow, 1949.

Grabar', I. E., and others, eds. *Istoriya russkogo iskusstva*. Vol. I. Moscow, 1953.

Gryaznov, M. *Drevnee iskusstvo Altaya*. Leningrad, 1958.

Herodotus. *History*. Translated by George Rawlinson. Edited by Manuel Komroff. New York, 1956.

Ivanova, A. P. *Iskusstvo antichnikh gorodov severnogo prichernomor'ya*. Leningrad, 1953.

Maskell, A. *Russian Art and Art Objects in Russia*. London, 1884.

Minns, Ellis H. *Scythians and Greeks*. Cambridge, 1913. A survey of ancient history and archaeology on the north coast of the Euxine from the Danube to the Caucasus.

Niederle, L. *Slavianskiye drevnosti*. Translated from the Czechoslovak *Rukovet Slovanskych starozitnosti* by T. Kovaleva and M. Khazanova. Edited by Mongait. Moscow, 1956.

Radlov, W. *Aus Sibirien*. Leipzig. 1884.

Rostovtzeff, M. *Iranians and Greeks in South Russia*. Oxford, 1922.

———. *The Animal Style in South Russia and China*. Princeton, 1929.

Rudenko, S. I. *Vtoroi Pazyryksky kurgan*. Leningrad, 1948.

———. *Kul'tura naseleniya Gornogo Altaya v skifskoye vremya*. Moscow, 1953.

———. *Kul'tura naseleniya Tsentral'nogo Altaya v skifskoye vremya.* Moscow, 1960.

———, and N. M. Rudenko. *Iskusstvo skifov Altaya.* Moscow, 1949.

Shakhovskaya, S. N. *Uzory starinnago sheetiya v Rossii.* Preface by Th. Buslaev; text in Russian and French. Moscow, 1885.

Shul'ts, P. N., ed. *Istoriya i arkheologiya drevnego Kryma.* Kiev, 1957.

Tolstoi, I. I., and N. P. Kondakov. *Russkiya drevnosti v pamyatnikakh iskusstva.* St. Petersburg, 1880–90. Vol. I: *Classical Antiquities of South Russia,* 1880; Vol. II: *Scytho-Sarmatian Antiquities,* 1889; Vol. III: *Antiquities of the Migration Period,* 1890.

Vernadsky, George. *Ancient Russia.* New Haven, 1943.

Architecture, Principally Before 1725

Alpatov, Mikhail. *Geschichte der altrussichen Kunst.* Augsburg, ca. 1932.

Andreev, A. M., ed. *Moskovsky Kreml'.* Moscow, 1958.

Arkhitektura i Stroitel'stvo. An architectural periodical, published by the Ministry of City Building, R.S.F.S.R.

Ashchepkov, E. A. *Russkoye narodnoye zodchestvo v vostochnoi Sibiri.* Moscow, 1953.

Bartenev, S. P. *Moskovsky Kreml' v starinu i teper'.* 2 vols. St. Petersburg, 1912–18. Vol. I: *Historical Outline of the Kremlin Fortifications, Walls, and Towers;* Vol. II: *The Court of the First Grand Princes and Tsars of the House of Rurik.* The best book in Russian on the subject; contains many illustrations and a good bibliography.

Cross, Samuel Hazzard. *Mediaeval Russian Churches.* Cambridge, Mass., 1949. Lectures, sponsored by the Mediaeval Academy of America, delivered at the Fogg Museum, Harvard University, in 1933.

Duncan, D. D. *The Kremlin.* Greenwich, Conn., 1960.

Eding, Boris von. *Rostov Veliky, Uglich, Pamyatniki Khudozhest-vennoi Stariny*. Moscow, 1913.

Grabar', I. E., ed. *Istoriya russkago iskusstva*. Moscow, 1910.

Ivanov, V. N., and others. *Sokrovishcha russkoi arkhitektury*. Moscow, 1950.

Krasovsky, M. V. *Kurs istorii russkoi arkhitektury: Derevyannoye zodchestvo*. Petrograd, 1916. Contains an extensive analysis of the elements of Russian wood construction, ancient fortifications, civil and religious structures; many illustrations and bibliography.

Lo Gatto, Ettore. *Gli artisti italiani in Russia*. 2 vols. Rome, 1934–43.

Lukomsky (Loukomski), Georgy K. *L'Architecture religieuse russe du XIe siecle au XVIIe siecle*. Paris, 1929.

———. *Pamyatniki starinnoi arkhitektury Rossii v tipakh khudoz-hestvennago stroitel'stva, Russkaya provintsiya*. Petrograd, 1915. Building activities in the Russian provincial cities of the eighteenth and nineteenth centuries—the cities of the Russian hinterland, where the Russian national spirit was more prevalent and lingered longest.

Martynov, A. *Environs de Moscou, Anciens Monuments*. Moscow, 1889. An album of drawings.

Moskva, sobory, monastyri i tserkvi. Moscow, ca. 1880. Collection of plates.

Moskva v yeiya proshlom i nastoyashchem. 12 vols. Moscow, 1910–17. An extensive, collective, illustrated work dealing with the various aspects of the growth and development of the Kremlin and Moscow from their legendary beginnings to the twentieth century. Contains essays on the geology and topography of the city's location and its architecture.

Opolovnikov, A. V. *Pamyatniki derevyannogo zodchestva Karelo-Finskoi SSR*. Moscow, 1955.

Pavlinov, A. *Istoriya Russkoi arkhitektury*. Moscow, 1894.

Pervukhin, N. *Tserkov' Ioanna Predtechi v Yaroslavle*. Moscow, 1913.

———. *Tserkov' Il'i Proroka v Yaroslavle.* Moscow, 1915.

Podkliuchnikov, V. N. *Tri Pamyatnika XVII stoletiya; Tserkov' v Filyakh, Tserkov' v Uborakh, Tserkov' v Troitskom-Lykove.* Moscow, 1945.

Réau, Louis. *L'Art russe.* Paris, 1921–22. Vol. I: *L'Art russe des origines á Pierre le Grand,* 1921.

Rikhter, F. F. *Pamyatniki drevnyago russkago zodchestva.* Moscow, 1850.

Rzyanin, M. I. *Arkhitekturnye ansambli Moskvy i Podmoskov'ya XIV–XIX veka.* Moscow, 1950. Many illustrations and extensive bibliography.

———. *Pamyatniki russkogo zodchestva.* Moscow, 1950. Many illustrations and extensive bibliography.

Shamurin, Yu. *Kul'turnyia sokrovishcha Rossii.* Moscow, 1912–14. Vol. I: *Yaroslavl', Romanov-Borisoglebsk, Uglich,* 1912. A monograph on seventeenth-century art and architecture of the Yaroslavl' region.

———. Vol. 10: *Veliki Novgorod,* 1914. A monograph on the early history, eleventh-fifteenth centuries, of Novgorod: its architecture, painting, iconography, and literature; the churches of Spas-Nereditsa, St. Theodore Stratilates, and the Cathedral of St. Sophia, its frescoes and its art treasures.

Shamurina, Z. *Kul'turnyia sokrovishcha Rossii.* Moscow, 1912. Vol. 2: *Kiev,* 1912. A monograph on the city of Kiev, ninth-twentieth centuries, its cultural life with special emphasis on its ecclesiastical architecture.

Snegirev, I. M. *Uspensky Sobor v. Moskve.* Moscow, 1856.

Snegirev, V. *Moskovskoye zodchestvo.* Moscow, 1948. Covers the period from the fourteenth to the nineteenth century.

Suslov, V. V. *Pamyatniki drevnyago russkago zodchestva.* St. Petersburg, 1897. Five folios of photographs and measured drawings, many in color.

———. *Tserkov' Vasiliya Blazhennago v Moskve.* St. Petersburg, 1912.

Tikhomirov, M. *The Towns of Ancient Rus'.* Moscow, 1959.

Viollet le Duc, E. *L'Art russe, Ses origines, ses elements constitutifs, son apogée, son avenir.* Paris, 1877.

Voyce, Arthur. *The Moscow Kremlin: Its History, Architecture, and Art Treasures.* Berkeley, 1954. A detailed study of the subject, containing many illustrations, tables, notes, and an extensive bibliography.

Zabelin, Ivan E. *Cherty samobytnosti v drevne-russkom zodtchestve.* Moscow 1900.

———. *Istoriya goroda Moskvy.* Vol. I. Moscow, 1905.

Zabello, S. Ya., and others. *Russkoye derevyannoye zodchestvo.* Moscow, 1942. A comprehensive study of Russian wooden architecture, richly illustrated.

PAINTING TO 1700

Alpatov, M. *Altrussische Ikonenmalerei.* Dresden, 1958.

Alpatov, M., ed. *Khudozhestvennyie pamyatniki Moskovskogo Kremlya.* Moscow, 1956.

Avinoff, A., ed. *Russian Icons and Objects of Ecclesiastical and Decorative Arts from the Collection of George R. Hann.* Carnegie Institute, Pittsburgh, Penna., 1944.

Farbman, M., ed. *Masterpieces of Russian Painting.* London, 1930.

Hackel, A. A. *The Icon.* Freiburg im Breisgau, Western Germany, 1954.

Kondakov, N. P. *The Russian Icon.* Oxford, 1927. Translated by E. H. Minns. Summary of the following work.

———. *Russkaya ikona.* 4 vols. Prague, 1928–33. A comprehensive survey of Russian iconography, with excellent plates in color and black and white.

Kornilovich, K. *Iz letopisi Russkogo iskusstva.* Moscow, 1960.

Lasareff (Lazarev), V., and O. Demus. *USSR Early Russian Icons.* New York, 1958.

Muratov, P. P. *Les Icones Russes.* Paris, 1927.

Onasch, K. *Icons*. New York, Leipzig, 1963. 151 color plates and an annotated catalog of illustrations.

Ouspensky, L., and V. Lossky. *The Meaning of Icons*. Boston, 1952. Many illustrations.

Pervukhin, N. *Stenopisniye Kompozitsii v tserkovnykh galereiyakh goroda Yaroslavlya i Borisoglebskogo sobora*. Tver'., 1905.

Pokrovsky, N. V. *Pamyatniki Khristyanskoi ikonographii i iskusstva*. St. Petersburg, 1900.

Russkaya ikona. A series of illustrated essays on iconography, edited by R. Golike and A. Vil'borg. St. Petersburg, 1914.

Schweinfurth, Philipp, *Russian Icons*. Oxford, 1953.

Svirin, A. *Drevnerusskaya zhivopis' v sobranii gosudarstvennoi Tretyakovskoi galereii*. Moscow, 1958. 65 plates.

ARCHAEOLOGY, DECORATIVE ARTS AND CRAFTS

Babenchikov, M. V. *Narodnoye dekorativnoye iskusstvo Ukrainy i ego mastera*. Moscow, 1945.

Bakushinsky, A. V. *Iskusstvo Palekha*. Moscow, 1934.

Barshchevsky, I. F. *Russkiya drevnosti*. St. Petersburg, *ca.* 1895. Photographs of decorative art objects.

Bogoyavlensky, S. F., and G. A. Novitsky, eds. *Gosudarstvennaya oruzheinaya palata Moskovskogo Kremlya*. Moscow, 1954. Numerous illustrations and extensive bibliography.

Boguslavsky, G. A. *Gosudarstvennaya oruzheinaya palata Moskovskogo Kremlya*. Moscow, 1958. 381 illustrations and commentary.

Botkin (Botkine), M. P. Collection. St. Petersburg, 1911. 103 plates in color, 38 pp. of text in French.

Butovsky, V. *Istoriya russkago ornamenta*. Paris, 1873. Based on ancient manuscripts.

Conway, Martin. *Art Treasures in Soviet Russia*. London, 1925.

Evdokimov, I. *Sever v istorii russkogo iskusstva*. Vologda, 1921.

Farmakovsky, B. V. *Arkhaicheskii period v Rossii*. Petrograd, 1914.

Iskusstvo i khudozhestvennaya promyshlennost'. Journal. St. Petersburg, 1901.

Khudozhestvennyia sokrovishcha Rossii. An illustrated monthly, edited by A. Benois and S. Prakhov, and published by the Imperial Society for the Advancement of Art. St. Petersburg, 1901–1907.

Lukomsky (Loukomski), G. K. *L'Art decoratif russe*. Paris, 1928. Richly illustrated.

———. *Mobilier et Decoration des Anciens palais imperiaux russes (Musees du peuple)*. Avec une preface de M. Louis Réau. Paris et Bruxelles, 1928. 84 plates.

Makarenko, N. E. *Iskusstvo drevnei Rusi u Soli Vychegodskoi*. Petrograd, 1918. 104 illustrations, bibliography.

Margeret, Jacques. *Estat de l'empire de Russie*. Paris, 1649.

Maskell, Alfred. *Russian Art and Art Objects in Russia. A Handbook*. London, 1884.

Mir Iskusstva. A monthly review, edited by S. Diaghilev and A. Benois. St. Petersburg. 1899–1904.

Motivy russkoi arkhitektury. Fifty plates of scale drawings of buildings and articles of furniture (plans, sections, elevations, and details), including a number of designs for projected church and house furniture in the "Russian" style. St. Petersburg, 1880.

Nekrasov, A. *Ocherki dekorativnogo iskusstva drevnei Russi*. Moscow, 1924.

———. *Vizanteiskoye i russkoye iskusstvo*. Moscow, 1924. Illustrated.

Obraztsy dekorativnago i prikladnogo iskusstva iz imperatorskikh dvortsov, tserkvei i kollektsii v Rossii. Thirteen folios of plates. St. Petersburg, Russian Ministry of Finance, 1908. The plates are chromolithographs from watercolors made by the pupils of the Art School of the Imperial Society for the Advancement of Art under the direction of Academician E. Sabaneiev, and from the watercolors of Academician M. Villie.

Polonskaya, N. D. *Istoriko-kul'turnyi atlas po Russkoi istorii s obyasnitel'nym tekstom.* Edited by M. B. Dovnar-Zapolsky. 3 vols. Kiev, 1913. Profusely illustrated.

Prokhorov, V., ed. *Materialy po istorii russkikh odezhd i obstanovki zhizni narodnoi.* St. Petersburg, 1881–85. Profusely illustrated, many plates in color.

Réau, Louis. *Russie: art ancien; Russie: art modern (L'Art et les artistes).* Paris, 1917.

Romanov. *L'Art byzantine chez les slaves.* Paris, 1932.

Ross, Marvin C. *The Art of Karl Fabergé and His Contemporaries.* Norman, 1965.

Rybakov, V. A. *Remeslo, Istoriya kul'tury drevnei Rusi; Domongol'sky period.* Moscow, 1948.

———, ed. *Treasures in the Kremlin.* London, 1962. 120 plates in color with comments.

Sakharov, I. *"Obozreniye russkoi arkheologii,"* an article in *Zapiski otdeleniya russkoi i slavyanskoi arkheologii I. A. O-va.* Vol. II. St. Petersburg, 1851.

Sbornik khudozhestvenno-promyshlennykh risunkov. 4 vols. St. Petersburg, Imperial Society for the Advancement of Art, 1886. The illustrated objects are from the Russian section of the Society's Industrial Art Museum in St. Petersburg.

Shakhovskaya, S. N. *Uzory starinnago sheetiya v Rossii.* Preface by Th. Buslaev. Text in Russian and French. Moscow, 1885.

Simakov, N. *Russky ornament v starinnykh obraztsakh khudozhestvenno-promyshlennago proizvodstva.* St. Petersburg, Imperial Society for the Advancement of Art, 1882.

Snowman, A. K. *The Art of Carl Fabergé.* London, 1962.

Sobolev, H. *Russkaya narodnaya rez'ba po derevu.* Moscow, 1934.

Solntsev, F. G., illustrator. *Drevnosti rossiiskago gosudarstva.* 6 vols. The text is a collective work edited by Count Sergei Stroganov, Mikhail Zagoskin, Ivan Snegirev, and Alexander Veltman. Moscow, 1849–53. The work contains more than five hundred colored and beautifully executed plates.

Staryie Gody. A monthly review, edited by P. Weiner, devoted to ancient and modern art. St. Petersburg, 1907–17.

Stasov, V. *Russky narodnyi ornament: sheetiye, tkani, kruzheva.* St. Petersburg, 1872. Text in Russian and French.

Sultanov, N. *"Istoricheskoye obozreniye finiftyanago i tseninnago dela v Rossii"* in *Zapiski,* vol. VI.

———. *Izraztsi v drevne-russkom iskusstve.* Monograph in the series of *Materialy po istorii Russkikh odezhd i obstanovky zhizni narodnoi.* St. Petersburg, 1885.

Wladimirov & Georgiyevsky. *Old Russian Miniatures.* Moscow, 1934.

Zapiski. Journal of the Imperial Archaeological Society. St. Petersburg, 1893.

Church and Religion

Bulgakov, S. *The Orthodox Church.* New York, 1935.

Fedotov, G. P. *The Russian Religious Mind.* Cambridge, Mass., 1946.

Golubinsky, E. *Istoriya russkoi tserkvi.* Moscow, 1881. A standard work on the history of the Russian church.

Miliukov, Paul. *Outlines of Russian Culture.* 3 pts. Philadelphia, 1942. Pt. I: *Religion and the Church in Russia.*

Stanley, Arthur Penrhyn. *Lectures on the History of the Eastern Church.* New York, 1884.

History, Biography, Literature, and Culture

Avvakum, Archpriest, the Life of, by Himself. Translated by Jane Harrison and Hope Mirrlees from the seventeenth-century text. London, 1924.

Chadwick, N. K. *Russian Heroic Poetry.* Cambridge, Mass., 1932.

Chancellor, Richard. *Description of Muscovy in the 16th Century,* in R. Hakluyt, *Principal Navigations and Voyages.* London, 1809.

Enciclopedia Italiana. (Edizioni Instituto G. Treccani). Roma, 1932–40.

Excerpts from the Russian Chronicles. Vol. I. St. Petersburg, 1767–92.

Grabar', I. E. *Feofan Grek*. Kazan', 1922.

Grekov, B. D. *The Culture of Kiev Rus'*. Translated by Pauline Rose, Moscow, 1947.

———. *Istoriya kul'tury drevnei Rusi*. Moscow, 1948.

Gudzii, N. K. *History of Early Russian Literature*. New York, 1949.

Hakluyt, Richard H. *Principal Navigations and Voyages*. London, 1809.

Herberstein, S. von. *Commentaries on Muscovite Affairs*. Edited and translated by O. P. Backus III. Lawrence, Kansas, 1956. Herberstein was ambassador from Vienna to the court of the Grand Prince Vasili Ivanovich in 1517 and again in 1526. His travel notes are considered to be the first authentic description of Muscovite life based upon long residence and experience by a European observer, and are a major source of information for the period.

Kliuchevsky, V. O. *A History of Russia*. 5 vols. London, New York, 1911–31.

———. *Kurs Russkoi istorii*. Petrograd, 1918.

Likhachev, D. S. *Kul'tura Rusi epokhi obrazovaniya russkogo natsional'nogo gosudarstva*. Moscow, 1946. Covers the period from the end of the fourteenth to the beginning of the sixteenth century.

Magnus, L. A. *The Heroic Ballads of Russia*. New York, 1921.

Mirsky, D. S. *Russia, a Social History*. Edited by C. G. Seligman. London, 1931.

Olearius, Adam. *The Voyages and Travels of the Ambassador from the Duke of Holstein to the Great Duke of Muscovy, and the King of Persia, 1633–39*. Rendered into English by John Davies of Kidwelly. London, 1669. Olearius visited Russia several times as secretary to embassies sent by Frederick, Duke of Holstein. While in Moscow, Olearius constantly wandered through the streets observing every phase of Muscovite activities and recording his impressions. His descriptive pen pictures of Moscow street life are perhaps the best we have.

Paul of Aleppo. *Travels of the Antioch Patriarch Macarius in Russia (1654–57)*. Translated from the Arabic into Russian. Moscow, 1896–1900. Archdeacon Paul, who accompanied the Patriarch, left a copious diary of all that occurred. It is particularly valuable as a record of the experiences and the impressions of a Syrian Orthodox Christian observing the Russian church and its clergy during the great schism.

Rambaud, A. *History of Russia.* 3 vols. Translated by L. B. Lang. Boston, 1888.

Riasanovsky, V. A. *Obzor Russkoi kul'tury.* 2 vols. New York, 1947–48.

Russky biografichesky Slovar'. St. Petersburg, 1896–1918.

Solov'ev, S. M. *Istoriya Rossii s drevneishikh vremen.* 3 vols. Moscow, 1851–53.

Tikhomirov, M. N. *Srednevekovaya Moskva v XIV–XV vekakh.* Moscow, 1957. A scholarly, well-documented history of medieval Moscow.

Trutovsky, V. K. *"Boyarin i oruzhnichii Bogdan Matveevich Khitrovo i Moskovskaya Oruzheinaya Palata,"* in *Staryie Gody.*

Vernadsky, George. *Ancient Russia.* New Haven, 1943.

———. *Kievan Russia.* New Haven, 1948.

———. *The Mongols and Russia.* New Haven, 1953.

———. *Russia at the Dawn of the Modern Age.* New Haven, 1959.

Voyce, Arthur. *Moscow and the Roots of Russian Culture.* Norman, 1964.

Wipper, Robert. *Ivan Grozny.* Translated by J. Fineberg. Moscow, 1922.

Zabelin, Ivan E. *Domashnei byt russkikh tsarei.* Pt. II. Moscow, 1915.

———. *History of Russian Life.* (in Russian) Moscow, 1876.

Index

Ecclesiastical and civil buildings will be found indexed under the name of the city, province, or region where they are located. Icons are listed under the general heading of Icon painting schools, and sublisted alphabetically under each particular school. Examples of decorative art are listed under the general heading of Decorative arts and crafts, and sublisted alphabetically under the subheading of each specific category. Numbers in *italics* refer to plates.

Index

Index

Prozorovsky, Prince Peter Ivanovich: 286
Prussus (Prus), brother of Augustus Caesar: 151, 228
Pskov: 21; "younger brother" of Novgorod, 113–15; churches, 113; river, 113; territory, 113; builders, 114, 162; painting, 138; chronicles, 301
Puchezhskaya (Puchenezskaya) *plashcnanitsa*): 271
Pulci, Luigi, Florentine poet: 148&n.

Radlov, V. V.: 62
Rambaud, historian: 19&n., 23&n.
Rastrelli, V.: 158
Ravenna of the North: 92
Red Square: 194–95&n.
Reims: 153
Religious dualism (*dvoeveriye*): 90
Renaissance period: 146
Requinus, Madgeburg artist: 111
Rhenish cathedrals: 21
Ridge beams: 171 f.
Riga: 113, 281
Rod: 78
Roman Capitolium: 153
Roman Empire: 70; Eastern, 76; Western, 76; East, 130
Roman, Prince: 248
Romanov-Borisoglebsk: 248, 250, 252
Romanov dynasty: 160n.
Romans: 75
Rome: 90, 146ff., Third, theory of, 150
Romny: 35, 38
Roof ridges: 73, 171, 175
Roshnov, F. N.: 159
Rostov-Veliki: 25, 67, 77, 127, 156, 246, 252; Kremlin at, 247
Rostovtzeff, cited: 34&n., 40, 55, 87&n.
Royal Tumulus (Tsarsky kurgan): 52
Rozhanitsy: 82
Rublev, Andrei: 163, 214–17, 221, 349f.
Rubruquis (William of Rubrouck), traveler: 103
Ruffo, Marco: 153, 163f., 191
Rurik dynasty: 151, 187
Russia, Great, style of: 290
Russia, medieval: 23; South region,

29; Central, 29; Galician, 104; pre-Mongolian, 116; North, 168
Russian Museum, Leningrad: 62, 110, 300
Russians, Great (Velikorussian): 6, 76, 116
Ryazan: 143
Ryananese princes: 141
Ryzhanovka graves: 38

Saints and their surroundings, portrayal of: 131
Saint Denis: 153
Sainte Chapelle: 153
Samodershets, meaning of the word: 151
Sarmatians: 46f., 67, 76; world, 67; motifs, 68; art, 70; period, 82
Sarmato-Gothic period: 75
Sassanian craftsmanship: 67
Sazykov, Paul: 288&n.
Scandinavia: 118
Schism (Raskol): 237&n.
Sclaveni: 75
Scripin brothers: 243
Scythian art: 40ff., influence of, 68; motifs in Russian decorative art, 74
Scythian current: 44
Scythian and Sarmatian Tumuli: Dnieper Group, 49–52; Kerch Group, 52–54; Kuban and the Don Groups, 54–57
Scythian Naples: 30
Scythians: 29ff.; plowmen (*Aroteres*), 32; Royal, 32; civilization, periods of, 42&n.; customs, dress, occupation, 51
Secularization, process of: 237
Sergius of Radonezh, St.: 222
Serogozy tumuli: 38
Sevastopol': 30
Seven Brothers Barrow: 45, 55
Shadrach: 299
Shatry: (pl.) *see* tent-shaped spires
Shatyor (*Shatër*): 161, 180f.
Shchusev, A, V.: 99, 109&n.
Shemyaka, Dmitri: 146
Sherwood, V.: 175
Siberia: 38; northern, 40; western, 58; southern, 59
Siberian Collection: 60

THE ART AND ARCHITECTURE
OF MEDIEVAL RUSSIA

was set on the Linotype in various sizes of Caledonia. This type-
face was designed by the distinguished American typographer
and lettering artist, the late William A. Dwiggins, who based
his drawings on Scotch Roman. The paper on which the text of
this book is printed bears the watermark of the University of
Oklahoma Press and is designed for an effective life
of at least three hundred years.